MILTON STUDIES

XLIV

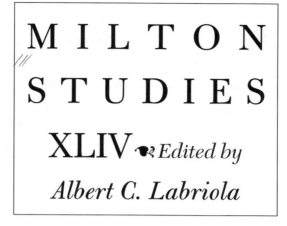

MILTON STUDIES

XLIV *Edited by*

Albert C. Labriola

UNIVERSITY OF PITTSBURGH PRESS

MILTON STUDIES

is published annually by the University of Pittsburgh Press as a forum for Milton scholarship and criticism. Articles submitted for publication may be biographical; they may interpret some aspect of Milton's writings; or they may define literary, intellectual, or historical contexts—by studying the work of his contemporaries, the traditions which affected his thought and art, contemporary political and religious movements, his influence on other writers, or the history of critical response to his work.

Manuscripts should be upwards of 3,000 words in length and should conform to *The Chicago Manual of Style*. Manuscripts and editorial correspondence should be addressed to Albert C. Labriola, Department of English, Duquesne University, Pittsburgh, Pa., 15282–1703. Manuscripts should be accompanied by a self-addressed envelope and sufficient unattached postage.

Milton Studies does not review books.

Within the United States, *Milton Studies* may be ordered from the University of Pittsburgh Press, c/o Chicago Distribution Center, 11030 South Langley Avenue, Chicago, Ill., 60628, 1-800-621-2736.

Published by the University of Pittsburgh Press, Pittsburgh, Pa. 15260

10 9 8 7 6 5 4 3 2 1

ISBN 0-8229-4241-0

ISSN 0076-8820

CONTENTS

MILTON STUDIES

XLIV

WHY MILTON MATTERS; OR,
AGAINST HISTORICISM

Stanley Fish

TO THE QUESTION assigned us—why does Milton matter?—I would add two additional questions: Matter to whom? And matter as what? The second—matter as what?—is the crucial one, for I take it to be true that things matter in particular ways—nothing matters in *every* way—and I also take it to be true that the particular way a thing matters is a function of what it is intended by its maker or author to be. That is to say, when evaluating a human production (as opposed to a natural phenomenon) one must begin with a precise understanding of its purpose. What was it meant to do? What task was it fashioned to perform? Once these questions have been answered, you are equipped with a framework from the perspective of which you can identify the relevant features of a performance. And once those features have been identified, you can go about the business of determining what they mean, all the while keeping in mind that the meanings you seek to establish will be meanings specific to the purpose of the agent or agents who set out to do something, not everything. (Here I reaffirm C. S. Lewis's assertion that, "The first qualification for judging any piece of workmanship from a corkscrew to a cathedral is to know *what* it is—what it was intended to do and how it is meant to be used."[1]) It is in relation to the something purposive actors set out to do that the end result must be evaluated. If the evaluation is strongly positive, you say, "that's a really good instance of X or Y or Z—a really good song, or a really good wine, or a really good automobile, or a really good movie." And if this positive evaluation is transmitted to, and shared by, generations subsequent to the initial appearance of the something someone set out to do, you can then say, "this really matters," by which you will mean that in the history of the effort to do that kind of thing, this is a shining and lasting and exemplary contribution.

With these general speculations (to which I shall return) as background, I can now answer the question "Why Milton Matters" by posing and answering the secondary (really primary) question, "matters as what?" Insofar as Milton matters, he matters as a poet, for it is poetry he set out to write; and, moreover, if this is so, then it seems to me that the best scholarship now being produced by the most intelligent, learned, acute students of Milton is de-

1

signed, not self-consciously of course, to ensure that in time he won't matter. No one will care.

How can this be? How can a scholarship at once be best and be (at least potentially) responsible for the diminishing of its object? There is no puzzle or paradox here: the scholarship I refer to is best because it is scrupulous, well informed, wide-ranging, illuminating, full of insights, pathbreaking. But its very virtues are likely to have the negative effect I predict because in the exercise of those virtues the authors of this scholarship pick up the stick from the wrong end.

It's time for an example, and remember, it's an example of something excellent in many respects except for the one respect that counts. The year 2002 saw the publication of an important (and award-winning) collection of essays entitled *Milton and the Terms of Liberty*, edited by Graham Parry and Joad Raymond. In the introduction to the volume Parry identifies it as the report of the International Milton Symposium, a conference assembled "to discuss the current state of Milton studies" and declares that "the collection of papers presented here reflects the predominance of interest in Milton's constant adjustment of his political ideas to the changing circumstances of the nation" (xv). This predominance is reflected, he points out, in the fact that "many of the conference papers considered the larger question of Milton's place in the history of political thought in early modern Britain and Europe." "This bias," he concludes, "seems likely to continue to influence the future direction of Milton studies." That's just what I'm worried about, for although Parry mentions, in passing, that there was some attention paid at the conference to "the interconnections between linguistic register, literary form and ideas in the expression of political concerns," it is clear that in his mind and the mind of his fellow contributors, political concerns came first, their expression in linguistic and literary form second.

That is what I mean by picking up the stick from the wrong end. If what is important is Milton's place in the history of political thought, the form taken by his political reflections will be a matter of (at most) secondary interest. If you think of Milton as being in competition with Thomas Hobbes, John Harrington, John Locke, John Lilburne, William Prynne—a competition he would most likely lose—the fact that he wrote in verse will no doubt be noted, but it will not take center stage, and the history of poetic conventions—along with the imperatives for performance encoded in those conventions and the meaning-making recipes they provide—will first become background and then, after a while, fade from sight; and fading with them will be any recollection of why—as an instance of what general purpose—Milton wrote these things in the first place. In short, if Milton's value—the degree to which he matters—stands or falls on his contribution to English and European political thought, it will fall. After all, the only reason anyone would care about "Milton's constant adjustment of his political ideas" is because he's the guy who wrote *Paradise Lost, Paradise Regained, Lycidas,* and *Samson Agonistes;* and if those poems are quarried for political or economic or agricultural or military views, the collection and analysis of those views *as* politics or economics or agriculture (as if those disciplines named the arena of Milton's ambitions) will displace any interest in their status as poems, and as a result we will have lost our grip on what kind of accomplishment they are.

I here give voice to a concern that has been expressed with some frequency in recent years. Michael Clark, commenting on the recent tendency to subsume literature in "a more general symbolic determinism," observes that when "the system as a whole, rather than anything specific to the literary text" takes front and center stage, "Literature as such simply disappears against a general background of material action or symbolic determination." Richard Strier is making the same kind of argument when he declares that in giving up formalism, we "give up both the question of value and the conception of 'the literary.'" Ellen Rooney is even more pointed when she insists that, "For a critical reader bereft of the category of form, the subject matter of literary and cultural analysis loses all standing as a *theoretical* object." Once the category of form has been attenuated, she concludes, every text is reduced "to its ideological or historical context," and "reading has been displaced by a project of sorting by theme."[2] Of course, themes can be found embedded in any form whatsoever, and if you make themes the focus of your analysis, the particular form that gives them experiential life will receive no attention whatsoever.

I can imagine at least two objections to the arguments I have just rehearsed: (1) Why couldn't it be the case that the inventorying of Milton's views on a number of subjects illuminated rather than overwhelmed the poetry? and (2) Isn't the idea of a distinctively literary performance a relic of a long-since-rejected aesthetic idealism with its built-in alibi for a poetic genius floating free of the entanglements of the world? The inventorying of Milton's views on history, politics, theology, and so on, will indeed have a chance to illuminate the poetry, but only if those views have been tabulated in response to a literary question: that is, you notice, as everyone since Addison has, that the God of *Paradise Lost* is a puzzlingly unsympathetic figure and you look in Milton's writings on theology and kingship for a key to the puzzle. If, on the other hand, you simply ask and then answer the question, "what did Milton think about X," you will have marshaled a good deal of information, but there will be no way to get from it to the poetry you want it to illuminate. Let me illustrate with another example, again a scholarly work that is in many respects impeccable: Jeffrey Shoulson's "Milton and Enthusiasm: Radical

Religion and the Poetics of *Paradise Regained.*"[3] Early on, Shoulson identifies his project by posing it as a question: "Is it possible to determine from *Paradise Regained,* a poem so deeply engaged in the matter of messianic salvation and its relation to history, Milton's attitudes toward these various enthusiastic movements?" (3). The answer is, "sure it's possible," and in fact Shoulson does it for the rest of an elegantly constructed and argued paper. But when it comes time for him to make good on his subtitle—"Radical Religion and the Poetics of *Paradise Regained"*—he has nowhere to go because nothing in his framing of the essay's question and therefore of its agenda is in touch with any poetic or aesthetic concern. The pages he devotes to *Paradise Regained* as a poem at the end of the essay are interesting and incisive, but they don't grow out of the longer exposition that precedes them. That exposition was the exposition of a historian of theology, and while it is certainly possible and indeed likely that the history of seventeenth-century theology will be relevant to *Paradise Regained,* that relevance will not emerge if you simply lay the exposition next to the poem. Rather, the relevance must be elaborated and *argued* for, and argued for in specifically literary terms. There is, to be sure, an argument in Shoulson's paper, but it is not, until the very end, a literary argument, and its materials will not transform themselves into poetically significant materials without the intervention and controlling guidance of the literary interrogation Shoulson never sets in motion. What he does set in motion is an interrogation that proceeds from quite a different angle; and as that angle takes over his paper any sense of *Paradise Regained* as a poem, as a production of a particular and distinctive kind, pretty much disappears and the aesthetic object is absorbed by the cultural materials that now surround it.

But isn't that just the point (and here I take up the second obvious objection). After all, it has been the project of cultural studies to achieve just such an absorption by denying to the literary object its splendid but irresponsible and historically impossible isolation. Raymond Williams stands in here for the innumerable proclaimers of the same sentiments: "We cannot separate literature and art from other kinds of social practice, in such a way to make them subject to quite special and distinct laws. They may have quite specific features as practices but they cannot be separated from the general social process."[4] Well, yes and no. While it is true that no discourse occupies a privileged, self-defining, independent, and autonomous place, and while it is also true that all discourses are both culturally constituted and constitutive of culture, participating in and productive of a "general social process" they affirm and modify, it can nevertheless be said of a particular discourse that it is separate and distinct; not distinct in the impossible sense of being free-standing, but distinct in the sense that it inflects the general and shared set of discursive practices in a way appropriate to its claimed function. Writing a sermon and writing a history and writing a poem are all conventional activities enabled by and feeding back into the same social conditions of articulation, and no one of them is finally independent of the others; but "finally" is a very abstract measure, and short of it the differences that attend different purposes are operationally real and result, despite what Williams says, in "quite special and distinct laws," the law, for example, that a sermon must have a homiletic and hortatory point, or the law that histories must offer explanations of the events they report, or the law that poems must at once utilize and display the resources of language, or the law that fictions can set aside the requirement of verisimilitude. To be sure, it is always possible to focus on the set of generally enabling conditions and to discover its traces in particular performances, but if you do only that and always do that you will lose sight of the conventional—not essential—differences that make things what they are; you will fail to ask the right questions and you are likely to be distracted by the wrong ones.

The lesson is simple and it is the one I began with: in the act of assessing a performance you must always be in mind of its point, of what it is trying to do. This was a lesson forgotten by those moviegoers who in 1967 criticized Mike Nichols's *The Graduate* because in a crucial scene the hero, played by Dustin Hoffman, drives his Alfa Romeo across the upper level of the Bay Bridge in a direction prohibited by the traffic laws. It was said that Nichols spoiled the movie by making this mistake, but it wasn't a mistake at all; it was a cinematic choice that had to do no doubt with the position of the sun, the quality of the light, the panorama available to the camera, and the relation of all of these to the film's dramaturgy. It was to those conventions and conventional resources—the conventions and resources of movie making—that Nichols was being responsible; he was not responsible to the conventions of the documentary or the conventions of news broadcasting or the conventions of history or the conventions of driving practices. Those viewers who held him to the decorums of another practice got hung up on something that was irrelevant to his achievement, and so they missed it.[5]

I would say the same about Raymond Williams's famous thesis about the pastoral, the argument that if we focus only on the formal and genre aspects of poems like *Lycidas* and *To Penshurst* we miss the fact that, by perpetuating the myth of an "enameled" country life, such productions functioned as screens and apologies for the reality of oppressive agricultural practices—enclosure, eviction, conditions of near-slave labor.[6] The accusation is that both the poets and the critics who follow the standard line of analysis are accomplices to the outrages they fail to address. They don't bring to light what was really going on at Appleton House or Tintern Abbey. My response is, right, they don't, and that wasn't what they set out to do. They set out to write poetry in a particular genre.

This doesn't mean that the poetry they produced is without any connection whatsoever to issues of agricultural reform, peasant labor, foreclosure, enclosure, and the like. Virgil's *Eclogues,* a model for would-be pastoral poets in the Middle Ages and Renaissance, are explicitly concerned with all of these matters, and after Virgil the formal/conventional properties of the pastoral genre are understood to include them. In his influential and authoritative *The Art of English Poesie* (1589), George Puttenham says of the pastoral that "under the veil of homely persons" it glances "at greater matters and such as perchance had not been safe to have been disclosed in any other sort." Thus, when Milton begins *Lycidas* with the words, "Yet once more," his readers know that the pastoral poet's lament will touch on matters greater than the "rustical manner" (Puttenham) the representation suggests. In short, substantive concerns are built into the formal signatures of the genre.[7]

What is not built into the formal signatures of the genre, however, are the concerns of the Marxist/materialist critics who, following Williams and others, focus on what the genre, at least in its classical instantiations, leaves out. Poems leave out many things—indeed the vast majority of things—but an account of what a poem leaves out cannot be an account of the intention of the author (and of the poem's meaning) unless it can be shown that the author wanted the reader to notice the exclusion and to make something of it. In general, anything *can* count as relevant to meaning (even an exclusion, if, for example, an allusion to a mythical hero leaves out half of his story) so long as it can be linked up to the author's intention. Something in the present, something in the past—it doesn't matter. Historical proximity to the act of composition is neither a requirement for nor a guarantee of relevance. The fact that an author said or did something does not make that something part of his intention even if what he did was causally productive of the object of interpretation.

This is a point missed, I think, by Stephen Dobranski in his learned and illuminating *Milton, Authorship, and the Book Trade;*[8] Dobranski forcefully argues that an overemphasis on the picture of Milton as a solitary genius (a picture, as he notes, Milton himself sometimes draws) has deflected attention away from "the material conditions of Milton's authorship" (3). Dobranski is particularly interested in the transactions between Milton and his printers and booksellers, and it is his project "to reconstruct such relationships based on his publications and personal letters, as well as documentary evidence about the book trade" (3). This project is organized, he tells us, by three questions: "What role did Milton play in the production of his texts? What can we learn about the author by examining his practices of writing and publishing? How does the material creation of Milton's books affect their meaning?" But if you will allow me a Sesame Street moment, question three is not like the others. Questions one and two are historical and empirical questions and are interesting in their own right. Question three is an interpretive question; it assumes that there is a relationship between the details of composition and publication—How long did it take to write? To whom were various drafts shown? What were Milton's negotiations with his printer?—and what the published product *means*. There is no such relationship, or, rather, there isn't any except in the case of two special circumstances: (1) When the history of composition and publishing is incorporated explicitly into the text or is rehearsed in a prefatory note; (2) When there is a question of attribution that requires an examination of compositional practices and the identity of booksellers or printers in order to determine who the author actually was, a determination necessarily preliminary to any specification of his or her intention. In any other circumstance information about the "practices of writing and publishing" will stand to the side of the interpretive effort, for while those practices are surely part of an author's biography, they are not evidence of what he or she set out to do even if they are evidence of the route pursued in the doing of it.

Again, it is not that information about compositional habits and publishing practices can never be relevant to interpretative concerns. Rather interpretative concerns must be in place *first;* otherwise, one could never establish relevance and one would be in the position (as many historicists, in fact, are) of considering relevant any and every fact that came one's way. It may be, as Jerome McGann contends, that authorship "takes place within the conventions and enabling limits that are accepted by the prevailing institutions of literary production," but those conventions, even if they are necessary to the production of meaning, are not what the literary work means; they are not the author of the work; they do not have intentions. Dobranski's claim that by "analyzing Milton's books as physical objects we gain new insights into the circumstances of their production" is certainly true and even tautological; but the assertion that follows in the same sentence is certainly false: "and thereby improve our understanding of the individual texts' meanings."[9] An understanding of a text's meaning can only be achieved by first understanding the purpose—literary or otherwise—that animates and impels its unfolding. In Milton's case, that purpose will *not* have been to contract with a certain bookseller or secure the services of a certain printer.[10]

Critics like Dobranski draw a wrong conclusion from a correct premise. The correct premise is by now a commonplace and I have already alluded to

it: literature is not a privileged, uniquely complex and transcendent discourse, but is rather "one of many culturally productive discourses susceptible to critical analysis"[11] and on that level no different from any of the others.
The wrong conclusion is *any* conclusion that follows from the premise, for all
the premise tells you is that literature is historically situated and produced.
But so is the sermon, the political pamphlet, the encyclopedia, the catechism,
the rhetorical handbook, the formal oration, the eulogy. In order to take the
next step, or any step, you have to attend to the specificity of the discourse
that has solicited your attention, and that means attending to its history, not to
history in general (there is no such thing) but to the history of a form.

Here we come, I think, to the crux of the matter. The mistake polemic
historicists often make is to think that there is an opposition between criticism that attends to history and politics and criticism that attends to aesthetic
forms. But as I have already argued, aesthetic forms have their own histories
and those histories are almost always more than "merely" aesthetic. The
debates in the period about stressed and unstressed verse, writing in Latin
and writing in the vernacular, the virtues and defects of the Senecan and
Ciceronian styles, the merits of rhyme and blank verse are unintelligible
apart from the issues of nationalism, political authority, and public morality
thought to hang on the choice between these forms; and we cannot understand the force and meaning of literary forms without first understanding
their implication in such issues. A criticism that focuses on aesthetic form is
no less historical than any other, and, therefore, there can be no opposition
between historical criticism and aesthetic criticism; rather, the opposition is
between different kinds of historical criticism; and to the question which of
the various histories is the one appropriate to the description and evaluation
of literary works, the obvious, and indeed tautological, answer is the history of
literary forms, so long as we remember that far from excluding social and
political concerns, literary forms are, more often than not, their vehicles. As
Ellen Rooney puts it, formalism, properly understood, "is a matter not of
barring thematizations, but of refusing to reduce reading entirely to the
elucidation, essentially the paraphrase, of themes—theoretical, ideological,
or humanistic."[12]

It is the tendency of much criticism that labels itself historicist to go
directly for those themes and to bypass the particular forms in which they are
expressed. But when this happens no pertinence whatsoever is given to the
fact that the discourse in question is a poem, and, therefore, there is no
possibility of gauging (because one does not even recognize) the particular
effectivity of poetic representation. Moreover, if one keeps in mind the laws
of poetic representation—the assumptions and requirements that are part

and parcel of a fully developed genre like the pastoral—one knows what questions to put to the materials that present themselves for incorporation into an interpretation. That is to say, literary criticism has the advantage of actually having a direction and a point (provided by the intentional structure of its object) while the historical criticism that has no method except to proclaim loudly, "we're historical and you're not," often has neither. Informed only by the conviction that if it's a historical item, it's relevant, such a criticism, as Richard Strier has observed, ends up being nothing more than a series of mentionings. The mention in the text of any "item . . . taken to be politically or culturally significant . . . is sufficient to get the machinery of 'archeology' and archive-churning going."[13]

That machinery does, of course, generate things to notice. As Strier declares, "Much that is rich and strange is turned up"; but what is turned up cannot settle anything, cannot determine or even help you to determine what the text means. The moral is not that historical investigation is to be opposed "as such." Rather, as Mark Cousins points out, "All that is opposed . . . is the claim that such investigations can *resolve* problems within the human sciences."[14] Of course, such investigations can indeed resolve problems within the discourse of history because it is within the framework of that discourse—a framework that defines the object of study and the appropriate means of studying it and identifying what is and is not relevant—that the problems are set and present themselves for consideration. What historical investigation as such cannot resolve are problems in other disciplines, for those other disciplines—literature, theology, anthropology, political science, and so on—come equipped with their own stipulations of what is relevant and noticeable. There is no *general* transferability of observation from discipline to discipline and, therefore, it is a mistake to assume that conclusions reached in historical investigation as such are relevant to investigations undertaken in other domains. The question one most always asks is, what is pertinent to this particular production of the human mind undertaken in response to a particular disciplinary agenda and purpose? A criticism that does not ask this question and then guide itself by the answer is a criticism that can say nothing because it can say anything.

I began by observing that the best minds of our profession are attracted to this kind of criticism and indeed believe not only in its methodological superiority—despite the fact that it is without method—but in its moral superiority. Why? The answer is politics. The practitioners of cultural studies or cultural materialism generally situate themselves on the left and for them the rejection of formalist criticism is a political act that demonstrates their political virtue. As Mark Rasmussen puts it, it is a "tendency of contemporary academics to find their own post-modern alienation mirrored in the anxieties of works produced at the inception of modernity."[15] If you can link the so-called literary work with revolutionary sentiments, or with the crisis of the nation state, or with the emancipation of the liberal subject from the hegemony of religion and political tyranny, you're doing the Lord's, or rather the proletariat's, work. And it follows then that you must enroll your poet in the same standing and marching army. That's why so many critics have a stake in demonstrating that the Milton they admire professionally has the right political values—their values—and believe that if he were alive today he would be against the war in Iraq and for multiculturalism. Actually, Milton probably would have been a cheerleader for the war in Iraq and he would have been horrified, I think, by the tendency of multiculturalism in its stronger versions to forgo judgments of right and wrong in favor of an ever-expanding ethic of mutual respect. Not that any of that matters, at least for the question of why Milton matters; for as I have said over and over again, any answer to that question must be a literary answer in relation to which historical and political matters matter chiefly as the material of an aesthetic achievement. Describing and evaluating that achievement, which while it is often inconceivable apart from historical and political concerns cannot be identified with them, is the proper business of literary criticism. It is not the proper business of literary criticism to pronounce grandly on the substantive issues an author chooses to raise in the course of implementing the intention to write a poem.

One last example, from popular culture. Jody Rosen has written a book entitled *White Christmas: The Story of an American Song.*[16] Rosen's interests are broadly cultural and sociological. He discusses the shift from the urbane popular sound of Cole Porter to the more nostalgic and sentimental music that began to appear in the early years of World War II when "White Christmas" was written and recorded; and he makes much of the fact that Irving Berlin, a Jewish immigrant from the Lower East Side, produced not only "White Christmas" but also "Easter Parade" and "God Bless America." But Rosen is a careful enough historian to note that Irving Berlin's thoughts about his music were of another kind. When Berlin finished "White Christmas" and showed it to his manager, he said, "Not only is it the best song *I* ever wrote, it's the best song *anybody* ever wrote." Or, in other words, I have soared above the Aonian Mount and written something the world will not willingly let die. That's his perspective on things, and it is also Milton's and it should be ours. If I might quote or misquote from the gospel according to James Carville, George Stephanopoulos, and Bill Clinton, "It's the poetry, stupid."

University of Illinois, Chicago

NOTES

1. C. S. Lewis, *A Preface to "Paradise Lost"* (Oxford, 1942), 1.

2. Ellen Rooney, "Form and Contentment," *Modern Language Quarterly* 61 (March 2000): 19, 26, 28; *Revenge of the Aesthetic: The Place of Literature in Theory Today,* ed. Michael Clark (Berkeley and Los Angeles, 2000), 5; Richard Strier, "How Formalism Became a Dirty Word," in *Renaissance Literature and Its Formal Engagements,* ed. Mark Rasmussen (New York, 2002), 209.

3. Jeffrey Shoulson, "Milton and Enthusiasm: Radical Religion and the Poetics of *Paradise Regained*" (unpublished essay, author's files).

4. Raymond Williams, "Base and Superstructure in Marxist Cultural Theory," *Problems in Materialism and Culture* (London, 1980), 44.

5. It is not that fidelity to historical fact can never be pertinent to the evaluation of a film as film. If, for example, verisimilitude is a part of the director's claim, if he or she signals us that his or her intention is a documentary one as well as a narrative one, the question of responsibility to fact will be relevant to the cinematic achievement. That is why the objections put to Oliver Stone's movies about JFK and Richard Nixon are to the point, while objections to Mike Nichols's flow-of-traffic error are not. To some extent it is a question of historical distance. The recent TV bio-pic about Ronald Reagan was criticized because some words spoken by the former president were obviously made up, or, at the very best, composite versions of what he might have said on one or more occasions. There was a feeling that there was something wrong about taking factual liberties with a still-living person. But when Reagan early in his career played George Custer to Errol Flynn's Jeb Stuart, no one seemed bothered by the fact that the two were far apart in age and had never actually met.

6. Raymond Williams, *The Country and the City* (New York, 1973), 15 ff.

7. See Douglas Bruster, "Shakespeare and the Composite Text," in Rasmussen, *Renaissance Literature,* 44: "New Formalism could be defined as follows: A critical genre dedicated to examining the social, cultural, and historical aspects of literary form, and the function of form for those who produce and consume literary texts. The New Formalism sees language and literary forms—from the single-lettered interjection 'O' to the stanza, the epic battle, and epic itself—as socially, politically, and historically 'thick.' " There is a danger that by arguing for the substantive content of literary forms, those forms are rendered merely instrumental in relation to that content. In this scenario attention to aesthetic form is legitimized, but at the cost of denying it a value of its own, a value we traditionally take note of with words like "beautiful," "powerful," "stunning," "ingenious," "innovative," and "wow." See on this point Heather Dubrow, "Recuperating Formalism and the Country House Poem," in ibid., 85: "The assumption that formalism may once again become respectable simply because it can serve the needs of its host, historical and political criticism, relegates the formal to a secondary, supplementary role that neglects the depth and range of its contributions to style and meaning."

8. Stephen Dobranski, *Milton, Authorship, and the Book Trade* (Cambridge, 1999).

9. Ibid., 181; Jerome McGann, cited in ibid., 105.

10. See on this point Edward Pechter, "Making Love to Our Employment; or, The Immateriality of Arguments about the Materiality of the Shakespearean Text," *Textual Practice* 11 (1997): 54: "They [materialist accounts] demonstrate merely that Shakespeare's texts *may* be studied as an aspect of the history of printing . . . and that if they are examined from within the assumptions of this discipline, Shakespeare will be produced not as an author . . . but as a product of the early modern printing industry." This is a materialist version of one thousand monkeys pecking away on typewriters for many years and accidentally producing King Lear.

11. Stephen Cohen, cited in Rasmussen, *Renaissance Literature,* 26.

12. Rooney, "Form and Contentment," 29.

13. Richard Strier, "How Formalism Became a Dirty Word," 213.

14. Mark Cousins, "The Practice of Historical Investigation," *Post-Structuralism and the Question of History,* ed. Derek Attridge, Geoff Bennington, and Robert Young (Cambridge, 1987), 128.

15. Rasmussen, *Renaissance Literature,* 2.

16. Jody Rosen, *White Christmas: The Story of an American Song* (New York, 2002).

BARBARA K. LEWALSKI ON
WHY MILTON MATTERS

Barbara K. Lewalski

IN 1642, IN THAT remarkable comment on poetics, poetic vocation, and public duty prefacing Book Two of his *Reason of Church-Government,* Milton voiced the earnest hope that he "might perhaps leave something so written to aftertimes, as they should not willingly let it die."[1] Nor *have* they— we—for over three centuries. Milton was thinking of the poetry, and especially the epic poetry, he was planning to write and it is of course that superb poetry that has always mattered profoundly to lovers of poetry—though they may be a "fit audience . . . though few" (*PL* 7.31) in any age.[2]

Professional literary scholars will always admire Milton's experimentation with many genres—sonnet, hymn, ode, masque, funeral elegy, diffuse and brief epic, tragedy—transforming each of them into something new and strange. We also admire his mastery of metrics and versification: From the same verse form (octosyllabic couplets) he was able to produce the utterly different tonal effects of *L'Allegro* and *Il Penseroso*. For *Paradise Lost* he created a sonorous, exalted, yet highly flexible blank verse suited to all its demands: high rhetoric, tender lyric, dramatic interchanges, hymnic praise, dynamic narrative. And the near free verse of his final tragedy is astonishing in its poignancy and power, as in Samson's long lament for his loss of sight:

> O dark, dark, dark, amid the blaze of noon,
> Irrecoverably dark, total eclipse
> Without all hope of day!
> O first-created beam, and thou great word
> Let there be light, and light was over all,
> Why am I thus bereaved thy prime decree?
> The sun to me is dark
> And silent as the moon,
> When she deserts the night
> Hid in her vacant interlunar cave. (*SA* 80–89)[3]

But readers have seldom approached Milton's poetry as pure art—if there ever is such a thing—apart from his life, his ideas, and his soon-attained status as a cultural icon of English literature. Milton the self-described *Iconoclastes* would hardly have appreciated being enshrined as a cultural icon, and that

13

construction of him has had some deleterious effects. One is the spate of bad eighteenth-century poetry in Miltonicks, and frigid would-be epics aiming at Miltonic sublimity. Another is the frequent misreading of Milton over several centuries as the organ voice of Christian orthodoxy, dramatizing the events of Genesis in terms of centrist Christian theology. Still another is the impulse, especially among English critics of the T. S. Eliot generation, to belittle the poet they thought tarnished by republicanism and Puritanism.

Yet Milton himself insisted upon intertwining life and art. In the *Apology for Smectymnuus* he famously declared that the high poet must write out of wide experience and can only make his poem out of the values and virtues he has cultivated within himself:

He who would not be frustrate of his hope to write well hereafter in laudable things ought him selfe to bee a true Poem, that is, a composition, and patterne of the best and honourablest things; not presuming to sing high praises of heroick men, or famous Cities, unlesse he have in himselfe the experience and the practice of all that which is praise-worthy. (1:890)

In the four proems to *Paradise Lost* he explores more explicitly than any other epic poet the problematics of authorship (an issue that concerned him from the beginning of his career), inserting himself and his own experiences —of blindness, of political danger, of writing, of inspiration—directly and extensively into the poem. In that spirit Wordsworth invoked Milton in his sonnet "London, 1802" as an exemplar in his life and his poetry of steadfast freedom of mind, noble ideals, virtue, and duty: "Milton, thou shouldst be living at this hour / England hath need of thee." American revolutionaries and transcendentalists also thought America had need of him in their times. Jefferson excerpted some forty-eight passages from *Paradise Lost* in his *Commonplace Book* (many of them dealing with Satan's revolt), and Emerson proclaimed him "The sublimest Bard of all," a poet-prophet who was an "apostle of freedom" in the house, state, church, and press.[4]

I think Milton should matter to us in the twenty-first century for many of the ideals he holds forth in his prose works. Though sometimes qualified and imperfectly realized in his texts and in his own day, they offer principles we can, have, and should further adapt and extend to our own needs and circumstances. And he should matter to us especially for the imaginative representation of human experience and human possibility rendered in his great poems.

In an era rife with efforts to restrict the free exchange of ideas—whether by harsh restrictions on speech and press in many totalitarian regimes, or fatwas against supposedly blasphemous Salman Rushdies; or, closer to home, by efforts to ban the teaching of *The Adventures of Huckleberry Finn* or of evolution in the schools, or efforts to block some speakers on university campuses, or government manipulation of news about the necessity for and costs of the war against Iraq, or efforts to demonize dissent in times of crisis as unpatriotic—we need the stirring testimony of *Areopagitica* to the vital importance of the free flow of ideas. We need to be reminded in Milton's graphic metaphor of the overarching wrong done by suppressing books and the ideas they contain, despite the danger some may find in them:

For Books are not absolutely dead things. . . . I know they are as lively, and as vigorously productive, as those fabulous Dragons teeth; and being sown up and down, may chance to spring up armed men. And yet on the other hand unlesse wariness be us'd, as good almost kill a man as kill a good Book; who kills a Man kils a reasonable creature, God's Image; but hee who destroyes a good Booke, kills reason it selfe, kills the Image of God, as it were in the eye. Many a man lives a burden to the Earth; but a good Booke is the pretious life-blood of a master spirit, imbalm'd and treasur'd up on purpose to a life beyond life. . . . Revolutions of ages doe not oft recover the losse of a rejected truth, for the want of which whole Nations fare the worse. (YP 2:402–3)

And if we can no longer quite believe (at least in the short run) that "Truth is strong, next to the Almighty" and will in free and open encounter surely defeat falsehood, we can probably agree that "Good and evill . . . in the field of this World grow up together almost inseparably," that there is no such thing as maintaining a blank innocence—"a fugitive and cloister'd virtue,"[5] and that conscientious choice, based on knowledge, is the cornerstone of any meaningful religion or ethics. As scholars and teachers we surely respond also to Milton's moving portrait of truth as a dismembered Osiris, and ourselves as seeking out such bits and pieces as we can find though we know we will never find them all. We can take inspiration also from Milton's representation of the duty and responsibility of scholars—a vision of some ideal MLA or Milton Society: "Behold now this vast City . . . the mansion house of liberty, . . . there be pens and heads there, sitting by their studious lamps, musing, searching, revolving new notions and idea's wherewith to present, as with their homage and their fealty the approaching Reformation; others as fast reading, trying all things, assenting to the force of reason and convincement" (YP 2:553–54). Even Milton's uneasy partial restrictions on Roman Catholics and (perhaps) Ranters and Antinomian Familists, arising from immediate circumstances, political fears, and perceived dangers, are instructive, reminding us that such compromises normally seem illogical and unnecessary from a later perspective. Milton's ringing testimony to intellectual freedom continues to resonate and is often closely paraphrased in our day by political dissidents living under tyranny: "Give me the liberty to know, to utter, and to argue freely according to conscience, above all liberties" (YP 2:560).

Also, given the strong presence in all the major religions of fundamentalists who find a literal basis in religious texts or in the pronouncements of an absolute authority for war, terrorism, land claims, devastation of nature, gay-bashing, subjugation of women, denial of human rights, and obstruction of scientific advances, we can appreciate Milton's touchstones for the interpretation of sacred texts. Forced by his own experience of an incompatible marriage to rethink the gospel prohibition against divorce in the light of the human pain that prohibition causes, he came to believe that religious texts, religious law, and civil law must be interpreted according to the overarching principles of charity, reason, and human good. Heaping scorn on those who rest "in the meere element of the Text" with an "obstinant literality" and an "alphabetical servility" (YP 2:279–80), he insisted that "it is not the stubborn letter must govern us, but the divine and softning breath of charity which turns and windes the dictat of every positive command, and shapes it to the good of mankind" (YP 2:602–3). Or yet again, "To those whose mind is still to maintain textual restrictions whereof the bare sound cannot consist somtimes with humanity, much lesse with charity, I would answer by putting them in remembrance of a command above all commands. . . . *I will have mercy and not sacrifice; for on that saying all the Law and profets depend*" (YP 2:365–66). And more emphatically, that "no ordinance human or from heav'n can binde against the good of man" (YP 2:588). He restates these interpretative principles throughout *De Doctrina Christiana,* clearly unable to imagine a God who would deal with humankind on any other basis.

Again, at a time when so many, especially the young, do not vote and attend almost exclusively to their private concerns, we might well ponder Milton's model of responsible citizenship. Associated as he was with forward-looking theorists who were working out theories of popular sovereignty, republicanism, and separation of church and state, he often called on his countrymen to eschew the servility he thought monarchical culture promoted, and to make themselves the informed and worthy electorate absolutely essential to a republic, according to the classical and Italian political theorists he read. In some early poems, notably *Comus,* and in some antiprelatical tracts of the early 1640s, he projected the artist's role in such a reformed society, producing the kind of art appropriate to it. In *The Reason of Church-Government* he explained that he felt a strong call to turn from poetry to polemic for a time so as to advance reformation in church and state, in full consciousness that in that endeavor he had the use, as he put it, "but of my left hand" (YP 1:808). And in 1660, on the very eve of the Restoration and despite his clear danger from vengeful royalists about to regain power, he made a last desperate attempt to persuade his countrymen to preserve a republic. It would have been easy, and prudent, for Milton to conclude that he needed to lie low in order to survive and be able to complete and publish *Paradise Lost,* probably well underway by 1660. But he did not.

Even more important for Milton's modern readers are the poetic worlds created by his major poems. Milton meant the imaginative experiences those poems offer to be educative, supposing that they could help produce discerning, virtuous, liberty-loving human beings and citizens. Great literary works wed highly significant content to a just and appropriate form. Milton's major poems portray in magnificent verse the intellectual and moral complexities of human life, engaging both characters and readers in the hard tasks of knowing and choosing amid such complexities.

In *Paradise Lost,* almost half the poem is given over to the education of Adam and Eve, prompted by Adam's questions and directed by Raphael before and Michael after the Fall. God the Father engages in Socratic dialogue with the Son about the Fall and the redemption of humankind, and with Adam over his request for a mate, prompting both to advance in self-knowledge. Adam and Eve's conversations with each other involve them in an ongoing process of self-education about themselves and their world. Also, by setting his epic in relation to other great epics and works in other genres, Milton involves his readers in a critique of the values associated with those works, as well as with issues of contemporary politics and theology. To take the most obvious case, with his striking portrait of Satan in Books One and Two, Milton prompts the reader to begin a poem-long exploration and redefinition of heroes and heroism, at length locating human heroism not in epic martial figures but in a domestic pair cultivating their garden and then venturing forth to meet the challenges of a harsh, fallen world.

Milton's modern readers—subjected to an onslaught of propaganda, political and commercial, fraught with misinformation and subtle plays on the emotions—can profit from experiencing the powerful rhetoric so prominent in *Paradise Lost.* Satan's brilliant speeches mesmerize his angelic companions, Eve, and the reader by using all the strategies of ethos and pathos recommended by the classical rhetoricians. His performances are marked by eloquence, power, and passion, and they are especially seductive when they echo the noble republican rhetoric of a Cicero or a Demosthenes denouncing tyrants, or of Milton himself in *The Tenure of Kings and Magistrates:*

> Who can in reason then or right assume
> Monarchy over such as live by right
> His equals, if in power and splendour less.
> In freedom equal? Or can introduce
> Law and edict on us, who without law
> Err not, much less for this to be our lord,

And look for adoration to the abuse
Of those imperial titles which assert
Our being ordained to govern, not to serve.[6]   (*PL* 5.794–802)

No man who knows ought, can be so stupid to deny that all men naturally were borne
free, being the image and resemblance of God himself, and were by privilege above all
the creatures, born to command and not to obey. (*Tenure*, YP 2:198–99)

In tempting Eve Satan is especially effective when he constructs a false
autobiography for the snake he inhabits, narrating its supposed experience of
being enabled to talk by eating from a marvelous tree. Then he dazzles her
with a rapid succession of difficult questions about God, death, aspiration to
knowledge, and good and evil. Milton also constructs a fascinating session of
an infernal Parliament, or rather House of Lords, in which all the speakers
make persuasive cases: Moloch for continued war whatever the cost, Belial
for peace through submissive inaction, and Mammon for establishing an
empire rivaling heaven. Sorting through such propositions, readers have to
judge what is said by standards of internal logic and outside evidence, and to
weigh many complex questions: When is monarchy appropriate and when is
it a species of idolatry? When is rebellion called for and when not? When and
how should we be "by experience taught" (5.826), as Abdiel advised, and
when is experience untrustworthy?

Paradise Lost is the only literary work that attempts a sustained representation of the prelapsarian world, setting forth Milton's version of an ideal
human life. Some aspects of it (notably the gender hierarchy) most of us
would not consider ideal. And of course the poem does not invite the belief
that prelapsarian practices could be replicated in an all-too-fallen world. But
that is precisely the point: Milton thought that efforts to "sequester out of the
world into *Atlantick* and *Eutopian* politics, which never can be drawn into
use will not mend our condition," but that we should rather "ordain wisely as
in this world of evill" (YP 2.526). Accordingly, his Eden is not a rigid utopian
scheme but rather a vision of human possibility for readers to relate as they
can to their own circumstances.

One component of that vision is the poem's evocation of sheer delight in
the beauty, variety, and frolic activity of plants, birds, animals, and all the
creatures of the world, rendered in the account of their generation from
Mother Earth in Book Seven and in the extended descriptions of Eden as
containing "In narrow room Nature's whole wealth" (4.207). Along with that
is the representation of Adam and especially Eve as gardeners, loving care-
takers of their world, propping and nurturing and pruning whatever needs
such actions to bring out Eden's full beauty or to reform luxuriant growth
"tending to wild" (9.212), though only as dictated by their own needs, not

more—"as wide / As we need walk" (9.235–36). Related to this is the concept of labor as essential to maintain the natural world—even in Eden—but also as an activity that should accord with the rhythms of human life:

> Yet not so strictly hath our Lord imposed
> Labour, as to debar us when we need
> Refreshment, whether food, or talk between,
> Food of the mind, or this sweet intercourse
> Of looks and smiles, for smiles from reason flow,
>
> . . . .
>
> To brute denied, and are of love the food,
> Love not the lowest end of human life.
> For not to irksome toil, but to delight
> He made us, and delight to reason joined.   (*PL* 9.235–43)

Monist that he was, Milton represents his human pair in Eden enjoying a range of pleasures that pertain at once to the senses and the spirit—food, sex, music, learning, and making poetry; and his angels in heaven enjoy the same pleasures in more delightful forms. Finally, *Paradise Lost* represents love and companionship as the highest human good: Adam complains to God that he can enjoy no pleasure in solitude but seeks fellowship "fit to participate / All rational delight" (8.390–91), and God himself testifies that he always "Knew it not good for man to be alone" (8.445). Yet even in Paradise Adam and Eve have constantly to think how to get all this right—how to manage their labor, and how to deal with the tension between loving interdependence and the proper sphere of individual choice and responsibility. The poem's brilliant representation of their efforts and their ultimate failure to resolve these tensions engages readers to think hard about such core problems of human life.

In portraying the poem-long debate between Jesus and Satan, Milton's brief epic, *Paradise Regained,* involves its readers in the experience of analyzing the full panoply of human goods—food, sex, wealth, kingship, glory, military power, empire, learning—in circumstances that highlight the moral complexities attending the pursuit of or enjoyment of any of them. When and how may they be tainted? When do they become idols? What considerations of circumstance and individual bent and duty govern their use? As they consider such issues, readers are also led to think about how to deal with the past, with history. Satan's temptations are usually posed in terms of past experience —what happened before must happen again: none has without aid survived in this desert; none has ascended a throne without wealth; only arms or imperial power have ever settled a king of Israel; only the (classical) learning of the past can be a means to convert the Gentiles. We know that argument well. It is a truism that we always prepare to fight the last war, that we expect history to repeat itself in economic cycles and in our personal lives. More tragically, in many areas of the world—the Middle East, Northern Ireland, the Balkans—antagonists reenact the same religious, cultural, or territorial conflicts for generations or even centuries. Milton's brief epic offers its readers the experience of working out (along with the hero, Jesus, in his terms and times) questions of how to honor the past without being bound by its mandate, how to redefine history not as cyclical repetition but as process and re-creation, and how to imagine the new.

Samson Agonistes ends with the Chorus's statement that Samson's drama has offered them (and the larger audience) a "new aquist / Of true experience" (1755–56). It does indeed offer an impressive exploration of the difficulties involved in making moral and political choices in the usual ambiguous circumstances in which they must be made. The issues are posed in historical terms appropriate to Samson's era and especially Milton's own: a flawed and now blinded hero, a defeated cause and a people subjected to and ridiculed by their enemies, a populace (Israelites, Puritans) whose inner servility has kept them from gaining and keeping their political liberty:

> But what more oft in nations grown corrupt,
> And by their vices brought to servitude,
> Than to love bondage more than liberty,
> Bondage with ease than strenuous liberty;
> And to despise, or envy, or suspect
> Whom God hath of his special favour raised
> As their deliverer; if he aught begin,
> How frequent to desert him, and at last
> To heap ingratitude on worthiest deeds?   (268–76)

But the questions posed by Samson, his several visitors (Manoa, Dalila, Harapha, the Philistine Officer), and the Chorus in those historical circumstances have continuing resonance: What *is* the connection between inner and outward freedom or servility (a constant refrain in Milton's work)? When is rebellion or revolution justified? How can we know when to follow a flawed leader in a good cause? How to negotiate the competing claims of various mandates: cultural norms, religious law, civil law, a higher moral or natural law, or a personal (presumed divine) inspiration to go beyond or reinterpret any of those? Samson's final act of pulling the theater down on the assembled Philistine nobility poses for modern readers as well as the Chorus the all-too-relevant question of how to tell the difference between a freedom fighter and a suicide terrorist. I think we can determine Milton's position on some of these questions, but, as there is no narrative or interpretative voice in this drama, it offers no ready and easy answers to any of them. Rather, it forces a profound engagement with them through the experience of the characters and the resonances of the deeply moving poetic language.

T. S. Eliot famously observed that Milton began a deplorable "dissociation of sensibility"[7] in English poetry, a separation of thought and feeling. I think Eliot could not have been more wrong. I know no other poet who makes us think so seriously about so many important matters, and at the same time engages our deepest emotions as we experience the imaginative worlds created by his great poems.

Harvard University

NOTES

1. John Milton, *The Reason of Church-Government,* in *The Complete Prose Works of John Milton,* 8 vols., ed. Don M. Wolfe et al. (New Haven, 1953–1982), 1:810. Hereafter designated YP and cited parenthetically in the text.

2. All quotations from *Paradise Lost* are from *John Milton: Paradise Lost,* 2nd ed., ed. Alastair Fowler (London, 1998); hereafter cited by book and line number in the text.

3. Quotations from Milton's shorter poems are from *Milton: Complete Shorter Poems,* 2nd ed., ed. John Carey (London, 1997); hereafter cited in the text by line number.

4. Emerson cited in Barbara K. Lewalski, *The Life of John Milton: A Critical Biography,* rev. ed. (Oxford, 2003), 542, 545.

5. YP 2:562–63, 514–16.

6. Satan's misapplication of this rhetoric is contextualized by Cataline's exhortation to his greedy and dissolute soldiers, as reported by Sallust: "Awake, then! Lo, here, here before your eyes is the freedom for which you have yearned, and with it riches, honor, and glory . . . unless haply I delude myself and you are content to be slaves rather than to rule." See *The War with Cataline,* 20.1–17, trans. J. C. Rolfe (Cambridge, MA, 1965), 35–39. Another is Caesar's speech upon crossing the Rubicon denouncing Pompey as a tyrant, as reported by Lucan: "we are but dislodging a tyrant from a state prepared to bow the knee." See *Pharsalia* 1.299–351, trans J. D. Duff (Cambridge, MA, 1928), 24–29.

7. T. S. Eliot, *Homage to John Dryden: Three Essays on Poetry of the Seventeenth Century* (London, 1924), 30.

JOSEPH WITTREICH ON
WHY MILTON MATTERS

Joseph Wittreich

> In the context of what appears to be a crisis . . . in the late twentieth-century university, the question of how, and still more *why*, we should still be reading [Milton] . . . seems to deserve a larger scrutiny.
> Annabel Patterson, *Early Modern Liberalism*

IF THEY DID NOT invent the question, "Why Milton?" the Romantics lent fashion to it, empowering Milton by making him whole again and, simultaneously, giving force to his poetry by reading it as if it were a true history; but also by reading it in the future tense so that poems emerging from one moment of crisis could reflect upon, and explain, another crisis in history when, once again, tyranny and terror ruled. In the early years of the twenty-first century, the sense of crisis is undiminished. "Why Milton?" is no less urgent; and the worry that Milton may have written poetry as propaganda for warfare remains intense. Witness the Web magazine essay, "*Samson Agonistes* (Confession of a Terrorist/Martyr)," and *The Boston Globe* piece, "Was [Milton's] Samson a Terrorist?" (both from November 2002), together with *The New York Times* article of the following month, "Is Reading Milton Unsafe at Any Speed?"[1] In view of this clamor, it is remarkable, yet no wonder, that *Samson Agonistes* had five announced performance readings, all in New York City, in February and April 2003, and one in Bryn Mawr, Pennsylvania, also in April 2003. Other readings were announced for August 2003 and April 2004, both in conjunction with assemblies of international literary organizations.[2] With various voices from the academy as well as the popular culture conspiring as one, it is as if Milton's tragedy were now being rescued by history *for* history—in this time, for this place—as another nation's poem unfurling *our* national drama. Evidently, we have not yet outgrown Milton's tutelage.

I

So I will start with what most of us agree on, *Milton matters*—but by way of acknowledging that disagreements emerge (and sometimes become disagreeable disputes) the moment we ask *why* Milton matters, and then entwine with this question another, "Who reads what how?"[3] We are caught by surprise, often dizzyingly so, when, still mired in the culture wars of the last century, we discover that the "who" on one side of the debate achieves consensus with the "who" on the other side in the claim that, even if he is (in our time) a monument to dead ideas, Milton is a reliable index to the starched theology and bruising politics, including sexual politics, of his own era. If, in *Paradise Lost*, the Son acts as God's emissary during the celestial battle, in his later-published tragedy, masked as Samson, Milton (it is sometimes said) performs the same role within a revenge fantasy. Thus, tearing down the pillars of church and state, he leaves in ruins a government whose restoration he had opposed and by which he had been incarcerated. The gist of such an argument is obvious: Milton's excellence is his relevance to the seventeenth century and irrelevance to our own—with Milton, then, seeming to embrace the very values that, having outgrown them, we now oppose. Whatever enlightened values may be today, Milton's, apparently, are the values of yesterday. But no news here: *Samson Agonistes* was, has been, and still is part of a culture war with Milton's tragedy, as Sharon Achinstein remarks, "bear[ing] the mark of that contest in its very name."[4]

Some 125 years ago, in the grip of what he calls "the Puritan Samson Agonistes," Peter Bayne concluded that "the spiritual depths of Christianity, the Divine power of kindness and self-sacrifice, were fully fathomed" in *none* of Milton's last poems, wherein dwells instead "the inspiration of Puritan battle."[5] And in the aftermath of 9/11 comes this bitter complaint from Michael Mendle:

I write in the wake of the terrorist attacks, which confirm in their way the full hideousness of Milton's fantasy of exterminatory hatred upon "all who sat beneath." . . . Even the details ring home: Milton subtly shifted the terms of the Samson story in Judges to exclude personal motives and denied the implication of suicide. Like the modern terrorist martyrs who deny their deaths constitute the sin of suicide, Milton's Samson's death is only "by accident" . . . , the cause of "dire necessity."[6]

John Carey, aware of the same harrowing ironies and analogies, asks, in his anniversary reflections on 9/11: "Is . . . [this] what *Samson Agonistes* teaches?"[7] Or, alternatively, are the lessons the poem supposedly teaches the same ones we learn from it?

A director's program notes to a recent reading are, within the context of such questioning, particularly astute:

Samson Agonistes is a troubling work at any time, for it is a timeless study of the self-righteous instinct urging all defeated men to vengeance and violence. As such, it is a work which remains curiously open, for who can without confounding ambivalence be sure just *who* this English Samson is meant to stand for, or who next might feel justified in invoking his example.[8]

Is Milton's poem a manual for killing? Is it a polemic on behalf of war? Is the history it reports a record of servitude or freedom, of history repeated—or renewed and transfigured? And does Samson's life distill into the resume of a terrorist? What are the consequences, we might go on to ask, of reverting to an earlier reading of *Samson Agonistes* as a poem in which the protagonist, not morally compromised, takes, in "a death so noble" (1724),[9] "magnanimous revenge upon his enemies";[10] a reading that finds in the tragic "action of *Samson Agonistes,* a moral greatness;—the sacrifice of oneself for the sake of others. . . . In the case of Samson," this critic continues, "the sacrifice is life itself, for the sake of God and country,—religion and patriotism."[11] What are the risks both here, and later, in ratcheting up our claims and applauding Samson as "a great guerilla leader"?[12] Is the Samson story—should it be allowed to become—a fuse for a much larger war of civilizations?

Margaret Thatcher seems to think so, as she invokes "the strong man" of *Areopagitica,* awakening from sleep and shaking his invincible locks. Most Miltonists are quick to identify this strong man as Samson; and Thatcher, as if in response to the Miltonic injunction, "Let not England forget her precedence of teaching nations how to live," is just as ready to invoke this image of Samson as a model for what America should be today: a nation acting "vigorously," "deploy[ing] its energies militarily," and moving against "aggressive ideology," while leaving such matters as the promotion of "civil society" and "democratic institutions" to others.[13] The good news (for Thatcher) is that America is a modern-day Samson, a superpower, eager to practice the politics of retaliation. The bad news (for us) is that America is still naive about the avenging hatred such power arouses, not to mention the fact that Thatcher herself uses Milton differently than he would be used, far differently than he (and others) had used Euripides against those who would reduce a city to ruin and desolation and therefore as part of an appeal not to tear down—to create rather than destroy and thereby revive "expiring libertie."[14]

Samson Agonistes is described repeatedly as Milton's "drama of denunciation and personal invective," as his left hand writing poetry, as his "scourge [on] a backsliding nation" and prophecy of "the vengeance to come," as ("angry, embittered, defeated") his "jeremiad on current affairs," and as his Puritan attachment to "the potency of a fanatical idea" in which, nourished by faith, true heroes surrender themselves to "an overruling Providence" as they claim "a *favoured* communion with the Divine Being."[15] As if it were a propaganda piece on behalf of a discredited regime and a failed ideology, Milton's tragedy is often read as a polemic against the Philistines and Dagon rather than (in parallel with the Book of Judges) as a critique of the English people, Milton's allies rather than his enemies—and as a scrutiny of their God. Moreover, through his own revisions and transgressions of the Judges narrative, Milton urges, as poets since have done, that his own poetry, not "univocal in a theological sense," is "pluralist" and "open"—an insistent questioning, the exact "opposite of the sealed . . . text of religion."[16] Milton's aim in *Samson Agonistes,* no less than *Paradise Regained,* is to stretch biblical stories beyond their existing parameters, in the process authorizing no single interpretation of a scriptural tale but, instead, privileging hermeneutical suspicion over complacent exegesis. As Margaret Kean so wisely observes, Milton puts "all authorities past and present under scrutiny, making them the subject of debate," as he then "strives to re-invest his telling of events with the full impact of a revolutionary moment."[17] Through reconfigurations of biblical stories, history, once reinterpreted by them, can then be made anew.

Accordingly, never forgetting Samson's swagger and bluster, Milton raises the issue of Samson's culpability and accomplishes an unveiling of it as he forces the questions: does God dispense with his laws, and to what extent has Samson's own aggression provoked aggression against his people? In *Pro Populo Anglicano Defensio,* Milton is insistent: "the law allows no exceptions," nor are such exemptions found in Scriptures, where "the law of God does most closely agree with the law of nature" (YP 4:365, 373, 422). Milton is unequivocal: "a law which overthrows all laws cannot itself be a law" (YP 4:401). Put simply: the law makes of Samson an outlaw, within which context it needs to be remembered (with Luke H. Wiseman) that "the first recorded act of Samson is one which involved a violation of the law," with his life, then, becoming a whole series of such violations.[18] Milton may even have remembered (with Maimonides) that, if he is to be revered, the judge must show reverence for the law; he "must not make himself contemptible" and, further, "is forbidden to do menial labor in public . . . or attend assemblies of ignorant people."[19]

Yoking together *The Doctrine and Discipline of Divorce* and *Samson Agonistes* through the sexual metaphor of grinding at the mill, Milton presents Samson, first, as going a-whoring in order to throw into contention Samson's own flouting of the laws he is expected to uphold and, then, as married for a second time in order to interrogate the lawfulness of those marriages. By simultaneously questioning whether Samson has a divine warrant either for his marriages or for going to the temple/theater, Milton brings into dispute the proposition justifying all that Samson does, namely that the most troubling of his actions are divinely motioned and approved; that his is a tragedy wherein Samson's mind is repeatedly subdued to the dispensations of providence. Rather, in keeping with one of Terry Eagleton's characterizations of modernist tragedy, in *Samson Agonistes,* "the pact . . . between fate and freedom begins to break up, as a self-determining subject," acting of his own accord, "squares up to an external compulsion"[20] when Samson feels some rousing motions within. In this interpretive calculus, Milton seems to be saying with Gregory Nazianzen: "I saw in the man *before* his actions exactly what I afterwards found him *in* his actions."[21]

II

It was still being said at the end of the nineteenth century (and it continues to be said today) that "Milton viewed himself . . . as raised up by Heaven."[22] Yet few who say so acknowledge, much less document, Milton's emerging suspicion of an idea that, for a while, had caught him within its embrace. Would that Milton "had considered . . . the wildness of fanaticism and enthusiasm," writes one of his eighteenth-century critics,[23] in that very complaint crafting the bold outlines of a critique, which Milton begins in *The Tenure of Kings and Magistrates,* suppresses in *Pro Populo Anglicano Defensio,* but eventually retrieves in *A Treatise of Civil Power,* and threads through his entire tragedy. Within its scaffolding, *Samson Agonistes* may contain assumptions previously credited by Milton; but the failure of the revolution seems to have left Milton with an urgent need to reexamine those assumptions—where they lead and how to modify them, especially those that breed contempt, foster cruelty, and foment violence. Kindled not by the energy of the historical moment but by its frustrations, *Samson Agonistes* is a protest poem in its every aspect: in its epistle, even in its generic and prosodic forms, directing "a counterblast"[24] at the Restoration, its aesthetics and politics, as well as the theological tenets and religious values subtending both.

It is as if Milton is here moving toward the more mocking posture, in another century, assumed by the American president John Adams, who thought it never should be pretended that any person employed in national leadership has interviews with the gods, or is in any sense under the inspiration of heaven. Milton matures into a position that is a far cry from the one now attributed to George W. Bush, for whom 9/11 is said to have provided authorization for his presidency, with Bush himself apparently believing that he had divine sanction for going to war against Iraq.[25] In one of the supreme ironies of the American journalistic press, Daniel Henninger avers that "what is now clear is that . . . [the churches] don't believe in evil as John Milton believed in it, and as does, evidently, George Bush."[26]

Identity between Milton and Bush is achieved by paralleling Bush's words, "Today our nation saw evil," with the words of the Elder Brother in *A Masque:* "evil on itself shall back recoil, / And mix no more with goodness" and, "if this fail, / The pillared firmament is rottenness / And earth's base built on stubble" (592–93, 596–98). There is no mention here of the generic tendencies of a mask to represent moral categories starkly, in black and white, as opposed to Milton's blurring of those categories when, in words from *Areopagitica,* he declares: "Good and evill we know in the field of this World grow up together inseparably," with "the knowledge of good . . . so involv'd and interwoven with the knowledge of evill" (YP 2:514). There is no awareness here that, in *Paradise Lost,* evil comes to be defined as revenge: "Revenge . . . / . . . long back on itself recoils," "spite then with spite . . . repaid" (9.171–72, 178). No recognition, either, that in a work where he cites *A Mask,* Milton, in *An Apology against a Pamphlet,* is insistent that an author's characters should be "ever distinguisht from the persons [like the Elder Brother] he introduces" (YP1:880). Perhaps *especially* this Elder Brother who, if he speaks in character, speaks as an adolescent, not as an Isocratic orator, and who, as it happens, maturing into a staunch royalist, came to think that Milton's *Pro Populo Anglicano Defensio* was "deserving of burning" and its author "of the gallows."[27] Surely Milton would detach his own complex moral vision from the likes of John Egerton, First Earl of Bridgewater, in the same way as he would eventually detach himself from the Samson legend in which others had wrapped him. Milton does not so represent himself but is represented by others as a Samson-like warrior steeling himself for another battle. Hence, Andrew Marvell, mediating Milton to his reading public, distances the poet from the very persona in which others had found him, and would continue to find him.

"The pre-eminent interest" of *Samson Agonistes,* A. Wilson Verity concluded well over a century ago, "is Samson's revenge on the Philistines,"[28] though, almost from the beginning, critics fretted less over this nominal than over what they supposed was the real subject of this tragedy, the revenge Milton himself would take upon his adversaries. If Milton had been mythologized as Samson well before the publication of *Samson Agonistes,* yet within some phase of the poem's composition, in defense of the poet or, more precisely, by way of protecting him, it was incumbent upon someone to say that Milton was not Samson. It was important to mount such a defense before anyone could say, as has been said so insistently through the centuries, that in *Samson Agonistes,* "a veiled presentment of . . . Milton's life," "Samson is Milton," yet "so subtly identified" with him "as almost to defy censorship."[29] Indeed, a whole series of meldings carry over into *Samson Agonistes:* Milton and Cromwell merging into one another in the letters of state, Milton and Satan becoming one at crucial moments in *Paradise Lost,* and Milton/ Samson/Cromwell/Satan blurring into one another as *Samson Agonistes* proceeds. Yet the dramatic form in which this poem is cast militates against such identifications, as do Milton's repeated declarations that characters speak in their own voices and not in the voice of their author. "Insistence on this distinction . . . may be meant to protect the writer," but as Paul Stevens goes on to explain, "the effect is to erase him."[30]

In view of this now centuries-old critical tradition, it is no wonder that Marvell's initial defense of the poet of *Paradise Lost* was that, no Samson, Milton would have no part in avenging the world for his loss of sight. This early reception of *Paradise Lost,* so finely calibrated, should now go on record as one of the earliest receptions of *Samson Agonistes,* perhaps forestalling but never quelling the personalized political reading Milton's tragedy was about to acquire. It should also be part of the record that Marvell's poem very carefully shields Milton from the charge of taking private revenge, not from what would be the numerous, now notorious, charges that Milton sought revenge, public not private, for indignities experienced by his allies, living and dead, in the aftermath of the Restoration. Indeed, against *those* charges *Samson Agonistes* is Milton's defense of himself.

Within Milton's own writings, the trajectory of the Samson image moves from the resurrected Samson of *Areopagitica* to the fallen Samson of *Paradise Lost;* from Charles I as Samson in *The Reason of Church-Government,* where his locks are likened to the law, to Milton as no Samson in *Samson Agonistes,* where the flash point of the Samson story is its hero's repeated and increasingly audacious claims to divine inspiration in contrast with Milton's growing reticence about making such assertions, let alone acting upon them. Just as in Milton's day Europe was asking what went wrong in England, in *Samson Agonistes* Milton asks the same question as now—through Milton and especially his tragedy—America is compelled to address similar questions about itself, as well as its religious assumptions, which have fostered self-righteousness and threatened mass violence. As darkness becomes visible, as we see where such assumptions lead, we may wish that earlier we had abandoned them. Indeed, as M. G. Lord says, our own wrestling with such questions understandably "recalls Milton in its effort to put a human face on the perpetrators of evil"[31] and, even more, in its eventual need to cast off error by annihilating the propositions by which cultures of violence are perpetuated.

While Milton may have believed that his *De Doctrina Christiana* is inspired by God, he also insists on the sparing use of his own words, "even when they arise from the context of revelation."[32] In *Paradise Lost,* Milton frets over those "feigning . . . to act / By spiritual [power], to themselves appropriating / The Spirit of God"; and in the same poem, for all its bravura when it comes to claiming inspiration, Milton must ask, *what if this all be a fiction:* "[what] if all be mine, / Not hers who brings it nightly to my Ear"

(9.46–47)? Those "what ifs" concerning divine promptings and motions from above form the very core of the uncertain world of *Samson Agonistes,* indeed are the signatures of uncertainty in a poem that asks whether Samson's "part" in this tragedy is really "from heaven assigned" (1217) and whether his actions in the play are truly a "command from heaven" (1212).

The defining feature of Samson's world is its uncertainty, Milton so preferring tragedy to determinism that he extends uncertainty to the very matters—Samson's divine warrant and renovated spirit—that the best of critics continue to invest with certainty.[33] In this poem, the shock of interpretive discovery comes when there is certifiably divine intervention, and from the accompanying realization that this intervention is not a sanction for Samson's politics of retaliation but, rather, a divine tempering of such. To ask about the lawfulness, as well as to examine the ramifications, of Samson's going to the temple/theater, then hurling it down, is to invite the answer (albeit to a different question) of *Eikonoklastes:* "the vulgar judge of it according to the event, and the lerned according to the purpose of them that do it" (YP 3:221).

By letting the vulgar escape, Milton's God places brakes on the very actions he supposedly sanctions and on the culture of violence he is sometimes thought to promote, thus illustrating what Terry Eagleton would probably call another instance of that "sweet violence" through which "mercy . . . flourish[es] without making a mockery of justice."[34] This signally important moment in *Samson Agonistes* resonates ironically not only with the prefatory slur against "trivial and vulgar persons" (CP, 356) but with the Chorus's earlier description of "the common rout, / That . . . / Grow up and perish, as the summer fly" (674–76); indeed, with those many disparaging comments, in prose and poetry alike, where the vulgar are "the inconsiderate multitude" of *The Readie and Easie Way* (YP 7:375) or "the miscellaneous rabble" of *Paradise Regained* (3.50).

In *Samson Agonistes,* apparently, it is an enlightened minority, persons of character, who escape or to whom Milton refers in *Pro Populo Anglicano Defensio* as the "sound" part (YP 4:317), the "uncorrupted" (YP 4:332), "the better, the sound part" or "the better part" (YP 4:457; compare 470), "the wise, that is, and the brave" (YP 4:343). They are perhaps that third class of people described by Manoa as "More generous far and civil . . . [for whom] / The rest was magnanimity to remit" (1469–70). By sparing three thousand of the people who, according to the Judges narrative,[35] perish, Milton's God restores both the justice and the compassion to religion that the Samson story had been used to hijack from it, at the same time making clear that God is neither defined, nor limited, by his would-be messengers; that, indeed, he is himself bound by the edicts and ethics his supposed messengers so readily defy. If Milton urges in *Eikonoklastes* that "God judges not by human fansy," in *Samson Agonistes* he seems to reiterate the idea that God asserts "his Justice . . . [only] to the magnifying of his own mercy" (YP 3:432).

With its uncertainties and contradictions, investigative sweep and bristling questions, *Samson Agonistes* mirrors an entire culture, while concurrently affording a critique of it, which is then reinforced outside the poem by the counterparadigm of *Paradise Regained,* its modifying context. The inverted order in which *Paradise Regained* and *Samson Agonistes* appear in the 1671 poetic volume, the implied regression, hints that the warning Milton issues in *Eikonoklastes* still pertains. In *Paradise Lost,* the story of the Israelites, wandering the desert for forty years before entering the Promised Land, culminates in the founding of "their government and their great Senate," chosen "Through the Twelve Tribes, to rule by Laws ordained" (12.226). But if now God's Englishmen should retreat into "a second wandring over that horrid wilderness," as Milton explains in *Eikonoklastes,* the risk is in reverting to their earlier "state of miserie" and to "more civil slaughter" (YP 3:580).

Old values persist, yet new values would displace them—with the Samson story, as told in the Book of Judges and then as retold by Milton, mirroring the changing consciousness of a nation, especially of a nation that, as Heymann Steinthal reports, has undergone "a radical revolution, extending over many important domains of ideas."[36] The Judges history may not repeat itself in the age of Milton; but these two panels of history, separated by centuries, do rhyme. The Samson story, in this context, represents history and values on the other side of the revolution, bygone events and conditions, earlier beliefs and values now ready to be overthrown. What we witness in the juxtaposition of Samson in the Bible, Hebrew and Christian, and the Samson of literary tradition and of Milton's poem, is the development of a legend, its connection to religious life and ethical systems over time, but also, in terms of the English revolution and 9/11, the relationship between ethical systems, the law, and political action. We witness the formation of a critique of culture, all the more remarkable if, begun before and finished after the Restoration, *Samson Agonistes* may be said to illustrate that "the poet writes the poem but major poems sometimes rewrite their authors."[37] Indeed, had F. R. Leavis not misinterpreted Milton's prophetic message in the last poems, or so badly miscalculated its thrust while reading *Paradise Lost* in the trenches during World War II, he may never have moved so unconditionally for the poet's dislodgment.

III

Milton *matters,* then, because with *Samson Agonistes* we see America, along with England, "responding to its tragedy," as Derek Walcott urges it to do, "with tragic poetry" that makes a nation's eyes "clear with grief."[38] Milton *matters* because, in facing tragedy, he forces us to reach beyond an axis of good and evil in the world to a more ambiguous reality. Milton's tragedy *matters* especially because it is a challenge to the past—an invitation to restore, even to establish, its relevance to the present time not by reinventing Milton but by recuperating his tragedy through reversion to earlier readings of *Samson Agonistes*. Those readings stretch from Andrew Marvell's Samson, "grop[ing] the temple's posts in spite"; to Dr. Johnson's Samson, whose plaudits come from "bigotry" and "ignorance"; to Shelley's Samson-like Prometheus ("eyeless in hate"); to Thomas Macaulay's *Samson Agonistes*, "the least successful" of Milton's efforts in part because of its "wild and barbaric" melodies; to George Gilfillan's Samson whose hand, as he stands at the pillars, "has few flowers in it. . . . His spirit is that of Abimelech," and whose actions within the poem itself bear "the wrath of Heaven" and "threaten to crush wonder . . . rather than to awaken . . . admiration."[39] And from here on to Bayne's "Puritan Samson Agonistes" (see note 6). But also back to Carey, whose own haunting analogies are a reminder that literary contexts, drawn from the textual field of Milton's last poems, are often biblical contexts as well, and that text and contexts are irrevocably involved.

Yet regardless of the context, whether it is afforded by Milton's tragedy or its source in the Book of Judges, each context eventually rivets attention to the moment of terror at the temple/theater when, having already slaughtered thirty, then a thousand, now in taking down a "Hostile City" (1561), Samson slaughters thousands more than in all his life he had slain before. It is one of the coincidences of history that the rhetoric of biblical commentary just before 9/11 will match with the rhetoric of some Milton criticism in its aftermath. Thus one commentator on the Book of Judges will proclaim that Samson is "like a modern suicide bomber" and, simultaneously, will advance his story as "a warning, not an example."[40] Just as England could find its tragedy in the figure of Samson, America can now find its tragedy in *Samson Agonistes*—a poem that without salesmanship, as Arthur E. Barker once expected, has become "a relevant tract for the times, in part because the story it enshrines has such pertinence."[41]

The Bible itself is mute on the details of this final "desolation" (1561); although for two centuries now, through its annotations, it sometimes invokes Milton's account as scriptural supplement:

> those two massie pillars
> With horrible convulsion to and fro,
> He tugged, he shook, till down they came and drew
> The whole roof after them, with burst of thunder
> Upon the heads of all who sat beneath.[42]   (1648–52)

That said, we can focus on questions underscored by Milton's tragedy: Is *Samson Agonistes* an embrace—or simply a representation—of violence, an incitement to—or indictment of—terror? Is revenge a divine instinct or a human impulse, and is it to be condoned or condemned? And what of anger in *Samson Agonistes?* Where is this poem's supposed politics of retaliation driving us? Is the poem itself caught in the paradox of asserting continuity with institutionalized religion as it contemplates, in the image of Dagon's temple destroyed, institutionalized religion in collapse? What image of deity here prevails, the God of the Apocalypse or the God of the Gospels: the figure of a wrathful, avenging God, "cultivated by the . . . self-righteous," or "the reverse . . . image of God as a broken body, as an executed political criminal"?[43]

What Philip Fisher seems to construe as a "vehement, spirited anger," working itself through progressive states until it reaches "finality" in the epitomizing line in Milton's tragedy, "calm of mind all passion spent" (1760), at times seems more like "uncompassionate anger" (818), "anger, unappeasable," raging like a "tempest never to be calmed" (963–64).[44] This trait of character may be better comprehended in terms of a question: Is Samson's anger "an excess" or "a defect," or, rather, a mark of Aristotle's honorable man, "angry at the right things, and with the right people, . . . as he ought, when he ought, and as long as he ought"?[45] If judges signal the invention of a legal system, as well as society's intervention with punishments meant to eliminate retaliation, it is of some moment that Samson in the Book of Judges, from whom Milton withholds the very appellation of judge, is engaged throughout his life in acts of revenge. With those acts escalating, the question becomes, to adapt one of Fisher's finest formulations, "Should . . . [they] be forgiven? Should . . . [they] be ignored? Must retaliation happen? If it happens, will it lead to a response and a spiral of violence that has no easy exit?"[46] Is Samson ultimately a person whose only exit, whose "dire necessity" (1666), is that he "inevitably" must pull down "destruction" on himself (1658)? Is this the bind in which Samson, supposedly "a person raised / With . . . command from heaven / To free my country" (1211–13), is finally caught? Are we, in turn, the ongoing victims of that anger?

And what *of* violence in Milton's tragedy? In the character of Samson, does Milton underwrite or undermine its practitioners, together with those cultural authorities and institutions that would validate them? Legitimating them, is he complicit in such practices; or, interrogating them, does he reject the cultural barbarism subtended by the Samson story and coded into the poem in the famous line, "And a thousand foreskins fell, the flower of *Palestin*" (144)—into the very indignity of counting dead bodies. To what extent are Milton's critics, as opposed to Milton himself, responsible for those harsh rebukes, over the centuries, from which John Carey and others have tried to shield the poet, with Carey, for one, reminding us that "Milton's drama is . . . a drastic rewriting of the Samson story":

[*Samson Agonistes*] calls into question Samson's motivation, and whether he has any divine sanction for his suicide attack. . . . Crucially, Milton omits Samson's prayer. . . . In this final stage of the drama we cannot know what is going on in Samson's mind. . . . All through this last phase Milton hides Samson's thoughts and, for that matter, God's. When he destroys the theatre Samson may think he is carrying out God's will, or he may be following his purely human impulse to revenge.[47]

"There is insufficient evidence to eliminate any of these possibilities" from a poem, concludes Carey,[48] that treats the Samson story less as a record than as an echo of history. In *Samson Agonistes*, Milton creates a tragedy that in its aftermath resonates with history—a poem in which there seems to be a causal relationship between personal tragedy and national disaster, between Samson defeated and a nation in ruins, and in which Milton not only stages the crises of his culture but structures a critique of them. Even by those who find in *Samson Agonistes* "the noblest conception of . . . [Samson] in modern poetry," we are reminded that "no . . . national renovation" is achieved by him.[49] That is not part of his story. Indeed, it may be Johann Gottfried Herder's own grasp of the intricacies of the Samson narrative, which caused him to conclude that "the life of man may be considered as a miniature of the fate of nations."[50]

Carey seems to get it just right when he concludes that seeing 9/11 under the lights of *Samson Agonistes* makes it all the more evident that the premises underlying each tragedy belong to a world that Milton has outgrown and would have us do the same. *Samson Agonistes* is not trivialized by politics, nor does it trivialize 9/11, so long as we remember that the lesson here is not that history repeats itself but that history rhymes and that within the vast complexities of their worlds, in the words of Salman Rushdie, "one man's hero is another's villain."[51] One nation's freedom fighters are another's terrorists. In fact, deriving its potency from the imprecision and incompleteness of such parallels, from "the principle of inexact analogy,"[52] *Samson Agonistes* helps explain not only what happened on 9/11, but why it happened and then how, in practicing a politics of resentment and retaliation, a nation compromises its own moral authority. Moreover, as Annabel Patterson would probably go on to say, *Samson Agonistes* does so by "offering . . . readers a *choice* of interpretations, arising out of a welter of conflicting textual directions," with Milton thus creating "the readerly equivalent of Arminianism, hermeneutical free will," in a poem that, as Patterson might say, becomes a swirling "vortex of possible or alternative meanings."[53]

Samson Agonistes is a reminder that we must refuse easy answers even as we resist uncomplicated allegiances; that poetry repeals traditions and voids conventions; and that the truths of poetry are plural not singular and, in Milton's tragedy, so resistant to easy ideological unravelings that they are not encapsulated by Samson, or Manoa, or the Chorus. If answers in their inconsistency are inadequate, questions in the poem, if insistent, are interconnected and, while usually unanswered, not always unanswerable. This is a poem that mirrors cultural violence without summoning us to mimic it. Thus, in a turn of the critical lens, Milton's tragedy may seem to unleash its subversive forces against the very system of beliefs others have thought it is meant to support. Not so much a rehearsal of existing interpretation but, instead, part of a contestatory tradition, *Samson Agonistes* tries the reader's aptitude for *re*interpretation.

Lest anyone think that the interpretation charted here is a distinctly postmodernist phenomenon, let us remember that "the reading" of Milton's tragedy we now associate with John Carey and Irene Samuel was already in place, embryonically, before Milton's death, in Andrew Marvell's dedicatory poem to *Paradise Lost*. What is widely regarded as the Carey-Samuel "reading" achieved major articulation more than a century ago when, as if in response to Peter Bayne, J. Howard B. Masterman in 1897 sought to free *Samson Agonistes* from a politics of violence and religion of retaliation. Here in Milton's poem is *the tragedy of Puritanism,* which, he says, "appears as the blind and discredited champion of Divine Vengeance," now a "brute secular force" that "might hope to strike one more blow" only to "perish in the overthrow of its enemies." The whole point of Milton's 1671 poetic volume, where each poem is a "fragment," neither complete without the other, as Masterman supposes, is to present as "a great alternative . . . [to revenge] the victory of patience and self-repression—the Divine overcoming of evil with good"; to choose as "the better part . . . to be patient" and, despite the penalty of disappointment, "to hope."[54]

An alternative tradition of *Samson* criticism is enabling just because it presses old questions upon us but also allows for new solutions to them, in this way drawing *Samson Agonistes* out of relative seclusion even as it releases meanings, over time embedded in literary works, through new and opportune contextualizations. In the process, misunderstandings are swallowed up in new understandings as, in his last poems, Milton casts his lot with those who worked not for the undoing of the human race but for its betterment and who, planting good where others had sown evil, would still build a new world on the wreckage of failed dreams. This last point, Milton's final poems—all of them—speak in a chorus. *Samson Agonistes* makes it in thunder.

The Graduate Center of the City University of New York

NOTES

1. See Adam Engel, *"Samson Agonistes* (Confession of a Terrorist/Martyr)," from the Web magazine *Counterpunch,* ed. Alexander Cockburn and Jeffrey St. Clair, November 2, 2002; available at www.Counterpunch.com; Christopher Shea, *The Boston Globe,* Sunday, November 3, 2002, D5; and D. D. Guttenplan, "Samson the Suicide Bomber," *The New York Times,* Saturday, December 28, 2002, B9. This article carries the caption, "Samson the suicide bomber," and is coupled with this remark: "More than 300 years after his death, John Milton is being accused of encouraging terrorism." In another piece, Milton is credited with having created a language for warfare; see Geoffrey Nunberg, "War-Speak Worthy of Milton and Chuck Norris," *The New York Times,* Sunday, April 6, 2003, WK 4; and in yet another, the Elder Brother's words on evil (see *A Mask,* 593–99) are juxtaposed with those of George Bush on 9/11, even as Milton's portrait here appears with the legend, "Milton: A Man for Our Time" (see Daniel Henninger, "Wonder Land: 'Know Ye Not Me?': The Face of Evil Is Seen, Defeated," *The Wall Street Journal,* Friday, April 18, 2003, Opinion). On Milton and terrorism, see also John T. Shawcross, "'What is Faith, Love, Vertue unassaid': Some Literary Answers to Our Ever-Present Evils" (paper presented at the Literature and Christianity Conference, New Orleans, 2003).

2. The last two of these performance readings were sponsored by the North American Society for the Study of Romanticism (New York, August 2, 2003) and by the Renaissance Society of America (New York, April 2, 2004). On performance history, see Timothy J. Burbery, "Intended for the Stage?: *Samson Agonistes* in Performance," *Milton Quarterly* 38 (March 2004): 35–49.

3. I borrow this phrase from Norman N. Holland, *5 Readers Reading* (New Haven, Conn., 1975), 1 (see chapter subtitle).

4. Sharon Achinstein, *"Samson Agonistes,"* in *A Companion to Milton,* ed. Thomas N. Corns (Oxford, 2001), 414.

5. Peter Bayne, *The Chief Actors in the Puritan Revolution* (London, 1878), 345.

6. Michael Mendle, review of David Loewenstein, *Representing Revolution in Milton and His Contemporaries,* in *Renaissance Quarterly* 55 (Summer 2002): 778–79.

7. John Carey, "A Work in Praise of Terrorism? September 11 and *Samson Agonistes,"* *Times Literary Supplement,* Friday, September 6, 2002, 15. Compare Stanley Fish, "Postmodern Warfare: The Ignorance of Our Warrior Intellectuals," *Harper's Magazine* 305 (July 2002): 33–40, and Fish, "Can Postmodernists Condemn Terrorism? Don't Blame Relativism," *The Responsive Community* 12 (Summer 2002): 27–31.

8. Robert Scanlan, "Director's Note," *Milton's "Samson Agonistes,"* 92nd Street Y, April 21, 2003, program insert.

9. All quotations of Milton's poetry are from *Milton: Complete Short Poems,* 2nd ed., ed. John Carey (London, 1997). Poetry from this edition will be cited by line (and where appropriate, book) numbers, parenthetically within the text. Prose passages accompanying Milton's poems, also from the Carey edition, are signaled by the abbreviation CP, followed by the page reference.

10. Walter Raleigh, *Milton* (1900; reprint, New York, 1967), 28; see also 29.

11. H. M. Percival, *Milton's "Samson Agonistes"* (London, 1890), xix.

12. See Ann Phillips, ed., *Samson Agonistes* (London, 1974), 24, and more recently Janel Mueller, "The Figure and the Ground: Samson as a Hero of London Nonconformity, 1662–1667," in *Milton and the Terms of Liberty,* ed. Graham Parry and Joad Raymond (Cambridge, 2002), 146.

13. For Margaret Thatcher's op-ed piece, see "Advice to a Superpower," *The New York Times,* Monday, February 11, 2002, A27. For the supposed Samson allusion, see *Areopagitica* (YP 2:557–58), and for Milton's injunction, see *The Doctrine and Discipline of Divorce* (YP 2:232). Hereafter, all quotations of Milton's prose (unless otherwise indicated) will be from *Complete Prose Works of John Milton,* 8 vols., ed. Don M. Wolfe et al. (New Haven, Conn., 1953–1982), hereafter designated YP and cited parenthetically by volume and page number in the text.

14. Tellingly, like Milton, Euripides has been invoked as a looking glass on 9/11; see, for example, Alexander Cockburn, "Euripides Joins Post 9/11 Debates," in the Web magazine *Counterpunch,* ed. Cockburn and St. Clair, May 23, 2003; available at www.Counterpunch.com.

15. A. Wilson Verity, ed., *Milton's "Samson Agonistes"* (Cambridge, 1892), xxvii; Edmund K. Chambers, ed., *Samson Agonistes* (London, 1897), 19; E. H. Blakeney, ed., *Samson Agonistes* (Edinburgh, 1902), xxviii (compare xxix); Rose Macaulay, *Milton* (1935; reprint, New York, 1962), 117; and I. P. Fleming, ed., *Samson Agonistes* (London, 1876), 34, 35.

16. Adonis ('Ali Ahmad Sa'id), "Poetry and Apoetical Culture," trans. Esther Allen, in *The Pages of Day and Night,* trans. Samuel Hazo (Evanston, Ill., 2000), 106–7. In his important commentary, *The Book of Judges,* trans. P. H. Steenstra (Edinburgh, [1868]), Paulus Cassel is supremely sensitive to the force of that tradition even as he complains of "the seventeenth and eighteenth century irreverence [toward Samson] too often called criticism, and [of] that frivolous insipidity . . . considered free inquiry. Aesthetic vapidness," Cassel laments, continues "to nestle in the exegesis of the Old Testament," as is strikingly evident in the Old Testament dialogues of Johann Gottfried Herder, *Oriental Dialogues: Containing the Conversations of Eugenius and Alciphron on the . . . Sacred Poetry of the Hebrews* (London, 1801), 225.

17. Margaret Kean, "Paradise Regained," in Corns, *A Companion to Milton,* 431, 429.

18. See Luke H. Wiseman, *Men of Faith; or, Sketches from the Book of Judges* (London, 1870), 312.

19. See also Maimonides, *The Code of Maimonides, Book Fourteen: The Book of Judges,* trans. Abraham M. Hershman (New Haven, Conn., 1949), 76.

20. Terry Eagleton, *Sweet Violence: The Idea of the Tragic* (Oxford, 2003), 118. Milton has the precedent of Peter Martyr, *Most Fruitfull & Learned Comentaries* (London, 1564), for using "of his own accord" to signify "of his own free will," with Martyr arguing that Samson's parents made vows "of their own fre will" and followed them "of their owne accorde" (f203v).

21. Gregory Nazianzen, "Second Invective against Julian," in *Julian the Emperor Containing Nazianzen's Two Invectives and Labanius's Monody,* trans. C. W. King (London, 1888), 105.

22. Thomas Keightley, *An Account of the Life, Opinions, and Writings of John Milton, with an Introduction to "Paradise Lost"* (London, 1855), 322. Compare "Samson was a hero raised up to Heaven" (322).

23. John Upton, cited by Francis Blackburne, *Memoirs of Thomas Hollis,* 2 vols. (London, 1780), 2:624.

24. The phrase and sentiment belong to A. J. Grieve, ed., *Samson Agonistes* (London, 1904), vi.

25. As reported on CNN's *Connie Chung Tonight,* March 10, 2003. For further documenta-

tion and alarmingly acute commentary, see Norman Mailer, *Why Are We at War?* (New York, 2003), 65, 111.

26. Henninger, "Wonder Land," Opinion. See also Mailer, *Why Are We at War?*, 51, 53, 55.

27. See William Riley Parker, *Milton: A Biography,* 2 vols. (Oxford, 1968), 2:975.

28. Verity, *Milton's "Samson Agonistes,"* xlii. Verity insists that, despite the strong "undercurrent of personal allusion" (164), which would seem to make Milton himself "the true protagonist of the drama" (165), "the parallel between Samson and Milton ceases when we investigate the respective causes of the failure of each, Milton . . . overthrown through the weakness and folly of others, Samson through his own" (lxi).

29. For the first quotation, see J. E. Bradshaw, ed., *Milton: "Samson Agonistes"* (London, 1949), 19; for the second and third quotations, see C. S. Jerram, ed., *Samson Agonistes* (London, 1898), x. In *Samson Agonistes,* Fleming traces Henry John Todd's notion that "MILTON must have a view to himself in Samson" (32) to the younger Jonathan Richardson, William Hayley, and Charles Dunster, with Hayley and Dunster reinforcing their views by the idea that Milton's tragedy is "at least three years anterior to 'Paradise Regained'" (34; see also 6). Compare Thomas Page, ed., *Samson Agonistes* (London, 1896), 13–14; Chambers, *Samson Agonistes,* 17. Believing that Milton speaks in all his characters, Grieve numbers Milton among the "quasi-dramatists"; see Grieve, *Samson Agonistes,* x.

30. Paul Stevens, "Pretending to Be Real: Stephen Greenblatt and the Legacy of Popular Existentialism," *New Literary History* 33 (Summer 2002): 502.

31. M. G. Lord, "The Fourth Target," *The New York Times Book Review,* Sunday, September 8, 2002, 12.

32. In this instance, I quote from the translation of *De Doctrina Christiana* by Charles R. Sumner as it is reprinted in *The Works of John Milton,* 18 vols., ed. Frank Allen Patterson (New York, 1933), 14:11; compare YP 6:122. In this very insistence, Milton may be said to have incited, even as he continues to fuel, the controversy over the authorship of *De Doctrina Christiana.*

33. See John T. Shawcross, *The Uncertain World of "Samson Agonistes"* (Cambridge, 2001), esp. 61, 95, 104.

34. Eagleton, *Sweet Violence,* 141.

35. There is a striking symmetry between the "three thousand men of Judah" who, in the Judges narrative (15:9), think that Samson is making trouble for the Israelites and the "three thousand men and women" (16:27) who, on the roof in the Judges narrative, are, in Milton's poem, saved from the final catastrophe.

36. Heymann Steinthal, "The Legend of Samson," in Ignác Goldziber, *Mythology among the Hebrews and Its Historical Development,* trans. Russell Martineau, 392–446 (New York, 1967), 440.

37. Balachandra Rajan, "The Poetics of Heresy," in *Osiris and Urania,* ed. Elizabeth Sauer (Toronto, forthcoming), ms. 78.

38. Derek Walcott quoted in Melanie Rehak, "Questions for Derek Walcott: Poet of the Ages," *The New York Times Magazine,* Sunday, May 12, 2002, 19.

39. See, respectively, Andrew Marvell, "On Mr Milton's 'Paradise Lost,'" in *Andrew Marvell: The Complete Poems,* ed. Elizabeth Story Donno (Middlesex, 1972), 192 (see esp. lines 5–10); Samuel Johnson, "The Rambler No. 139. Tuesday, July 16, 1751," as excerpted by Ralph E. Hone, ed., *John Milton's "Samson Agonistes": The Poem and Materials for Analysis* (San Francisco, 1966), 103; Percy Bysshe Shelley, *Prometheus Unbound,* in *Shelley's Poetry and Prose,* ed. Donald H. Reiman and Sharon B. Powers (New York, 1977), 136, act 1, line 7; Thomas Macaulay, *An Essay on the Life and Works of John Milton: Together with the Imaginary Conversation*

between Him and Abraham Cowley (London, 1868), 20–21; George Gilfillan, "Critical Estimate of the Genius and Poetical Works of John Milton," in *Milton's Poetical Works,* 2 vols., ed. Charles Cowan Clarke (Edinburgh, 1853), 2:xxx. Of Marvell's poem, it needs to be remembered that he is marking not Milton's identity with, but distinction from, Samson; and of Johnson's remarks, that his harsh words come on the heels of his observation that Samson "declares himself moved by a secret impulse to comply, and utters some dark presages of a great event to be brought to pass by his agency, under the direction of Providence" (102); and later, in "the Rambler No. 140. Saturday, July 20, 1751," he explains that his severest censure is for "the solemn introduction of the Phoenix . . . which is . . . incongruous to the personage to who it is ascribed," hence the poet's "grossest errour" (104).

40. See F. Calvin Parker, "Formations Lesson for August 26: Samson," *Biblical Recorder,* August 3, 2001, 1. Parker cites the example of Keito Yoshida, imprisoned as a traitor by the Japanese in the aftermath of Pearl Harbor, thereupon swearing vengence, only to discover in prison that forgiveness is superior to the way of Samson and that vengeance is God's alone. The rhetoric of terrorism is already a feature of Milton criticism in the 1990s as both Noam Flinker and Jackie Di Salvo illustrate; see Flinker, "Pagan Holiday and National Conflict: A Philistine Reading of *Samson Agonistes,*" *Milton Quarterly* 25 (December 1991): 160, and Di Salvo as cited by Roy Flannagan, ed., *The Riverside Milton* (Boston, 1998), 795. Worries about Samson, if focused by 9/11, were in the air months before: see Eric Lewin Altschuler et al., "Did Samson Have Antisocial Personality Disorder," *Archives of General Psychiatry* 58 (February 2001): unpaginated Internet essay; available at http://archpsyc.ama-assn.org; and Cullen Murphy, "Second Opinions: History Winds Up in the Waiting Room," *The Atlantic Monthly* (June 2001): unpaginated Internet essay; available at www.theatlantic.com.

41. Arthur E. Barker, "Calm Regained through Passion Spent: The Conclusions of the Miltonic Effort," in *The Prison and the Pinnacle: Papers to Commemorate the Tercentenary of "Paradise Regained" and "Samson Agonistes," 1671–1971,* ed. Balachandra Rajan (London, 1973), 34. See also Joseph Berger, "Orthodox Jews Temper Views on Gaza Pullout," *International Herald Tribune,* Wednesday, June 16, 2004, who writes, "It was in Gaza that Samson brought the house down. Some Israelis say with gallows humor that in killing hundreds of Philistines he was the first suicide bomber" (4).

42. See, for example, J. J. Lias, *The Book of Judges, with Maps, Notes, and Introduction* (Cambridge, 1882), 175.

43. Eagleton, *Sweet Violence,* 210.

44. Philip Fisher, *The Vehement Passions* (Princeton, NJ, 2002), 193, 36; see also 10, 154. "Calm of mind," Rees, *Aristotle's Theory and Milton's Practice,* reports, is a cliché of Italian criticism and, as such, reinforces the platitudinous nature of the final words of the Chorus (10).

45. Fisher, *The Vehement Passions,* 173. Fisher quotes from the Loeb Classical Library edition of Aristotle's *Nicomachean Ethics,* 4.5.1125b30–35.

46. Fisher, *The Vehement Passions,* 185.

47. Carey, "A Work in Praise of Terrorism," 15.

48. Ibid., 16.

49. See Cassel, *The Book of Judges,* 225, 183.

50. Herder, *Oriental Dialogues,* 322.

51. Salman Rushdie, "Getting into Gang War," *The Washington Post,* Wednesday, December 25, 2002, A29.

52. Patterson, *Censorship and Interpretation: The Conditions of Writing and Reading in Early Modern England* (Madison, 1984), 81; compare 47.

53. Patterson, *Reading between the Lines* (Madison, 1993), 272. The last quotation is from *Censorship and Interpretation,* 156.

54. John Howard Bertram Masterman, *The Age of Milton* (London, 1897), 72. Compare J. H. Hexter, *Reappraisals in History,* 2nd ed. (Chicago: University of Chicago Press, 1979), 248. Masterman underscores the interdependency of the two poems by referring to each of them as a "fragment" (69, 70).

TOLERATIONISM, THE IRISH CRISIS, AND MILTON'S *ON THE LATE MASSACRE IN PIEMONT*

Elizabeth Sauer

T HE POOR OF LYONS, called "Waldensians" by their detractors,[1] resided in the seventeenth century in two Piedmontese valleys of the Alps bordering on Italy and France. While they had been granted toleration within defined geographical boundaries, the Waldensians were not legally entitled to occupy the lower parts of the valley of the Pellice or the open plain. In 1655 Carlos Immanuel II, Duke of Savoy, at the instigation of his mother, Grand Duchess Christina of Lorraine, sent an army of four thousand, led by the Marquis of Pianezza from Turin, to expel the Waldensians from the regions outside the tolerated limits. Assisted by a communal militia and Irish Catholics who had been oppressed under Oliver Cromwell's orders in their homeland, Pianezza's army in the name of Louis XIV and Catholicism slaughtered the Waldensians in the Piedmontese Easter massacre of April 1655. On May 3, the marquis commemorated this civilizing Counter-Reformation conquest by raising a cross "as a sign of the faith and the might of his Royal Highness."[2] When news of the atrocity reached England, the nation, though divided along political and religious lines, found cause for a show of solidarity for its Protestant brethren, who had been slaughtered or had fled to the wintry mountain wasteland. Cromwell himself declared a day of humiliation, contributed generously to a collection of over 38,000 pounds for the victims, and produced letters of protest to European rulers, a task in which his Latin secretary, John Milton, had a formative role. As well as participating in the letter-writing campaign, Milton was said to have drafted an address delivered by Cromwell's envoy, the mathematician and philosopher Sir Samuel Morland, to the court in Turin, and he also composed *On the Late Massacre in Piemont*.[3] As I demonstrate in the following study of the poem's dialogue with the conflictual cultural and political milieu in which it was generated, *Sonnet XVIII* offers a tribute to the Waldensians in Milton's own native English tradition while promoting English Protestant nationalism on the Continent and at home.[4]

Milton's response to the atrocities committed against the Waldensians takes on new meaning when set in relation to the controversial acts and expressions of nation building in Cromwellian England. Slavoj Žižek attributes an "ambiguous and contradictory nature" to "the modern 'nation,'" which he defines as a "community delivered of the traditional 'organic' ties, a community in which the pre-modern links tying down the individual to a particular estate, family, religious group, and so on, are broken." In a reformulation of Benedict Anderson's influential theory that "from the start the nation was conceived in language, not in blood," Žižek argues that nationhood cannot "be reduced to a network of purely symbolic ties: there is always a kind of 'surplus of the Real' that sticks to it—to define itself, 'national identity' must appeal to the contingent materiality of the 'common roots,' of 'blood and soil,' and so on." "The crucial point," he avers, is "to conceive both aspects in their interconnection: it is precisely the new 'suture' effected by the Nation which enables the 'desuturing,' the disengagement from traditional organic ties."[5]

As England's champion writer, Milton contributed substantially to the forms of nationhood produced in conjunction with the imperatives and the "contingent materiality" of "blood and soil."[6] In the historical narrative on the Piedmont massacre, the discursive and symbolic constructions of nationhood meet the material that becomes in turn anglicized and Protestantized even as the colonization of Catholic territory in Ireland reemerges as a subject of heated discussion in the kingdom, and as England's confrontation with cultural, political, and religious difference reaches an apex. The "new 'sutures'" that Žižek associated with the evolving nation stitch the gaps together, but they remain under stress. To replace "organic ties," these sutures must draw heavily on emotional binding, as illustrated in my reading of Milton's *On the Late Massacre in Piemont,* in which the otherwise conventional turn from octave to sestet is generated by an emotional onrush rather than being allotted a formal space.

The result of situating *Sonnet XVIII* in the political and cultural milieu in which it was produced—one that highlights the Cromwellian government's politics of religion—is a new facet to the poem's critical tradition and the work it performs in the history of tolerationism and nationalism.[7] The Miltonic voice in the sonnet merges with those of the martyrs and those of the nation, as the verses resonate with Hebraic, Christian, journalistic, homely, nationalistic, and apocalyptic imagery. At the same time, the outrage that characterized the historical and literary reactions to the Piedmont massacre provokes the cry for divine retribution in the sonnet and offers a pretext for the reinforcement of an imperialist ideology that materialized in the colonization of Ireland and proposed transplantation of Irish Catholics. The first section of this essay, then, establishes a framework for interpreting Parliament's reaction to the Piedmont massacre and to the corresponding English-Irish crisis; the second historicizes the "resolution" Milton presents in the "sestet," specifically the advancement of the Reformation through the planting of Protestantism in Catholic soils.[8]

THE IRISH CRISIS

English nationalism emerged in conjunction with a culture of toleration and, paradoxically, a climate of intolerance and imperial ambition. "Toleration" was a vexed term in the early modern era, and most often used pejoratively. Debates on liberty and diversity focused instead on "liberty of conscience," the aim of which was religious union. "There hath been much these dayes bygone concerning a general *Toleration,* and liberty of Conscience," James Hays begins in his address to Parliament, which quickly becomes a plea for "uniformity in Religion": "by granting too large a *Toleration,* you dishonour God, and disorder the State."[9] True liberty was not synonymous with contemporary notions of liberalism but with the freedom to act according to God's laws. In the configuration of nationhood, which originated in conjunction with tolerationism, certain groups were pushed outside the Christian pale while others were assimilated.

Cromwell's 1648 desire for religious unification characterizes this early notion of tolerationism: "I profess to thee [Colonel Robert "Robin" Hammond] I desire from my heart, I have prayed for it, I have waited for the day to see union and right understanding between the godly people (Scots, English, Jews, Gentiles, Presbyterianism, Independents, Anabaptists, and all)."[10] Cromwell's promotion of the Protestant League in 1654–1655 anticipates his strong appeal in 1655 for Protestant unity: In denouncing the Piedmont massacre, Cromwell urges that warring Protestant parties "by brotherly consent and harmony unite into one" (YP 5:680). The realization of such a vision necessitated the management of any threats to liberty of conscience or religious harmony. It also makes conceivable the link between events as seemingly diverse as the English transplantation of Irish Catholics in the mid-1650s and the Interregnum government's protestation against the atrocities committed upon the Waldensians. The Irish crisis and the persecution of the Waldensians are historically related insofar as these events, along with England's military alliance with France, dominated Cromwell's agenda and Continental politics in the mid-1650s. But they are also connected by virtue of the new sutures of nationalism and by the debates about tolerationism, which made possible the curious juxtaposition of Cromwell's support of a culture of dissent; his anti-Catholicism in the European theater; the proposed readmission of the Jews in the 1655 Whitehall conference; his campaign against the Irish and war against the Spanish; and the Rump's hostility toward English Levellers and Quakers.[11] These apparently contradictory positions are integral to the Interregnum government's political, ecclesiastical, and imperial mission to advance the Reformation movement with which notions of nationhood and tolerationism became entangled. Their juxtaposition affords insights into England's "election," its policies on religious and cultural toleration, and its development of a national and international Protestant and imperial identity.

The various politico-religious campaigns of the Cromwellian government were extensions of the century-long war against popery, anti-Catholicism having become entrenched in the rhetoric and practices of England's nation formation. The history of the conflict with Catholicism generated what Joad Raymond describes as a "typology of accounts of atrocities against Protestants" to which narratives of suffering and persecution conformed to various degrees.[12] Journals thus compared the Piedmont massacre to the oppression of the Cathars in France, the slaughter of Huguenots in Paris on Saint Bartholomew's Eve in 1572, and to the attacks on Protestants by Catholic Irish rebels in 1641. The martyrologies from the Marian era also haunted the nation's cultural imagination. John Foxe's *Actes and Monuments*—a 1563 version of the *Book of Martyrs* —documented the history of Protestant martyrdom and remained influential in Milton's day. *Actes and Monuments* connects itself strongly to Milton's sonnet through its accounts of the Babylonian woe and through the idea that the blood of Marian martyrs nourished the soil in which the seeds of the nation were planted.[13] Stephen Greenblatt explains that if Foxe's book "dwelt lovingly upon scenes of horror, if it insisted again and again that beneath the institutions and symbolic language of the Catholic Church lay 'mere power and violence,' it was . . . because the revelation of such violence attacked that consensual unity for which More went to the scaffold."[14] At the same time, however, by encouraging their own consensual unity, *Actes and Monuments* and the seventeenth-century Protestant counterparts it inspired reiterated Cromwell's call for "brotherly consent and harmony," thereby supplying some of the stitches for the sutures for the elect nation.

In the age-old battle against Babylonian powers, the Waldensians as the original defenders of the Reformed religion, resisted Catholic oppression longer than any other of the Protestant sectarians who, in a demonstration of compassion and unity, felt compelled to defend the cause of their ancestral brethren. "It may easily be gathered from the premises," *Mercurius Politicus* reported,

what a sad and lamentable condition they are now in, after long and heavy sufferings; all the true Protestants being bound by charity to have a fellow feeling of their miseries: so much the more, by reason that it will appear by good proofs, that they have retained among them the purity of the Gospel ever since the Apostles time, notwithstanding many cruel persecutions raised against them, by the malice of the Devil & Antichrist, without any mixture of Idolatry or Superstition. These are those who were cruelly persecuted by the Papists, about five hundred years since, and then were called *Vaudois* and *Albigois*.[15]

In combination with details of specific atrocities and catalogs of individual martyrs, widely circulated journalistic reports of the violence against Waldensian women and children sparked a national outcry for vengeance. Morland's 1655 speech to the Duke of Savoy, a version of which was printed in his 1658 *History,* identifies details of the atrocities that also informed Milton's sonnet. "Those wretched creatures," complains Morland, "are now wandering, with their wives and children, houseless, roofless, poor, and destitute of all resource, through rugged and inhospitable spots and over snow-covered mountains. . . . what was not dared and attempted against them? . . . some infants were dashed against the rocks, and the brains of others were cooked and eaten . . . heaven itself seems to be astounded by these cries."[16] Blending his voice with the nationwide appeal for justice, Milton calls out not as a supporter of independency or as a harsh critic of Anglicanism but as an "enraged Protestant citizen . . . forgetting for the moment, like most Englishmen, the wars against the Irish and the massacres at Drogheda."[17] The speaker of *Sonnet XVIII* thus cries: "Avenge, O Lord, thy slaughter'd Saints, whose bones / Lie scatter'd on the Alpine mountains cold" (1–2). The Waldensians were "Slain by the bloody *Piemontese* that roll'd / Mother with Infant down the Rocks. Their moans / The Vales redoubl'd to the Hills, and they / To Heav'n" (7–10), the sonnet continues, offering further evidence of the shared imagery on which political testimonies, martyrologies, journals, newsbooks, and literary accounts all relied.

One of the most popular and extensive histories of the massacre was produced by a Swiss minister and friend of Milton, Jean Baptiste Stouppe. Stouppe's *A Collection of the Several Papers* (1655) lists in its subtitle the nations involved in the tragedy: "The Bloody and Barbarous Massacres . . . by the Duke of *Savoy's* Forces, joyned therein with the French Army, and severall *Irish* Regiments."[18] This triple alliance serves as an additional gloss on Milton's "triple Tyrant" (*Sonnet XVIII,* 12), validly glossed by Miltonists as an image for the pope and his three-tiered crown.[19] Of particular concern in Stouppe's analysis is the unexpected participation of the Irish in the assault. In his dedication to Cromwell in *A Collection,* Stouppe observes that the slaughter of the Waldensians should enrage the Protector all the more "because this cruell action was chiefly executed by the Irish, as in revenge to those who have driven them out of their own Country for the cruell Massacres they there committed." In listing alleged causes for the massacre of the Waldensians, Stouppe cites and then dismisses the claim *"That the Reformed have cruelly murthered the Catholiques in Ireland, and have wholly expelled them"* (40); he continues by observing that the Catholics' revenge involves *"murther[ing] the Reformed in Piedmont, and clear[ing] the State of them, to lodge the Irish in their place."* The Irish are described shortly thereafter as enraged rebels who were justly "banished out of their Country, for Massacring the Protestants there" (Stouppe, 41, 3; Abbott, 3:707).

Stouppe's estimation in "To the Christian Reader" that the dead Waldensians numbered six thousand was a huge inflation of the actual figure.[20] The casualty rate was among the many aspects of *A Collection of the Several Papers* that Stouppe's critics disputed. *A Short and faithfull Account of the Late Commotions in the Valleys of Piedmont* (1655) evaluates Stouppe's arguments without, however, dismissing them altogether.[21] The author concludes that Stouppe's papers "describe the punishment, and not expresse the crime" (6). Among the explanations for the slaughter that he provides is the Waldensians' denial to the Catholics of "a Liberty of Conscience," which entailed "not permitting their Priests to say *Masse,* but us[ing] many revilings and mockeries towards their *Masse,* and religious people; as at *La Tour,* they dressed an Asse in a *Monks* habit" (3). *A Short and faithfull Account,* however, was no match for Stouppe's popular treatise, which was heavily steeped in anti-Catholic sentiment. On George Thomason's copy of *A Short and faithfull Account,* one mischievous reader inserted "un" to the word "faithfull" and added "written by a papist" to the end of the title.

Still, as Stouppe's history reluctantly suggests, the English government was actively involved in denying "a Liberty of Conscience" to those outside the faith, that is, those who opposed the Reformed religion. When approached by Morland about the Piedmont massacre, the Duchess Christina, mother of Carlos Immanuel II, chastised the English government for doling out criticism while persecuting Catholics at home.[22] In the final period of negotiations for the treaty between England and France in 1655, Antoine de Bordeaux-Neufville reminded English commissioners of the persecution of Catholics in England (Abbott, 3:718). But such accusations and chastisements were out of line; as Samuel Gardiner explains, the "doctrine that each prince was responsible to no external Power for his treatment of religious questions arising in his own dominions had not only been consecrated by the recent Treaties of Westphalia, but was firmly rooted in the conscience of Europe."[23] No foreigner as a result was entitled to judge Cromwell's treatment of the inhabitants of his kingdom. Nevertheless, such political critiques, particularly about the oppression of Irish Catholics, serve as a subtext in the history of the Piedmont massacre.

From August 1649 to May 1650, Cromwell led an army against the Irish, allegedly in retaliation for the 1641 rebellion, anti-Catholicism having been "energized by first allegations and then legends of Irish rebellions and massacres."[24] Exposing the depths of his hostility, Cromwell accused the Irish clergy of having ignited the early revolt: "You are a part of Antichrist, whose Kingdom the Scripture so expressly speaks should be laid in blood; yea in the blood of the Saints" (Abbott, 2:199). He probably obtained his convictions about the Irish from Sir John Temple's *The Irish Rebellion* (1646), a popular Protestant martyrology that presented a national myth hostile to the Irish Catholics.[25] The ongoing holy war against the Catholics in Ireland would in turn avenge "the innocent blood that hath been shed" and also "hold forth and maintain the lustre and glory of English liberty in a nation where," Cromwell insisted, "we have an undoubted right to do it."[26]

Ireland had long served as a thorn in the side of those English citizens who invoked the example of the uncivilized, rebellious Irish to justify imperialist acts in the kingdom and abroad. For Milton in particular, Ireland obstructed the establishment of a Protestant, Anglocentric, British nation. "Whole massachers have been committed on [the king's] faithfull Subjects" (YP 3:197), Milton reminds the readers of *The Tenure of Kings and Magistrates* in defending Cromwell's reconquest of the rebellious Irish in 1649. Then, just over a month later on March 28, 1649, Milton was appointed to advance the national cause by offering "some observations upon the Complica[ti]on of interest wch is now amongst the severall designers against the peace of the Commonwealth."[27] *Observations upon the Articles of Peace with the Irish Rebels* served as a response to a January 1649 treaty between the king's lord lieutenant, James Butler, the Earl of Ormond, and the Confederate Catholics of Ireland, a treaty that threatened the new government. Milton refers to the articles as one of the late king's "Masterpieces" (YP 3:301) in anticipation of his deconstruction of *Eikon Basilike* in the same year. The main targets, however, are the authors of the Articles of Peace and the "Papist Rebels of *Ireland*" (YP 3:300). Milton presents a cultural, national, and imperial mandate to attack those whom he characterizes as "barbarous, savage, uncouth, but, worst of all, papistical in religious belief,"[28] thus feeding anti-Irish antipathy. *Observations* is in turn preoccupied with "a crucial phase of English domestic politics,"[29] one intimately connected to a nationalist sentiment that defined itself in relation to the European theater and beyond.

Leaving the Irish "ashamed / To see themselves in one year tamed," Cromwell, England's Gideon, returned victorious to England where preparations would begin yet again for the transplantation of the Irish and the colonization of their country in the early and mid-1650s. Indeed, as Raymond

Tumbleson remarks, "the blood of the martyrs was the seed of colonialism."[30] The incursion into Ireland represented something more than simply a foreign intrusion: inextricably entangled with the domestic affairs of England, it involved the English at the most basic level as a Protestant and imperial nation.

The "Complica[ti]on of interest" in Ireland was translated in the case of the Piedmont massacre into what Cromwell called "one common Interest" in which the cause of all Protestants was at stake.[31] Foreign correspondence about the tragedy, political dispatches and state papers to which Milton himself contributed, and the letters of protest he wrote, speak of the "fraternal bond" between the English and the Waldensians, who had been murdered or banished to a wintry wasteland for their refusal to embrace the "Roman religion" (YP 5:684–701). Reformers in turn identified the victims as ur-Protestants. Like his contemporaries, Milton locates the Waldensians in the line of the early Christians: "those Churches in *Piemont* have held the same Doctrin and Goverment, since the time that *Constantine* with his mischeivous donations poyson'd *Silvester* and the whole Church. Others affirme they have so continu'd there since the Apostles."[32] The sect remained pristine and constant throughout the centuries, resisting Catholicism and Constantine, who "marr'd all in the Church," as acknowledged "even among men professing the Romish Faith." Morland's *History of the Evangelical Churches* (1658), modeled on *Actes and Monuments,* features the Waldensian massacre while also quoting from writers attacking the Catholic Church from within.[33] Morland highlights Petrarch's derisive comments on the church in various Petrarchan sonnets, including "Sonetto 110," *"Fontana di dolore."* Milton translates the first five lines of the sestet in *Of Reformation* as follows:

> Founded in chaste and humble Poverty,
> 'Gainst them that rais'd thee dost thou lift thy Horn,
> Impudent Whore, where hast thou plac't thy Hope?
> In thy Adulterers, or thy ill-got wealth?
> Another *Constantine* comes not in haste.[34]

Petrarch's image of the papal court as Babylon—an identification that resonates throughout the Protestant literature of suffering—is in turn appropriated by Milton for his Petrarchan *On the Late Massacre in Piemont,* which he converts into a memorial for the ur-Protestant martyrs.

Sonnet *XVIII* calls on God to avenge the "slaughter'd Saints, whose bones / Lie scatter'd" (1–2), reminiscent of God's chosen, who were dispersed by their enemies. Morland likewise echoes this cry for justice and vengeance throughout *The History of the Evangelical Churches,* from the title page on which he connects the Waldensians with the martyrs under the throne of God in Revelation 6:9: "I saw under the Altar the souls of them that were slain for the word of God, and for the testimony which they held; And they cried with a loud voice, saying, How long O Lord, holy and true, dost thou not judge and avenge our bloud on them that dwell on the earth." In dialogue with contemporary accounts of the massacre and with biblical prophecies (Psalms, Jeremiah, Daniel, and Revelation), Milton in *Sonnet XVIII* develops an alternative genealogy for the contemporary heroes.[35] As defenders of the truth "so pure of old" (*Sonnet XVIII*, 3), the Waldensians "in their ancient Fold" (6) represent at once the Old Testament Israelites and New Testament Christians who suffer "for truths sake." Thus, while their founder, Pierre Valdes, did not secede from Catholicism until 1179, Milton sinks the sect's roots (and thus Protestantism) in a more ancient tradition. Essentially, he generates a history for the Reformed religion that competes with a primitive Catholicism. The Waldensians' origin is predicated on their renunciation of idolatry, the speaker maintains, appealing for their preservation and inscription into "heav'nly Records" or the "Books of Life" (*PL* 1.361, 363):

> Ev'n them who kept thy truth so pure of old
> When all our fathers worship't Stocks and Stones,
> Forget not: in thy book record their groans
> Who were thy Sheep and in their ancient Fold.   (3–6)

Those who violate the sheepfold are the enemies of the Good Shepherd. In *Lycidas*, they are corrupt clergy who "Creep and intrude and climb into the fold" (115), while in *Paradise Lost* the poet-narrator compares Satan to "a prowling Wolf" who steals his way into God's "Fold" (4.183, 187). This first "grand Thief" reappears as the "lewd Hirelings" of Milton's day (*PL* 4.193); while in the case of the Waldensian massacre, the "bloody *Piemontese*" (*Sonnet XVIII*, 7) perform Satan's part.

The rewriting of the Protestant history and specifically that of the Waldensians involved a typological identification with the elect of the Old Testament. Anti-Catholic literature frequently cited the example of the Israelites' liberation from Babylon, their fall prophesying divine vengeance against the Roman church. Stouppe's *Collection* takes advantage of this Protestant interpretation by casting the Waldensians as "poor banished men, who like the faithfull of old, are wandering in the wildernesses, in the Dens, in the Mountains and in the clefts of the earth: *That they might sing as those that returned from the Babylonian Captivity,* When the Lord turned again the Captivity of *Zion,* we were like them that dream: Then was our mouth filled with laughter, and our tongue with singing" (Stouppe, 43–44). Also drawing on the second book of Hebrews, Morland's *History* repeats the passages to describe the persecuted Waldensians (b). Noting that the psalmist interspersed "divers bitter complaints throughout the whole Book of Psalms," Morland invokes Psalm 137 to characterize the persecuted Waldensians as a chosen people who carry on the tradition of the exiled Israelites in Babylon: *"they sat down and wept* (as they had good reason) *by the waters of* Babylon, *when they remembered* Sion" (Morland, b2). The appeal of the "Committee for the Affairs of the Poor Protestants in the *Valleys of Piedmont"* echoes this popular sentiment, and the committee implores God "to raise up *Sion* upon the Ruins of *Babylon,* hastening his work, and blessing the means to it."[36]

Recalling the deliverance from Babylonian captivity, Milton's sonnet correspondingly refers to the Waldensians' flight from the *"Babylonian* woe" (14). Woe, which reverberates throughout the biblical texts (Isa. 5:8–22; Luke 11:42–52; Rev. 8:13), as it does in the poem, is ceremonial, melancholic, and prophetic. The octave's end rhymes reinforce the elegiac nature of the verses: "bones," "cold," "old," "Stones," "groans," "Fold," "roll'd," "moans." Sonically, then, the poem is dominated by the "o" sound, which both begets and sustains its avalanche. For the most part, the sonnet is only Petrarchan by virtue of its rhyme scheme. Through the enjambment of the word "moans," the poem in fact resists Petrarchan containment as the octave is melded to the sestet, in which the sound and sense of "sow" and "grow" are checked by the final "woe." A seventeenth-century reader, susceptible to fears of international Catholic conspiracy, would have received an "additional emotional charge" when reading Milton's concluding couplet, Joad Raymond maintains.[37]

TOLERATION AT HOME

Though sown in sorrow, the seeds take root and mature, ultimately yielding a hundredfold crop. While the themes of dispersal and death predominate both in the octave and the sestet, the latter focuses more on planting and growing and enacts a final judgment on popery. "Plant" specifically denotes the founding or establishing of a city, or more relevantly, a colony; 2 Samuel 7:10 states, "I will appoint a place for my people . . . and will plant them, that they may dwell in a place of their own." Milton himself frequently uses the term in reference to the planting of Christianity (YP 1:651; 3:490, 493), of faith (YP 2:567), of the gospel (YP 5:219), of churches (YP 3:518), and of colonies (YP 5:5). Such practices are most controversial, of course, when they involve displacing or transplanting an existing people.

The planting or colonization of Ireland in the mid-1650s through the establishment of English plantations involved the transplanting, or what

Francis Bacon had earlier called "displanting," of the natives, namely Irish Catholics. While James Harrington recommended in *The Commonwealth of Oceana* that Panopea (Ireland) be "farmed out unto the Jews" for pay[38]— Jews being, unlike Catholics, marginally tolerable; and while Cromwell wrote to his son-in-law Charles Fleetwood about settling Ireland with Piedmont refugees (Abbott, 3:715), proposals resurfaced for the transplantation of Catholic Irish. Of central concern was the segregation of Catholics in Connaught and Clare. Vincent Gookin, surveyor-general of Ireland, and Cromwellian MP in the Irish Parliament, opposed forced transportations to Connaught in *The Great Case of Transplantation in Ireland Discussed* ([January] 1655)[39] and in *The Author and Case of Transplanting the Irish into Connaught Vindicated from the Unjust Aspersions of Col. Richard Laurence* (May 12 , 1655). Gookin produced the latter in response to colonial fantasies of the Cromwellian Colonel Richard Lawrence, who in *The Interest of England in the Irish Transplantation* (March 9, 1655) staunchly supported the segregation of the Irish and the English settlement of Ireland. Homeland security and the defense of English interests become refrains throughout Lawrence's work as he recounts in graphic detail the atrocities committed by the Irish against the English, and insists that "some of the *Irish* should be removed out of some parts of *Ireland,* to make way for the *English* Plantations, and if so, then a Plantation must be admitted to be essential in order [to maintain] the security of the *English* interest and People there."[40]

In his earlier work, Gookin already doubted the purity of the colonizers' motives. Acknowledging the failure to evangelize the Irish in their own country, Gookin entertained the possibility that the English themselves might be at fault: "as if our business in Ireland was only to set up our own interests and not Christs." Then several months later, in his lengthy refutation of Lawrence's argument, Gookin recommends a more civil form of colonization: "We may overspread them and incorporate them into ourselves, and so by an oneness take away the foundation of difference and fear together . . . we have opportunities of communicating better things unto them."[41] Gookin's solutions to the problems seem to accord with Milton's sowing of Protestant seeds in Catholic territory.

Gookin did recognize the difficulties involved in the colonizing act: "The unsetling of a nation is an easy work; the setling of a nation is not, it has cost much Blood and Treasure there."[42] Some of his contemporaries were, however, more critical of even such cautious and "benevolent" acts of colonization, assimilation, and apartheid, which Gookin advanced in dealing with Irish Catholics and other religious "detractors." Lord Cork, a proroyalist who was nevertheless involved with the new Cromwellian order and attended the memorial in the city of Cork for the slain Waldensians, protested in 1658 against the "wickedness of many of this nation to fetch poor Irish people out of their beds and sell them into the Barbadoes."[43] During the 1650s, Irish priests, Tories, and "vagrants" were exiled to the colonies, including Jamaica and Barbados, where they were sold to planters for less than the price of black slaves.[44] At the same time that Cork decried such practices, he was also known to have disagreed with a fellow magistrate's ruling that a troublesome Quaker should be imprisoned. In general, however, the lament for England's own "slaughter'd Saints"—Quakers, other dissenters, Catholics, and Jews— fell on deaf ears.

Parliamentary newsbooks of the 1650s effectively illustrate England's negotiation of cultural and religious differences in its management of such international and domestic affairs. The *Weekly Post* of early August 1655 documents or "impartially communicat[es]" a range of foreign events, from the "great and lamentable Engagement between the English and the Spaniards"[45] in the wake of the collapse of the Western design, to the inflamed relations between England and France, to the subduing and taming of Ireland. The self-congratulatory remarks on the subjection of Ireland are particularly revealing: "By Letters further from Ireland was certified, that the business of setling the Military and Civil Affairs, and Course of Justice being now well over, the Lord Deputy *Fleetwood* is preparing for *England* with all speed. . . . The Officers of the New Militia Troops in every Country, have been feasted at White hall, and great expressions of joy there were at the celebration thereof: *May they not well laugh that wins?*" (1908). As for the encounter between Protestant and Catholic forces in the European theater, the *Weekly Post* reports: "Mr. Moreland, Agent from his Highness, to the D. of Savoy, hath received his Answer, and is returning towards England, he is expected suddenly. The poor Protestants are still in Arms in the mountains and grow numerous, their brethren who fled returning to them from all parts. And whilest the Dukes forces were spoyling of their harvest in the valleys, they descended from the Hills, and after a hot dispute routed them, and took many prisoners" (1910).

Between these news reports on international events is a section titled "Quaking Intelligence," which marks George Fox's entrance onto the nation's political stage (1906–7). The newsbook characteristically links Fox with sorcery, witchcraft, and Catholic priesthood. Victimized from the time of their emergence by the government's policies and judicial system, Quakers consciously recorded their experiences. Their testimonials as persecuted saints in England are written alongside the history of the Waldensians' tragedy in a Great Book of Sufferings. As sufferers for truth's sake as they publicly identified themselves, Quakers issued a counter-plea to "forget not" and to record their trials in God's book, as Milton's speaker urges for the Waldensians

(*Sonnet XVIII*, 5).[46] Moreover, Quakers made connections between various kinds of oppression in England and on the Continent to which Milton and governmental officials of his day turned a blind eye. *False Prophets, Antichrists, Deceivers, which are in the World* (1655), the first work of Margaret Fell, Fox's future spouse, exposes the hypocrisy of the English who allegedly aided their fellows on the Continent while persecuting the Friends in their own country. Her addressees are "the Heads and Governours of this Nation, who have put forth a Declaration for the keeping of a Day of Humiliation for the Persecution (as they say) of poor Inhabitants in the Valley of *Lucerna, Angrona,* and others professing the Reformed Religion."[47] Fell emphasizes the emptiness of the government's fast to mark the event of the Waldensians' massacre, noting that the officials' inner condition remained unchanged and their correspondingly oppressive internal policies unaltered (17). Reminding Cromwell of his commitment to toleration, Fell, in anticipation of the accounts in the Great Book of Sufferings, states:

And whereas you take it into your consideration, the sad persecution, tyrany and cruelty exercised upon them, whom you call your Brethren, Protestants, and therein do contribute and administer to their wants outwardly . . . we who are sufferers by a Law derived from the Pope, are willing to joyn, and contribute with you to their outward necessities . . . but in the mean time while you are doing this, and taking notice of others cruelty, tyrany and persecution: turn your eye into your own bosoms, and see what is doing at home. (18)

Descriptions of the Friends' suffering are interspersed throughout, justifying Fell's harsh, ironic accusations of the government's alignment with popery: "Therefore honestly consider what is done, whilest you are taking notice of others Cruelties abroad, lest you overlook what is done at home: for there is much difference in many things between the Popish Religion and the Protestant (as they call it) but in this persecution there is no difference" (20). In an appeal she repeats throughout her Restoration writings, Fell urges the English government to abandon its "Popish law" (21), which oppresses those in the homeland.

During the remaining years of the Interregnum, royalists, Catholics, and Quakers alike continued to expose the limitations of Cromwell's policies on civil liberty and religious toleration. Samuel Fisher's *The Scorned Quakers True and honest account* describes the silencing of the Quaker after this famous September 17, 1656, parliamentary sitting. Identified by both Margaret Fell and himself as a sufferer "for Truth's sake," Fisher calls the magistrates to justice and repentance.[48] God, he warns, will "seek to snap and suppress them, as the old *Israel* their Type did upon *Pharaoh* and the *AEgyptians,* so that the more ye slay them, the more they shall grow and multiply; &

their Blood shall be the Seed of that Church, that shall be called *The Sion of the Lord*" (8). Here Tertullian's statement, "The blood of the Christians is the seed of a new life," finds new ground in the testimony of a victim of Cromwell's policies.[49] As Milton lamented the Waldensians' fate and demanded revenge for the "slaughter'd Saints," whose "bones / Lie scatter'd" (1–2), so Fisher bemoans the "Remnant of *Jacob*," left in the wilderness and "scattered, and shattered up and down in the dark and Gloomy day" and "every where complained on, and accused by proud *Haman*'s Generation that ever hated them" (18). The English government's denunciation of the Piedmont massacre did not lead to greater toleration in the homeland. As well as policing what was outside of the pale, England's national self-fashioning involved acts of internal colonization designed to suppress religious and cultural difference.[50]

The main accounts of the Piedmont massacre locate the slain Waldensians in a providential narrative. Morland concludes his *History of the Evangelical Churches* with images of the empty fields and barns of the Waldensians, while also deploying the language that "*Peter* sometimes used of the scattered Churches in *Pontus, Galatia, Cappadocia, Asia,* and *Bithynia*." The evangelist thereby assures the persecuted that God will reward their faithfulness in the midst of trial (709). Milton in *Sonnet XVIII* has a different type of consolation in mind, one reminiscent of, but not specific to, the experiences of Fisher, and English dissenters generally. The Waldensians undergo a series of conversions from faithful Israelites scattered by the enemy,[51] to New Testament martyrs, to ardent defenders of the Reformed religion. Their death is avenged through the advancement of the Reformation as their remains are sown "O'er all th'*Italian* fields" (11) and as the blood of martyrdom seeps into Catholic soils.

The concluding images in *Sonnet XVIII* combine the classical and biblical accounts of regeneration: the legend of Cadmus, the Phoenician prince who grew an army of soldiers, which led to the founding of Thebes; Ezekiel's prophecy of the Israelite nation springing to life from dry bones (37:1–14); the parable of the sower from the New Testament (Matt. 13:3–8; Mark 4:3–8; Luke 8:5–8). The martyred Waldensians' "blood and ashes" (10) cry for vengeance in the sestet (much like Abel's blood in Genesis, chapter 4). The blood of ritually slain animals described in Mosaic law and the ashes of sacrificed animals feature prominently in Hebrew rites as the agents and seeds of atonement and purification.[52] In the poem, the imagery of blood and ashes applies to the Waldensians as sacrificial, slaughtered sheep. The "bones . . . scatter'd on the Alpine mountains" (1–2) metamorphose into the "blood and ashes sow– / O'er all th'*Italian* fields" (10–11) where they regenerate.

"*Italian* fields" is no innocent reference: its significance harkens back to the "*Celtic* and *Iberian* fields," that is, the French and Italian fields in which Comus roved and preyed (*Comus*, 60); and it anticipates the reference to "th'*Hesperian* Fields" where Saturn fled, as recorded in a catalog of the possessed and possessors of hell in *Paradise Lost* (1.520). In *Sonnet XVIII*, the image is topical and politically charged, marking the site both of the tragedy and of a newly planted Reformation. Superimposed on the meaning of the "*Italian* fields" is a biblically inflected typological reading of a transition from the valley of dry bones (Ezek. 31) and the valley of the shadow of death (Ps. 23) to the fields ripe for harvest (Matt. 9:37–38) and the field where the kernel of wheat is planted and then dies to produce new life (John 12:24). "Neither is it therfore true," Milton insisted in 1649, when he denounced the violence associated with the tyranny of kingship, that "Christianity is planted or watred with Christian blood" (YP 3:490). But a few years later, Tertullian's famous adage serves as his consolation, conveyed by the sowing and reaping trope from the New Testament that he adopts (10–13). Throughout his prose works Milton uses the term "sowing" much more in a metaphorical than literal sense as he speaks about sowing opinions (YP 2:432), diversity (YP 2:751), "spiritual things" (YP 7:300), and sowing sedition or dissension (YP 3:322; 5:392). Now, in his most powerful application of the term, he implores God to sow the seeds of vengeance, resulting in the "hundredfold" regeneration of Protestantism "O'er all th'*Italian* fields."

"Hundredfold" (13) refers to the growth of the fourth portion of seed cast by the sower of the synoptic Gospels, a portion divided into three categories, yielding a hundredfold, sixtyfold, and thirtyfold. The seed is the Word of God, which is received in various ways, with the hundredfold yield being the most fruitful. In accordance with Saint Cyprian's interpretation of the parable of the sower, the hundredfold harvest is the result of the incarnation of the Word as blood through martyrdom.[53] This transformation is effected by God through the poet, the sower of the seeds, which, like books, are invested with a "potencie of life" (YP 2:492). The meaning of sowing thus multiplies through the words of the poem itself. Blood stains the path to the Promised Land while the fertile language of *Sonnet XVIII* serves as seed for an ascent: "hundredfold" is the hundredth word in the sonnet, leaving eleven words to complete the sonnet.[54] Presented in these terms, Milton's verse memorial of the tragedy marks a transition from death and destruction to rebirth.[55] At the same time, by using a monosyllabic *native* English diction and Protestant imagery, Milton "Englished" his Petrarchan sonnet, converting eroticism into passion and turning his notes to a tragic lament for all Protestants.

Milton composed the sonnet, as noted earlier, while participating in the Cromwellian government's Pentecostal mission to spread the word about the Waldensian crisis. In his capacity as Latin secretary, Milton wrote letters of protest, which were transmitted under Cromwell's seal on May 25, 1655. His address to the United Provinces describes the letter-writing campaign to European heads of state, ranging from "Protestant princes and magistrates" to the (Catholic) Duke of Savoy and the king of France. A companion letter was directed to Cardinal Mazarin (Morland, 553). For reasons of political expedience more than anything else, the correspondence to the French officials is gracious and cautious rather than vindictive, the English government having been involved at this time in negotiations with France to develop a military alliance against the Spaniards.[56] In a plea for Protestant solidarity, Cromwell explains to the duke,

> we must acknowledge that we are joined with them, not only by the communion of humanity, but also by the same Religion and indeed by a deeply felt fraternal bond, [and thus] we have judged it impossible to satisfy our duty toward God, or brotherly charity, or the profession of the same religion, if in this calamity and misery of our brethren we are affected solely by a sense of grief and do not also exert all our efforts to relieve, as much as in us lies, their many unexpected evils. (YP 5:686)

The desired outcome of a united response to the assault on the Waldensians is cast as a triumph for Protestant diplomacy designed to yield much fruit: "if the Duke of Savoy will allow himself to be appeased and prevailed upon by the prayers of us all, we shall carry away a noble and plentiful harvest and reward from this labor which we have undertaken" (YP 5:693), Cromwell announces in his address to the Netherlands.

Under pressure from the international European community and in reaction to the Waldensians' recent military victories, the French government ordered an end to the persecution and restored the Waldensians' rights at the 1655 "pacification" of Pignerol (Abbott, 3:717). But within no time, the duke resumed his assaults on Protestants, prompting Cromwell's intervention again in 1658.[57] In the meantime, the Cromwellian government rejected the proposal to readmit the Jews, declared war on Spain and the house of Austria, aggressively advanced "Western design," extended the transplantation policy in Ireland, and suppressed dissenters at home. Such practices remind us of the exclusionary thinking that marked the evolution of elect nationhood. While retaining a strong commitment to free-will theology, Milton, too, increasingly and paradoxically reserved his designation of the chosen for the fit though few (see, for example, YP 3:339–40). Though unrelated in all other regards, the Grand Duchess Christina of Lorraine, Antoine de Bourdeax-Neufville, Vincent Gookin, Lord Cork, and Samuel Fisher exposed attitudes and incidents of English intolerance, though their words fell on stony ground. And at the same time, Margaret Fell identified the kinds of connections between domestic and foreign policies on toleration that Milton

and other governmental officials disregarded in their response to the Irish
and in their ready assimilation of the Waldensians into the Protestant providential narrative.

In conclusion, I have sought in this study to reread *Sonnet XVIII* in
terms of the "complication of interest"—a phrase applied to the supporters of
the Articles of Peace—[58] implicit in political, religious, and tolerationist policies advanced by the Cromwellian government and championed by Milton
in the 1650s. By studying *Sonnet XVIII* in the context of English cultural
politics of the day, we discover how "the blood of the martyrs becomes the
seed of colonialism," thus capturing the imperial potential implicit in the acts
and expressions of reformation/regeneration. Having admitted them into the
(sheep)fold, Cromwell in 1655 defended the cause of the Waldensians, and
Milton memorialized their suffering in his political and literary canon. As
English colonizers proposed the planting of Protestants in Catholic Irish
soils, Milton grafted the Protestant nation's outrage about the Piedmont
massacre onto an Italian poetic form and tradition. The rhetorical dexterity in
fulminating against the Catholics while justifying the colonization of the Irish
and the internal colonization of the sectarians and, in the same year, of the
Jews marked the agendas and writings of early modern nationalists.[59] The
chosen, imperial nation·generates and sanctions territorial imperatives of
blood and soil while, as we have seen, sowing the seeds of intolerance abroad
and at home. Indeed, the measure of the emerging nation lies then as now in
its foreign relations and policies as well as in its management of internal
difference.

Brock University

NOTES

For their generous, penetrating responses to earlier versions of this essay, I am very grateful
to John T. Shawcross, Paul Stevens, Balachandra Rajan, and Nabil I. Matar. I also acknowledge
my indebtedness to the anonymous *Milton Studies* reader of this essay. Research for this study
was made possible by the generous support of the Social Sciences and Humanities Research
Council of Canada.

1. See Gabriel Audisio, *The Waldensian Dissent: Persecution and Survival c. 1170–c. 1570*,
trans. Claire Davison (Cambridge, 1999).

2. Ibid., 205. For the phrase "civilizing Conquest" in Milton's writings on Ireland, see John
Milton, *Complete Prose Works of John Milton*, 8 vols., ed. Don M. Wolfe et al. (New Haven,
1953–1982), 3:304; hereafter designated as YP and cited parenthetically by volume and page
number in the text.

3. Robert Thomas Fallon, *Milton in Government* (University Park, PA, 1993), 139–51,
argues for the attribution of Morland's speech to Milton. Compare Michael Lieb, *Milton and the*

Culture of Violence (Ithaca, NY, 1994), 30 n. 27. Fallon concurs with the Columbia editors about the "suggestive parallels between the sonnet and the speech to the duke, both composed at about the same time" (143, 144). Barbara K. Lewalski, *The Life of John Milton: A Critical Biography* (Oxford, 2000), 330, 664 n. 38, supports Fallon's reading.

4. No manuscript version of *Sonnet XVIII* exists. The only text of the poem is that of 1673. The edition used in this essay is John Milton, *Sonnet XVIII*, "On the Late Massacre in Piemont," in *John Milton: Complete Poems and Major Prose*, ed. Merritt Y. Hughes (New York, 1957). All references to Milton's poetry are to this edition, hereafter cited in the text by work and line number.

5. Benedict Anderson, *Imagined Communities: Reflections on the Origin and Spread of Nationalism* (1983; rev. ed. London, 1991), 145. Slavoj Žižek, *For They Know Not What They Do: Enjoyment as a Political Factor* (London, 1991), 20. Otherwise, Anderson and Žižek address unrelated subjects and do not cite each other's works.

6. Paul Stevens, "Milton's Janus-Faced Nationalism: Soliloquy, Subject, and the Modern Nation State," *Journal of English and Germanic Philology* 100, no. 2 (2001): 247–68. Stevens offers a brilliant application of Žižek in his study of Milton, which complicates the differentiation between civic and ethnic nationalisms (256–68). David Loewenstein and Paul Stevens's discussion in their panel on "Milton and Early Modern Nationalism" (presented at the Seventh International Milton Symposium, South Carolina, 2002), of the reinvention by civic nations of the imperatives of blood and soil in more exclusionary forms also informed my study.

7. The vast majority of studies on *Sonnet XVIII* contextualize the poem in terms of the Judeo-Christian tradition; see, for example, John K. Hale, "Milton's Sonnet 18 and Psalm 137," *Milton Quarterly* 29, no. 3 (1995): 91; John R. Knott, "The Biblical Matrix of Milton's 'On the Late Massacre in Piemont,'" *Philological Quarterly* 62 (1983): 259–63; John S. Lawry, "Milton's Sonnet 18: 'A Holocaust,'" *Milton Quarterly* 17 (1983): 11–14; Kathryn Gail Brock, "Milton's Sonnet XVIII and the Language of Controversy," *Milton Quarterly* 16 (1982): 3–6; Charles E. Goldstein, "The Hebrew Element in Milton's Sonnet XVIII," *Milton Quarterly* 9 (1975): 111–14; Joseph G. Mayer offers a dialectical reading of the sonnet in "Doubleness in Milton's Late Sonnets," in *Milton Studies* 39, ed. Albert C. Labriola (Pittsburgh, 2001), 26–49, esp. 41–49. On the sonnet's dialogue with contemporary accounts, drawn from newsletters, journals, or political pamphlets, see *Milton's Sonnets*, ed. E. A. J. Honigmann (London, 1966), 164–66; Joad Raymond, "The Daily Muse; or, Seventeenth-Century Poets Read the News," *The Seventeenth Century* 10, no. 2 (1995): 189–218, esp. 203–11; John T. Shawcross, "A Note on the Piedmont Massacre," *Milton Quarterly* 6, no. 1 (1972): 36; Anna K. Nardo, *Milton's Sonnets and the Ideal Community* (Lincoln, NE, 1979), 132–33; Lieb, *Milton and the Culture of Violence*, 29–32.

8. Milton's variations on the Petrarchan sonnet form resist the octave-sestet. The section of the poem to which I refer in this sentence constitutes what Lewalski, *The Life of John Milton* (353), identified as the verses following the "volta" in the poem, which can be said to have a three-part structure: lines 1–4, 5–10a, 10b–14.

9. Blair Worden, "Toleration and the Cromwellian Protectorate," in *Persecution and Toleration*, vol. 21 of *Studies in Church History*, ed. W. J. Shields (Oxford, 1984), 210; *Collonel James Hays Speech to the Parlament upon the Debate concerning Toleration* ([London], 1655), 4, 5. On the progress of religious liberty and toleration in seventeenth-century England, see David S. Katz, *Philo-Semitism and the Readmission of the Jews to England 1603–1655* (Oxford, 1982), 161, esp. 158–89; *Tracts on Liberty of Conscience and Persecution 1614–1661*, introduction by Edward Bean Underhill (1846; reprint, New York, 1966). This debate takes a new direction in William Dalrymple's *From the Holy Mountain: A Journey among the Christians of the Middle East* (New York, 1998), which is notable in its depiction of Ottoman tolerance of Christianity. Dalrymple identifies the limits of the European Christian response to difference:

How easy it is today to think of the West as the home of freedom of thought and liberty of worship, and to forget how, as recently as the seventeenth century, Huguenot exiles escaping religious persecution in Europe would write admiringly of the policy of religious tolerance practised across the Ottoman Empire. The same broad tolerance that had given homes to hundreds of thousands of penniless Jews, expelled by bigoted Catholic kings from Spain and Portugal, protected the Eastern Christians in their ancient homelands, despite the Crusades and the continual hostility of the Christian West. (188)

I am grateful to Balachandra Rajan for drawing my attention to this quotation.

10. *The Writings and Speeches of Oliver Cromwell*, 4 vols., ed. W. C. Abbott (New York, 1970), 1:677. Subsequent quotations from Abbott's edition are cited parenthetically by volume and page number.

11. Christopher Hill, *God's Englishman: Oliver Cromwell and the English Revolution* (Harmondsworth, 1970), offers a suggestive list of Cromwell's political policies and positions on toleration: "The British Empire, the colonial wars which built it up, the slave trade based on Oliver's conquest of Jamaica, the plunder of India resulting from his restitution and backing of the East India Company, the exploitation of Ireland; a free market . . . religious toleration, the non-conformist conscience, relative freedom of the press . . . none of these would have come about in quite the same way without the English Revolution, without Oliver Cromwell" (262–63).

12. Raymond, "The Daily Muse," 208.

13. John Foxe, *Actes and monuments of matters most speciall and memorable*, 3 vols. (London, 1641), 2:7.201–23. The account of the persecuted Waldensians during the period 1555–1561 includes a letter appealing to the Duke of Savoy for toleration (7.210–11). On Foxe and national election, see William Haller, *Foxe's Book of Martyrs and the Elect Nation* (London, 1663), esp. 224–28.

14. Stephen Greenblatt, *Renaissance Self-Fashioning: From More to Shakespeare* (Chicago, 1980), 79.

15. *Mercurius Politicus*, no. 257 (May 10–17, 1655), in *Making the News: An Anthology of the Newsbooks of Revolutionary England, 1641–1660*, ed. Joad Raymond (Gloucestershire, 1993), 283.

16. [The First Draft of Samuel Morland's Address to the Duke of Savoy, and His Mother], Additional State Papers, in *The Works of John Milton*, ed. Frank Allen Patterson et al. (New York, 1937), 13:479–81.

17. As far as I have determined, Don M. Wolfe's introduction in volume 4 of *Complete Prose Works of John Milton* is the only study on Milton that juxtaposes—if only in passing—the 1655 events at Piedmont with those in Ireland at this time (YP 4:1.273).

18. J[ean] B[aptiste] Stouppe, *A Collection of the Several Papers . . . Concerning the Bloody and Barbarous Massacres . . . of many thousands of Reformed, or Protestants dwelling in the Vallies of Piedmont* (London, 1655), title page. Subsequent quotations from Stouppe are to this edition and are cited parenthetically by page number.

19. Among the critics who gloss line 8 accordingly are: Lewalski, *The Life of John Milton*, 353; Goldstein, "The Hebrew Element," 111; Nardo, *Milton's Sonnets*, 133, 153–56; Mayer, "Doubleness in Milton's Late Sonnets," 44; Lieb, *Milton and the Culture of Violence*, 34; Lieb notes Milton's previous reference: "*In Eandem (In Proditionem Bombardicam),*" line 3.

20. Stouppe, *Collection*, A3v. Compare Samuel Morland, *The History of the Evangelical Churches of the Valleys of Piemont* (London, 1658), 362–79, who lists about 257 names of the massacred and an additional 113 victims who died in prison (380–83). David Masson, *The Life of Milton: Narrated in Connexion with the Political, Ecclesiastical, and Literary History of His*

Time, 6 vols. (London, 1880), 5:39, cites a figure of 300, while Abbott, *Writings and Speeches of Oliver Cromwell,* estimates "two or three hundred" (3:707). Also see Samuel Rawson Gardiner, vol. 6, *1655–1656, History of the Commonwealth and Protectorate 1649–1656,* 4 vols. (New York, 1965), 4:185.

21. *A Short and faithfull Account of the Late Commotions in the Valleys of Piedmont, with the Dominions of the Duke of Savoy. With some Relections on Mr. Stouppe's collected Papers touching the same businesse* (Printed for W. P. and G. L., 1655). References following immediately are to this pamphlet and cited parenthetically in the text.

22. Gardiner, *History of the Commonwealth,* 4:189; Morland, *History of the Evangelical Churches,* 568–80.

23. Gardiner, *History of the Commonwealth,* 4:187

24. Raymond D. Tumbleson, *Catholicism in the English Protestant Imagination: Nationalism, Religion, and Literature, 1660–1745* (Cambridge, 1998), 11.

25. See T. C. Barnard, "Crisis of Identity among Irish Protestants, 1641–1685," *Past and Present* 127 (May 1990): 52–59. Temple thus regarded the 1641 rebellion in the context of a much larger clash between Catholicism and Protestantism. See I. J. Gentles, *The New Model Army in England, Ireland and Scotland, 1645–1653* (Oxford, 1992), 371–72, 542 n. 126.

26. Abbott, *Writings and Speeches of Oliver Cromwell,* 2:205; Gentles, *New Model Army,* 372.

27. PRO, Order Book of the Council of State, SP Dom 25/62, p. 125; also see Masson, *The Life of Milton,* 4:87, 98. Also see *The Life Records of John Milton,* ed. J. Milton French (New York, 1966), 2:240.

28. See Wolfe, introduction (YP 1:169). Willy Maley, "Milton and 'the complication of interests' in Early Modern Ireland," in *Milton and the Imperial Vision,* ed. Balachandra Rajan and Elizabeth Sauer (Pittsburgh, 1999), 155–68, argues that the representation of Ireland is a testing-ground for theories of British identity. Critics repeatedly confront the issue of Milton's response to Ireland as a compromise of his liberalism and radicalism. Milton's own "fierce polemical engagement in the politics of the Irish crisis," as David Loewenstein, *Representing Revolution in Milton and His Contemporaries: Religion, Politics, and Polemics in Radical Puritanism* (Cambridge, 2001), observes, is "part of his disturbing complexity as a godly revolutionary writer" (200). Christopher Hill, "Seventeenth-Century English Radicals and Ireland," in *Radicals, Rebels and Establishments: Historical Studies* 15, ed. Patrick J. Corish (Belfast, 1985), observes that even liberal thinkers like Milton assumed "the total inferiority of the Irish and their culture" (35). Also see Paul Stevens, " 'Leviticus thinking' and the Rhetoric of Early Modern Colonialism," *Criticism* 35, no. 3 (1993), who notes that "In Ireland, Milton's revolutionary rhetoric becomes colonizing rhetoric" (456). The early notion of tolerationism as religious unification may help explain to some degree, however, why even nonconformist thinkers like Milton did not apologize for their hostility toward Irish Catholics.

29. Thomas N. Corns, "Milton's *Observations upon the Articles of Peace:* Ireland under English Eyes," in *Politics, Poetics, and Hermeneutics in Milton's Prose,* ed. David Loewenstein and James Grantham Turner (Cambridge, 1990), 123–34.

30. Andrew Marvell, "An Horatian Ode," in *The Complete Poems,* ed. Elizabeth Story Donno (1972; reprint, Harmondsworth, 1985), lines 73–74; Tumbleson, *Catholicism,* 40.

31. State Papers II, Letter 53, in Patterson, *The Works of John Milton,* 13:169. "*Pene unam esse*" (13:168) is translated in the Yale edition as "cause . . . common to . . . all" (YP 5:688).

32. YP 3:514; also see *Of Reformation,* YP 1:559–60; *The Likeliest Means,* YP 7:291, 306, 308. In the second reference from *The Likeliest Means,* Milton mentions the author of the standard history of the Waldensians, Peter Gilles, who produced *Histoire Ecclesiastique des Eglises Reformees* (Geneva, 1644).

33. Samuel Morland used similar images to those of Stouppe, and both his and Stouppe's discussions of the duke's motives reveal that his mother, Grand Duchess Christina, a granddaughter of Catherine de' Medici, and the sister of Henrietta Maria, was the real force behind the massacre. See Morland, *History of the Evangelical Churches*. Subsequent quotations from Morland's work are cited parenthetically by page number.

34. YP 1:559; in *Of Reformation* Milton translates the first five lines of the sestet of Petrarch's Sonnet 108, which is numbered 110 in Morland, who quotes the entire "Sonetto" (C3r). In *Of True Religion*, Milton mentions that "One of their own famous Writers" characterized the Romish church as *"Mother of Error, School of Heresie"* (YP 8:421).

35. John R. Knott refers to the Waldensians as Milton's "best contemporary examples of martyrdom" in "'Suffering for Truths Sake': Milton and Martyrdom," in Loewenstein and Turner, *Politics, Poetics, and Hermeneutics*, 163.

36. "Committee for the Affairs of the Poor Protestants in the *Valleys of Piedmont* " (London, 1658), 4.

37. Joad Raymond, "Daily Muse," 207. John K. Hale, "England as Israel in Milton's Writings," *Early Modern Literary Studies* 2, no. 2 (1996), argues that Milton reserves some of the few positive references to Old Testament Israelites found in his later works for these ancestral Protestants who fly the *"Babylonian* woe" (14).

38. James Harrington, *The Commonwealth of Oceana: The Political Works of James Harrington*, ed. J. G. A. Pocock (New York, 1977), 159.

39. Vincent Gookin, *The Great Case of Transplantation in Ireland Discussed* (London, [January] 1655), 3.

40. Richard Lawrence, *The Interest of England in the Irish Transplantation* (London, March 9, 1655), 16. On the significance of "planting," also see Mary Fenton, "Hope, Land Ownership, and Milton's 'Paradise Within,'" *Studies in English Literature, 1500–1900* 43, no. 1 (2003): 151–80.

41. Gookin, *The Great Case of Transplantation*, 3; Vincent Gookin, *The Author and Case of Transplanting the Irish into Connaught Vindicated from the unjust Aspersions of Col. Richard Laurence* (London, May 12, 1655), 41. See *Mercurius Politicus* (March 15–22, 1655), 5197; (March 29–April 5, 1655), 5241.

42. T. C. Barnard, "Crisis of Identity among Irish Protestants, 1641–1685," *Past and Present* 127 (May 1990): 72.

43. Gookin, *The Great Case*, 29.

44. John W. Blake, "Transportation from Ireland to America, 1653–60," *Irish Historical Studies* 3 (1942–1943): 275. Colonization and conversion were part of the same mandate. Cromwell himself proposed that upon being transported abroad, Irish girls would have to be restrained but Irish boys could potentially be educated to be "Englishmen, I mean rather, Christians." See Thurloe, *State Papers*, 4.23–4, 40, quoted in Blake, 271 n. 3.

45. *The Weekly Post*, no. 283 (London, Tuesday, July 31 to Tuesday, August 7, 1655), 1905. References following immediately are to this document and cited parenthetically.

46. In 1657 George Fox encouraged Quakers to present their sufferings to judges of assize, and in 1658 he organized a system of recording sufferings, which would be incorporated by Ellis Hookes into the Great Book of Sufferings. But Quakers like Margaret Fell were already documenting their trials before 1657.

47. Margaret Fell, *False Prophets, Antichrists, Deceivers, which are in the World* (London, 1655), title page. Subsequent quotations from Fell are cited parenthetically in the text by page number.

48. Samuel Fisher, *To all the Worthy Gentlemen who . . . were violently kept out of the Parliament-house etc.* ([London], September 17, 1656), 1. Subsequent quotations from Fisher

are cited parenthetically in the text by page number. See also Margaret Fell, "*A Letter to Samuel Fisher, 1656,*" *A Brief Collection of Remarkable Passages and Occurrences Relating to . . . Margaret Fell, but by her second Marriage M. Fox* (London, 1712), 99–100. Fisher reports in his tract that one of the two justices who confronted him labeled him a Jesuit (2), with whom Quakers were not infrequently aligned. See the above-mentioned *Weekly Post* report on Fox.

49. *Apologeticus,* 50; A. S. P. Woodhouse and Douglas Bush, eds., *A Variorum Commentary on the Poems of John Milton,* 2 vols. (New York, 1972), 2:440. Also see Lawry, "Milton's Sonnet 18," 11–14.

50. Michael Hechter, *Internal Colonialism: The Celtic Fringe in British National Development, 1536–1966* (Berkeley and Los Angeles, 1975), 9.

51. Knott, "The Biblical Matrix," 260.

52. Goldstein, "The Hebrew Element," 112–13. On the Waldensians and the Israelites, see Knott, "The Biblical Matrix," 259–63.

53. "The first fruit, that of a hundred-fold, belongs to martyrs; the second, sixty-fold, is yours"; see Saint Cyprian, *The Dress of Virgins,* trans. Sister Angel Elizabeth Keenan, in *Saint Cyprian: Treatises,* trans. and ed. Roy J. Deferrari (New York, 1958), chap. 21, p. 49; Manfred Siebald, "Sower, Parable of," in *A Dictionary of Biblical Tradition in English Literature,* gen. ed. David Lyle Jeffrey (Grand Rapids, MI, 1992), 732–34.

54. I am much indebted to John T. Shawcross for this observation about the sonnet in our correspondence (2002). Also see John T. Shawcross, ed., *The Complete Poetry of John Milton* (Garden City, NY, 1963), 215 n. 6.

55. Lieb, *Milton and the Culture of Violence,* 29.

56. An appeal directed at Cardinal Mazarin of France refers to "an even closer bond between this Commonwealth and the Kingdom of France," the initial bond having been established through negotiations resulting in the November 1655 Treaty of Westminster; see YP 5:700–701 and Charles Harding Firth, *The Last Years of the Protectorate, 1656–1658,* 2 vols. (1909; reissued New York, 1964), 1:268–301, 2:177–222.

57. Fallon, *Milton in Government,* 150–51.

58. See Maley, "Milton," 155–68.

59. On Milton and the question of Jewish readmission, see Don M. Wolfe, "Limits of Miltonic Toleration," *Journal of English and Germanic Philology* 60 (1961): 834–46, and Elizabeth Sauer, "Religious Toleration and Imperial Intolerance," in Rajan and Sauer, *Milton and the Imperial Vision,* 214–30.

THE MASQUING OF GENRE IN *COMUS*

Heather Dubrow

Speak—
But keep yes and no unsplit
And give your say this meaning:
Give it the shade.

. . . .

He speaks truly who speaks the shade.

Paul Celan

we felt the old need
to charm, to literally enchant
which also means subdue.

Stephen Dunn

I

THE GENERIC PEDIGREE OF *Comus* is as "tangl'd" as the forest itself and as sticky as the heroine's "marble venom'd seat": readers of this masque must navigate a perilous course to arrive at its family origins.[1] At first glance, to be sure, it would appear that such debates have been happily resolved: older theories that the Ludlow production is a Cavalier masque have apparently been conclusively displaced by the recognition that Milton, anticipating or arguably even exemplifying the radical sympathies characteristic of his later work, instead fashioned a Reformed and hence reformed version of the genre. More specifically, until around 1980 many readers unhesitatingly categorized *Comus* within the courtly tradition of the masque, in some instances expanding that classification to comment as well on interactions with other forms, notably opera and ballet.[2] The 1980s, however, witnessed a number of challenges to such assumptions. Pioneering and often persuasive, David Norbrook's "The Reformation of the Masque" uncovered critiques of the form within certain versions of the masque that preceded *Comus;* Milton's text, Norbrook went on to argue, achieves a more radical reinterpretation of the masque. At around same time, Maryann Cale McGuire traced Puritan components in *Comus*, while a number of other critics buttressed these studies by cogently citing further evidence that Milton had effectively reconceived the courtly masque as a very different genre.[3]

With a handful of exceptions, in the two subsequent decades the readings of Norbrook, McGuire, and many others have been embraced.[4] Indeed, David Norbrook has developed his original contentions in important and influential subsequent writing,[5] while the widespread critical consensus about classifying *Comus* as a reformed masque is manifest at many junctures in *The Politics of the Stuart Court Masque*, a collection of essays edited by David Bevington and Peter Holbrook that appeared in 1998. Here, with her usual thoroughness and thoughtfulness, Barbara Kiefer Lewalski enriches and expands earlier work on the text, concluding that "Milton's *Comus* is in every respect a reformed masque, a generic tour de force." The editors of the volume concur with neither qualification nor hesitation, ending their teleological survey of the genre by contrasting *Comus*, "a reformed masque reflecting Puritan religious and political sympathies," with conventional courtly masques.[6]

Yet if we reexamine this text from a perspective that has generally been neglected—studying its approach to the masque in relation to how it negotiates the generic norms of romance and pastoral—we are impelled to revise the revisionists.[7] Its affiliations to both courtly masques and reformed masques, as well as the workings of both those categories, prove more complex and fluid than either the earlier theories or the revisionist challenges to them would suggest. If, as J. Martin Evans recently emphasized, the text of this masque is "in a constant state of flux," we find similar and not unrelated instability in its approach to genre.[8] An examination of this type of flux will also gesture toward larger issues: the relationship of generic lineage to linear progress and, above all, Milton's negotiation of formal and political problems and of the connections between them.[9]

II

To reconsider Milton's deployment of the generic norms of the masque in terms of how he approaches romance and pastoral in *Comus*, we need to reconsider as well certain presuppositions that have shepherded critics through the thickets of the formal issues raised not only by that masque but by many of his other texts as well. The first contender for the role of beneficent Attendant Spirit is the assumption that a process of judicious choice, an ethical model for Milton in so many other venues, is the predominant norm for his approach to genre. To be sure, this model is in fact sometimes apt. Previous critics, notably Lewalski, have cogently demonstrated how the dialogue among genres throughout Milton's canon does indeed demonstrate his lifelong concern with choice.[10]

Yet, as Satan's sibling rivalry with God's favored Son famously reminds us, Milton is also concerned with rivalry throughout his career, and questions of liberating choice, when reformatted in the fonts more popular in contemporary criticism, may reemerge as bitter competition among alternatives. If genres present themselves relationally, as many theorists of literary form have persuasively maintained, that relationship is often a conflictual one: the epyllion insists it is not an epic; satire defies—and in so doing helps to define —pastoral; city comedy assertively distinguishes itself from other comedic forms; and so on.[11] But in no writer's canon are such patterns more apparent than in Milton's. Much as languages compete with each other in the 1645 *Poems* and much as the mourners in *Lycidas* or the speakers in *L'Allegro* and *Il Penseroso* offer alternative perspectives, so, too, genres struggle with alternative forms and alternative versions of the same literary type throughout Milton's career. "Si teneris vacat inter praelia Musis" [if there is leisure for the delicate Muses in the midst of the fighting] (*Elegy IV,* 51), he writes when only eighteen, and while the sentiment may be conventional in its origins, its frequency and intensity throughout his canon irrefutably establish it as close to the bone. The chain of disjunctive "or's" when Milton lists generic options in the preface to the second book of *The Reason of Church-Government* flags the competition among the formal possibilities Milton saw waiting for him. Anticipating the fateful choice Adam and Eve will shortly make, Book Nine opens on the happier generic choices its author has made—but does so, as we will see, in language that implies continuing rivalries. And, developing an analysis different from but in some ways compatible with my own, Nancy Lindheim reads *Comus* itself in terms of a conflict between the Neoplatonic values of the masque and the more earthly preoccupations of pastoral.[12]

In short, Milton is as consistently preoccupied with conflicts among literary forms as with other types of ethical trial and decision: he has no patience with fugitive and cloistered genres. In the instance at hand, as we will see, he struggles within and among the conventions of romance, pastoral, and masque, displacing onto the plot his anxieties about being seduced by certain generic conventions. Or, to put it another way, his negotiations with generic norms and the values they embody belie, not buttress, Stanley Fish's recent insistence on a Milton whose core values are so firm, even so monolithic, that apparent ambiguities are more likely to symptomize critical misconceptions than authorial ambivalences.[13]

Similarly, the valuable work by previous critics on generic choices often assumes, as it were, resolution and independence. This second would-be Attendant Spirit, in other words, encourages us to expect clear-cut triumphs

in Milton's approaches to genre, with better versions unseating their alternatives as decisively as the older gods are superseded in the Nativity ode. But
Paradise Lost, demonstrating as it does the recurrence of error and sin, warns
us that such struggles with literary form, like so many other battles, are
unlikely to culminate in secure victories.[14] And the plot of *Comus* itself
gestures toward the way genre will be approached. It is telling that the villain,
like some of his Spenserian grandfathers, escapes. It is no less telling that our
villain deceives his victim not simply by changing his appearance but by
sprinkling a magic dust that changes her own perceptions: "When once her
eye / Hath met the virtue of this Magic dust, / I shall appear some harmless
Villager" (164–66). Although assessing the culpability, if any, that these lines
attribute to the Lady is as problematical as interpreting the more famous
"glutinous heat" (917), the lines at least hint that we are all betrayed by our
own senses, agents in, not merely victims of, destruction.[15] Blake's extraordinary illustrations for the text emphasize this possibility, for in the first picture
of the series the Lady, present at the reveling, leans toward Comus and his
band with an expression suggesting that she is transported, not disgusted or
frightened.[16]

But whatever Blake's interpretation, Milton's own emphasis on the fallibility of our senses has clear implications for the writer attempting to avoid
problems in other, lesser versions of a literary type. Two apostrophes—"List
mortals, if your ears be true" (997) and the concluding address, "Mortals that
would follow me" (1018)—distinguish those who can appreciate the lessons
of the masque from those who cannot or will not, while suggesting that even
the elect group must continue to struggle for virtue.[17] If the hope of creating
reformed genres is potentially imperiled by the fallen man who writes them,
it is threatened as well by the fallen reader liable to misinterpret them,
especially if the glitter of courtly values has been sprinkled before her or his
eyes.[18] And if such readers' hermeneutical skills are threatened by that dangerous dust, their political capacity to evaluate the aristocracy and monarchy
is also called into question.

Previous approaches to the genres of *Comus* have also been guided by
assumptions about its sibling *Arcades,* now widely seen as an early instance of
the reformed masque. Although a detailed discussion of *Arcades* is necessarily outside the scope of this essay, even a brief examination suggests that
the earlier masque anticipates *Comus* above all in representing not a per-
fected new type of masque but rather an uneasy and imperfectly resolved
interaction between more traditional and revisionist approaches to its genre.
Admittedly, the assertion that it celebrates moral worth rather than physical
beauty, locating that quality in a worthy aristocrat rather than a dubious
monarch, is particularly persuasive.[19] This "rural Queen" (108) outshines

even Syrinx, a figure who clearly gestures toward the monarchy.[20] In some important respects, then, the case that this text distinguishes itself from the courtly masque is indisputable.

But it is no accident that the critics who attribute to *Arcades* a wholly successful rejection of the flattery associated with that form seldom quote much of its language: the assertions that its heroine is "clad in splendor as befits / Her deity" (92–93), like the command to "attend ye toward her glittering state" (81), cannot be said to demonstrate ironic distance from courtly compliment. Witness, too, the apostrophe to the other players on which the text opens:

> Look Nymphs, and Shepherds look,
> What sudden blaze of majesty
> Is that which we from hence descry,
> Too divine to be mistook.   (1–4)

This is hardly the language of someone eager to demonstrate his rejection of the court and its discourses: while lines like these do not definitively establish their author's willingness to bestow similar compliments on the monarch, they do manifest his willingness to participate in the sycophantic hyperbole of the court. Moreover, the term "majesty" (2), though laden with multiple meanings, arguably hints that the countess is herself a kind of substitute for Charles, as does the emphasis on her as a centralized figure from which all else radiates. It is by no means clear that the text presents the praise of this noble lady as an alternative rather than a supplement to that of the king. What's a nice boy like Milton doing in literary and social conventions like these? By insistently posing that same question in relation to a number of literary forms, *Comus* offers some answers.[21]

III

Although the varieties of romance complicate attempts to generalize about Milton's, or any writer's, engagement with it, it is clear that the ambivalence about this form latent in the anxious discrediting of it in Book Nine of *Paradise Lost* emerges as well throughout his canon. To begin with, if romance had not existed, Milton would have invented it, if only because its preoccupation with the relationship of good and evil was so congenial to him. With spatial place often troping social place and amorphous locales the geographical equivalent of deferred closure, romance is the genre of displacement. Milton's preoccupation with that issue is manifest: the plots of *Paradise Lost* and *Paradise Regained* pivot on it (and on its cousin surrogacy), and it surfaces as well in Milton's early saga of lost homes, *On the Morning of Christ's*

Nativity, where "*Peor* and *Baalim* / Forsake their Temples dim" (197–98) and run into quite a traffic jam of refugee deities in doing so. As I have argued elsewhere, *protecting what is threatened* is no less central to romance than the underlying plot structure more commonly attributed to it, *finding what is lost,* and this too helps to explain Milton's attraction to that genre.[22] For the emphasis on curative agents—moly, Sabrina, the poem itself—in *Comus* recalls the dynamic of lurking threats and cures elsewhere in Milton's canon; the relationship between *L'Allegro* and *Il Penseroso,* for example, might well be diagrammed in such terms. Moreover, the genre was congenial because it characteristically stages a tension in Milton himself, the pull between the apocalyptic closure of the prophet and the anticlosural propensities of the Christian who believes that the first disobedience generated a cycle of repetitions.[23]

The very strength of Milton's attraction to romance glosses the virulence of his attacks on it. In the opening section of Book Nine of *Paradise Lost,* like the banqueting temptation in *Paradise Regained,* he lashes himself to the mast as he sails by romance and explains his reasons for doing so: it is a world of "tinsel Trappings" (36) and above all not morally serious enough, he writes in a passage that hints at the appeal of the very characteristics he is at pains to reject. Mimetically enchanting its listeners even as it tells stories of the dangers of enchantment, romance gave a local habitation and a name to the anxieties about art repeatedly experienced by a poet who, as we will see, characteristically describes poesy as a dangerous charm. And, more specifically, the writer whose fellow students had apparently termed him the "Lady" surely knew that the siren that is romance, like other sirens, was gendered female in early modern culture. Indeed, in uncovering and resisting romance's gendered temptation of that quintessentially masculine and putatively superior genre, the epic, the opening of Book Nine foreshadows Eve's allurement of that putatively superior genre of human being, Adam, later in the book.

But rather than merely choosing to let others sing of knights and paladins, in *Comus* Milton negotiates his ambivalence about romance both by playing versions of it against one other and by gesturing toward the inaccessibility of the most attractive of those versions.[24] To begin with, the romance elements in it are apparent throughout the text: Comus is the enchanter whose courtly castle is a kind of underworld; the prologue and epilogue provide an unusually clear example of the corresponding higher spheres that Frye in particular associates with the genre; the plot reinterprets the convention of bringing home the lost child, common in many though not all versions of romance; and so on. The imprint of the pastoral romances that flourished on the stage and in print during Milton's youth is often apparent:

we find here the interspersed songs so characteristic of that hybrid mode and also, of course, the infusion of heroic adventure into the pastoral world. But throughout the text Milton rejects one form of romance in favor of another, a pattern culminating in the epilogue's allegorized gesture toward romance, which at once distances and acknowledges it. Thus the Brothers' inability to effect a military rescue, a surgical strike, enacts Milton's refusal of chivalric romance; their youthfulness, more apparent in performance than on the page, might even hint that chivalric romance is itself a childish game.[25] This refusal is all the more telling given that Milton could have eaten his cake and had it too; that is, he might have introduced Sabrina earlier in the poem, perhaps as a beneficent spirit who gives the Brothers the magical potion they need to rescue their sister. By not doing so, he rejects as well the usual gendering of subject positions in romance: the hapless victim is indeed a virginal woman, but the male world and the subgenre that celebrates it are denied their usual roles, perhaps out of anxiety about separating the aggression of a Comus from that of a romance hero. Moreover, the rejection of chivalric romance is one of the most significant components of the rejection of courtly values that marks the putative Reformed masque.

What supersedes the courtly romance? Notwithstanding the dichotomy of nature and grace that Woodhouse's reading of the text famously asserts, I maintain that Sabrina's connection with that baptismal agent water in itself establishes at least some links with the spiritual world, though they do not preclude also associating her with nature.[26] Hence turning to her involves turning to a more overtly providential romance, replacing as it were the search for the woman's body with the Grail quest. At its culmination the text apparently adds a new but consistent dimension to the redefined genre represented by Sabrina. Bringing the Lady home deploys the romance convention of returning the lost child, a plot device beloved of writers in the genre ranging from Edmund Spenser to the twentieth-century detective writer Robert Parker, who signals his debts to romance by naming his hard-boiled hero Spenser. Because of the emphasis on the version of family values promulgated in numerous sixteenth-century marriage manuals—*"Heav'n hath timely tri'd their youth, / Their faith, their patience, and their truth. / And sent them here through hard assays"* (970–72; italics in original)—the passage links the godly magical world of Sabrina with its domestic analogue, the godly Protestant family. Thus, not only the revisions of the masque traced by earlier critics but also cognate changes in romance apparently signal generic and social reform.

But only apparently, only partially: "wisest fate says no, / This must not yet be so" (Nativity ode, 149–50). Like its villain, the text remains in motion.

Traces of the aristocratic roots of romance, to which we will return below, cling to the scene as well. The return of the child, after all, typically implies aristocratic as well as Protestant family values; when, for example, the princess discovered in lowly circumstances is returned to her castle, the restoration of her geographical place enables a restoration of social place. Moreover, whereas the Blake drawings of the final episode present the parents as elderly and worn, the performance would surely have drawn attention to the dignified aristocratic presence of the "Noble Lord, and Lady bright" (966) to whom the children return.[27] The stately dance that immediately follows the return of the children, integrating romance and masque conventions, was surely closer in mood to Whitehall festivities than to prayer sessions within the Protestant family. This is not to say all these elements are totally incompatible with a reformed romance—after all, courtly romances often have a spiritual dimension—but Milton would surely have been aware that they, like the presence of the sirens near Sabrina, at the very least risk incongruity.

That awareness may explain why in all its versions his epilogue assumes an ambivalent and ambiguous relationship to the reformed romance conventions developed so carefully earlier. In effect rephrasing the earlier command to the shepherds as "Back, Courtiers, back, enough your play," the Attendant Spirit's final words manifest some anxiety about the courtly dance and the world it represents—and also about the extent to which the romance motif of the returned children is an ethically satisfactory conclusion. On the one hand, the epilogue stresses the limitations of all earthly achievements, presumably including those of romance and of its usual forms of termination: it offers a vision of realms far removed from Ludlow and recommends not the closure and enclosure of the returned children but, rather, transcendence resulting from continuing movement and striving—"She can teach ye how to climb" (1020). Indeed, David Norbrook relates the closural strategies of this text to Protestant apocalyptic visions.[28] On the other hand, this divagation from the genre of romance circles back to it, again acknowledging a debt. For romance no less than pastoral often culminates on a movement, spatial and ontological, away from its world—in Malory, the retreat to a monastery, in Chaucer's *Troilus*, the palinode—a movement determinedly and defiantly anticlosural. And the mythological stories told by the Attendant Spirit do display some romance motifs (for example, the reference to "wandr'ing labors" [1006] and to the pending wedding).

In short, the conclusion neither insistently rejects nor, for all the other embraces on which the text ends, unequivocally embraces the version of romance it has been privileging.[29] When discussing Milton's attitudes to song, Marc Berley imputes to him an intense awareness of the dangers of aspiring to heavenly song, intensified by his recognition of how it differs from its earthly counterpart; the author of *Comus* is, I suggest, not coincidentally no less aware of the dangers and difficulties of attaining an idealized romance.[30]

IV

The text's approach to pastoral is equally complicated and ambivalent. The author of *Comus* might well have termed Spenser "mine owne auctor," and Milton's interest in pastoral is as predictable and profound as Spenser's: the genre typically engages with many problems central to him throughout his career, from the ecclesiastical issues conveniently figured by shepherds to the concern we explored earlier, the loss of home and other versions of place and displacement. If the shepherds in *On the Morning of Christ's Nativity* just don't get it, elsewhere in the canon their counterparts and their genre often are loci of positive values.

Nonetheless, *Comus* stages Milton's anxiety about two entwined questions, whether the pastoral genre and its values are accessible and whether they are desirable in a fallen world. Recurring frequently elsewhere in his canon, those questions about accessibility register in *Comus* through repeated allusions to the diseases and discomforts of the postlapsarian nature, the woods being a "tangl'd" (181) garden contaminated by "urchin blasts" (845) and liable to "Summer drouth or singed air" (928). Such physical ailments are the counterpart to the mental confusion that is, as Jeffrey Theis has acutely shown, associated with this environment, and one might add that both forms of turmoil provide a kind of lyricized antimasque.[31] Implicitly drawing on the concept of *silva* as chaos, *Comus* raises the question of whether the woods represent not an alternative to the more customary sylvan pastoral but rather the inevitable landscape of a fallen garden. Moreover, if the Fall turned ideal gardens into targets for disease and drought, it also transformed man's work from gardening to harder labor, and in *Comus* the repeated emphasis on georgic gestures toward that consequence as well. In lieu of achieved pastoral *otium*, we have "the labor'd Ox" (291) and his companion, "the swink't hedger" (293).

When the Attendant Spirit and his mirror image Comus disguise themselves as shepherds, they hint at the performativity of pastoral (with the clothes they discard arguably figuring alternative genres and hence again suggesting the competitiveness of literary forms). Deployed to establish the wearer's identity in the eyes of those with whom he will relate in his role of shepherd, the clothes also establish genre as a form of social communication and interaction, a focus seconded by students of genre ranging from Bakhtin to recent composition specialists. But more to our purposes, this costuming figures another threat to the achievement of a positive pastoral vision: like a shepherd's garments, the genre can be appropriated—or misappropriated— and in making that point Milton is, I suggest, gesturing toward the misappropriation by Caroline pastoral of values he respects. As critics have observed, it is no accident that *The Faithful Shepherdess* was apparently revived shortly before *Comus*.

Though it thus qualifies and delimits the potentialities of the genre, *Comus* does hint that pastoral is in fact accessible in some forms. The Brothers' anxiety generates a fantasy of pastoral tranquility—

> Or if our eyes
> Be barr'd that happiness, might we but hear
> The folded flocks penn'd in their wattled cotes,
> Or sound of pastoral reed with oaten stops,
> Or whistle from the Lodge, or village cock
> Count the night watches to his feathery Dames. (342–47)

—that is bracketed by the conditional mode but remains vivid nonetheless. The chain of adjectival past participles in line 344 ("folded . . . penn'd . . . wattled") suggests that for Milton, as for Spenser, not the least attraction of a pastoral vision is its ability to transfer the verbs of strife and movement into the adjectival participles of stasis. In a passage that describes folding, action is thus folded into rest, the epistemological confusions identified by Theis and the visual illusions of the woods penned up and dismissed; or, to put it another way, this description of confinement literalizes the process of asserting control by turning unmarked space into marked and mapped place, thus anticipating the movement from the amorphous woods to that clearly defined locale Ludlow Castle.[32] Not surprisingly, even while he stresses continuing ethical and literary struggles, Milton finds its opposite appealing.

Comus also recuperates pastoral by associating both the natural world and the genre in question with cure no less than disease: haemony may be more beautiful in another country, but it is accessible even in this one, and the pharmacist in question is, tellingly, a shepherd who dispenses many other healing herbs as well.[33] In addition to all the other roles she assumes in the poem, including her association with the spiritual, Sabrina embodies the curative potentialities of the natural world: visiting nurse to the imperiled herds, she helps "all urchin blasts" (845) and of course cures the Lady, a process anticipated in its demonic parody shortly before Comus's insistence that his cup will "cure" (811) melancholy and all other ailments.

Comus dramatizes as well the association of those cures through song. The shepherds in *Comus* devote far more energy to tending their pipes than their sheep, and song becomes the core of the pastoral world, the repository of many of its values and the font of much of its power. Particularly striking is the instrumentality bestowed upon pastoral song: it performs apotropaic and curative functions. Louis Martz even suggests that haemony represents sacred song.[34] Thyrsis signals the connection between the pastoral world and the power of song when he declares that he will, so to speak, cross-dress as a shepherd who, Orpheus-like, "Well knows to still the wild winds when they roar, / And hush the waving Woods" (87–88). Although such passages do not assign political potency to poesy, they, like cognate comments about the instrumentality of lyric, anticipate Milton's later deployment of literary types sometimes considered apolitical or quietist for political ends.

Comus negotiates the contrasting visions of pastoral it proffers not simply by juxtaposing them but rather by establishing a dialectical hermeneutics in which one interpretation of pastoral is countered by its opposite, a pattern that typically is succeeded by another interwoven dialectic.[35] Thus the initial opening implies that pastoral is not accessible in "the smoke and stir of this dim spot, / Which men call Earth" (5–6): its values are, tellingly, associated instead with the "calm and serene Air" (4) from which the Attendant Spirit descends, with their absence on earth signaled by the noun ironically used in "this pinfold here" (7), a phrase whose doubled deictics insist that the listener and text are trapped in the dim region in question. But shortly afterward that same spirit changes into the garb of Thyrsis, reminding us that good shepherds are indeed alive and well on earth and for the first of many times signaling that connection between pastoral and apotropaic song. Yet the fact that Comus enters immediately afterward in turn reminds one that such song, though efficacious to some extent, has not rid the natural world of all its threats. Thyrsis's real, though limited, reassurance about the positive effects of poesy, however, becomes the thesis against which the antithesis of Comus's own role as shepherd and musician is cast.

Similarly, the instrumental power of pastoral music is played against its dark twin, the equally potent music of the "Wassailers" (179) whom the Lady fears. Later on she offers a tribute to the courtesy of "lowly sheds" (323) that is sometimes cited as yet more evidence of Milton's successful creation of a Reformed masque. Yet an apparent tribute to pastoral is again succeeded by its palinode: in this instance the lowly shed to which she gratefully follows Comus is in fact a courtly underworld, with the setting itself thus enacting the misappropriation of pastoral values by the courtly world. And if Sabrina's song represents the curative agency of the pastoral world, the "wily glance" (884) of the nymphs associated with her—and arguably the presence of those ambivalent and ambiguous figures the sirens in her invocation—reminds us of the dangers of pastoral song, especially gendered pastoral song.

Until its conclusion, then, the text expresses some reservations about the accessibility and attractiveness of pastoral in the fallen world but nonetheless shapes a version of it that stresses its most beneficent potentialities. Yet much as the conclusion of *Comus* complicates its earlier development of a re-formed romance, so, too, a passage near the end of the masque emphasizes tensions between pastoral and the courtly practices closely related to it, thereby demonstrating the imbrication of political and generic predilections:

> *Back, Shepherds, back, enough your play,*
> *Till next Sunshine holiday;*
> *Here be without duck or nod*
> *Other trippings to be trod*
> *Of lighter toes, and such Court guise*
> *As Mercury did first devise*
> *With the mincing Dryades*
> *On the Lawns and on the Leas.*   (958–65; italics in original)

Although *"Till next Sunshine holiday"* (959)—a line not surprisingly ignored by the critics committed to convicting Milton of social snobbery—does prom-ise a reintegration of low and high denizens and genres, the fact remains that one dance supersedes another.[36] To be sure, the movement from the pastoral world to the court is itself a convention of pastoral, and this passage may simply be read that way.[37] But "such Court guise" (962), a line that might easily have been omitted, emphasizes the values of the aristocracy and gentry over those of their shepherds, naturalizing those values by associating them with a mythological past and thus colonizing the lawns and leas of pastoral. One could argue, then, that the promise of a return engagement by the shepherds merely mystifies that colonization, but the other ambivalences in the text, like those in *Arcades,* make it more likely that the choreography of the rival dances is, in effect, yet again a struggle between pastoral and more courtly values. That struggle involves, too, the conflict between two perspec-tives on pastoral, a recognition of its lowliness and a nod toward the aristo-cratic employ into which it is often impressed. Here, as throughout the text, the dynamic of illness and palliation that characterizes the fallen pastoral world mirrors the poem's continuing and unresolved relationship to the court, as well as to pastoral. But whereas *Comus* privileges the reformed version of romance that it shapes despite the ambivalence of the epilogue, here we have no sense that a better type of pastoral emerges from the tensions between perspectives on the court, as well as between generic alter-natives.

V

It is precisely the imbrication of achievement and limitation manifest in Milton's engagement with romance and pastoral that exposes and explicates the problem of whether *Comus* is a Reformed masque as so many recent critics have asserted. That question is, however, further complicated in part by the standards one erects for such a hybrid creature. Critics developing the argument about Milton's revisionist masques have assumed that proto-radical doubts about monarchy need not involve a comparable rejection of aristocracy; the linkage of social hierarchy and republicanism developed by figures like Winstanley is, after all, associated with later decades. Yet that argument is liable to objections, as my earlier commentary on *Arcades* demonstrates. Aristocrats often were seen as dim echoes of monarchical radiance ("To some you are reveal'd, as in a friend, / And as a vertuous Prince farre off, to mee," Donne writes in "To the Countesse of Huntingdon" ["Man to Gods image," 43–44]); and reservations about monarchy are likely to imply doubts about courtly behavior and rhetoric.[38] From some important perspectives, then, a masque that praises aristocrats in courtly language may well imply a monarchism in conflict with the text's more radical agendas.

Moreover, the question of whether *Comus* should be classified as radical or proto-radical or curiously hybrid politically is complicated by the recognition that, as I noted above, masques before Milton were more varied than the common contrasts between them and *Comus* admit, with many masques offering textbook examples of the sycophantic monarchism associated with the form while some of Milton's predecessors anticipated the types of revision and reformation often attributed exclusively to him. In arguments buttressed by the admonitions to the queen some scholars have acutely uncovered in *The Faerie Queene* and the criticism of James I that may be implicit in Donne's sermons, critics have demonstrated that certain participants in the genre do offer some admonitions.[39] And whereas some masques culminate in the stasis best represented by Jonson's allegorized Perfection, others murmur or even announce that *wisest fate says no, / This must not yet be so:* for example, anticipating the conclusion of *Comus*, Jonson's *Pleasure Reconcil'd with Virtue* ends on an exhortation to seek virtue, which is described as a denizen of heaven but a stranger on earth.

In another sense, too, many masques anticipate *Comus* more than most critics have acknowledged, with the challenges to the form staged in the literal antimasque echoed in three intrusive and discordant questions the genre raises about its own workings. First, the emphasis on permanence explicated through Platonism, visualized through tableaux, and emblematized through allegorical figures is played against the temporariness of the masque's spectacle, tellingly termed by that master and slave of the form, Jonson, the "short braverie of the night."[40] And second, if, as John G. Demaray points out, masques often celebrate the triumph of restraint over excess, they do so with scenery and mechanical devices that are hardly restrained.[41] Above all, masques trope not only the commercialization of their own culture but also the analogous paradoxical materialism of their own workings. That is, they typically cause allegorical embodiments, figures who represent an escape from "the smoke and stir of this dim spot" (5), to rise up by means of the most material and most costly of mechanical devices. Thus, the abstract and ideal are the creatures of the material—and, more specifically, given the extraordinary cost of such devices, from another perspective the ostensibly ethical values of the masque are brought into being by material wealth. The material produces the illusion of the immaterial and spiritual. Masques trope, too, their own duplicity.[42]

The texts of this literary type that precede *Comus*, then, can fruitfully be positioned on a spectrum between uncritical celebration of courtly and monarchical values on the one hand and on the other a critique of those values that may involve the substitution of spiritual ones; most instances are closer to the first of the poles but fall somewhere between them. Thus, if Milton does recuperate the masque form, his project is not sui generis; and thus, too, other texts encourage us to think in terms of degree of reform, not its simple presence or absence.

And, as the approaches to pastoral and romance would suggest, *Comus* should be analyzed precisely in terms of those degrees of reform, not as a stable achievement in the new genre of Puritan or reformed masque. As I have already suggested, Milton's second masque, like his first, differs from many other Jacobean and Caroline contributions to the genre, not in kind but in degree: it is closer than they to the ideal form of a masque that replaces courtly with spiritual values, yet it never completely achieves that ideal: *But wisest Fate says no, / This must not yet be so.* Masque writers often express cultural anxieties about hybridity, fears activated perhaps by their genre's exemplification of *genera mista;* and *Comus*, that bestiary of animal-like humanoids, is itself a hybrid of versions of the masque.

Indubitably the text insists on distinctions from many earlier masques, much as elsewhere it insists on its rejection of certain types of romance. As many critics have pointed out, the principal action of *Comus* culminates in a celebration of the virtue of the Bridgewater children, not the majesty of the king or even of their parents. Implied in the rejection of courtly romance and the substitution of Sabrina for an aristocratic male rescuer is an alternative spatial sense encoding an alternative conception of power as adhering not in a centralized figure as in *Arcades* and so many courtly masques, but in Foucauldian capillaries.[43]

But the political implications of this diffusion of power remain ambiguous and ambivalent. The Earl of Bridgewater is distant from court and, as some scholars have reminded us, distant from some of the king's policies as well, but the image of Neptune reminds us that the existence of far-flung tributaries may be a compliment to, not a denial of, the potency of such a centralized figure.[44] This ideology is realized visually: *Comus*, like *Arcades*, moves toward the chair of state, and one critic has maintained that Inigo Jones would have attempted to make Ludlow Castle look as much like Whitehall as possible. And surrogates typically not only fill but also flag a lack.[45] Thus, Bridgewater's position vis-à-vis the court is as double and ambiguous as that of the masque in his honor. And whereas the climactic rescue by Sabrina calls into question monarchical values and the form that celebrates them, in the denouement the text moves toward that chair of state and toward a castle and a seat of power, thus narrativizing Milton's own attraction to that movement; it offers, in other words, alternative and unreconciled conceptions of where power lies and how it should be evaluated. While *Comus* clearly shifts away from courtly romance to its purified cousin, in juggling various possibilities for the masque it abjures that teleological progress from shadowy types to truth, or at least to something closer to truth.

The conclusion of the plot is equally ambiguous. As I briefly suggested earlier, bringing the lost child home is potentially a celebration both of the values of Protestant middle-class domesticity and of aristocratic romance. On the one hand, the text establishes the former (*"Heav'n hath timely tri'd their youth"* [970; italics in original]) as its primary gloss; but on the other hand we saw that whereas the Blake drawings of the final episode present the parents as elderly and worn, the performance would surely have drawn attention to the dignified aristocratic presence of the "Noble Lord, and Lady bright" (966) to whom the children return.[46] This is not to say that the masque was of Comus's party though it knew it not. But if, as critics have astutely demonstrated, Milton fears that better forms of government tend to revert to their faulty antecedents, *Comus* stages a comparable statement in literary politics, the tendency of genres to revert to earlier forms.[47] In this instance, the strongest affiliations of the text are undoubtedly to spiritual, not courtly, values; yet the return of the children hints as well at the tendency of the masque form—even when all its makeup seems to be scrubbed off in the interest of piety—to glitter with courtly values and assumptions. Or, to put it another way, McGuire is quite right that *Comus*'s emphasis on the dynamic rather than the static distinguishes it from many other court masques; but her observation could be extended to recognize that this dynamism includes a critique of the very achievements she locates securely within the text.[48] *Comus,* like so many of its author's other texts, is *genre en procès.*

Nothing in the text more clearly demonstrates that viewpoint than its closural gestures. In the return to the castle romance and the masque are closely connected, as is so often the case; adapting Jameson's analysis of the mystification of romance, one might even argue that the masque makes more overt the social hierarchies and ideologies implicit in romance.[49] But *Comus* also stages a struggle between them in several respects. We have already observed the tension between the aristocratic dance on which the masque ends and some of the romance values Milton has been developing. However latent and ambiguous that conflict is, other elements in the text intensify it. Whereas, for example, romance typically evokes certain locales, especially the dens of enchanters, with the Technicolor intensity of nightmare, it often enacts as well the difficulty the good characters have in finding and remaining in any stable, defined place, the spatial, horizontal analogue to the temporal and vertical problem of achieving narrative closure. In contrast, whereas masques often associate their evil characters with demonized locales like Ireland and with the urge to intrude into places they do not belong, resolution and closure are typically, though not universally, effected precisely through the transformation of the fictive world of the masque into the historical world of the court, dovetailing spatial and social place. Indeed, the relationship between the untoward interruptions of the antimasquers and the so-called discovery of the masquers stages the social contrast between those who are out of place at court, whether they be the professional actors professing the parts of antimasquers or the lower-class and foreign characters they portray, and those whose place is at the court. Having banished the villain whose very name is based on *komos,* a processional movement out into the streets, the end of *Comus* moves from the insistently closural emphasis on place characteristic of the masque—the children are returned to their parents, the action to the chair of state in particular and Ludlow Castle in general—to an epilogue that suggests all wayfaring Christians are displaced from their true home but may nonetheless strive for its values. Although, as I have demonstrated, *Comus* calls into question a number of Stanley Fish's assertions, its conclusion thus offers a textbook example of his observation about Milton's predilection for privileging interior truths over those discovered through externalized aspiration and adventure.[50]

In other words, here, as in *As You Like It,* it is above all the multiplicity of closural statements that testifies to the anticlosural anxieties of the author and the text, anxieties that in this case pivot on whether the Reformed masque, like the ideal landscape of the pastoral and the genre associated with it, can indeed be achieved in the fallen world. In *Arcades* the masquers' preliminary promise that "Here our solemn search hath end" (7) is realized as the text moves to its unchallenged culmination at the seat of the Countess of Derby, the physical movement toward her paralleling the temporal movement toward resolution. In contrast, as we have seen, in *Comus* the climactic return of the children to their parents celebrates the values of a new type of masque, but some faint traces of the older version remain.

This conclusion locates a new masque in the world of the Bridgewaters and the values associated with them—that is, in a power that replaces (yet, as I have argued, also represents) that of the monarch, in the dignity of the virtuous members of the aristocracy, and in achieved virtue on earth. Bridgewater replaces Charles, the Protestant home replaces the Cavalier court. As many readers have recognized, however, behind Milton's decision to expand and move the epilogue lies the implication, informed by both Christian and Platonic denigrations of "this dim spot, / Which men call Earth" (5–6), that true virtue cannot be achieved in and through any earthly world, including presumably the castle of the Bridgewaters.[51] He implies, in other words, that his first version of the reformed masque is not reformed enough, much as the type of romance that would culminate on the good offices of Sabrina and the return of the children is incomplete. If we cannot sign a second lease on the garden or write securely in the genre of gardens, so too the virtuous Christian, like the text itself, cannot achieve the closure of true virtue in sites and genres connected with earthly power.

Hence, in its double closure the text plays two double versions of the Puritan masque against each other, much as it juxtaposes variants of other genres. And the contrast between the closural force of the return of the children and the anticlosural emphasis on a continuing struggle in the Attendant Spirit's conclusion—"She can teach ye how to climb / Higher than the Spherey chime" (1020–21)—suggests that the spiritual goals of the Reformed masque are exactly that. And thus the text itself enacts a process comparable to that of the wayfaring Christian: a continuing struggle for a new type of masque, graced by many victories yet always liable to the siren call of the courtly practices common in other masques.[52]

Recognizing that undertow crystallizes a pattern that recurs throughout Milton's canon: alluding as it does to the ominous borderlands of the Severn, *Comus* reminds us that Milton himself dwelt on several borders throughout his career. To begin with, the assumption that *Comus* is a reformed masque is sometimes cited to substantiate the argument that its author's radical sympathies were firmly established even early in his career. Complex and contested, that credo cannot be examined at length in this essay, but my reading of *Comus* does at least gesture toward the shifting and at times ambivalent political attitudes that some critics, notably Annabel Patterson, have found in his early career.[53]

Whether or not we locate Milton on political thresholds, *Comus* does unambiguously reveal his preoccupation with other kinds of borders. Had he designed a Monopoly board, players who strove for secure tenure in that commodified Eden, Park Place, would have continually pulled cards that denied their title. For the perverse polyphony that interweaves Sabrina's sunny melodies with hints of peril exemplifies and explicates Milton's mental geography of ominous borderlands. *Comus*, a poem whose villain is iconographically represented in doorways, reminds us that in other Miltonic arenas as well as this text threats are always lurking just at the threshold.[54] Whereas Eve demands, "If this be our condition, thus to dwell / In narrow circuit strait'n'd by a Foe, / . . . How are we happy" (*PL* 9.322–23, 326), Milton removes the conditional and traces the consequences of such a condition. Not the least reason he substituted *Paradise Lost* for his Arthuriad is that the image of Satan at the door of Paradise was as central to his imagination throughout his career as, say, the image of the Canadian cabin was for Malcolm Lowry or that of the revenant for Seamus Heaney; not the least reason he incorporated an episode involving Satan into Book Three was to stress the ubiquity of threats. His rhetoric, too, stages this preoccupation with his negative constructions, like the Freudian *not*, often serving at once to introduce and then to contain the threat, while at the same time warning us that it may imperil us again in the future ("No voice or hideous hum / Runs through the arched roof in words deceiving" [*On the Morning of Christ's Nativity*, 174–75]; "not in the bought smile / Of Harlots . . . / . . . Or Serenate" [*PL* 4.765–66, 769]).[55] As we have seen, Milton's generic struggles not only mime but also explore and enact political ones, and this awareness of dangers lurking at the borders of literary forms recalls his conception of political change as constantly threatened by an attraction to older forms of government.

Comus is, in short, a draft for a reformed masque, not its polished realization, though it is much closer to that goal than *Arcades* or the masques by Milton's contemporaries. For all the ethical and aesthetic triumphs of *Comus*, enough of the court's magic has been sprinkled in front of Milton's eyes to prevent him from completely escaping the glamour of that world and the attraction of praising it. Moreover, even when he does want to escape courtly sycophancy, the undertow in the genre itself pulls the text back.[56]

The dialectic between achieving and questioning generic reform crystallizes another recurrent pattern in Milton's canon. Populated by so many apotropaic agents, typically his poems are themselves apotropaic, attempting, often with only partial success, to ward off ethical, spiritual, political, and literary dangers, including the perils associated with the literary types that they themselves variously test and attempt to discard. In the instance of genre, as in so many other arenas, apparent solutions are grasped only to be variously revised, rejected, and relinquished in the knowledge that *wisest Fate says no, / This must not yet be so*. Like haemony, like the Reformation and the English Revolution, even the reformed versions of genres prove at once efficacious and imperfect "in this soil" (633).

University of Wisconsin at Madison

NOTES

I thank Sarah Armstrong, David Loewenstein, and Donald Rowe for extensive assistance with this essay. I am also indebted to the audience at the 1999 Newberry Milton seminar at which an earlier version of this essay was presented.

1. *Comus,* 181, 916. All citations from Milton are to *Complete Poems and Major Prose,* ed. Merritt Y. Hughes (Indianapolis, 1957), hereafter cited parenthetically in the text. Translations of his Latin and Italian poems are also from this volume.

2. For a sample of earlier discussions of genre, see Don Cameron Allen, "Milton's 'Comus' as a Failure in Artistic Compromise," *English Literary History* 16 (1949): 104–19, who claims that this is not a true masque; C. L. Barber, *"A Mask Presented at Ludlow Castle:* The Masque as a Masque," in *"A Mask at Ludlow": Essays on Milton's "Comus,"* ed. John S. Diekhoff (Cleveland, 1968), argues, alternatively, that it is a true masque; and John G. Demaray, *Milton and the Masque Tradition: The Early Poems, "Arcades," and "Comus"* (Cambridge, MA, 1968), presents the case that *Comus* is a masque and as such heavily influenced by ballet and dance.

3. David Norbrook, "The Reformation of the Masque," in *The Court Masque,* ed. David Lindley (Manchester, 1984); Maryann Cale McGuire, *Milton's Puritan Masque* (Athens, GA, 1983). Among the other presentations of the revisionist argument about a revised masque are Cedric C. Brown, *John Milton's Aristocratic Entertainments* (Cambridge, 1985), chap. 7; Eugene R. Cunnar, "Milton, *The Shepherd* of Hermas, and the Writing of a Puritan Masque," *Milton Studies* 23, ed. James D. Simmonds (Pittsburgh, 1988), 33–52; two essays by Barbara K. Lewalski, "Milton's *Comus* and the Politics of Masquing," in *The Politics of the Stuart Court Masque,* ed. David Bevington and Peter Holbrook (Cambridge, 1998), and "How Radical Was the Young Milton?" in *Milton and Heresy,* ed. Stephen B. Dobranski and John P. Rumrich (Cambridge, 1998). John Creaser, " 'The present aid of this occasion': The Setting of *Comus,"* in Lindley, *The Court Masque,* attempts to negotiate a middle position, maintaining that *Comus* does not criticize other masques but is nonetheless a reformed masque.

4. One challenge comes from Annabel Patterson, *Pastoral and Ideology: Virgil to Valéry* (Berkeley and Los Angeles, 1987), who comments briefly but suggestively on *Comus* in the course of her argument that Milton's responses to aristocratic pastoral are divided, not simply negative (159). Michael Wilding, "Milton's 'A Masque Presented at Ludlow Castle, 1634': Theatre and Politics on the Border," *Milton Quarterly* 21 (1987): 35–51, finds the text ambiguous politically, as I do, but we part company on certain readings, and he traces the ambiguity by examining conflicts in particular episodes rather than genre.

5. See, for example, the commentaries on the politics of the 1645 volume in David Nor-

brook's major study, *Writing the English Republic: Poetry, Rhetoric and Politics 1627–1660* (Cambridge, 1999), esp. 162–64.

6. Bevington and Holbrook, "Introduction," 15. Barbara K. Lewalski, "Milton's *Comus* and the Politics of Masquing," in Bevington and Holbrook, *The Politics of the Stuart Court Masque,* 315.

7. One exception to this neglect is an important article that I encountered only after drafting this essay, Nancy Lindheim's "Pastoral and Masque at Ludlow," *University of Toronto Quarterly* 67 (1998): 639–68. Her approaches and arguments are, however, very different from mine: she traces a conflict between the otherworldly values she sees as normative in the masque and the more earthly perspectives of pastoral.

8. J. Martin Evans, *The Miltonic Moment* (Lexington, 1998), 40.

9. The issue of linearity in the poem is discussed from a perspective different from but compatible with my generic one in Nancy Lindheim, "Milton's Garden of Adonis: The Epilogue to the Ludlow *Maske,*" in *Milton Studies* 35, ed. Albert C. Labriola (Pittsburgh, 1997), 21–41.

10. Barbara Kiefer Lewalski, *"Paradise Lost" and the Rhetoric of Literary Forms* (Princeton, NJ, 1985), writes cogently on how genres are associated with choice in *Paradise Lost* in particular; though we read *Comus* very differently, I am indebted to her arguments on Milton's approach to genre. While his argument that *Paradise Lost* should be read largely as pastoral is unpersuasive, Barry Weller, "The Epic as Pastoral: Milton, Marvell and the Plurality of Genre," *New Literary History* 30 (1999): 143–57, also comments intelligently on generic choice.

11. Many critics have traced such patterns; one of the most influential recent studies is Michael McKeon, *The Origins of the English Novel 1600–1740* (Baltimore, 1987). A valuable instance of an earlier approach is the theory of countergenres developed by Claudio Guillén in *Literature as System: Essays Toward the Theory of Literary History* (Princeton, NJ, 1971), chap. 5.

12. Lindheim, "Pastoral and Masque at Ludlow," 639–68.

13. Stanley Fish, *How Milton Works* (Cambridge, MA, 2001), esp. chap. 1.

14. Jeanne S. Martin, "Transformations in Genre in Milton's *Comus,*" *Genre* 10 (1977): 212–13, argues persuasively that the end of the masque emphasizes the inaccessibility of an ideal world, the pervasiveness of deception, and the impossibility of dissolving the antimasque; she adduces this conclusion to distinguish *Comus* from other masques but does not pursue the central question explored in my essay, the implications of that pessimism for his approach to other genres in particular and genre in general.

15. Compare Stephen Orgel, "The Case for Comus," *Representations,* no. 81 (Winter 2003), who observes that those transformed by Comus are responsible for their sorry fate (35). On Milton's interest in the fallibility of vision, compare McGuire, *Milton's Puritan Masque,* 117–18. Debora Shuger, " 'Gums of Glutinous Heat' and the Stream of Consciousness: The Theology of Milton's *Maske,*" *Representations,* no. 60 (Fall 1997), esp. 7–9, also argues that Milton is concerned with the propensity for sin that arises within the sinner, but her reading, unlike mine, asserts that he is concerned to play down that propensity in this text.

16. These illustrations are in the print collection of the Boston Museum of Fine Arts; the item I describe is 90.119.

17. In interpreting such passages, Stanley E. Fish, "Problem Solving in *Comus,*" in *Illustrious Evidence: Approaches to English Literature of the Early Seventeenth Century,* ed. Earl Miner (Berkeley and Los Angeles, 1975), emphasizes the education of the audience. Also compare Brown, *John Milton's Aristocratic Entertainments,* 148, on the hortatory position of the conclusion of the masque.

18. Brown, *John Milton's Aristocratic Entertainments,* 77, also comments on the Protestant sense of the ubiquity of evil and corruption but does not acknowledge how this calls into question the viability of a Puritan masque.

19. For an intelligent presentation of this case, see McGuire, *Milton's Puritan Masque,* 36–38.

20. Compare Brown, *John Milton's Aristocratic Entertainments,* 46.

21. For a brief discussion from a perspective very different from mine of the connections between romance and masque elements in *Comus,* see, for example, Enid Welsford, *The Court Masque: A Study in the Relationship between Poetry and the Revels* (1927; reprint, New York, 1962), 284–92. A thought-provoking argument that *Comus* also engages with traditions of the country-house poem may be found in Hugh Jenkins, *Feigned Commonwealths: The Country-House Poem and the Fashioning of the Ideal Community* (Pittsburgh, 1988), 104–25.

22. See my *Shakespeare and Domestic Loss: Forms of Deprivation, Mourning, and Recuperation* (Cambridge, 1999), 101–4.

23. Many critics have discussed repetition in Milton; see especially Regina M. Schwartz, *Remembering and Repeating: On Milton's Theology and Poetics,* rev. ed. (Chicago, 1993).

24. For a discussion of the romance elements in *Comus* from a perspective different from but compatible with mine, see, for example, John Arthos, *On "A Mask Presented at Ludlow-Castle," by John Milton* (Ann Arbor, 1954), 20–23, 30–31.

25. Many critics have offered alternative and often compatible explanations for the Brothers' failure. See, for example, Evans, *Miltonic Moment,* 69.

26. See A. S. P. Woodhouse's long influential though contested argument that Sabrina represents divine grace in "*Comus* Once More," *University of Toronto Quarterly* 19 (1949): 218–23. Also see his "The Argument of Milton's *Comus,*" *University of Toronto Quarterly* 11 (1941): 46–71, reprinted in Diekhoff, "*A Maske at Ludlow.*"

27. See 90.126 in the collection of the Boston Museum of Fine Arts.

28. Norbrook, "The Reformation of the Masque," esp. 105–6.

29. Compare Lindheim's different but compatible thesis about a conflict between the Platonic transcendence of the masque and the this-worldly values of pastoral ("Pastoral and Masque at Ludlow"). Her otherwise astute essay is, however, limited by a tendency to play down the variations in the two literary types she contrasts.

30. Marc Berley, *After the Heavenly Tune: English Poetry and the Aspiration to Song* (Pittsburgh, 2000), esp. 180–205.

31. See Jeffrey Theis, "Betrayed by Pastoral? Comus, the Attendant Spirit and Pastoral Disguise in Milton's *A Masque*" (paper presented at the Graduate Student Conference, University of Wisconsin at Madison, May 1999).

32. On containment in *Comus,* compare Fish, *How Milton Works,* esp. 144–45.

33. The association of pastoral with cure is also discussed in Theis, "Betrayed by Pastoral"; also compare Lindheim, "Pastoral and Masque at Ludlow," on the pastoral motifs of care and human compassion (esp. 642–43).

34. Louis L. Martz, "The Music of *Comus,*" in Miner, *Illustrious Evidence,* 106–7. The shift from Martz's assertion that the text valorizes and celebrates poesy to my emphasis on Milton's anxieties about lyric aptly marks a shift in critical paradigms.

35. Barbara K. Lewalski, "How Radical Was the Young Milton?" 57, notes one instance of this dialectic, the way the shepherds' dance rescues pastoral from Comus.

36. For the argument that the passage shows Milton's class biases, see esp. Michael Wilding, *Dragons Teeth: Literature in the English Revolution* (Oxford, 1987), 64; and his essay "Milton's 'A Masque Presented at Ludlow Castle, 1634,'" 50.

37. For an acute statement of this case and other useful comments about pastoral in the text, see Leah S. Marcus, *The Politics of Mirth: Jonson, Herrick, Milton, Marvell, and the Defense of Old Holiday Pastimes* (Chicago, 1986), esp. 209.

38. John Donne, *The Satires, Epigrams and Verse Letters,* ed. W[esley] Milgate (Oxford, 1967).

39. See, for example, Hugh Craig, "Jonson, the Antimasque, and the Rules of Flattery," in Bevington and Holbrook, *The Politics of the Stuart Court Masque;* Norbrook, "The Reformation of the Masque," 96, 104. On the criticism of James I in Donne's sermons, see *John Donne's 1622 Gunpowder Plot Sermon: A Parallel-Text Edition,* ed. Jeanne Shami (Pittsburgh, 1996), 34–35.

40. "To Sir Robert Wroth," in *Ben Jonson,* 11 vols., ed. C. H. Herford and Percy and Evelyn Simpson (Oxford, 1925–1952), 10. The line in question may, of course, refer to other court entertainments besides the masque.

41. Demaray, *Milton and the Masque Tradition,* 91.

42. For a different but related argument relevant to the duplicity of masques, see the discussions of the dangers of allegory in Theresa M. Kelley, *Reinventing Allegory* (Cambridge, 1997), esp. chaps. 1–3. Also compare Theis, "Betrayed by Pastoral?" on how pastoral disguise is the source of pastoral truths.

43. Helen Cooper, "Location and Meaning in Masque, Morality, and Royal Entertainment," in Lindley, *The Court Masque,* offers a different but not incompatible gloss on the substitution of Sabrina for other rescuers, reading it as a tribute to "the harmony of man and countryside" (146).

44. Marcus, *The Politics of Mirth,* 183, argues unconvincingly that the text undercuts the identification of Neptune and Charles.

45. Willa McClung Evans, *Henry Lawes: Musician and Friend of Poets* (New York, 1941), 99.

46. See 90.126 in the collection of the Boston Museum of Fine Arts.

47. On Milton's attraction to this theory of regression, see Norbrook, *Writing the English Republic,* chap. 10.

48. McGuire, *Milton's Puritan Masque,* esp. 6–7, and chap. 2.

49. In *The Political Unconscious: Narrative as a Socially Symbolic Act* (Ithaca, NY, 1981), chap. 2, Fredric Jameson famously develops a materialist reading of romance.

50. See Fish, *How Milton Works,* esp. 31–36.

51. On these issues, see, for example, Lindheim, "Milton's Garden of Adonis."

52. Jenkins, *Feigned Commonwealths,* 124–25, notes the focus on process in *Comus* but offers a perspective different from though compatible with my own, tracing that focus to Milton's engagement with history and finding a comparable focus in the country-house poem.

53. See the brief but suggestive comments in Patterson, *Pastoral and Ideology,* 159; and her essay "'Forc'd fingers': Milton's Early Poems and Ideological Constraint," in *"The Muses Common-Weale": Poetry and Politics in the Seventeenth Century,* ed. Claude J. Summers and Ted-Larry Pebworth (New York, 1988), esp. 14–19.

54. Compare Stanley Fish's observation in "The Temptation to Action in Milton's Poetry," *English Literary History* 48 (1981): 524, that keeping watch is a central and strenuous activity in Milton.

55. In typing this passage, I wrote "Sabrinate" for "Serenate," thus enacting one of the central arguments of the essay.

56. For an argument that genres often work this way, see Peter Rabinowitz, "'Reader, I blew him away': Convention and Transgression in Sue Grafton," in *Famous Last Words: Changes in Gender and Narrative Closure,* ed. Alison Booth (Charlottesville, VA, 1993).

"THE REFORMING OF REFORMATION": THEATRICAL, OVIDIAN, AND MUSICAL FIGURATION IN MILTON'S *MASK*

Joseph M. Ortiz

Surely, if [Pythagoras] held any doctrine of the harmony of the spheres, or taught that the heavens revolve in unison with some sweet melody, it was only as a means of suggesting allegorically the close interrelation of the orbs and their uniform revolution in accordance with the laws of destiny for ever. In this he followed the example of the poets, or (what is almost the same thing) of the divine oracles, who never display before the eyes of the vulgar any holy or secret mystery unless it be in some way cloaked or veiled.

On the Harmony of the Spheres

The Bible . . . answers dubiously and darkly to the common reader.

Areopagitica

MILTON'S COMMENTS ON MUSIC and Scripture in the *Prolusions* and *Areopagitica* constitute a defense of allegory, based upon a careful understanding of figuration. Just as the Bible represents divine truth elliptically or "darkly," music—as it is understood and experienced by a human audience—has a figural relation to cosmological and divine knowledge, not a literal one. And while Milton couches his defense with references to the "vulgar" or "common reader," his other remarks in the same lecture on harmony suggest that this figural way of understanding truth is essential for almost *any* human reader or auditor: only Pythagoras, who was "worthy to hold converse with the gods themselves," could hear the true music of the spheres directly.[1] In this way, Milton's two essays posit figuration, defined as an indirect and imperfect way of presenting immutable concepts through poetic or musical forms, as necessary for the human attainment of knowledge, which on earth must always be considered incomplete.

This essay argues that Milton's conception of music and knowledge in his early writings elucidates a subtle, but ardent, defense of figuration in *A Mask at Ludlow*. Like the essay on harmony and *Areopagitica*, Milton's *Mask* represents earthly music both as a heavily mediated form and as an indispensable component of human understanding. Moreover, Milton expresses this complex attitude toward music and figuration in the *Mask* through a concurrent exploration of theatricality and Ovidian typology. Like music, Ovidian poetry and theatricality are frequently characterized in Renaissance England (in both laudatory and proscriptive contexts) as opaque, indirect forms of representation; Peter Lavinius's description of the *Metamorphoses* as truth hidden under "fictitious covers" (*fabulosa velamenta*) exemplifies a common rhetorical formulation in Renaissance representations of Ovid and in Milton's early references to music.[2] As I will attempt to show, Milton emphasizes the performative and dynamic aspects of theater, Ovid, and music in the *Mask* in order to demonstrate their shared status as intensely sensuous and imperfect modes of apprehending knowledge. In this way, the *Mask* dramatizes the pitfalls *and* benefits of theatrical, Ovidian, and musical representation—and, more generally, of figuration itself.

Much recent Milton criticism has focused on the complex evolution of typology and iconology in his prose and poetry.[3] The present essay contributes to these studies by examining Milton's own self-conscious evaluation of the usefulness of figural and iconological forms of representation. Equally important, this essay argues that the *Mask* identifies figuration as a central concern of Reformist ideology. Ovid and music were themselves often politicized and moralized in early modern antitheatrical literature, a fact of which Milton was well aware. As early as 1579, Stephen Gosson had included Ovid and complex music in his attack on plays. Likewise, Prynne's *Histriomastix*, published the year before *A Mask*, severely condemns both Ovid and polyphonic music.[4] Critical work on early modern antitheatricalism has seldom explored in depth the inclusion of music and Ovid in the Puritan attacks on the theater, even though these sections of the tracts often sparked the most violent responses at the time of publication.[5] This is an unfortunate omission, since the debates over music and Ovid bring into sharp focus a sustained hostility toward figuration and performance that is crucially relevant to an understanding of Protestant ideology. Early modern antitheatricalism systematically articulates a strong suspicion about pedagogical modes that rely upon fictive, sensuous veils to impart divine precepts. For this reason, heavily mediated discourses such as music and Ovidian allegory routinely fall under Reformist censure. In *A Mask*, Milton's attitude toward knowledge and figuration leads to a sympathetic (at least in part) representation of music, Ovid, and theatricality, and his sustained attention to these three subjects prompts us to consider the basis of their frequent proscription in Reformist polemic. In this respect, by unleashing Puritan, Prynnian rhetoric in the vicinity of Ovid and music, the *Mask* illuminates some of the ideological currents that inform early modern antitheatricalism.

By showing how the *Mask* interrogates Puritan antitheatrical polemic, this essay revises the prevalent critical notion that Milton "reforms" the Stuart court masque. David Norbrook suggests that, by radically departing from standard masque practices, Milton "rethink[s] masque conventions in the light of an apocalyptic Protestant ideology" and attempts to reinstate "a new moral purity and integrity in art." Likewise, Leah Marcus argues that *A Mask* is "designed . . . to win arts and pastimes back from the domination of the court and the Laudian wing of the church" and make them more compatible with Puritan political and moral ideology. It is certainly the case that the court masque, as a genre, embodied precisely those elements most disturbing to Puritan sentiment: theater, mixed dancing, women-actors, emphasis on visual spectacle, lavish monetary expenditure, and the replenishment of royalist iconography. It is also evident that Milton assigns the most conventional masquing idioms not to the masque proper, but to the central figure of the antimasque. As Norbrook remarks, "Milton puts the defence of 'high solemnities' in the mouth of the antimasque villain while his heroine calls for the redistribution of wealth." Thus, whether taking *A Mask* as an emblem for financial excess, sexual immorality, or Laudian politics, these interpretations generally presume that Comus the "anti-masque villain" represents those elements that Reformist ideology—and Milton—ultimately reject.[6]

However, Milton does not purge the masque of its intense reliance on figuration and iconology, even as he acknowledges that these "magic structures" may be championed and co-opted by someone like Comus.[7] Rather, Milton identifies the imperfect nature of these modes as a direct consequence of the Fall. In the next two sections, I show how the *Mask* uses theatricality and Ovidian allusion to demonstrate the radical instability of figurative knowledge, in a way that makes complete "moral purity in art" impossible. In the essay's last section, I suggest that Milton uses music—in many ways the most figurative art form—to confirm this instability, but in a way that establishes figuration as essential to *any* postlapsarian aesthetic. This acceptance of figurative "dubiousness" emphasizes the precariousness of Milton's project (because it denies authoritative claims to universal meaning), but it also enables Milton to stage a *critique* of the antitheatrical tracts for their refusal to acknowledge the impact of original sin on the transmission of knowledge. In the case of music, recent Milton criticism has generally aligned Milton's sympathies with Protestant ideology as put forth in the antitheatrical tracts. Stephen Buhler, discussing the repression of polyphony in *Paradise Lost,* argues that "the controversies over counterpoint—and Milton's participation in them—help to illustrate Milton's developing and sustained allegiances to Puritan principles."[8] Yet, the aesthetic-theological politics of the *Mask* may be ideologically closer to a work like *Areopagitica,* in which the narrow proscription of classical authors and music is cited as reason for "reforming the reformation itself." Despite Milton's obvious Puritan sympathies and his need to "reform" the court masque, *A Mask at Ludlow* responds to Protestant ideology more fully—and more critically—than has previously been recognized.

I

When Milton's Lady ironically tells Comus to "enjoy [his] dear wit, and gay rhetoric" (790), she effectively sums up his crime as a devotion to figurative, theatrical language.[9] In this way, Milton arms his heroine with contemporary antitheatrical polemic in order to establish a recognizable opposition between theatrical representation and plain, Puritan "honesty." Throughout the *Mask*, the Lady draws on Puritan political and moral ideology to vilify Comus on the basis of his mutability, manipulation of vision, and ability to transform others—all qualities that traditionally distinguish the Stuart masque. For example, when the Lady rebukes Comus for pretending to be a shepherd, she calls him "false traitor" and "imposter" (690, 762). William Prynne says as much about actors in *Histriomastix:* "what else is an *hypocrite, in his true etimologie, but a Stage-player, or one who acts anothers part."*[10] The Lady goes on to say:

> Hence with thy brewed enchantments, foul deceiver,
> Hast thou betrayed my credulous innocence
> With vizored falsehood, and base forgery,
> And wouldst thou seek again to trap me here
> With lickerish baits fit to ensnare a brute?   (696–700)

Here, "vizor" suggests "mask," and "base forgery" recalls the Platonic bias against the theater, often cited in the tracts, in which theater's mimetic nature makes it an inferior, "base" copy of an original. This Platonic distrust of appearances underscores the Lady's statement that Comus "canst not touch the freedom of my mind / With all thy charms, although this corporal rind / Thou hast immanacled" (663–65). The Lady's reference to "corporal rind" sustains Comus's allusion to Ovid's Daphne in the preceding lines (by recuperating a latent pun on rind/skin in the *Metamorphoses*), but in a way that deflates the Ovidian comparison: Comus may transform the Lady into a second Daphne, but only on the insignificant level of corporal surfaces. Thus, by filtering Comus's rhetoric through Protestant ideology, the Lady not only counters Comus's use of allusion; she also undermines the mode of figuration that enables him to traffic in fictive iconographies in the first place.

At the same time, the attempt to vilify Comus via a Puritan critique of

theatricality is risky business. By aligning the Lady with contemporary Reformist attitudes, Milton makes her vulnerable to a more damaging textual
contamination: the most radical Puritan antitheatrical rhetoric, which seeks
to dissolve the theater entirely. Indeed, early twentieth-century Milton criticism suggests the extent to which the *Mask* is susceptible to contamination
by Reformist polemic. Enid Welsford writes that "there is in *Comus* a subtle
incongruity between the symbolism and the idea that it is meant to sym-
bolise, and of this incongruity Milton seems to be entirely unaware. He could
not see that the masque, whose presiding deity was Hymen, was a most
unsuitable vehicle for the unfolding of the 'sage and serious doctrine of
virginity.' "[11] This reading of the Lady's harsh rhetoric, although it problematically denies the possibility of Milton's awareness of his masque's incongruities, foregrounds the fact that the masque is fully realized only in performance. Milton's Lady, for all her rebukes, *is* acting in a masque, after all, and
within this performative context mimesis is unavoidable. Welsford's sense of
a "subtle incongruity" hits at a conflict between content and context in the
Mask that must be considered—namely, what the Lady argues as being beyond theatrical representation *is* being represented. In contrast to Welsford's
reading, arguments about *Comus* as a "Puritan" or "anti-Laudian" masque
often avoid the problem of how one can articulate a rejection of figuration
and appearance, particularly in a dramatic medium. Such arguments tacitly
assume that Milton's masque is somehow exempt from contemporary Puritan
antitheatricality. For example, Maryann McGuire acknowledges the relevance of William Prynne's notoriously antitheatrical *Histriomastix* to Milton's
Comus, but she then confidently asserts that "Milton was no Prynne" in order
to avoid the possibility of literary or ideological contamination.[12] Accordingly,
when Milton's Lady rejects the argument that Beauty "must be shown / In
courts, at feasts, and high solemnities" (745–46), we are expected not to
dwell on the fact that she herself is conspicuously on display to the Bridgewater court. McGuire admits Prynne's applicability to *masques,* only to foreclose on his applicability to *A Mask.*

Milton does not, however, evade the potential conflict between the
Lady's argument and the physical occasion of its utterance. Rather, he intensifies this conflict by making theatrical self-consciousness (at least for the
audience) nearly unavoidable, as in the Lady's final repudiation of Comus's
theatricality:

> Enjoy your dear wit, and gay rhetoric
> That hath so well been taught her dazzling fence,
> Thou art not fit to hear thyself convinced;
> Yet should I try, the uncontrollèd worth

> Of this pure cause would kindle my rapt spirits
> To such a flame of sacred vehemence,
> That dumb things would be moved to sympathize,
> And the brute Earth would lend her nerves, and shake,
> Till all thy magic structures reared so high,
> Were shattered into heaps o'er thy false head.   (790–99)

As the Lady calls attention to Comus's "dazzling fence," which she brands as lacking substance, she also implies the performativity of her own response. For one thing, the effects of the "sacred vehemence" she describes are remarkably Orphean. While such language gestures toward prophecy, the Orphean parallel firmly places the Lady in the context of a listening *audience:* like Orpheus, Milton's Lady stands before an enraptured audience that will be "moved to sympathize" if she is successful. By emphasizing the dramatic nature of the Lady's utterance, Milton comes close to suggesting the self-contradictory theatricality of much radical antitheatricalism itself, which, as Jonas Barish has noted, often constitutes the very thing it aims to suppress.[13] In a sense, the sincerity of the Lady's argument depends on a deliberate unawareness of its occasional context—an unawareness that is far less appropriate to a masque performance than to a book like *Histriomastix.* As Stephen Orgel points out, theatrical self-consciousness is systemically more pronounced in the court masque than in any other dramatic genre; the hero of a Stuart masque conventionally triumphs by virtue of *"know[ing]* that he is an actor in a masque and is conscious of the presence and significance of the audience."[14] The masque, which for Orgel is radically self-conscious, is for Milton's Lady a remarkably unreflexive event.

In threatening to bring down Comus's "magic structures," the Lady reiterates a brand of antitheatricality typical of Ben Jonson in his attacks on Inigo Jones, whose magic structures Jonson begrudged as the most popular element of the Stuart masque.[15] Similar to Jonson's expressions of "unresolved ambivalence" toward the stage,[16] the Lady's implicit criticism of the masque paradoxically belies the fact that she is one of the principal entertainers of the evening: the magic structures falling on Comus's head would presumably fall on hers, too. This self-referential backfiring, which nearly amounts to a dramatic contradiction, may very well suggest the stage's inherent limitation: the masque cannot represent an attack on figuration without undermining its own message. In this way Milton demonstrates the masque's profound inability to advance a strict, Puritan aesthetic. Even further, Milton's dramaturgy during the temptation scene shows how the rejection of figuration might be indistinguishable from its authorization. In performance, the Lady's immobility and silence can register iconologically as a reminder of monarchical form. As the silent center and object of many of the spoken and sung words in the second half of the masque, the Lady takes on the visual qualities of the Stuart masque's sustaining icon: the "non-dramatic" monarch or other royal figure who conventionally "stays in the center of the masque universe" and silently authorizes the entertainment that is taking place.[17] Thus, even if the Lady's silence is intended as an assertion of the superiority of contemplation over linguistic display, the *Mask* exposes the impotence of silence when placed in a theatrical context. Taken all together, the Lady's silence and immobility effectively suggest the only logical outcome of her vehement antitheatricalism. The Lady's antitheatrical rhetoric, taken to its extreme conclusion, is ultimately self-negating, and the fact that she is literally stuck to her chair even after Comus is expelled suggests that a public condemnation of theatricality fatally ignores the condition of its utterance. It is worth noting that the Lady has no more lines for the rest of the masque. As she sits stuck to her chair in a gum of self-contradiction, forced to repudiate theatricality and demonstrate its effectiveness simultaneously, she visually emblematizes what a Puritan poetics, in the most radical Prynnian sense, must be.

II

Milton compounds the problematizing effects of the masque's theatricality with a sustained use of Ovid that emphasizes the pitfalls of figural representation. In this respect, Milton astutely identifies the proscription of Ovid in the antitheatrical tracts as an attack on figuration. At the same time, Milton makes figural representation in his masque unavoidable. In the previous section I suggested how the *Mask*'s iconographic and theatrical modes (the *appearance* of the Lady as an Orphean or monarchical figure) can undercut its poetic or argumentative ones (the Lady's antitheatrical polemic).[18] The *Mask*'s Ovidianism operates in much the same way, since, as Milton shows, poetic allusions to Ovid can spawn a series of figural or iconological associations that exceed any single ideological or political message.

Early in the masque, Milton's Lady alludes to two Ovidian myths that, despite their tragic associations, function largely as innocent poetic metaphors:

> Sweet Echo, sweetest nymph that liv'st unseen
> Within thy airy shell
> By slow Meander's margent green,
> And in the violet-embroidered vale
> Where the love-lorn nightingale
> Nightly to thee her sad song mourneth well.   (230–35)

As Richard DuRocher has noted, the Lady's allusion to Philomela ("the love-lorn Nightingale") is potentially gloomy: in the *Metamorphoses,* Philomela becomes a nightingale only after Tereus has brutally raped her and removed her tongue.[19] The apparent figural similarity between the nightingale and Milton's Lady, who both sing a sad song to Echo, does not suggest a happy outcome. In context, however, the Lady's allusions do not evoke any real sense of danger or compromise her intended meaning. Rather, they are contained by a pastoral, lyrical tradition that keeps tragedy at bay.[20] A darker Ovidianism comes to the foreground with the entrance of Comus. Comus's association with Circe, his intemperate sensuality, and his transformative powers all encourage Milton's audience to see him as an Ovidian prototype. Likewise, when Comus first hears the Lady singing, he imaginatively evokes an Ovidian world that is far more morally suspect than Philomela or Echo:

> I have oft heard
> My mother Circe with the Sirens three,
> Amidst the flowery-kirtled Naiades
> Culling their potent herbs, and baleful drugs,
> Who as they sung, would take the prisoned soul,
> And lap it in Elysium; Scylla wept,
> And chid her barking waves into attention,
> And fell Charybdis murmured soft applause.   (252–59)

Comus's references to Circe and the Sirens, and his own self-identification with Scylla, register Milton's construction of the antimasque through Ovidian models. Citing Scylla's transformation into a self-consuming monster in the *Metamorphoses,* DuRocher recognizes the moral appropriateness of Ovid's Scylla as a figure for Comus, since "for Milton the 'restless' circularity of the process—to flee, but drag along what one flees; to be self-fed and self-consumed—is both the condition and the horror of evil."[21] Thus, while Milton makes associations between the Lady and Ovid's Philomela and Echo, his use of Ovidian typology in his representation of Comus initially distinguishes pastoral humility from sensuous, "restless" mutability.

The tendency to view Comus as an Ovidian prototype—and his seduction as an Ovidian plot—is partly an effect of the masque's iconographic mode. In other words, Comus's legibility as a Circe or Scylla figure is enhanced by a mode of aesthetic reception, endemic to the Stuart court masque, in which the characters on stage are "read" as mythical or allegorical personifications.[22] However, in contrast to masque convention, Milton's recourse to Ovid does not ultimately stabilize the allegorical meanings in the *Mask.* As Comus elaborates his attempt to seduce the Lady, he incorporates the Ovidian associations so far established into a larger pattern that serves *his* immoral designs. For example, even though Comus recognizes a "sacred delight" in the Lady's pastoral singing, such delight does not reform him. Instead, Comus's memory of Circe and the Sirens contaminates that delight and refigures it as sensual. He imagines the Lady as someone who improves upon, but does not redeem, the sensuous qualities of Circe, the Sirens, and Scylla ("and she shall be my queen," 265). In this respect, Comus's attempt to seduce the Lady is tantamount to his representation of her as an Ovidian *figura*. The example of Ovid's Scylla is especially illustrative of Comus's subversive use of allusion. In Book 14 of the *Metamorphoses,* Glaucus attempts to seduce the virgin Scylla and appeals to Circe for help. When Circe offers herself instead and is rejected, she poisons Scylla's favorite wading pool and transforms her into the half-woman, half-Cerberean monster that terrorizes Odysseus. Like Ovid's Glaucus, Comus is enchanted by the Lady and appeals to Circean magic to trap her. Additionally, Circe's "liquids brewed," mentioned in Ovid (*latices pressos, Met.* 14.56), become Comus's "brewed enchantments" (*A Mask,* 696), and her "maze of uncanny words" (*obscurum verborum ambage novorum, Met.* 14.57) suggests his "dear wit, and gay rhetoric" (*A Mask,* 790).[23] Like his mother, Circe, Comus draws on occult magic to pollute a virgin and transform her into the object of her own horror. In the process, Comus promiscuously invests the figure of Ovid's Scylla—already identified with himself—with the Lady's own plight.

The special violence of Comus's allusiveness is that he repeatedly uses Renaissance moralizations of Ovid for immoral purposes. Whereas Renaissance moralizations often attempt to control the meaning of classical poetry and assimilate it to a Christian ideology, Comus takes advantage of the inherent figurativeness (and hence, the potential instability) of this mode of allegory. Although Ovid's Scylla is a helpless victim, the moralized Scylla of the Renaissance mythographies is appetitive; the slipperiness of this allegorical association opens up an imaginative space for Comus through which he can suggest the Lady's susceptibility to temptation. Judith Browning notes that the Renaissance moralizations of Scylla "associate her Circean 'pollution' with her inability to withstand 'bewitching pleasure,' "[24] and Comus evokes a similar association when, having "immanacled" the Lady in his hall with "charms," he tempts her with "all the pleasures / That fancy can beget on youthful thoughts" (664–69). In this way, the Renaissance Scylla not only provides Comus with a model for his own seduction plot; it also enables him to imagine the Lady—who parallels Ovid's Scylla—as someone who both succumbs to *and is a figure for* appetite. After all, Comus does not intend to rape the Lady. He attempts to seduce her and make her a willing accomplice in her own pollution. To this end, Comus encourages his audience to see the Lady not as

Chastity (as she is conventionally known), but as Appetite. Comus's allegorical Ovidianism (in contrast to a lyrical use of Ovid), aided by the Renaissance moralizations, enables him to shift the masque's figural politics in a way that aligns the Lady (and not merely himself) with Ovid's Scylla. The Lady's nondramatic immobility in performance corroborates this mode of Ovidian association: "fixed, and motionless" in Comus's chair just as Ovid's Scylla is fixed in the water with her barking dogs, the Lady replicates Scylla's fate (819). Likewise, the "glutinous heat" that binds the Lady to her chair (917) recalls the gluttonous heat that Renaissance mythographers associate with Circe and Scylla.[25] This is Ovidianism with a vengeance: in a medium as intensely iconographic as the Stuart masque, where visual association is nearly equivalent to meaning, Comus's "posing" of the Lady as Scylla amounts to an imaginative rape. His Ovidian "moralization" of the Lady engenders an iconological pollution of her before the actual event, effectively evacuating the Renaissance allegories of their moral efficacy by using their colorful rhetoric to stage an immoral scene.

Through Comus's manipulation of Ovidian *figurae,* Milton appears to confirm temporarily the depiction of Ovidian poetry in the antitheatrical tracts as morally unsalvageable. On the one hand, Comus's allusiveness does much to justify Puritan suspicion of Ovid, since for him Ovidian mythology provides a literary model for sexual corruption. On the other hand, Protestant critiques of Ovid (and, to a lesser extent, of Virgil) also reject the allegorization of classical poets by expressing a deep-seated suspicion of veiled, "figured" truth, regardless of how morally conservative that truth may be. Milton's *Mask* initially bolsters this suspicion by suggesting that the Renaissance moralizations, rather than having strict control over poetry's meaning, actually depend on a mode of figuration that is profoundly unstable and susceptible to abuse. Comus's eagerness to use this instability to his advantage, demonstrated in the allusions to Scylla, is even more pronounced in his reference to Ovid's Daphne:

> Nay lady sit; if I but wave this wand,
> Your nerves are all chained up in alabaster,
> And you a statue, or as Daphne was
> Root-bound, that fled Apollo.   (659–62)

This allusion serves Comus in two ways. First, it allows him (and the audience) to imagine at least a half-successful outcome to his pursuit of the Lady, since Daphne ultimately became the symbol of Apollo's poetic power. Second, and more importantly, by aligning the Lady with Ovid's most famous poetic *figura,* Comus emphasizes the Lady's role—entirely appropriate to the masque genre—*as figure.* It is precisely amid the shifting meanings of *figura/*

forma that Ovid's Apollo is able to possess Daphne. Once transformed into a poetic and corporal figure, Daphne "consents" to Apollonian ownership: "the laurel waved her new-made branches, and seemed to move her head-like top in full consent" [factis modo laurea ramis / adnuit utque caput visa est agitasse cacumen] (1.566–67). Similarly, Comus's figurations of the Lady allow him to "read" her as a second Daphne or, even worse, a second Gallathea ("all chained up in alabaster").[26]

Milton's reference to Daphne hints at the reason for Ovid's particular aptness for subversive allusion and for his prominence in the antitheatrical tracts. Ovid's Daphne episode plays on the potential conflict between form and content (Apollo's selfish interpretation of the tree's nodding is one of the master strokes in the *Metamorphoses*), a conflict that Ovid develops throughout the rest of his poem.[27] This instability of figural meaning, which Puritan polemicists rightly suspect as being encouraged by Ovidian poetry, makes deception in poetry possible. Milton glosses this possibility of deception in the exchange between the two brothers by showing how even the most straightforward articulation of ideology may be contaminated by the masque's Ovidian figurations. Realizing they have lost their sister, the Second Brother fears that she is "within the direful grasp / Of savage hunger, or of savage heat" (357–58). After learning his sister's predicament from the Attendant Spirit, the Elder Brother correctly identifies his sister's captor as a metamorphic power:

> But evil on itself shall back recoil,
> And mix no more with goodness, when at last
> Gathered like scum, and settled to itself
> It shall be in eternal restless change
> Self-fed, and self-consumed. (593–97)

Like someone versed in the antitheatrical tracts, the Elder Brother indicates his distaste for metamorphosis by equating moral evil with "eternal restless change."[28] As DuRocher correctly notes, the Elder Brother's depiction of evil ("self-fed, and self-consumed") points to Comus's earlier self-identification with Ovid's Scylla.[29] However, the Elder Brother cannot control his own metaphors, since his words also suggest the image of the Lady herself, who at this moment is visually surrounded (as Ovid's Scylla is) by a rout of barking monsters. The Lady, "within the direful grasp" of a Scylla figure, is also in danger of being read *iconologically* as the Scylla of the Renaissance mythographers.[30] This iconological identification, whose persuasiveness must be recognized as an effect of the masque's visual, performative nature, frustrates the easy *poetic* association of Comus with Scylla that the Elder Brother attempts to convey.[31] Thus, poetic terms in the masque that would enable an easy distinction between chastity and contagion threaten to collapse into each other by way of their figural semblance when the masque is performed.

Milton raises the crisis of figuration to its highest pitch at the end of the temptation scene by making a striking parallel between the Lady and Ovid's Philomela. The Lady's final assertion that she will raise "such a flame of sacred vehemence, / That dumb things would be moved to sympathize" (795–96) echoes Protestant formulations of inspiration, but it also imitates Ovid's Philomela immediately after her rape by Tereus:

> ipsa pudore
> proiecto tua facta loquar: si copia detur,
> in populos veniam; si silvis clausa tenebor,
> inplebo silvas et conscia saxa movebo;
> audiet haec aether et si deus ullus in illo est! (6.544–48)

[I will myself cast shame aside and proclaim what you have done. If I should have the chance, I would go where people throng and tell it; if I am kept shut up in these woods, I will fill the woods with my story and move the very rocks to pity. The air of heaven shall hear it, and, if there is any god in heaven, he shall hear it too.]

The Ovidian quotation here recalls the Attendant Spirit's earlier reference to the Lady as a "poor hapless nightingale" and the reference to "love-lorn nightingale" in the Lady's song—except that the metaphor now carries all its tragic associations. Whereas earlier the Lady could unproblematically allude to Philomela within the context of pastoral, at this point in the masque it is much more difficult to ignore the Lady's role as a second Philomela. In a sense, Milton's Lady is tricked into "speaking" Ovid. The fact that Ovidian quotation and antitheatrical rhetoric converge in the Lady's final speech suggests that her repudiation of Comus has somehow backfired. Paradoxically, Ovidian quotation and Puritan polemic *are* saying the same thing here, in that they both pressure a reading of the Lady as already contaminated. For one thing, Philomela's statement in the *Metamorphoses* that she will move rocks to pity is directed at a condition (rape) that Ovid represents as "unspeakable" (*nefas*).[32] Thus, although Milton's Lady refers to a subject (chastity) she believes to be beyond the representational limits of the stage, the Ovidian context makes her ensuing silence indistinguishable from the shame (*pudor*) Philomela casts aside. For Ovid's Philomela, it is the violation of chastity, not its essence, that is truly unspeakable. At the same time, Puritan polemic as put forth by Prynne categorizes the Lady as a "notorious whore" by virtue of her performance in a masque. Under this harsh view of theatricality, the Lady's "sacred vehemence" represented onstage would look very much like Comus's "dazzling fence" and would undoubtedly evoke more

Ovidian resonances. Given this impasse, Milton seems to suggest a profound weakness of Protestant ideology—or at least of the articulation of Protestant ideology—in the face of figural representation. Stuck between Comus's profligate Ovidianism and the radical Puritanism of her own arguments, between a figural context that reads silence as *pudor* and an ideology that suspects female declamation as "whorish," Milton's Lady finds herself with no critical space in which to move.[33] To put it glibly, she finds herself between Scylla and Charybdis.

III

The failure to appreciate the urgency of the Lady's ideological dilemma, represented by her immobility, inevitably leads to a failure to appreciate her very real need for deliverance. Such a failure causes Stanley Fish to remark, after a lengthy discussion on the meaning of haemony, that the Lady is "fixed but free."[34] However, just as haemony as a magical device is insufficient in the *Mask,* the "fixed but free" argument would hardly satisfy the Earl of Bridgewater as to why his daughter cannot return home. The point is that Milton has created an ideological and aesthetic crux in which allegorical Ovidianism, royalist iconography, and zealous antitheatricalism all compete for the meaning of the Lady's theatrical presence. Milton's awareness that neither an inward reversion to the "freedom of [the Lady's] mind" nor a prophecy-inspired shattering of magic structures is an acceptable *occasional* solution (that is, they will not get us to the evening's festive dances) suggests that they are insufficient moral responses as well, if we believe that the *Mask* sustains its moral-ideological trial through the end. Indeed, the *Mask* continues to work out the difficulties of figuration raised in the scenes with Comus and it finally resolves these issues in the context of a third, related contemporary debate: the controversy over music. Milton's masque, it should be noted, ends with a dense sequence of musical interludes: the musical invocation to Sabrina, the spell that frees the Lady from her chair, the restoration of the children to their parents, and the song that the Attendant Spirit sings as he returns to the heavens. As Louis Martz suggests, music in *Comus* "gives one the power to penetrate disguises, guard from evil, and rescue from enchantment. . . . Music serve[s] to create a harmony in which the oppositions of life are reconciled."[35] We should not take Martz's reference to "harmony" to conclude that music for Milton is merely a metaphysical conceit or a metaphor for rejuvenation—in the *Mask,* the *performance* of music exemplifies the need for figural modes of knowledge in a postlapsarian world.

There are many reasons why music is, for Milton, an appropriate context for the close examination of Protestant ideology. Through its constitutive performativity—the fact that it cannot be reduced to verbal rhetoric or visual icon—music achieves an illustrative force that effectively clarifies the theological and political debates over Ovid and theater as arguments over the transmission of knowledge. Thus, unsurprisingly, the debate over certain kinds of music appears in Puritan attacks on the theater as early as 1579. Stephen Gosson, writing about chromatic harmony in *The Schoole of Abuse,* decries the technical complexity of contemporary music (which also approaches illegibility through its notational excessiveness):

Terpandrus and Olimpus used instruments of seven strings . . . [but] Timotheus . . . toke the seven-stringed harp, that was altogether used in Terpandrus time, and increaced the number of the strings at his owne pleasure. . . . Were the Argives and Pythagoras nowe alive, and saw how many frets, how many stringes, how many stops, how many keyes, how many cliffes, how many moodes, how many flats, how many sharps, how many rules, how many spaces, how many noates, how many restes, how many querks, how many corners, what chopping, what changing, what tossing, what turning, what wresting and wringing is among our Musicians, I beleve verily, that they would cry out with the country man: *Heu quod tam pingui macer est mihi taurus in arno.* Alas here is fat feeding, and leane beasts.³⁶

Likewise, in *Histriomastix,* William Prynne castigates any kind of harmonization that is too complex, calling it a "dishonest art of warbling the voyce," a "whorish musicke crowned with flowers." What is being attacked in these tracts is not just complex harmonization or conventional polyphony, but any composition or decorative style that has the effect of undermining the text's authority over music. Excessive trilling, the repetitions of words, and contrapuntal settings all come under fire by Protestant reformers. Thomas Becon, translating Erasmus, vehemently criticizes the use of polyphonic settings in church, asking, "But nowe what other thing doth the common people heare, than voyces signifying nothing?" In a passage later quoted by Prynne, Becon (translating Agrippa) rails against the use of polyphony in divine services by remarking that these singers "barke a counterpoynt as it were a number of dogges." Here, Becon's references to "dogges," "bulles," and "hogges" come close to Milton's Comus and the Renaissance Circe, who change people "into some brutish form of wolf, or bear, / Or ounce, or tiger, hog, or bearded goat" (70–71). According to Becon and Prynne, if sexual incontinence transforms people into beasts allegorically, as the moralizations of Ovid teach, then polyphonic music ("counterpoynt") disfigures people aurally.³⁷

Most readers of Milton view the *Mask* as upholding the Reformist attitude toward music, noting that the characters' descriptions of Comus echo contemporary attacks on polyphony.³⁸ For example, when the Elder Brother says that his sister has "no gross ear" (458), he suggests that the Lady's chastity depends on her ability to discriminate among different kinds of sound, an observation that is consistent with the masque's repeated references to ears and hearing. This sensitivity to various kinds of music arguably explains Milton's removal of the word "counterpoint" from the Lady's song to Echo at the beginning of the masque. In the Bridgewater manuscript, the Lady's song has "Sweet queen of parley, daughter of the sphere. / So mayst thou be translated to the skies / And hould a Counterpointe to all heav'ns harmonies" (241–43), whereas in the 1637 publication of the masque, Milton replaces "hould a Counterpointe" with "give resounding grace."[39] As Stephen Buhler suggests, "Milton apparently decided, counterpoint should not be approvingly mentioned in a song that" is clearly monodic. The settings that Henry Lawes wrote for the masque's songs, Buhler notes, conform well to the "pattern advanced by the Reformist critique of polyphony."[40] Nonetheless, readings of the *Mask* as simply extolling a "monodic," Reformist style tend to downplay the many other kinds of music that are sanctioned by the masque, including the loud "jigs" and "rural dance" that are foregrounded by the Lady's return to the court (952).[41] Moreover, while Milton clearly evokes Lawes through the figure of the Attendant Spirit ("a swain, / That to the service of this house belongs" [84–85]), he is careful to distinguish this figure from the other, equally necessary "artists" that preside over the Lady's resuscitation. Before examining the role of music in the masque's final scene, however, it will be useful to consider briefly Milton's treatment of music in a few other representative works.

In *At a Solemn Music*, Milton distinguishes between heavenly and earthly music:

> That we on earth with undiscording voice
> May rightly answer that melodious noise;
> As once we did, till disproportioned sin
> Jarred against nature's chime, and with harsh din
> Broke the fair music that all creatures made
> To their great Lord, whose love their motion swayed
> In perfect diapason, whilst they stood
> In first obedience, and their state of good.   (17–24)

The pun on "broken" at line 21 is particularly revealing: in technical terms, "broken" music consists of several parts played by different instruments (hence the term "broken consort").[42] Even if such music is written monodically, each part is still heard distinctly, thus approaching the effects of conventional polyphony. Milton is aiming at more than a mere poetic conceit: by "breaking" its "first obedience" to God, humanity necessarily distanced itself from the "undisturbèd song of pure concent" (6) in which multiple voices are indistinguishable from perfect unity. Broken or polyphonic music should not accordingly be rejected, but recognized as an imperfect imitation (figuration) of divine harmony. This imitative music will not be made perfect "till God ere long / To his celestial consort us unite, / To live with him, and sing in endless morn of light" (26–28). Milton's poem thus defines the inherent difference between heavenly and earthly music as ontological, and it authorizes the figure-making activity of the imagination ("high-raised fantasy" [5]) as a noble striving toward the divine ideal.

A similar distinction is made in *Arcades,* only this time the focus is on hearing rather than performing music. Here, music has the power to draw "the low world in measured motion . . . / After the heavenly tune, which none can hear / Of human mould with gross unpurgèd ear" (71–73). As a "lesser god" (79), the poem's Genius of the Wood can hear the celestial harmony, but only "in deep of night when drowsiness / Hath locked up mortal sense" (61–62), presumably when imagination or fantasy is given reign over the faculties of sun-clad reason ("mortal sense"). At the same time that the poem commends earthly music's aspiration toward perfection, it also emphasizes a dissociation between the "inimitable sounds" (78) of divine music and human (or semidivine) music made by "inferior hand or voice" (77). A much harsher view of earthbound music appears in *Lycidas,* where Milton denounces the empty ceremony of the Laudian church:

> What recks it them? What need they? They are sped;
> And when they list, their lean and flashy songs
> Grate on their scrannel pipes of wretched straw,
> The hungry sheep look up, and are not fed,
> But swoll'n with wind, and the rank mist they draw,
> Rot inwardly, and foul contagion spread.   (122–27)

These lines closely follow Gosson's critique of polyphony in the *Schoole of Abuse* (both allude to Virgil's *Eclogues*), and the references to "scrannel pipes" and "swoll'n wind" echo the Protestant bias against wind instruments. But Milton seems more critical of the use such music is put to than of any inherent moral deficiency in it; the "oaten flute" and "rough" satyrs' dances are positively mentioned in the description of Lycidas's youth (33–34). Moreover, as in *At a Solemn Music* and *Arcades,* Milton carefully distinguishes between heavenly and earthly music: the Apollonian music that interrupts the poem is "of a higher mood" than the shepherd's piping (87), and heaven's "unexpressive nuptial song" is apprehensible to Lycidas only after death (176).

Milton's persistent classification of music in the early poems adumbrates the idea that earthly music is ontologically inferior, since it can gesture toward celestial harmony but never articulate it.[43] In this respect, polyphonic music is different from monody in degree, not kind—both are expressive figurations of heaven's "*un*expressive nuptial song" (my emphasis). However, to respond to music's inarticulateness by overregulating it (as if attempting to pin down its meaning) or by shunning it altogether (as a vain or idolatrous figuration) is for Milton clearly inappropriate, as he indicates in *Areopagitica* (1644):

> If we think to regulate printing, thereby to rectify manners, we must regulate all recreations and pastimes, all that is delightful to man. No music must be heard, no song be set or sung, but what is grave and Doric. . . . It will ask more than the work of twenty licensers to examine all the lutes, the violins and the guitars in every house. . . . And who shall silence all the airs and madrigals that whisper softness in chambers? . . . The villages also must have their visitors to inquire what lectures the bagpipe and the rebec reads, even to the balladry and the gamut of every municipal fiddler. (251)

Milton's mock proposal to inspect every fiddler's "gamut" (range of notes) is a sardonic answer to Gosson's contempt for the historical creation of new musical strings.[44] Milton revises Gosson's near-hysterical list of musical innovations so that it is the attempted *control* of music that threatens to spin into confusion. The indeterminacy of music (especially polyphonic music) with respect to language, which underscores the Protestant proscription on polyphony, is in fact extremely consonant (no pun intended) with Milton's representation of Truth in *Areopagitica:*

> Truth indeed came once into the world with her divine master, and was a perfect shape most glorious to look on; but when he ascended, and his apostles after him were laid asleep, then straight arose a wicked race of deceivers, who, as that story goes of the Egyptian Typhon with his conspirators, how they dealt with the good Osiris, took the virgin Truth, hewed her lovely form into a thousand pieces and scattered them to the four winds. (263)

In the musical sense of the word, Milton's Truth is distinctly "partial." Accordingly, Milton's ardent rejection of the Puritan attitude toward music in *Areopagitica* reflects his more general theme that Reformist attitudes in England may have gone too far, threatening to make England "the latest and the backwardest scholars, of whom God offered to have made us the teachers" (265).

  Areopagitica provides an instructive context for Milton's attitude toward music in the *Mask,* which is less deferential to Protestant ideology than has generally been recognized. For one thing, Milton's removal of "counterpoint" at line 243 may suggest a Reformist attitude toward polyphony, but it may also suggest—somewhat at odds with Reformist attitudes—a fundamental incongruity between heavenly music and Echo's earthly music. In musical practice, "counterpoint" implies two lines of equal stature, which do not accord with Milton's conception of earthly (or semidivine) music in the early poems. For its own part, the *Mask* maintains distinctions between heavenly and earthly experience, particularly in the case of the Attendant Spirit, whose language closely resembles Milton's representation of earth in *Areopagitica:* "but for such, / I would not soil these pure ambrosial weeds, / With the rank vapours of this sin-worn mould" (15–17). The Attendant Spirit's identification with Henry Lawes is an appropriate compliment, since, as Milton suggests in *Sonnet XIII,* Lawes's essentially homophonic style represents a noble striving for the heavenly ideal of unity between words and music. Yet, by associating Lawes with specifically divine music, the *Mask* also enables the articulation of a *positive* relationship between heavenly music and its inferior, earthly figuration. In other words, Milton's praise of Lawes and monody is not restrictive. After all, while the Attendant Spirit shows a marked preference for the monodic style of the Lady's song (a preference that would have registered as a charming joke in performance, since he composed it), he is still content to listen to the "barbarous dissonance" of Comus's music for "a while" (550–51).

Even more than *Areopagitica,* Milton's *On the Harmony of the Spheres* explicitly addresses the distinction between divine and earthly music, in language that frequently resonates with the poetry of the *Mask.* In his early essay, Milton defends the well-known Pythagorean theory of *musica mundana* as a useful allegory: "Surely, if he held any doctrine of the harmony of the spheres . . . it was only as a means of suggesting allegorically the close interrelation of the orbs" (235). Under this interpretation, earthly music is desirable because it approximates or figures heavenly harmony, not because it can boast a literal identification with it. Building upon this defense of figurative knowledge, Milton describes the rejection of Pythagorean theory in terms that are remarkably similar to Comus's defense of pleasure:

If you rob the heavens of this music, you devote those wonderful minds and subordinate gods of yours to a life of drudgery, and condemn them to the treadmill. And even Atlas himself would long since have cast down the burden of the skies from his shoulders to its ruin, had not that sweet harmony soothed him with an ecstasy of delight as he panted and sweated beneath his heavy load. Again, the Dolphin would long since have wearied of the stars and preferred his proper element of the sea to the skies, had he not well known that the singing spheres of heaven far surpassed Arion's lyre in sweetness. And we may well believe that it is in order to tune their own notes in accord with that harmony of heaven to which they listen so intently, that the lark takes her flight up into the clouds at daybreak and the nightingale passes the lonely hours of night in song. (237)

In this paragraph, the Aristotelian dismissal of *musica mundana* amounts to both a rejection of figurative knowledge and a harsh asceticism reminiscent of the Lady's attack on Comus. Taken together with the *Mask* (a comparison made more appealing by Milton's reference to the "lonely nightingale"), *On the Harmony* proffers a critique of the Protestant bias against theatricality and allegory, insofar as it suggests that Protestant ideology crucially misunderstands the relationship between divine truth and human understanding. Milton argues that only an indirect and imperfect apprehension of divine truth is possible on earth, which explains why heavenly music can never be experienced as actual sound: "The fault is in our own deaf ears, which are either unable or unworthy to hear these sweet strains" (238). As in *Areopagitica*, Milton here applies the idea of the Fall (registered by his specific use of the word *incusare*) to construct a defense of figuration. In other words, the Fall makes figured truth—and earthly music—necessary, rather than things to be rejected for their lack of plainness. In language that strongly recalls the description of the Attendant Spirit in the *Mask*, Milton again in *On the Harmony* evokes Pythagoras to suggest that figured knowledge is a gift from heaven itself: "Pythagoras alone among men is said to have heard this music— if indeed he was not rather some good spirit and denizen of heaven, sent down perchance by the gods' behest to instruct mankind in holiness and lead them back to righteousness" (238). Like the Attendant Spirit, Milton's Pythagoras represents cloaked, "disguised" knowledge. The singularity of Pythagoras's aural experience makes his gift of harmony valuable while confirming the ontological distance between heavenly and earthly music.

While consideration of Milton's early writings on music effectively reorients the Lady's antitheatrical polemic in the *Mask* as a debate over the merits of figuration, we should note that the *Mask* advocates a defense of earthly music on its own terms as well. Along these lines, Milton's critique of Reformist polemic in the *Mask* might best be summarized in a line shortly before the invocation to Sabrina. Here, the Attendant Spirit reveals that the Lady can only be freed through an earthly water nymph who must be "right invoked in *warbled* song" (854; my emphasis). "Warbled" here is a loaded word: it appears consistently in Reformist polemic as an indicator of immoral, seductive sound. In *Histriomastix*, Prynne refers to chromatic harmony as "a dishonest art of warbling the voice." In Henry Burton's sermon against conformity to the English cathedrals, he calls their musical services a "Long Babylonish Service, so bellowed and warbled out." Likewise, Christopher Dow's attack on Burton sarcastically calls attention to his "distaste" for music that is "bellowed and warbled out." And in Owen Feltham's *Resolves* (1631), a text that is particularly uncongenial to music's sensuous qualities, a "warble" is nothing short of demonic: "Damned Sathan! that with Orphean ayres, and dextrous warbles, lead'st us to the Flames of Hell."[45] In these contexts, "warble" appears to denote a kind of utterance that undermines language (particularly scriptural language) in favor of purely physical sound.[46] This preference for sensuous experience partly explains warbling's "fallen" associations in certain Miltonian contexts. In Book Two of *Paradise Lost* (in a passage that echoes Feltham's *Resolves*), for example, Milton characterizes the insincere praise that the fallen angels render to God as "warbled hymns" (2.242). In a very different setting, Milton's *Sonnet I*, "warbling" becomes the sign of amorous (not necessarily chaste) love: "O nightingale, that on yon bloomy spray / Warblest at eve, when all the woods are still" (1–2). As here, "warbling" occurs frequently in Ovidian contexts in Renaissance poetry, particularly those that allude to Philomela. Marlowe's translation of Ovid's *Amores* has in the invocation a call to the "Elegian muse, that warblest amorous lays." In *The Complainte of Phylomene* (1576), George Gascoigne uses alliteration to emphasize the pure sonority of Philomela's irregular yet melodious lament: "And many a note, she warbled wondrous wel." Likewise, Shakespeare describes the post-rape Lucrece as a "lamenting Philomel [who] had ended / The well-tuned warble of her nightly sorrow."[47] As the special province of rebel angels, concupiscent lovers, and mutilated women, "warbled" song is, in these particular contexts, "fallen" song. Through its resonance in Marlowe, Gascoigne, and Shakespeare, "warbled song" returns Milton's audience to the scene of Ovid's Philomela and to the kind of sensuous Ovidianism that characterizes Comus himself.

This is not to say that "warble" does not carry positive connotations, particularly in Milton's early poems and elsewhere in *Paradise Lost*. Yet, even in these cases, "warble" often appears in contexts that emphasize the distance between heaven and fallen humanity. In *Arcades,* for example, the "warbled string" represents the Genius of the Wood's attempt to imitate, but not replicate, "the heavenly tune, which none can hear" (87, 72). Likewise, in *On the Morning of Christ's Nativity,* "divinely-warbled voice" signals an unprecedented, startling conjunction of heavenly song and earthly sensuous experience, by which the "crystal spheres" almost "have power to touch our senses" (96, 125, 127); only an event as momentous as Christ's Nativity can effect such a conjunction. In *L'Allegro,* "warbling" comes to stand for a kind of utterance that calls attention to its own sonority, irrespective of the words that only partially structure it. Here, Milton contrasts a "warbling" Shakespeare with "learnèd" Jonson, anticipating Samuel Johnson's famous portrayal of Shakespeare as a wandering Atalanta entranced by the sonorous indeterminacy of language (132–34). As John Guillory has noted, this section of *L'Allegro* bears more affinity with Comus's artistry than with the Attendant Spirit's or the Lady's.[48] Milton's deliberately ambivalent moralization of "warbling" can be gauged by its proximity to the word "lapse" in *Paradise Lost* (a similar association between "warble" and "lap" occurs in *L'Allegro*):

> And liquid lapse of murmuring streams; by these,
> Creatures that lived, and moved, and walked, or flew,
> Birds on the branches warbling; all things smiled,
> With fragrance and with joy my heart o'erflowed.   (8.263–66)

For prelapsarian Adam, the "warbling" sounds of birds are unproblematic because they are intelligible, just as every speech or sound act in heaven is immediately articulate ("my tongue obeyed and readily could name" [272]). In the same way, the soundful "lapse of murmuring streams" has an unqualified innocence. After the Fall, however, "warbling" sound becomes inarticulate and "lapse" assumes its negative meaning. Although evocative of heavenly experience, postlapsarian warbling (and earthly music in general) represents the loss of simultaneity between uttering and "naming" that Adam once enjoyed.[49]

In a poem that bears such a heavy intertextual relationship with contemporary attacks on music and theater, as well as with Milton's other early poems, the characterization of the Attendant Spirit's song as "warbled" has far-reaching implications. "Warbled song," as early modern antitheatricalism rightly suspects, does not presuppose the inviolability of language, but rather calls attention to the gap between sound and word through its own imperfect imitation. Thus, by making "warbled song" a prerequisite for the Lady's freedom, Milton recognizes the fallen condition of his human protagonists and ties the masque's divine resolution to a kind of music that Reformist polemic repeatedly condemns. Whether or not Henry Lawes's music for the masque is strictly monodic in its composition (as has been argued), the *Mask* repeatedly tempts its audience to hear this music as earthly and sensuous; Milton's emphasis on shepherds' "play" (958) and "court guise" (962) in the closing songs is closer to the raucous wedding masque of Shakespeare's *A Winter's Tale* than to the angelic (homophonic) choirs of the Nativity ode. In fact, the musical associations at the end of the *Mask* do not support a strict adherence to rigid, Puritan aesthetics. The invocation to Sabrina includes the appeal to "songs of sirens sweet" (878), recalling Comus's earlier praise of siren (polyphonic) music, and the "mincing Dryades" (964) at the end of the masque recall Becon's characterization of polyphonic music as "mynsed." As David Lindley has shown in his study of the musical politics of the court masque, a performance of *Comus* would have intensified the correspondences between Comus's music and the celebratory music at the end (in contrast to the music composed by Lawes): "the musical markers of social class and moral probity slip and slide in this masque. The problem is embodied in the person of Henry Lawes himself . . . [who] is disguised as a shepherd, but employs a musical language in the masque's surviving songs which is emphatically removed from the taint of the popular."[50] In effect, Milton "tricks" our ears, capitalizing on music's performance in the masque in order to loosen the traditional associations between monody and "divine," unfallen song. The point is not only that performed music introduces indeterminacy of signification (which it surely does), but also that Milton is aware of this indeterminacy and attributes it to music's ontological status after the Fall. For Milton, music's indeterminacy results from its status as an imitation of celestial sound, which is inaudible on earth.

As imitation, "warbled song" is for Milton profoundly theatrical and figural. Likewise, Sabrina's appearance in the *Mask* is intensely theatrical in a way that emphasizes earthly, sensuous experience:

> Thrice upon thy finger's tip,
> Thrice upon thy rubied lip,
> Next this marble venomed seat
> Smeared with gums of glutinous heat
> I touch with chaste palms moist and cold,
> Now the spell hath lost his hold. (914–19)

Sabrina's focus on the Lady's fingertip and lip suggests rejuvenation of the senses of touch and taste which the Lady's ascetic Puritanism has stifled. Finger and lip also signify the two body parts that perform earthly music, either on a string instrument or by singing. This implicit sanctioning of sensuous experience (especially musical experience), which is fulfilled by the "jigs" and "rural dance" at the end of the *Mask*, corresponds to the dense profusion of mythological, mostly Ovidian figures that characterize the invocation to Sabrina and the closing hymeneal scene. As Christopher Kendrick has noted, "[Sabrina's] presence lifts at least part of the fairy world from Comus's copious ambit."[51] But Milton does more than "lift" Comus's stock figures: he rechannels the musical and Ovidian elements of the antimasque in order to free the Lady, thus authorizing the modes of figuration and performativity—which Comus had abused—as necessary and valuable aspects of human experience. It is this acceptance of figuration and theatricality, despite their moral ambivalence, that arguably stands behind the Attendant Spirit's warning to the Lady's brothers that "without [Comus's] rod reversed, / And backward mutters of dissevering power, / We cannot free the Lady" (816–18).

Milton's *Mask* intuits an ideological connection between the Puritan critiques of classical poetry and polyphonic music, and it finds the basis of this connection to be a deep-seated anxiety over the fundamental indeterminacy of artistic expression. Again, the masque shares this outlook with *Areopagit-*

ica, where the defense of "wanton" Ovid appears in close conjunction with the defense of musical innovation (241–42). In this work, as in *A Mask,* the mythological figure of Psyche stands as a reminder of the distance between heaven and humanity and of the inapprehensibility of divine knowledge; like Truth in a thousand pieces, knowledge is represented here as "those confused seeds which were imposed upon Psyche as an incessant labour to cull out and sort asunder" (247). Humanity's fallen nature partly explains why Milton unanxiously presents Cupid and Psyche, and Venus and Adonis, at the end of the *Mask,* as analogous—but not identical—examples of love. In both cases, men and women imitate divinity in a way that creates an unending proliferation of voices and *figurae.* This mode of figuration is certainly precarious and creates an "incessant labour," as the example of Comus makes clear, but a "marble-like" retreat into nonperformative contemplation impedes the reintegration of Truth rather than furthers it. Milton's rejection of an aesthetics based on Puritan ideology in the *Mask* reminds us that we are after all in a fallen world, and it is a fact of our fallen condition that we speak and hear several voices. In doing so, Milton forecloses on the rigidly antitheatrical and antifigural rhetoric of the Lady's attacks on Comus. Despite his need to repudiate an intemperate sensuality, and despite his need to reform the masque in the face of Laudian politics, Milton recognizes that Reformist extremism—whether directed against theater, Ovid, or music—can lead to a debilitating stasis, as the Lady's immobility iconologically suggests.

Princeton University

NOTES

1. *The Complete Prose Works of John Milton,* 8 vols., ed. Don M. Wolfe et al. (New Haven, 1953–82), 1:238. All quotations of *On the Harmony* are from this edition, hereafter cited parenthetically in the text.

2. P. Lavinius, *P. Ovidii Nasonis poete ingeniosissimi Metamorphoseos Libri XV* (1527), 19.

3. See, for example, recent essays by Stella P. Revard, Kent R. Lehnhof, Raymond B. Waddington, and Lauren Shohet in *Milton Studies* 41, ed. Albert C. Labriola (Pittsburgh, 2002).

4. See also Phillip Stubbes, *The Anatomie of Abuses* (1583), sigs. O3v–4O3, who condemns all music. For an interesting discussion of the role of Ovid in the antitheatrical tracts, see Mary Ellen Lamb, "Ovid and *The Winter's Tale:* Conflicting Views Toward Art," in *Shakespeare and Dramatic Tradition: Essays in Honor of S. F. Johnson,* ed. W. R. Elton and W. B. Long (Newark, DE, 1989), 69–87. A good summary of Reformist attacks on polyphonic music is Diane McColley's chapter on the church music controversy in *Poetry and Music in Seventeenth-Century England* (Cambridge, 1997), 53–93.

5. See, for example, an account of William Prynne's trial in Stephen Buhler, "Counterpoint

and Controversy: Milton and the Critiques of Polyphonic Music," in *Milton Studies* 36, ed. Albert C. Labriola (Pittsburgh, 1998), 22–25. The preeminent study of early modern anti-theatricalism remains Jonas Barish, *The Antitheatrical Prejudice* (Berkeley and Los Angeles, 1981), but see also Jean E. Howard, *The Stage and Social Struggle in Early Modern England* (London, 1994), and Laura Levine, *Men in Women's Clothing: Anti-Theatricality and Effeminization, 1579–1642* (Cambridge, 1994).

6. David Norbrook, "The Reformation of the Masque," in *The Court Masque*, ed. David Lindley (Manchester, 1984), 106–7; Leah S. Marcus, *The Politics of Mirth: Jonson, Herrick, Milton, Marvell, and the Defense of Old Holiday Pastimes* (Chicago, 1986), 20. Marcus recognizes Milton's desire to reconcile aspects of Comus's art with his own theological outlook, although she generally upholds the oppositional Puritan-Laudian schematic by aligning Milton with contemporary Protestant ideology.

7. On the phenomenological aspect of mediation in the Stuart masque, particularly Milton's *Comus*, see Lauren Shohet, "Figuring Chastity: Milton's Ludlow Masque," in *Menacing Virgins: Representing Virginity in the Middle Ages and Renaissance*, ed. Kathleen Coyne Kelly and Marina Leslie (Newark, DE, 1999), 146–64.

8. Buhler, "Counterpoint and Controversy," 18.

9. Except for *On the Harmony*, all quotations of Milton's works are from *John Milton*, ed. Stephen Orgel and Jonathan Goldberg (Oxford, 1991), unless otherwise noted.

10. William Prynne, *Histriomastix: The Players Scourge or Actors Tragedie* (London, 1633), 158.

11. Enid Welsford, *The Court Masque* (Cambridge, 1927), 320. Other early critics who find the Lady too prudish include Sir Walter Raleigh, *Milton* (New York, 1900), 28; and Douglas Bush, *The Renaissance and English Humanism* (1933; reprint, Toronto, 1968), who remarks that "one would rather live with Comus than the Lady" (108).

12. Maryann C. McGuire, *Milton's Puritan Masque* (Athens, GA, 1983), 22. See also William S. Miller Jr., *The Mythography of Milton's Comus* (New York, 1988), 169–212.

13. See, in particular, Barish's discussion of *Histriomastix* in *The Antitheatrical Prejudice*, 83–89.

14. Stephen Orgel, *The Jonsonian Masque* (Cambridge, MA, 1967), 13; my emphasis.

15. For an excellent discussion of Jonson's antitheatricalism, see Barish, *The Antitheatrical Prejudice*, 132–54. Also see D. J. Gordon, "Poet and Architect: The Intellectual Setting of the Quarrel between Ben Jonson and Inigo Jones," in *The Renaissance Imagination*, ed. Stephen Orgel (Berkeley and Los Angeles, 1975), 77–101.

16. Barish, *The Antitheatrical Prejudice*, 133.

17. Orgel, *The Jonsonian Masque*, 18. Joseph Loewenstein, *Responsive Readings: Versions of Echo in Pastoral, Epic, and the Jonsonian Masque* (New Haven, CT, 1984), also notes that the Lady's immobility recalls "the ironic image of the monarch enthroned in the royal seat" (139). Although it runs somewhat counter to my claims, his argument that this identification actually suggests a deficiency in royalist masque convention (by forestalling the more dynamic aspect of the quest) is persuasive.

18. Cedric Brown, *John Milton's Aristocratic Entertainments* (Cambridge, 1985), 132–52, suggests that the text of the *Mask* is primarily intended for reception in a *poetic* (literary) mode rather than a theatrical or iconological one, citing the fact that Milton made several strategic changes and elaborations for the 1637 publication. The distinction is not trivial, since reading the *Mask* poetically leads Brown (and many other critics) to assert the work's "ardently, idealistically reformist spirit" as well as the "Protestant radicalism of Milton's writing" (2, 11), thus evading the possibility of a critique of Reformist ideology's attitude toward theater and figuration. On the other hand, Brown sensitively points out a number of dramatically "awkward" moments that

Milton's emendations create—an effect that Milton may have very well intended, even if he did not expect them to be fully realized in performance.

19. Richard DuRocher, *Milton and Ovid* (Ithaca, NY, 1985), 50–51. DuRocher also notes the dark implications of the Lady's invocation to Echo, comparing it to Ovidian soliloquies "in which an isolated female character reveals her wavering personality."

20. However, Loewenstein, *Responsive Readings*, 142, notes that often "Milton's associations with echo have an odd morbidity, as if he recognized only the lamenting strain in the traditions of echo," suggesting that this darker strain of the pastoral-echo tradition profoundly inflects the Lady's performance of her song. On the role of Ovid in *Comus*, see Davis P. Harding, *Milton and the Renaissance Ovid* (Urbana, IL, 1946), 58–66; DuRocher, *Milton and Ovid*, 47–58; Leonora Leet Brodwin, "Milton and the Renaissance Circe," in *Milton Studies* 6, ed. James D. Simmonds (Pittsburgh, 1974), 46–54. See also Judith E. Browning, "Sin, Eve, and Circe: *Paradise Lost* and the Ovidian Circe Tradition," in *Milton Studies* 26, ed. James D. Simmonds (Pittsburgh, 1991), 135–58. Although Browning's article focuses on the Ovidian elements in *Paradise Lost*, her discussion of Ovid's Scylla and Circe has been particularly helpful for the present essay.

21. DuRocher, *Milton and Ovid*, 49.

22. See Barbara K. Lewalski, "Milton's *Comus* and the Politics of Masquing," in *The Politics of the Stuart Court Masque*, ed. David Bevington and Peter Holbrook (Cambridge, 1998), 296–300.

23. Miller translates *latices* as "liquors." All Ovidian quotations are from the *Metamorphoses*, trans. Frank Justice Miller (Cambridge, MA, 1984).

24. Browning, "Sin, Eve, and Circe," 139.

25. Harding, *Milton and the Renaissance Ovid*, 59.

26. DuRocher, *Milton and Ovid*, on the other hand, while acknowledging Comus's "depth of imaginative power and ethical perversion," argues that the Lady is never contaminated by Comus's Ovidianism:

> To anyone familiar with Ovid's myth, however, Comus's attempt to heighten his putative mastery over the Lady by the comparison [to Daphne] must seem vain, if not ludicrous. Daphne actually avoided Apollo's seduction precisely by becoming "root-bound," and her transformation into the laurel, though unwelcome, was not a result of Apollo's power. . . . By ascribing to Comus this and other perverse uses of Ovidian myth, Milton undercuts the power of the seducer while channeling the Ovidian material so that it contaminates only Comus. (51–52)

Yet, it is precisely the "ludicrousness" of Comus's Ovidian perversions, I argue, that reveals the potentially radical instability of Ovidian figuration in the poem, which Comus seeks to exploit. By contaminating the myth of Daphne and Apollo with that of Pygmalion (which DuRocher does not note), Comus takes the elements in the Daphne and Apollo story that do not support his sinister agenda and reworks them to his advantage.

27. See Lynn Enterline, "Pursuing Daphne," *The Rhetoric of the Body from Ovid to Shakespeare* (Cambridge, 2000), 1–38.

28. See Barish, *The Antitheatrical Prejudice*, esp. 80–131.

29. *Milton and Ovid*, 48. However, in contrast to my interpretation, DuRocher's analysis strictly identifies the moralized Scylla with Comus, not the Lady.

30. George Sandys, in his edition of the *Metamorphoses*, writes: "How *Circe* was said to bee the daughter of *Sol* and *Persis*, in that lust proceeds from heat and moisture, which naturally incites to luxury; and getting the dominion, deformes our soules with all bestial vices; alluring some to inordinate Venus; others to anger, cruelty, and every excess of passion" (cited in

Harding, *Milton and the Renaissance Ovid,* 59). Brodwin, "Milton and the Renaissance Circe," argues that Milton's treatment of Circe differs from the Renaissance mythographers' "easy moralising" of Circe, asserting that the Homeric source, which enumerates "temptations . . . on three different levels of intensity [swinish metamorphosis, effeminizing sex, and enervating idleness], of which the swinish metamorphosis is only the most debased" (23), is the version closest to Milton's. For the same reason, she prefers Homer to Ovid as Milton's most direct model. However, like the Renaissance mythographers (and to a lesser extent, Ovid), Milton tends to conflate the three Homeric temptations. Browning's study of the Circe figure in *Paradise Lost,* cited above, by foregrounding the specifically Ovidian association of Scylla with Circe, offers a good corrective to Brodwin in reestablishing Ovid as a preeminent source for Milton's Circe in both *Comus* and *Paradise Lost.*

31. For an analogous example of how visual, iconographic meanings may override textual ones in the masque, see Orgel's discussion of Hunnis's *The Ladie of the Lake,* in *The Jonsonian Masque,* 39–42.

32. Enterline, "Pursuing Daphne," 3.

33. In the same vein, Marcus, *The Politics of Mirth,* reads the Lady's immobility as a visual representation of the "Puritan dilemma in the face of Laudian power—the plight of those who were locked into rigid rejection of all arts and pastimes because those which were most culturally conspicuous seemed tainted with political and sexual corruption" (198). Whereas Marcus's interpretation is primarily informed by political context, my argument is more directed at the Lady's poetic and rhetorical effects. In this respect, I argue that the Lady's harsh absolutism and antitheatricalism are as much (if not more) responsible as Laud for her immobility.

34. Stanley Fish, "Problem Solving in *Comus,*" in *Illustrious Evidence: Approaches to English Literature of the Early Seventeenth Century,* ed. Earl Miner (Berkeley and Los Angeles, 1975), 127.

35. Louis Martz, "The Music of *Comus,*" in ibid., 108.

36. Stephen Gosson, *The Schoole of Abuse* (1579), sigs. Bv–B2.

37. Prynne, *Histriomastix,* 275; Thomas Becon, *The Reliques of Rome* (1563), 120r–121v.

38. See Buhler, "Counterpoint and Controversy"; Norbrook, "The Reformation of the Masque"; and Mary Elizabeth Basile, "The Music of *A Maske,*" *Milton Quarterly* 27 (1993): 86–98.

39. For the Bridgewater text of the Lady's song to Echo, see *Milton's Dramatic Poems,* ed. Geoffrey and Margaret Bullough (London, 1978).

40. Buhler, "Counterpoint and Controversy," 26–27.

41. Likewise, John Creaser, " 'The present aid of this occasion': The Setting of *Comus,*" in Welsford, *The Court Masque,* argues that positive, royalist imagery runs throughout the masque, going so far as to say that "the final scene is not a charmingly parochial touch, but a symbol of vice-regal authority" (113).

42. The validity of this musical meaning of "broken" in seventeenth-century England has been questioned, but see *Troilus and Cressida,* 3.1.50–55, where "broken music" clearly seems to have been understood in relation to "part-music." Polyphony, of course, should not be confused with polyvocality (music with several voices); see Buhler, "Counterpoint and Controversy," 18–19, for the frequent association of "partial" music with "counterpoint."

43. Marc Berley also argues that early poems such as *L'Allegro* and *Arcades* are concerned with making distinctions between divine and earthly music, although he tends to emphasize less than I do the value Milton attaches to performed, audible music. See his excellent chapter on the influence of *musica speculativa* on Milton's poetry in *After the Heavenly Tune: English Poetry and the Aspiration to Song* (Pittsburgh, 2000), 141–205.

44. "Gamut" is the lowest note, or the lowest string of a violin, so that to inspect the "gamut" of every fiddler, as Milton says, would require inspecting every string on every string instrument.

45. Prynne, *Histriomastix*, 275; Henry Burton, *For God, and the King* (1636), 160; Christopher Dow, *Innovations Unjustly Charged upon the Present Church and State* (London, 1637), 9; Owen Feltham, *Resolves* (1631), 86.

46. This sense of "warble" is corroborated a few years after Milton's masque in a poem by Edmund Waller that is addressed, somewhat coincidentally, to Henry Lawes himself. Praising Lawes for his (presupposed) rejection of florid ornamentation in musical settings, Waller writes, "Let those which only warble long, / And gargle in their throats a song, / Content themselves with *Ut, re, mi:* / Let words, and sense, be set by thee." See the preface to Henry Lawes, *Ayres and Dialogues* (London, 1653), lines 25–28.

47. Christopher Marlowe, *Ovid's Elegies*, in *The Complete Poems and Translations*, ed. Stephen Orgel (London, 1971), 1.33; George Gascoigne, *The Complainte of Phylomene*, ed. William L. Wallace (Salzburg, 1975), 90; Shakespeare, *The Poems*, ed. John Roe (Cambridge, 1992), 1079–80.

48. John Guillory, *Poetic Authority: Spenser, Milton, and Literary History* (New York, 1983), 68–93. Guillory does not, however, note the resonance of "warbled song" in *Comus* with "warbling" Shakespeare in *L'Allegro;* rather, his reading of *Comus* proffers the whole Sabrina episode as a reversion to Spenserian (and occasionally Ovidian) influence.

49. See, however, *Il Penseroso,* where the speaker's reference to Orpheus's "warbled" notes forms part of a vision of divine reunion (106). Here, "warbling" is a distinctly sound-producing—not language-producing—activity, but one that points beyond the realm of sensuous experience ("where more is meant than meets the ear" [120]).

50. David Lindley, "The Politics of Music in the Masque," in Bevington and Holbrook, *The Politics of the Stuart Court Masque*, 282. Peter Walls, *Music in the English Courtly Masque 1604–1640* (Oxford, 1996), also notes that the actual music given to the Attendant Spirit introduces an unusually ambiguous mode of musical signification in the masque, although he finally concludes that "by and large, however, the use of music and dance corresponds to normal masque usage" (298).

51. Christopher Kendrick, "Milton and Sexuality: A Symptomatic Reading of *Comus,*" in *Re-membering Milton: Essays on the Texts and Traditions,* ed. Mary Nyquist and Margaret W. Ferguson (New York, 1987), 51.

GO ASK ALICE: DAUGHTER, PATRON, AND POET IN *A MASK PRESENTED AT LUDLOW CASTLE*

Ronald Corthell

A *MASK PRESENTED AT LUDLOW CASTLE* is a work at once strange and familiar. An aristocratic couple is entertained by the spectacle of their fifteen-year-old daughter resisting seduction in a dark wood while she and her brothers philosophize on the topic of her virginity. The occasion, the performers, and "the sage / And serious doctrine" promulgated have inspired prodigious feats of historical scholarship and imagination, and yet both Milton's conception and the Egertons' pleasure in seeing it realized seem almost impossibly removed from our full understanding in the twenty-first century. At the same time, how close to us this work can appear. Witness the controversy over the question of sexual abuse in the *Mask,* a debate that engages with very pressing social and psychological issues as well as with more professional and theoretical concerns raised by feminism, new historicism, and psychoanalysis in literary studies. In what follows I hope to contribute to this debate at both levels by proposing a loosening of critical focus, from what has been the predominant concern with Milton's relationship to the Lady to a network of relationships between author, patron, and the patron's family. I should emphasize that I am not proposing a reading grounded in Milton's biography or the Bridgewater family history, work already undertaken by Milton biographers and, for *A Mask,* by William B. Hunter and Leah Marcus.[1] My focus is rather upon the structure of relationships that shapes the work. In a sense, the figure of the Lady remains at the center of my study, but by placing her in the position of the daughter of Milton's patron, instead of surrogate for the Lady of Christ's College, I hope to open the mask to a more difficult relationship to patriarchal culture than has been traditionally thought or than even Milton may have intended. Although Milton's mask concludes with celebrations of marriage and family, the ambulating and finally silent virgin daughter is not confined to her usual place in this ideological formation. Milton's poetic idealization and identification with the virgin daughter of his patron work across the lines of the sex/gender system: *A Mask* creates a cross-gendered fantasy of empowerment that inverts or at least suspends conven-

111

tional hierarchies within patriarchy and patronage by transposing daughters, fathers, poets, and patrons as signifiers of cultural authority.

The controversy about sexual abuse in *A Mask* has abated, but it is not resolved. In 1991 John Leonard challenged William Kerrigan's psychoanalytic reading of the work on the grounds that, in solidarity with psychoanalytic tradition, it focuses analysis on the victim rather than the perpetrator of sexual abuse and, what is more, it misreads the Lady's "no," making it "both too weak and too strong."[2] "Too weak" because Kerrigan wants "no" to mean "yes" in the time-honored tradition of psychoanalytic interpretation; "too strong" because Kerrigan wants the "no" to signify a vow of celibacy on the part of the Lady and of Milton, who is assumed to be the Lady in drag, and thereby "to admit a 'yes' through the back door of her [that is, *his*] unconscious."[3] As Leonard acknowledges, Kerrigan's reading is a strong psychoanalytic version of a rather long tradition of suspicious, if not prurient, commentary on the possibility of the Lady's complicity, mainly focused on the notorious "gumms of glutenous heat" that bind the Lady to the enchanted chair in Comus's stately palace. Kerrigan's reply accuses Leonard of political correctness, denying a close fit between the Lady's ordeal and the rape case of Margery Evans, explored by Leah Marcus and featured in Leonard's article; Kerrigan admits the "originality" of Leonard's reading of the Lady's line, "Good men can give good things," as "way off on the outskirts of entailment, a suggestion of sexual temperance," a concession that Leonard presses in his 1996 reply to Kerrigan.[4] Although she does not directly engage in this debate, Debora Shuger, in a more recent essay, has offered a new perspective on the question of will and desire by locating the "gumms" conundrum within a tradition of finely wrought and frequently paradoxical Augustinian moral theology spun from the experience of nocturnal emissions, a moral theology that Shuger goes on to relate to a discourse of inwardness that was surprisingly reconstituted in the poetry of the English Renaissance.[5]

One way into the critical debate between Kerrigan and Leonard is to ask, following Shuger's lead, "Whose inwardness?" That is, critics suspicious of the Lady's possible complicity with Comus's desires, including Kerrigan, have tended to read the mask as something like a chapter from a bildungs-roman of John Milton (the Lady as the Lady of Christ's who experiences a temptation), while Leonard, Marcus, and Catherine Belsey treat the Lady as a female victim (albeit a resourceful and resistant one) of sexual assault.[6] Leonard appears to make the issue one of reading as a man (in a masculinist psychoanalytic mode) or reading as a woman (using Marcus as representative), a strategy strenuously objected to by Kerrigan in his reply to Leonard.[7] This exchange helpfully connects problems of Miltonic identification and representation with a politics of reading Milton. It matters a great deal whether the body imprisoned by Comus is imagined as male (as Kerrigan assumes) or female (as Leonard asserts), or both—as Katherine Eisaman Maus has it, a male "imagining himself as *inhabiting* the Lady's body."[8]

What also complicates the question of gender in the mask is the familial economy that positions the three young speakers in the mask script but that also framed the performance at Ludlow Castle on Michaelmas night in 1634 and is textually memorialized in the printed editions of 1637, 1645, and 1673. As already suggested, I am not proposing a "local" reading of the Bridgewater family at play here, but rather a reading of the mask that apprehends the full range and interplay of what Harry Berger has termed "positional" and "ethical" discourses. As Berger notes of what he calls "the family drama," "any single position in the system is not an integer but the fraction of a dyadic bond—'parent' and 'child,' for example, require and co-define each other— the differential logic of the drama speaks through the speakers inscribed in it, limits their autonomy, ambiguates their love, and intensifies their desire for self-representation while diminishing their control over it."[9] In the case of *A Mask* this requires reading the speeches particularly of the Lady and the brothers both as expressions of beliefs that motivate their actions and as statements situated within a system of familial relationships.

I think it is a mistake to think about that Lady without also remembering that the character is carefully placed as a sister and daughter in the various texts of the mask. What happens to a reading that tries to keep the focus on the *daughter,* who is typically dissolved into some idea of Woman or transformed into Milton in drag? A reading of Milton as Woman must forget the character's relationships to men; it may be that one aspect of Milton's originality in the mask is the degree to which he encourages this forgetfulness, but we are not permitted to forget entirely that the Lady is valued as a sister and daughter, and, by Comus himself, as potentially a wife and queen. The Lady of the *Mask* is not the figure of an essentialized woman. In the Michaelmas night performance of 1634 she was Alice Egerton, the fifteen-year-old daughter of the Earl of Bridgewater and older sister of Lord Brackley and Mr. Thomas Egerton, and in all published or performed versions she is a sister separated from her brothers during a journey home and, in the final scene at the President's Castle, a daughter "presented" with her brothers to their father and mother. It behooves us to remember these positions in the family economy when we read the *Mask.*

This is, in a way, to return to the implications of comments made long ago by David Masson, who suggests that some of the omissions of the Bridgewater manuscript "are such as the Earl and Countess of Bridgewater would hardly have liked to hear their young daughter, on the stage in Ludlow Castle, speaking aloud or having addressed to her."[10] As John Creaser notes, Masson's comment makes sense, except that much sexual innuendo survives the Bridgewater manuscript cuts and some of those cuts are not sexual in nature. Even so, Creaser admits the adequacy of Masson's explanation, extending it to cover plausibly an omission not cited by Masson, Comus's carpe diem speech of lines 737–55. The logic of Creaser's remarks (debatable as they are in today's permissive popular culture) goes to the heart of my question about the mask:

Even now, adolescent girls not "hardened" to the stage (to use the term from *Mansfield Park*) can be embarrassed by having to utter or be the subject of openly sexual passages in school plays. Social decorum of the period would have made all the more sensitive the addressing of the *carpe diem* to any young and unmarried aristocratic woman, all the more so on a state occasion and with Comus played by an actor who was not an aristocrat.[11]

My question issues from this point of social decorum, though I hope it has a broader relevance to the culture of the *Mask*. The question is this: What is gratifying or congratulatory to the family of Milton's *patron* in these speeches of a daughter and sister or, beyond the Michaelmas performance, what are the effects of these speeches on the reader's sense of the familial relationships represented in the *Mask?* While I share some of Kerrigan's and Leonard's criticisms of Marcus's argument, her essays on the *Mask* seem to me to be salutary in their shift of focus away from the poet who made the mask in collaboration with Henry Lawes to this broader set of family and cultural effects. Critical tradition has tended to read this work as an intensely private, even idiosyncratic, expression of Milton's ideals and struggles as a young writer.[12] This tradition is in part a response to such conundrums as the "gumms of glutenous heat" and the omissions from the Bridgewater manuscript, but, as Christopher Kendrick has suggested, a "symptomatic reading of *Comus*" may gesture toward a "politico-cultural reading" without denying the legitimacy of a biographical interpretation.[13]

What happens when we enter the work through the family—parents, daughter, brothers—instead of the Lady of Christ's? To begin with an analogy, we might think of some proud parents watching their daughter perform an especially difficult individual feat that at once displays her budding sexuality and her mastery of her body—a performance on the ice, say, or the balance beam. Add to this feat a sense of its imbrication in sexual awakening (an aspect not irrelevant to the gymnastic and skating analogies I am invoking). Given this aspect of the performance, Stephen Orgel's argument about spectatorship at court masks seems on the mark; at the Michaelmas 1634 performance I imagine an audience of townspeople and officials watching the Earl of Bridgewater watch his daughter "rehearse" a first sexual encounter.[14] If we shift focus for a moment from the Lady's point of view, with which Milton is typically held to be aligned, to that of her parents (and of her brothers), the mask's curious overinvestment in virginity and chastity makes a new kind of sense. Still a young man, Milton unexpectedly captures the combination of parental apprehension and pride that would accompany witnessing one's daughter's successful handling of a first sexual challenge/experience. Instead of a Miltonic fantasy of self-sufficiency, the mask can also, given the circumstances of its original production, work as a parental (and filial) fantasy. Attending to this larger familial framework recuperates some of the affective force of the mask, which tends to get obscured in readings that emphasize its intellectual, political, and even autobiographical implications.

How might these investments in a daughter and sister be bound up with the controversy between Leonard and Kerrigan? As Kerrigan suggests, running just beneath the surface of their debate is the old controversy regarding Freud and the seduction theory. In treating the action of the mask as a matter of sexual assault and by charging psychoanalysis with shifting attention from the perpetrator to the victim, Leonard aligns himself with critics of psychoanalysis who accuse Freud of denying actual paternal abuse in favor of a theory that overemphasized the sexual fantasies of women.[15] Taking a cue from the original circumstances of performance (though not limiting interpretation to that occasion), I suggest that the *Mask* stages a tangle of intrafamilial desires—father/daughter, daughter/father, brother/sister, sister/brother, son/mother. Conspicuously missing, to the reader of today, is mother/daughter love, covered in the mask by the action performed by the exogenous (in terms of both the fiction and the original performers) figure of Sabrina.[16] This is a work about love in the family, a sexual threat to this from the outside and, finally, a chaste same-sex female love that parallels and finally overpowers the heterosexual extrafamilial predation of Comus. While the mask concludes by restoring order to the family, the restoration is effected by a female agent outside the family, and the desires explored in the dark wood linger to complicate the metaphysical patriarchy so grandly asserted in the conclusion.

Parent-child relationships permeate this work. Even Comus himself, a parent's nightmare of a pick-up artist, displays considerable depth in this regard. Kerrigan's reason for not putting Comus on the couch (as Leonard proposes) is that "the tempter's desire seemed to me relatively straightforward. He hears the Lady sing, thinks of his mother, falls in love, and decides to make her his queen."[17] There are, however, some twists and turns in Comus's advance toward the Lady and its connection with his relationship to Circe. He claims a magical power to discern her virgin presence:

> Break off, break off, I feel the different pace,
> Of som chast footing neer about this ground.
>
> . . . .
>
>   som Virgin sure
> (For so I can distinguish by mine Art)
> Benighted in these Woods.   (145–46, 148–50)

At first the Lady's virginity seems only to make her an acceptable addition to the "fair" herd that he soon hopes, in imitation of his mother, to gather about him. In a beautiful irony that anticipates the effect on Comus of her speech on the mysterious power of virginity later in the mask, the Lady in fact quickly enchants the enchanter with her ensuing song to Echo. As Kerrigan notes, the song reminds Comus of his mother as well but focuses his advance on making the Lady his queen. It seems significant, however, that Comus's recollection of the songs of Circe and the Sirens is both like and unlike his response to the song of the Lady. As already suggested he immediately confesses to "Divine enchanting ravishment" (245), but, after working through his memories of Circe and the Sirens, he realizes a difference:

> Yet they in pleasing slumber lull'd the sense,
> And in sweet madnes rob'd it of it self,
> But such a sacred, and home-felt delight,
> Such sober certainty of waking bliss
> I never heard till now. Ile speak to her
> And she shall be my Queen.   (260–65)

Comus's desire for the Lady is not contained by the Oedipal complex.[18] His pursuit of the Lady also appears to be a way of escaping the Siren-song aura of his mother, and thus at least at this juncture, his words contradict John Rumrich's thesis that Comus represents a maternal dependence rejected by the good characters in the mask.[19] One might say Comus wants to grow up and be a good man. His attraction to the "sober certainty of waking bliss," together with his initial sensing of the Lady's "chaste footing," oddly presents a Comus who, for a moment anyway, longs to escape the life of illusion and "vain deluding joys" bequeathed by his mother and her circle and move ahead into adulthood, authenticity ("home-felt delight"), and reality.

Just what such a move would entail probably comes home to Comus after the Lady's great reality check in lines 755–78 and the declaration of "the sage / And serious doctrine of virginity" that accompanies it in the published versions. Both parts of the speech clarify to Comus what he had only glimpsed earlier—what it would mean to live a life of "sacred, and home-felt delight" in the "sober certainty of waking bliss," to deal with a straight-talker ("She fables not") instead of a charmer like his mother. He is shaken to whatever core of identity can be attributed to him, experiencing something like self-division:

> I feel that I do fear
> Her words set off by som superior power;
> And though not mortal, yet a cold shuddring dew
> Dips me all o're. (800–803)

Thus his resolve to "dissemble" (805) is at once a paradoxical return to his "true" self ("I must dissemble," since that is what I am, a dissembler) and a confession of his need to conceal from the Lady that curious feeling "that I do fear." If we have been following Comus's own struggle with himself, it is possible to hear his final rebuke and offer of relief as a speech addressed to *himself* as well as to the Lady:

> I must not suffer this, yet 'tis the lees
> And setlings of a melancholy blood;
> But this will cure all streight, one sip of this
> Will bathe the drooping spirits in delight
> Beyond the bliss of dreams. Be wise, and taste. (809–13)

In the end, the challenge to a Circean life of illusion represented by the Lady proves too frightening to Comus, who instead opts for a seventeenth-century version of sex, drugs, and rock 'n' roll.

The text pushes me to hedge Kerrigan's "bet" that "Milton's deepest feelings and beliefs were engaged in the representation of the Lady."[20] It may be that, as is sometimes the case in his later poems, Milton's feelings were distributed more or less evenly among his main characters, and here I am including the brothers as well as Comus and the Lady.

In her song to Echo, the Lady describes her brothers as "a gentle Pair / That likest thy Narcissus are" (236–37), but the figures of Echo and Narcissus just as obviously govern the relationship between her and her Elder Brother.[21] The rapt speech of the Elder Brother on the "hidden strength" (415) of his virgin sister, echoing her own apostrophe to "unblemish't form of Chastity" (215), epitomizes a narcissistic fantasy underlying Milton's text:

> 'Tis chastity, my brother, chastity:
> She that has that, is clad in compleat steel,
> And like a quiver'd Nymph with Arrows keen
> May trace huge Forests, and unharbour'd Heaths,
> . . . .
> Yea there, where very desolation dwels
> By grots, and caverns shag'd with horrid shades,

She may pass on with unblench't majesty,
Be it not don in pride, or in presumption.   (420–23, 428–31)

This fantasy of a hidden, quasi-magical female power captures the attributes of mystery, self-sufficiency, and inaccessibility that Freud attaches to female narcissism, and, more to the point, with the "charm" of female narcissism for men.[22] Freud's theorizing on female narcissism, particularly as it has been critiqued by the feminist theorist Sarah Kofman, offers a powerful model for the work's mobilization of male fantasies, while, paradoxically, also supporting a feminist reading of the Lady as a figure of power. In her book on Freud and women, Kofman demonstrates that Freud's earlier writings on women, including the essay "On Narcissism," evince a balance of fascination and fear on the topic of female power. Over the years, she argues, Freud moved away from an earlier receptivity and ambivalence to insist, notoriously, on female inferiority.[23] Milton's mask displays female power and a range of male fantasies that arise in response to it. Like Freud, Milton continued throughout his career to revert to binary opposition of male and female; although the later struggles with sex and gender in *Paradise Lost* and *Samson Agonistes* lie beyond the scope of this essay, I would suggest that, perhaps again like Freud, Milton seems in contradiction with himself on his insistence on male superiority.

Milton's empowered Lady is wrapped in a discourse of narcissism. Brilliantly underscored by Milton's use of Echo in the song, it includes the Lady's own narcissism, Elder Brother's mirroring and echoing of his sister, Comus's attraction to the power of the virgin, and Milton's investment in the daughter of his patron. In his text "On Narcissism," Freud suggests a link between the development of female narcissism and the social restrictions placed upon women: "Women, especially if they grow up with good looks, develop a certain self-contentment which compensates them for the social restrictions that are imposed upon them in their choice of object. Strictly speaking, it is only themselves that such women love with an intensity comparable to that of the man's love for them."[24] The narcissistic structure of the Lady's devotion to the Idea of chastity is evident in her insistence, highlighted by the text's redundancy, that "I see ye visibly" (216). Even more directly than its Freudian analogue, the Lady's narcissistic devotion to chastity and the sense of empowerment that accompanies it grow out of sociocultural restrictions placed on female sexuality. The Lady's narcissism derives from her attachment to the ideal she calls chastity or, climactically, virginity. Out of the restrictions placed on female sexuality, Milton's Lady fashions a devotion to this ideal, a sense of her sexual invulnerability so powerful that it continues to disturb commentators on the work.

Freud goes on to associate this self-contentment and inaccessibility with the bliss of childhood. The charm of female narcissism for men, he then argues, derives from a sort of reversal of the infamous "penis envy": "It is as if we envied them for maintaining a blissful state of mind—an unassailable libidinal position which we ourselves have since abandoned."[25] The Elder Brother seems to be susceptible to this "charm" in his first remarks about his sister. However, after learning from the Attendant Spirit that his sister has been deceived by Comus, he qualifies his belief in her unapproachability, using language that also revises Freud's characterization of the "charm." Elder Brother's earlier speech to his brother affirms his sister's freedom from even attempted violation—"No savage fierce, Bandite, or mountaineer / Will dare to soyl her Virgin purity" (426–27), a view supported most emphatically by his allusion to Minerva's "*Gorgon* sheild" (447).[26] The later speech, revised in light of the Attendant Spirit's narrative and the testy questioning of the younger brother ("Is this the confidence / You gave me Brother?" [583–84]), admits that "Vertue may be *assail'd*, but never hurt" (589; my emphasis), while it also ramps up the investment in his sister's inviolability: "if this fail, / The pillar'd firmament is rott'nness / And earths base built on stubble" (597–99). Hearing the report of the Attendant Spirit, Elder Brother is forced to acknowledge Comus's attempt on his sister; she is a sex object, whether he wishes to think of her as such or not. His response to this state of affairs is to ground the universe on her inviolability.

Milton's irresolution about what to call the ideal, virginity or chastity, to which the Lady is devoted may be related to this distinction between what Theodora Jankowski has characterized as a quasi-magical notion of the unassailable virgin, "neither desired nor desiring," and the slightly tempered view of the Elder Brother's later speech.[27] My scan of Flannagan's text, based on the 1645 edition, yields eleven occurrences of "virgin" or "virginity" and eleven uses of "chaste" or "chastity." In some cases, the use of different terms is easily explained, as, for instance, in Elder Brother's rhapsody on "the sacred rayes of Chastity" that will prevent the soiling of his sister's "Virgin purity" (see 425, 427). Chastity, a virtue, is held to ensure the preservation of a physical and moral condition—the purity of the virgin sister. In another instance, on first encountering the Lady, Comus appears to make a subtle, less obvious distinction. He first feels "the different pace, Of som chast footing neer about this ground," and then asserts that the different pace announces "Som Virgin sure / (For so I can distinguish by mine Art)" (148–49), perhaps suggesting as well a magical aura of virginity that ironically is perceptible to a magician like himself.[28] Finally and most problematically, while "chastity" predominates in speeches in which the Lady and Elder Brother refer to her virtue, in the famous extension of the Lady's final speech, added to published versions of the mask, she refers first to "the Sun-clad power of Chastity" and, five lines later, to "the sage / And serious doctrine of Virginity" (782, 786–87).

John Rogers has argued that this added speech can be regarded as "a temporal origin" of a remodeling of virginity by English revolutionaries; in the added speech the Lady "wrests the subject of her speech away from the virtue of moderation central to the doctrine of married chastity and bends it to the unyielding, absolutist virtue of sexual abstinence." What is more, Rogers insists, instead of serving as a mode of patriarchal control of female desire, this new model virginity expresses a "faith . . . in the connection between sexual purity and human power, a power that for some could potentially alter forever the religious and political face of the English nation."[29] Rogers's thesis intersects in interesting ways with Jankowski's *Queer Virginity in Early Modern English Drama,* which reminds us that chastity and virginity were also regarded as competing ideals in the seventeenth century, at least in their reference to female sexuality.[30] Both scholars emphasize a continuing investment in virginity in the face of the rise and eventual dominance of married chastity as the Protestant ideal, though, given her focus on gender politics in the period, Jankowski understandably worries the distinction between the two terms. Her emphasis on *competing* ideals makes Milton's use of the two terms in the Lady's speech all the more intriguing. Not only does Milton's Lady announce a new and powerful model of virginity, but she would appear to be restricting the meaning of chastity to abstinence. While her collapsing of the two terms into abstinence might be seen as appropriate given her present situation in the drama as a sexual hostage, her emphasis is picked up in the ensuing scene with the virginal Sabrina and in the concluding speech of the Attendant Spirit with its contrasting images of, on the one hand, the sexually experienced Adonis and Venus and, on the other, the embracing couple Cupid and Psyche, who miraculously produce the twins Youth and Joy "from her fair unspotted side" (1009).

Echoing his sister's language, the Elder Brother finds mirrored in her his own desire for self-sufficiency. In a sort of double-helix of narcissism, brother and sister, libidinally inaccessible to each other, envy each other's narcissistic inaccessibility: the sister fancies her brothers to be "likest thy [Echo's] Narcissus," while Elder Brother imagines his sister to be the invulnerable, cross-dressed goddess, an armored and "quiver'd Nymph with Arrows keen." Brother and sister also mirror one another as keepers of the secret of chastity, mystifying it through a paradoxical language of hiddenness and vision. Elder Brother calls it a *"hidden* strength," whose possessor is privy "in *cleer* dream, and solemn *vision*" to the revelations of "A thousand liveried Angels" (415, 457, 455; my emphases). His sister, after toying with the question of disclosing her secret to Comus, finally decides *not* to "unfold the sage / And serious doctrine of Virginity" (786–87), although she, like her brother, is convinced of her omnipotence:

> Yet should I try, the uncontrouled worth
> Of this pure cause would kindle my rap't spirits
> To such a flame of sacred vehemence,
> That dumb things would be mov'd to sympathize,
> And the brute Earth would lend her nerves and shake,
> Till all thy magick structures rear'd so high,
> Were shatter'd into heaps o're thy false head. (793–99)

In one of the several brilliant ironies of the mask, the fantasist Comus is charmed by this fantastic speech and assents to the Lady's marvelous claims: "She fables not" (800).

Both Comus and Elder Brother are thus charmed by the Lady's libidinal invulnerability. As already noted, the brother rhapsodizes it into a test of the moral order of creation: "if this fail, / The pillar'd firmament is rott'nness" (597–98). Comus, on the other hand, is divided against himself by its power. Both men also fail in their attempted relationships to the young woman— Elder Brother to protect her, Comus to violate her. She mysteriously eludes the projects of the men attracted to her.

What about the other two men centrally involved in the mask—the Lady's father and John Milton? The triangulated transaction involving poet, father-patron, and daughter foregrounds one of the fundamental relationships in Western familial and social organization. As Lynda Boose has observed, the daughter is "the figure upon whose mobility the whole kinship structure rests," yet she is, paradoxically, "specifically absent" within patriarchy.[31] The conspicuous presence of the daughter in the mask commands special attention, then. Moreover, while the treatment of the Lady can certainly be contained within a patriarchal narrative, it is not entirely congruent with the family plot of the Egertons. To be sure, the daughter of *A Mask* rehearses her function in the marriage system by securing a homosocial bond between men—here, the poet and his patron. In the patronage relationship, however, the direction of the "traffic in women" is reversed from its "normal" path in the marriage transaction: instead of the daughter being handed over from the father to the groom, the daughter is produced (as it were) by the poet, who by rights occupies the position of the exogamous male/groom, in order to be "presented" (to borrow an important word from *A Mask*) to the patron/father. Where the marriage ritual enacts a separation of father and daughter, the transaction between poet and patron, mirrored in the plot of the work, returns or restores the daughter to the father as a sexual property. In this act of presentation, the poet's reproduction of the patron's emotional investment in his daughter grows into an overvaluation of the daughter; thus, the normally marginalized, "specifically absent" daughter assumes a central position and presence. Making the daughter a focus of idealization and narcissistic identification, the mask, then, represents the relationship between father and daughter as, in Boose's words, "a conflicted text of desire and sanction." Far from simply affirming the structure of patriarchy, *Comus* displays its contradictions and fantasizes about empowering alternatives for both poet and daughter.[32]

Milton's Lady is discovered walking alone at night in a "wilde Wood" (stage direction, line 1). Like a forest in a Shakespearean comedy, the setting functions as a liminal space where the girl makes her passage from virgin daughterhood to married womanhood.[33] The details of those passages are, to be sure, sharply contrasting. Milton's Lady must, depending on your position in the *Comus* debate, fight off her own fears of sex (Kerrigan), an attempted rape (Marcus, Leonard), or an unauthorized marriage proposal of a brutal landlord,[34] before returning to the rightful lord of her sexuality. Whichever position the reader holds, it remains the case that the mask allows the father to have and have not, to see his daughter (one is tempted to add, to see her visibly) as both an "unblemish't form" and an object of desire. The conflicted nature of his investment in her is captured with precision in the botched rescue scene: the brothers ("O ye mistook" [815]) shatter Comus's glass instead of snatching his wand; Comus escapes with his wand; the daughter and sister sits "In stony fetters fixt" (819), still inaccessible but nonetheless stuck to the "marble venom'd seat / Smear'd with" those much remarked upon "gumms of glutenous heat" (916–17). The conundrum about those hot gums is perhaps exactly the point and renders the daughter/sister inaccessible in another sense—father and brothers are locked out, as it were, of the Lady's experience. They are caught in the contradiction of regarding the daughter/sister in terms of an *ideal* defined by a relation to *sexuality*.[35] In defining one's daughter or sister exclusively in terms of chastity—that is, her (invulnerable, to be sure) libidinal position, one is paradoxically defining her as a primarily sexual being. The brothers' discovery of their "root-bound" sister, fixed in Comus's "inchanted Chair," followed by their rash, ineffectual response, is a brilliant enactment of the contradiction underlying the investment of the Bridgewater males in their virginal sister/daughter as well as their fundamental separation from the experience she has undergone.

The impasse cannot be overcome by agents within the family; the Lady is utterly silent and alone. At this point in the mask Milton exercises a magnificent tactfulness, one might even call it sensitivity, in stepping away from his identification with his youthful characters—the brothers and their sister—even as he assumes control over the conclusion of his work. From this point on, he speaks as the poet—the Attendant Spirit (played in the original performance by his collaborator) who, in turn, learned from "*Melibaeus* old" (822) a way to free the Lady by the power of song. The power of the poet, however, is exercised indirectly. He can summon Sabrina, "a Virgin pure" (826) from a place outside the family circle to dissolve the gums, anoint the Lady's erogenous zones,[36] and thus allow him to return the daughter to the control of his patrons, her parents.

What might that anointing signify? In his compelling reading of the mask as a rite of passage, William Shullenberger suggests Eliade's notion of "the revelation of sexuality."[37] This comes close to my understanding of the force of Sabrina's act, but I want to place more emphasis on the Lady's isolation and silence as a signifying of her new inwardness, an inwardness that is bound up with her sexuality and that remains, like the precise meaning of "gumms," hidden from us. As Jean E. Graham points out, "a silent person is still an unreadable person."[38] If Milton, in the person of the Attendant Spirit, presents the children to their father and mother and proclaims victory "O're sensual Folly, and Intemperance" (975), he has the great good sense *not* to put this account of their experiences in the mouths of the children themselves, all of whom remain silent as the mask draws to its end and the Attendant Spirit rockets to his myth-drenched home, where Adonis is on the mend and Psyche gives birth to twins "from her fair unspotted side" (1009).

I agree with Kerrigan that the Psyche reference is bound up with parent-child relationships, though I see the "unspotted" allusion to Ephesians, noted by Leonard, as well as the euphemistic "side" issuing from a Milton who, for a moment, speaks for the patronizing parents (pun intended), not the children.[39] This is not another attempt to argue that the Lady's "no" meant "yes," but Milton does seem to allow for the possibility of alternative feelings about the timely trials of youth, thoughts quite different from the triumphalism and glorious vision of the Attendant Spirit, in the silence of the young Bridgewaters (or the fictional Lady and Elder and Second Brothers in subsequent performances/readings) at the end of the mask. The Attendant Spirit leads them to the dance, but the Lady's own powerful argument for the untouchable "freedom of my minde," her intensely self-regarding manner, creates a space between her compliant actions and her silence. She has endured a sexual assault[40] and the mysterious ministrations of her female deliverer; these experiences may or may not have affected her sense of autonomy. Her brothers have seen their sister as a prisoner, and they seem to be witnesses of the rites performed by Sabrina. They too may have interesting comments, new perspectives on their experiences in the dark wood. Milton is not talking (for them). Perhaps he does not know. In either case, how admirable of him not to presume.

What he does speak of at the end of the work is his desire for the power and authority of the bard. He abandons his identification with his patron and imagines transcending the temporary relationship with him. Flying, running, soaring "To the corners of the Moon," climbing "Higher then the Spheary chime" (1017, 1021), he adopts the sublime and mysterious mode of the Lady in her final speech in order to express his fantasy of poetic independence.[41] The audience or reader may wonder whether *she* too still feels such a sense of independence at the end. Or is she happy to return to her culturally pre-scribed position, "specifically absent" in her father's house? We do not know what she or her brothers are thinking. *A Mask Presented at Ludlow Castle* is a work at once strange and familiar.

Kent State University

NOTES

1. See William B. Hunter, *Milton's "Comus": Family Piece* (New York, 1983); Leah Marcus, "The Milieu of Milton's *Comus:* Judicial Reform at Ludlow and the Problem of Sexual Assault," *Criticism* 25 (1983): 317. See also Marcus, "The Earl of Bridgewater's Legal Life: Notes toward a Political Reading of *Comus*," *Milton Quarterly* 21 (1987): 13–23, and "Justice for Margery Evans: A 'Local' Reading of *Comus*," in *Milton and the Idea of Woman*, ed. Julia M. Walker (Urbana, IL, 1988), 66–85.

Citations of Milton's poetry in this essay are by line number from *The Riverside Milton*, ed. Roy Flannagan (Boston, 1998), hereafter cited parenthetically in the text. The copy-text for the Flannagan edition, the 1645 edition of the mask, is, as both Flannagan and Hunter note, the furthest removed version from the context of the original performance and patronage relationship. See Flannagan's comments on the texts of *Comus*, including Hunter's reconstruction of a "promptbook" for the original performance, at 114–16. While I am not concerned with the specifics of Milton's relations with the Bridgewaters in this article, I do want to consider the emotional risks and rewards of the situation: parents being entertained by their children's performance of a play created by a rising poet.

2. John Leonard, "Saying 'No' to Freud: Milton's *A Mask* and Sexual Assault," *Milton Quarterly* 25 (1991): 129. Leonard is referring to Kerrigan, *The Sacred Complex: On the Psychogenesis of "Paradise Lost"* (Cambridge, MA, 1983).

3. Leonard, "Saying 'No,'" 133.

4. Kerrigan, "The Politically Correct *Comus:* A Reply to John Leonard," *Milton Quarterly* 27 (1993): 150. On the Evans case, see Marcus, "The Milieu of Milton's *Comus*," 317. Leonard's reply to Kerrigan is "'Good Things': A Reply to William Kerrigan," *Milton Quarterly* 30 (1996): 117–27.

5. Debora Shuger, "'Gums of Glutinous Heat' and the Stream of Consciousness: The Theology of Milton's *Mask*," *Representations* 60 (Fall 1997): 1–21. Shuger's reading assumes the gums are exuded by the Lady, but might they instead be emissions from Comus, whose spell is

compared to bird-lime ("the very lime-twigs of his spells") by the Attendant Spirit (646)? Such a reading might allow for some access to the desire, the inwardness of Comus, a possibility I touch upon later in this essay. Comus's immobilization of the Lady with his "gumms of glutenous heat" would represent a male rape fantasy (another type of "spell" or "hellish charm" [613]) of the most graphic sort, a fantasy finally dissolved by Sabrina (significantly, not by the brothers) with the purifying drops from her fountain. For a different perspective on bodily fluids in the mask, see B. J. Sokol, " 'Tilted Lees,' Dragons, Haemony, Menarche, Spirit, and Matter in *Comus*," *Review of English Studies* 41 (1990): 309–24.

I would like to thank John Leonard for challenging my thoughts on the gums in his helpful reading of this essay for *Milton Studies*—specifically for the suggestion that the gums can be regarded as external to the Lady and for the connection between the gums and bird-lime.

6. Catherine Belsey: "*Comus* is about rape"; see Belsey, *John Milton: Language, Gender, Power* (New York, 1988), 46. Leonard, "Saying 'No,' " argues that "A consciousness of sexual assault will change the way in which we read many parts of the poem" (130) after quoting with approval Leah Marcus: "Her [the Lady's] fate is not that of a victim of rape, but her predicament is morally identical." See Marcus, "Judicial Reform at Ludlow," 317; quoted in Leonard, "Saying 'No,' " 130.

7. "Kerrigan's confidence would presumably be unshaken by the fact that women see a very different Lady from the one he sees." See Leonard, "Saying 'No,' " 130. For Kerrigan's objection to this approach, see "The Politically Correct *Comus*," 150.

8. Maus, "A Womb of His Own: Male Renaissance Poets in the Female Body," in *Sexuality and Gender in Early Modern Europe: Institutions, Texts, Images*, ed. James Grantham Turner (Cambridge, 1993), 284. Maus clearly articulates the potential benefits and risks afforded by a male poet's identification with a woman; the invisibility of the woman's sexual body (her hidden, inward-turning sexual organs) "can become a topos of a *resistance* to scrutiny, of an inner truth not susceptible to discovery or manipulation from the outside" (273). In the case of the *Mask*, "Milton's identification with a virginal character allows him to enjoy the advantages of the secure interior space associated with the female body without suggesting . . . that the interior need be compromised in order to obtain a poetic result. . . . He thinks of his poetic vocation in terms of inhabiting the Lady's physical position" (278–79). As Maus points out, however, Milton's appropriation of the female virgin body contradicts another topos of woman as "leaky vessel." Male wombs give birth—to poems—but they do not get impregnated (275). This contradiction is related to ambiguities regarding the body and soul; the inviolate virginal body seems to express a spiritual condition, but at the same time the work insists on an inviolate mind that is independent of the body. In Maus's words, "Milton keeps the pressure on by emphasizing the corporeality of the Lady, by making it difficult to idealize her virginal body too completely" (283). Again, the difficulty is exemplified in the mysterious "gumms." A revised version of this essay forms the last chapter of Maus's *Inwardness and Theater in the English Renaissance* (Chicago, 1995), 182–209.

9. See Harry Berger Jr., *Making Trifles of Terrors: Redistributing Complicities in Shakespeare*, ed. Peter Erickson (Stanford, 1997), 228–36. "Local" readings include three essays by Marcus ("The Milieu of Milton's *Comus*"; a condensed and revised version of this piece, "Justice for Margery Evans"; and "The Earl of Bridgewater's Legal Life"); Cedric C. Brown, *John Milton's Aristocratic Entertainments* (Cambridge, 1985); John Creaser, " 'The present aid of this occasion': The Setting of *Comus*," in *The Court Mask*, ed. David Lindley (Manchester, 1984), 111–34; Barbara Breasted, "*Comus* and the Castlehaven Scandal," in *Milton Studies* 3, ed. James D. Simmonds (Pittsburgh, 1971), 201–24; Creaser's critique of the Castlehaven thesis, "Milton's *Comus*: The Irrelevance of the Castlehaven Scandal," *Milton Quarterly* 21 (1987): 24–34; and William B. Hunter, *Milton's "Comus": Family Piece* (New York, 1983).

10. Quoted in Creaser, "Irrelevance," 29.

11. Ibid., 29.

12. One of the chief projects of historicist criticism of the mask has been a refutation of Milton's idiosyncrasies on the matter of "faith, hope, and chastity." See, for example, Maryann McGuire, *Milton's Puritan Masque* (Athens, GA, 1983); and John Rogers, "The Enclosure of Virginity: The Poetics of Sexual Abstinence in the English Revolution," in *Enclosure Acts: Sexuality, Property, and Culture in Early Modern England,* ed. Richard Burt and John Michael Archer (Ithaca, NY, 1994), 229–50.

13. Christopher Kendrick, "Milton and Sexuality: A Symptomatic Reading of *Comus,*" in *Re-membering Milton: Essays on the Texts and Traditions,* ed. Mary Nyquist and Margaret W. Ferguson (London, 1987), 43–73.

14. Orgel, *The Illusion of Power: Political Theater in the English Renaissance* (Berkeley and Los Angeles, 1975), esp. chap. 2. Again, I do not mean to limit my discussion to the effect of the mask on Michaelmas night 1634. That is Marcus's project in her *Comus* essays of the 1980s, but, as she argues in a more recent book, we ought to be wary of privileging one version, even the original performance version, at the expense of the other extant texts of the work. See Marcus, *Unediting the Renaissance: Shakespeare, Marlowe, Milton* (London, 1996). While the *Mask* was an occasional piece, Milton's collaborator, Henry Lawes, and the Bridgewater family decided not to limit its presentation to the occasion of performance when Lawes published it with their permission in 1637, and Milton apparently felt the same in publishing it with the 1645 *Poems* and again in the 1673 *Poems.*

15. Many of the issues raised by Jeffrey Masson's attack in *The Assault on Truth: Freud's Suppression of the Seduction Theory* (New York, 1984) are reviewed in David Willbern, "*Filia Oedipi:* Father and Daughter in Freudian Theory," in *Daughters and Fathers,* ed. Lynda E. Boose and Betty S. Flowers (Baltimore, 1989), 75–96. While my reading departs from Kerrigan's in important respects, it affirms his attempt to uncover the emotional and psychic energy that drives the mask.

16. For a suggestive reading of Sabrina's position outside the aristocratic family, see Lauren Shohet, "Figuring Chastity: Milton's Ludlow Mask," in *Menacing Virgins: Representing Virginity in the Middle Ages and Renaissance,* ed. Kathleen Coyne Kelly and Marina Leslie (Newark, DE, 1999), 154–57.

17. Kerrigan, "Politically Correct *Comus,*" 153. While my reading departs from Kerrigan's in important respects, I mean to affirm his powerful attempt to describe the emotional and psychic energy that drives the mask.

18. Kerrigan, *Sacred Complex,* writes that Comus "has transcended incestuous love in the only way men do, choosing his 'Queen' out of a 'home-felt delight' that identifies her with his mother, yet also valuing the difference and uniqueness of his choice ('never heard till now')" (52). I would place more emphasis on the difference between Circe and the Lady: "home-felt" more likely is a contrast to the delights of Circe's song, not an association with it, since it was "never heard till now." See also the suggestive note on the phrase in Flannagan, *The Riverside Milton,* 135 n. 171.

19. Rumrich, *Milton Unbound: Controversy and Reinterpretation* (Cambridge, 1996), 91 et passim.

20. Kerrigan, "Politically Correct *Comus,*" 153.

21. Thomas O. Calhoun, "On John Milton's *A Mask at Ludlow,*" in *Milton Studies* 6, ed. James D. Simmonds (Pittsburgh, 1974), 171, commented on the unusual character of the references of the Lady's song: "This is an extremely unusual set of references [to the grieving and aggrieved lovers Echo and Philomela, "the love-lorne nightingale,"] for a young woman to use in calling for her brothers, but the allusions are fitting and expressive if the young woman has been

contemplating, perhaps not even consciously, the problems of erotic love." Calhoun's focus on adolescent eroticism interrupted by parental alarm harmonizes with my emphasis on familial eros in the mask.

22. Freud, "On Narcissism," quoted in Sarah Kofman, *The Enigma of Woman: Woman in Freud's Writings,* trans. Catherine Porter (Ithaca, NY, 1985), 51. My reading of Freud is indebted to Kofman's analysis.

23. See esp. Kofman, *The Enigma of Woman,* part 2, chap. 5.

24. Quoted in ibid., 51.

25. Ibid., 51.

26. The effect of this slight, yet significant shift may be usefully compared to the adjustment in Adam's perspective in the great debate scene with Eve in Book Nine of *Paradise Lost.* In expressing his desire "to avoid / Th'attempt itself, intended by our Foe" (*PL* 9.294–95) on his wife, Adam has generally come under criticism for such an un-Miltonic recommendation of avoidance. But it could be that Adam is admitting Eve's charming power, experienced on that first day when she appeared to be so self-contented and inaccessible, so narcissistic. He in turn feels empowered in her eyes: "I from the influence of thy looks receave / Access in every Vertue, in thy sight / More wise" (9.309–11). Since Milton also emphasizes that Eve is made in Adam's image ("shee for God in him" [4.299]), it is possible to argue that narcissism plays a constructive role in "Matrimonial Love" (9.319). Venturing forth alone, Eve is no longer unassailable, if still inviolate: Adam's narcissistic fantasy of her unassailability is broken (though, as we know, Eve's narcissism becomes a major weapon employed by Satan against her).

27. Theodora Jankowski, " 'Where there can be no cause of affection': Redefining Virgins, Their Desires, Their Pleasures in John Lyly's *Gallathea,*" in *Feminist Readings of Early Modern Culture: Emerging Subjects,* ed. Valerie Traub et al. (Cambridge, 1996), 255.

28. Stanley Fish, *How Milton Works* (Cambridge, MA, 2001), 175–77, derives his reading of this passage from an allusion to Aeneas's recognition of Venus by her step; Fish continues by describing the Lady's "chast footing" as "a footing that takes its direction from itself rather than from some external roadway to whose turnings it must conform." Although Fish does not and would not relate his description of the Lady to narcissism, his emphasis on her self-sufficiency harmonizes with my reading of her self-regard (and Elder Brother's regard of her).

29. Rogers, "The Enclosure of Virginity," 231, 229, 230. I have two narrow objections to Rogers's argument, which branch into broader concerns. First, Rogers hinges his argument on the framing of the speech by the Lady's question, "Shall I go on? / Or have I said anough?" (779–80). This expression of uncertainty, he asserts, "signals quite pointedly the thematic excess of her new argument"; her claim to power "far surpasses the strength required to destroy a petty magus such as Comus" and leads into "a proclamation of virginal strength that logically overrides any need for the sanctioned transition to marriage and married chastity" (231, 232). But this "apocalyptic power" (231) has already been asserted earlier in the mask by Elder Brother (see esp. lines 593–99). As I shall argue below, brother and sister are a narcissistic dyad on this question of invulnerability. What is more, Rogers elides the Lady's indifferent use of the terms "chastity" and "virginity" to describe the source of this power. Milton's slippage between the two evidences an irresolution about sexuality. It is not clear to me whether this irresolution issues from the point of view of the Lady, her parents, or the author.

30. Theodora Jankowski, *Pure Resistance: Queer Virginity in Early Modern English Drama* (Philadelphia, 2000), esp. chaps. 3–4. In John Leonard's edition of *The Complete Poems* (London, 1998), in a note to the *Mask,* Leonard points out that in Protestant parlance, both the words "virginity" and "chastity" could include marriage (787). However, it seems equally noteworthy that the characters in the mask echo the language of a virginal aura researched by Jankowski in their references to the physically intact, unmarried Lady.

31. Lynda Boose, "The Father's House and the Daughter in It," in Boose and Flowers, *Daughters and Fathers*, 20.

32. Ibid., 46. Julie H. Kim, "The Lady's Unladylike Struggle: Redefining Patriarchal Boundaries in Milton's *Comus*," in *Milton Studies* 35, ed. Albert C. Labriola (Pittsburgh, 1997), 1–20, discusses the mask's testing of patriarchal structures from an economic perspective.

33. On *Comus* as a rite of passage, see William Shullenberger, "Into the Woods: The Lady's Soliloquy in *Comus*," *Milton Quarterly* 35 (2001): 33–43.

34. Hugh Jenkins, "Milton's *Comus* and the Country-House Poem," in *Milton Studies* 32, ed. Albert C. Labriola (Pittsburgh, 1996), 176–78. Jenkins argues well for the influence on *Comus* of the Jonsonian country-house poem with its "mediating female figure" (170).

35. Kim emphasizes the link between female sexuality and economics as the source of male anxiety in the mask. While I accept this connection, I do not believe it can entirely account for the Elder Brother's ascription of quasi-magical powers to his virgin sister's chastity.

36. I owe this observation to Shullenberger, "Into the Woods," 39.

37. Eliade is quoted in ibid., 37.

38. Jean E. Graham, "Virgin Ears: Silence, Deafness, and Chastity in Milton's *Maske*," in *Milton Studies* 36, ed. Albert C. Labriola (Pittsburgh, 1998), 14.

39. See Kerrigan's summary of his earlier, *Sacred Complex*, reading of this passage in "Politically Correct *Comus*," 154, and Leonard's reply, which provides the Ephesians allusion, in " 'Good Things,' " 125.

40. I agree with Leonard, " 'Good Things' ": "the Lady's confinement and paralysis are themselves a form of sexual assault" (120).

41. On Milton's magus fantasy, see Thomas M. Greene, "Enchanting Ravishments: Magic and Counter-Magic in *Comus*," in *Opening the Borders: Inclusivity in Early Modern Studies, Essays in Honor of James V. Mirollo* (Newark, DE, 1999), 298–323.

GALILEO IN ACTION:
THE "TELESCOPE" IN *PARADISE LOST*

Maura Brady

P*ARADISE LOST* is famously concerned with the difficulties of seeing and knowing. "What in me is dark / Illumin," the narrator exhorts his muse (1.22–23), a task made both arduous and urgent by his blindness. A clear view through the "glass of Galileo," similarly, is hard to achieve; the picture is repeatedly clouded by the instrument's associations with Satan, by morally and epistemologically ambiguous "spots," and by implied doubts about Galileo's scientific method. Nevertheless, while the problems of telescopic vision suggest that the search for knowledge holds very real moral and epistemological dangers, they do not foreclose the search or invalidate its results, any more than the narrator's blindness precludes insight.

Like the instruments of *Paradise Lost,* the first telescopes with which Galileo conducted his astronomical observations produced troubled visions and considerable controversy, yet they nevertheless participated in the construction of knowledge. As we shall see, they did so because of the very difficulties that would seem likely to have undermined them. In this essay, I will argue that Milton evokes Galileo's earliest instruments in order to develop them as signs for the labor by which knowledge is constructed, and to recover for his own purposes the epistemological problems that arose in the course of Galileo's work with the instrument. In *Paradise Lost,* as I hope to show, occlusions can facilitate vision, illusions can lead to truth, and the hard work of intellectual inquiry, with all of its attendant confusions and limitations, is unavoidable.

Galileo's instruments would have been within recent memory for both Milton and the first readers of *Paradise Lost.* Galileo developed his telescopes during Milton's lifetime, and the poet appears to have visited him on his trip to Italy in 1638–1639.[1] The two were contemporaries, or nearly so, and in the context of *Paradise Lost* it is reasonable enough that critics have treated them as such, since Galileo is the only seventeenth-century figure mentioned in the poem. The scientist continued to be a prominent figure in the public imagination even after his death in 1642, and the telescope he had helped develop was by midcentury a commonplace instrument of astronomical observation.

Yet that instrument may be said to have receded from view even as it came to be accepted as a valid tool of scientific investigation. Bruno Latour has argued that scientific instruments are most highly visible at moments of controversy and dissent, and fade from the public consciousness when they are no longer needed to justify the facts or interpretations of them. He offers the telescope as a case in point, asserting that, once the problems have receded,

[a] picture of moon valleys and mountains is presented to us as if we could see them directly. The telescope that makes them visible is invisible and so are the fierce controversies that Galileo had to wage centuries ago to produce an image of the Moon. . . . Once the fact is constructed, there is no instrument to take into account and this is why the painstaking work necessary to tune the instrument often disappears from popular science.[2]

Galileo's instrument was initially greeted with considerable skepticism, even active resistance. Within a few years, however, objections were rarely heard, even though the underlying theoretical and philosophical problems had not yet been solved. In this sense, the quickly waning debate over Galileo's telescope signifies a dwindling public awareness of the physical, intellectual, and social labor by means of which both the instrument and the knowledge it supported were constituted. I hope to make the early instrument visible again as a problematic site for the production of knowledge by examining the material, intellectual, and rhetorical labor that Galileo put into it. I will sketch some of the problems Galileo encountered in making his instruments, and give particular attention to the rhetorical instrument he constructed in *The Starry Messenger,* the treatise in which he first presented his astronomical observations to the public. In the process I hope to reveal Galileo in action, carefully assembling the instrument; this will allow us, in turn, to see how Milton, over half a century later, takes it apart again, opening the mysterious "black box" to remind the readers of *Paradise Lost* of the difficulties of producing an instrument that accurately mediates the world.[3]

It is no doubt evident by now that I am distinguishing both Galileo's astronomical instruments and those of *Paradise Lost* from what are commonly called "telescopes." I do not mean to suggest by this that Galileo did not see what he claimed to see in the night sky, or that Milton later found his observations unreal or untrue. I make the distinction to underscore the point that there was once a moment when the instrument was new and before audiences knew how to use it, and that the discourse in which it was embedded differed in significant ways from the discourse of the telescope. Generally speaking, I will use the term "instrument" to refer both to Galileo's first telescopes and to the telescopes of *Paradise Lost,* except when I designate the latter by the names Milton gives them. I mean the term to carry both a common and a more specialized meaning. In common usage, an "instrument" is simply a tool; the designation is neutral on the question of how the device works or what it does.[4] In this sense, it suits Galileo's early telescopes, about whose inner workings there was no immediate consensus. Within the discourse of the sociology of science, however, the "instruments" of modern science are understood as tools that make new matters of fact manifest as objects of perception; as such, these instruments may be said to have performed or inscribed knowledge, to have made it plain to the observers who would judge and verify it.[5] An "instrument" in this sense is most "instrumental" when it makes new contributions to a body of knowledge, establishes new facts, and expressly mediates this knowledge to an audience. As I will apply it, the distinction between "instrument" and "telescope" is meant to suggest that Galileo's *instrument* did not become a *telescope* until it and the facts it helped to establish had been accepted by the scientific community.

Until quite recently, critical discussions of Galileo and his "glass" have tended to elide the differences between the instruments of *Paradise Lost* and the telescope. Within the poem the instruments have commonly been read as a sign for Copernican cosmology or for Galileo's science, and thus as an index to Milton's attitudes toward these things; Marjorie Hope Nicolson, for example, argued that the telescope was responsible for the vast backdrop of the poem's imagined spaces, which she identified as Copernican.[6] More recently, both Roy Flannagan and Neil Harris have argued that the associations of the instrument, Satan, and "artistry" suggest that Milton was offering a strong critique of the new science.[7]

A growing body of criticism, however, has suggested that the "glass of Galileo" differs in some important respects from a telescope, though for the most part the point has not been argued explicitly. The instrument has been associated less with astronomy per se than with the broader project of envisioning the world anew. Thus, for example, the "optic glass" in *Paradise Lost* is often compared with the poet's own art and read for what it suggests about the role of the imagination in the search for knowledge. Linda Gregerson offers the "glass" as a simile for simile itself: "an artifact and an instrument with which to see," while Judith Herz reads it as confirmation of Milton's own artistic practice, "which depends upon the tension between certainty and doubt." In a similar vein, Donald Friedman argues that the "optic glass" stands as a sign for both the dangers and the potential rewards of imaginative projection.[8] Other critics have interpreted the instrument as one that resists paradigms of domination and scientific objectivity. Regina Schwartz argues that the would-be voyeur "cannot successfully possess the object of his sight because what he sees is at best a fabrication, an idealized image composed at an ideal point in a telescope, another fabrication." For Denise Albanese, the identification of "glass" as "telescope" obscures "a historical process . . . of sorting out the difference between . . . subject and object that is the work of an emergent scientific ideology." Amy Boesky reads Galileo's "glass" as holding in tension both the possibilities and the dangers of scientific certitude; the instrument presents a model of open-ended inquiry that Boesky describes as a form of "situated knowledge."[9]

In none of these readings is the "optic glass" a telescope, if by "telescope" we mean either the instrument that transparently reveals hard truths about the cosmos, or, to borrow Albanese's definition, "a neutral conduit for previously constituted visual phenomena to be examined with dispassion."[10] Rather, it is an instrument that participates in the active reconstruction of meaning amid the epistemological upheaval of the seventeenth century. I hope to further this discussion by explicating some of the specific differences between Galileo's "glass" and the telescope, detailing some of the points of connection between the instruments of Milton's poem and those developed by Galileo earlier in the century, and then moving into a discussion of the poem's complex epistemology, in which, as Herz argues, the telescope "enables [vision] precisely because it baffles it."[11]

GALILEO'S INSTRUMENTS

The instruments Galileo constructed and presented to audiences in 1610 and 1611 are distinguished from the telescope by nomenclature. In *The Starry Messenger* (1610) Galileo refers to his device as "organum," "instrumentum," and "perspicillum," while in his Italian correspondence of the period his most common name for it is "occhiale."[12] These terms do not specify how the device worked or what it did: "instrumentum" and "organum" designate simply a tool; "perspicillum" means something that is looked through; and "occhiale" indicates spectacles or eyeglasses. By contrast, the term "telescope" is fairly specific; it is a Greek neologism meaning, literally, "to see from afar."[13] It was proposed at the feast celebrating Galileo's induction into the Accademia dei Lincei in the spring of 1611, an occasion that has also been taken to mark the certification of his discoveries.[14] The adoption of the term "telescope" would thus seem to indicate that the scientific community was ready to accept "seeing from afar" as a fair description of what the instrument did, and to affirm the veracity of Galileo's vision. By the same token, the earlier multiplicity of competing terms suggests some uncertainty about what the instrument did and how it worked (and whether, indeed, it did work).

The mechanical problems with the early instruments would only have exacerbated audiences' doubts. The logician Jacob Christmann, for example, wrote in 1612 that upon turning a telescope toward Jupiter, " the body . . . was seen completely on fire, so that it appeared separated into three or four fiery balls, from which thinner hairs were spread in a downward direction, like the tail of a comet." Looking for Saturn's moons, he says, he saw through three different telescopes a single "long star," three "scintillations," and four "fiery balls," which he was unwilling to concede were planets.[15] Kepler commented that "to us Jupiter . . . appeared four-cornered. For one of the angular diameters was blue-green, and the other purple, while in the middle a flaxen body with a wonderful fulgor."[16]

There were many inferior instruments on the market during this period that might have produced such visual experiences, but even Galileo's own instruments, the best of their day, could produce problematic images. Their lenses contained air bubbles, marks, and pits, all of which would have introduced stray light into the tube and interfered with observations.[17] Spherical and chromatic aberrations produced hazy images irradiated with colored light, since light rays passing through a spherical lens do not focus at a single point on the optical axis, and because any curved piece of glass refracts the various colors of light to different focal points. The sources of these difficulties were accurately theorized later in the seventeenth century—spherical aberration by Descartes in 1637 and chromatic aberration by Newton in 1671—and it was rightly surmised that mirrors would be able to focus light refracted through a lens.[18] However, since Galileo was designing refractive instruments, not reflective ones, and since, in practice, lenses could only be ground as portions of spheres, he could not eliminate spherical and chromatic aberration altogether.

Galileo's solutions to these problems are instructive because they indicate the extent to which his instruments were the product of craftsmanship, trial and error in the workshop as opposed to theory.[19] To reduce spherical aberration, for example, he made longer instruments, and refractive telescopes grew to even greater lengths after his death. This remedied one problem but exacerbated another; Galileo's instruments had small fields of vision, and it could be difficult to locate and hold an object in the sky with them, particularly the hand-held instruments. To address chromatic aberration he hit on the idea of fitting the objective lenses of his instruments with cardboard rings; since the colored fringes were worse at the outer edges of the lenses, these "stops" reduced the colored halos and thereby clarified the images. Stillman Drake has suggested that Galileo arrived at this solution by analogy with his own eye trouble; it seems that from an early age he saw colored rings around bright objects, and had learned that looking through a small aperture such as a clenched fist would eliminate them and improve his vision.[20] Be that as it may, Galileo clarified and sharpened the images his instruments generated, paradoxically, by partially blocking their lenses.

Even after Galileo had managed to produce clear images of reasonably sharp definition, there were still obstacles. Some viewers refused to look through the instrument at all. Some who looked through it would not credit what they saw; Martin Horky, who had seen Galileo demonstrate his instrument at Bologna in April 1610, wrote to his mentor Magini that it performed well on earth, but failed when turned toward the heavens.[21] The Jesuit mathematician Clavius is reported to have said that in order for Galileo to see the things he claimed he saw with the instrument, he would have had to put those things inside it.[22]

These men may seem refractory to us; they appear to be denying the evidence of their eyes. It is important to remember, however, that the telescope was not just a new instrument but a new *kind* of instrument as well. It was the first instrument of experimental philosophy; the microscope and the air pump would follow later. As a group, these were termed "philosophical" instruments because their application was primarily theoretical rather than practical. The designation also distinguished them from the "mathematical" instruments that had long been in use in natural philosophy. While mathematical instruments quantified the readily observable phenomena of nature (measuring distance, weight, and angle, for example), philosophical instruments created new perceptual objects.[23] There was no precedent in natural philosophy for dealing with these phenomena; moreover, since they were distortions of nature—either magnifications of objects of the sort produced by the telescope or "unnatural" conditions such as the vacuum—their status was uncertain at best.

This was in part because the method by which they should be ordered and interpreted was not yet fully developed, and also because the assumptions about visual images under which early viewers operated differed markedly from the ones we make today about telescopic images. Up until the seventeenth century there was a long-standing tradition of skepticism about the reliability of vision under certain conditions, a tradition in which images created by lenses were particularly suspect. Galileo's instruments were widely thought to deceive when pointed at the sky because, in Aristotle's account of nature, substances of the lower, earthly sphere differed in their composition and behavior from substances of the heavenly spheres. Under the abnormal conditions imposed by the telescope, the senses were thought to give abnormal responses. Thus most medieval philosophers denied "real" existence to optical images; reflections in mirrors and refractions through glass were understood to be illusions, since by definition an optical illusion was an image out of its proper "place." This is why even the relative clarity of the images produced by Galileo's instruments was not, in and of itself, proof of their veracity, because expectations and assumptions could discredit even the clearest of images.

The images produced by Galileo's first instruments, then, were not self-evidently true. Viewers had to be persuaded of their veracity, and this was done by rhetorical and pedagogical means rather than through theoretical demonstration or improvements in the technology.[24] Significantly, Galileo does not argue in *The Starry Messenger* that the instrument works because it reveals "reality" transparently. He suggests that his labors with the instrument have produced a new vision, a corrected view of the night sky. Galileo presents the telescope as a register of the material and intellectual work by means of which his view was changed for the better. Like the "optic glass" of *Paradise Lost,* it is an emblem of human artistry and agency in the production of knowledge.

Galileo's account of constructing his instruments in *The Starry Messenger* emphasizes the general difficulty of constructing instruments of good quality and suggests the pains he himself took to make them. Early in the treatise, before describing his astronomical observations, he tells how he came to make his first instrument.

About ten months ago a report reached my ears that a certain Fleming had constructed a spyglass by means of which visible objects, though very distant from the eye of the observer, were distinctly seen as if nearby. Of this truly remarkable effect several experiences were related, to which some persons gave credence while others denied them. A few days later the report was confirmed to me in a letter from a noble Frenchman at Paris, Jacques Badovere, which caused me to apply myself wholeheartedly to inquire into the means by which I might arrive at the invention of a similar instrument. This I did shortly afterwards, my basis being the theory of refraction.[25]

He freely admits that the original idea was not his, but claims essentially to have reconstructed the instrument from scratch. The challenges here were not just theoretical, as he asserts, but mechanical and material. Although he does not discuss the difficulties of finding materials and producing good lenses, these challenges were significant. Galileo obtained relatively good glass from a source in Florence, but recent examination of his instruments shows that even his lenses were not without flaws, some attributable to raw materials, others to the processes of grinding and polishing.[26] While lenses for reading glasses had been available for some years, the range of strengths available was not adequate to meet the needs of the telescopes; therefore Galileo taught himself how to grind and polish his own lenses.[27] In the early seventeenth century most of the work of lens production was still done by hand. A blank disk of glass was first ground to the specified curvature with abrasives against a metal disk, a convex or a concave partial hemisphere; the operator would press the glass down hard against the tool to shape it to the tool's curvature. Finer abrasives were used in the polishing process, with heavy pressure still applied by hand, and finally the lens was buffed on a lathe worked by a treadle. The process was lengthy and exacting, and the smallest of mistakes could produce an unusable lens.[28]

Galileo suggests in the passage quoted above that he first reasoned out the theoretical principles of the instrument and then constructed it. Historians, however, have found that he designed his instrument through trial and error, working as much as a craftsman as a theoretician or scientist, a reading of the instrument that presents it as a sign for the halting and circuitous process of producing knowledge.[29] Galileo himself declines to give specific details of material production in *The Starry Messenger;* however, he does offer an account that makes a significant point of the labor involved. He points out that he made three instruments, the first "a tube of lead . . . fitted [with] two glass lenses," through which he noted the magnification of objects, his second, "more accurate, which represented objects as enlarged more than sixty times," and then a third: "Finally, sparing neither labor nor expense, I succeeded in constructing for myself so excellent an instrument that objects seen by means of it appeared nearly one thousand times larger and over thirty times closer than when regarded with our natural vision" (*Discoveries and Opinions,* 29). In this account, the enlargement of the images and the excellence of his instrument are direct results of "labor [and] expense." He adumbrates these difficulties of construction in an indirect fashion, by issuing a warning of the rigorous standards of clarity and brightness that must be met if an instrument is to work properly.

Here it is appropriate to convey certain cautions to all who intend to undertake observations of this sort, for in the first place it is necessary to prepare quite a perfect telescope, which will show all objects bright, distinct, and free from any haziness, while magnifying them at least four hundred times and thus showing them twenty times closer. Unless the instrument is of this kind it will be vain to attempt to observe all the things which I have seen in the heavens, and which will presently be set forth. (*Discoveries and Opinions,* 30)

The Starry Messenger thus gives us a partial picture of Galileo in action, showing readers the pains he took to achieve clear vision, laying the groundwork for the rhetorical case he will make for the validity of the instruments and his observations with them. In the subsequent presentation of the heavenly phenomena, he offers an additional argument. The instrument is to be trusted because it is an instrument like the eye—with one crucial difference. Whereas the naked eye is subject to certain illusions when it looks at the heavens, the astronomical instrument corrects these distortions. It does so by means of its own counterdistortions, corrective illusions of the sky's objects.

This paradox emerges when Galileo addresses the question of why the instrument does not seem to enlarge the bodies of the stars in the same proportion as it enlarges the moon, a problem that seemed to demonstrate the instrument's inconsistent operation. His answer is that to the unaided eye the stars seem larger than they are because they are "crowned" with radiance that the instrument removes.

When stars are viewed by means of unaided natural vision, they present themselves to us not as of their simple (and, so to speak, their physical) size, but as irradiated by a certain fulgor and as fringed with sparkling rays, especially when the night is far advanced. From this they appear larger than they would if stripped of those adventitious hairs of light, for the angle at the eye is determined not by the primary body of the star but by the brightness which extends so widely around it. . . . Therefore the stars are seen crowned among shadows, while daylight is able to remove their headgear; and not daylight alone, but any thin cloud that interposes itself between a star and the eye of the observer. The same effect is produced by black veils or colored glasses, through the interposition of which obstacles the stars are abandoned by their surrounding brilliance. A telescope similarly accomplishes the same result. (*Discoveries and Opinions*, 46)

The suggestion here is that the stellar rays seen by the naked eye do not belong to the star itself but are accidental by-products of visual circumstances; thus the star the viewer sees without the instrument is a false image, insofar as its size is concerned, and whatever device eliminates those rays generates a truer image of its size and shape.

Galileo is careful not to suggest that the star seen with his instrument is the "real" star; whatever the eye sees, with or without the instrument, is an image, since the stars themselves only offer "appearances." In fact, the terms of his explanation strongly imply that the image produced by the telescope is also an illusion, since the clouds, black veils, and colored glasses with which he associates it were also commonly linked with the production of illusions. On this point, it is worth noting the similarities between Galileo's account and that of the skeptic Magini: "since colored glasses showed three suns in an eclipse, doubtless Galileo's glasses had similarly deceived him."[30] Here Galileo is taking the old assumptions about lenses that deceive and standing them on their heads; truthful illusions correct for deceitful ones.

The Starry Messenger thus presents Galileo's instruments as a sign of the intellectual and mechanical labor that produces a more perfect vision of nature. The text (re)constructs the instrument before the reader is allowed to use it; it describes its lenses, their magnification, and their configurations, emphasizing the work involved in their production. This investment of labor permits the instruments to produce clear (hence, the author suggests, accurate) images of the heavenly bodies. In linking them with instruments of illusion, moreover, Galileo is acknowledging that they mediate between eye and object to change what is seen. Like the cardboard rings Galileo fashioned for his lenses, like a veil or a cloud, or like the clenched fist through which he peered at bright lights, the instrument produces truer images of objects precisely because it intervenes between the object and the eye looking at it, changing vision, producing new and more perfect images.

THE INSTRUMENTS OF *PARADISE LOST*

The poem's instruments resemble Galileo's early ones in at least two respects. First, as Denise Albanese has pointed out, the word "telescope" never appears in the body of *Paradise Lost*. Milton calls the instrument an "optic glass," a "glass," and an "optic tube," but never a "telescope." "Telescope" appears in the editors' glosses as a translation of the poem's other designations for the instrument. Since the term "telescope" had decisively supplanted all other designations in both popular and scientific discourse by the time *Paradise Lost* was published, Milton's choices of nomenclature may reasonably be interpreted as deliberately archaic. Moreover, in offering such a variety of terms, the poet evokes some of the early uncertainty about how (and whether) the instrument worked, uncertainty that is elided when all of the locutions are interpreted as telescopes.[31]

Secondly, the poem consistently yokes Galileo with the instruments; the "Optic Glass" is wielded by the "*Tuscan* Artist," the "optic tube" is the tool of the "Astronomer," and the "Glass of *Galileo*" scans the moon. This conjunction not only qualifies them as *early* astronomical instruments (which belonged exclusively to Galileo), but also indicates that they do not stand on their own as tools. There is something prosthetic about it, as Denise Albanese has observed, a sense in which Galileo is not altogether separable from his "glass."[32] When read in light of the early struggles to produce clear images, the repeated couplings of Galileo and instruments recall the work of constructing the instrument and winning legitimacy for it. They also recall the pedagogical function Galileo performed. As Albert Van Helden has argued, early viewers had to be taught how to see through a telescope, in part because the placement of the image was not straightforward.[33] Galileo was "instrumental" in teaching his audience how to see through his instruments and convincing them to validate what they saw. Whereas Albanese reads the instrument as prosthetic to Galileo, and thus a sign for the fallible subject, I want to reverse the order and emphasis of this coupling, and read Galileo himself as prosthetic to his "glass," a supplement whose rhetorical and pedagogical activities are crucial to the instrument's production of knowledge. Galileo is part of what Latour would call the instrument's *retinue*, a figure whose presence in *Paradise Lost* signifies that the instrument does not yet work reliably because it is, in a sense, still under construction.[34]

To claim such correlations between Milton's and Galileo's instruments does not imply that the former can be reduced to the latter. Although the difficulties that circumscribed early observations can help us see how Milton is using the "optic glass," such problems do not, by themselves, suffice to explain the poem's instruments. In the following examination, we shall see that at times the view of the sky seems to be occluded by Galileo's labors with the instrument, and that the poem's representations of the instrument are sometimes accompanied by disorientations and illusions that recall those produced by Galileo's own instruments. These passages should not be read in isolation from one another, however, but as part of an epistemology (albeit a precarious one) that unfolds over the course of the narrative. The doubts that shadow the instrument are most in evidence in Books One and Three, where, as has often been remarked, the instrument is associated with Satan's journey out of hell, and where vision is circumscribed by disruptions of scale, the possibility of illusion, and questions about methodology. In Book Five, however, where telescopically enhanced vision is linked with the angel Raphael, the aforementioned limitations and disorientations are reorganized and developed into a workable vision, a risky and limited but nonetheless powerful method of coming to understand the world.

In the passage in which Galileo and his instrument first appear in *Paradise Lost*, the astronomer's activities are highlighted in ways that recall the historical Galileo's methodological, rhetorical, and pedagogical labors with the instrument, and suggest that these labors may interfere with or distort vision. Early in Book One the viewer's gaze is trained on Satan and follows him as he moves through the burning lake of hell; Galileo and his instrument are introduced in the simile that compares Satan's shield with the moon.

> He scarce had ceas't when the superiour Fiend
> Was moving toward the shoar; his ponderous shield
> Ethereal temper, massy, large and round,
> Behind him cast; the broad circumference
> Hung on his shoulders like the Moon, whose Orb
> Through Optic Glass the *Tuscan* Artist views
> At Ev'ning from the top of *Fesole*,
> Or in *Valdarno*, to descry new Lands,
> Rivers or Mountains in her spotty Globe.   (1.283–91)

Here we have three suggestions about the ways in which the astronomer actively participates in the production of vision. First, the purposive infinitive "to descry" suggests that the "Tuscan Artist" has already conceived such features in the moon and seeks to confirm their existence with the telescope. "To descry" describes a scientific methodology that is not purely inductive, since it is inflected by the "art" of imagination; thus Donald Friedman has interpreted this passage as revealing Milton's doubts about Galileo's methodology.[35]

Second, the allusion to the "spotty Globe" of the moon—and, indeed, the passage as a whole—calls to mind the particular historical circumstances of Galileo's first application of the telescope to the heavens. It recalls Galileo's announcement in *The Starry Messenger* of spots in the moon that were smaller and more numerous than the "large" or "ancient" spots that had always been visible with the naked eye. These smaller spots led him to conclude that the moon's surface was "uneven, rough, and full of cavities and prominences, being not unlike the face of the earth, relieved by chains of mountains and deep valleys" (*Discoveries and Opinions*, 31), a judgment that proved controversial because it directly contradicted the Aristotelian doctrine of the immutable perfection of the heavens and its bodies, and because it was seen as an imagined projection of what Galileo hoped to see.

Third, the periphrasis "Tuscan Artist" suggests that Galileo's activity is at least in part inventive; the term has both positive and negative connotations. The term "artist," as has often been noted, was used during this period to describe someone who was skilled or knowledgeable in a general way, such as a master of the liberal arts, or a skilled practitioner, as opposed to a theorist; it also signified one who practiced a fine art such as poetry.[36] In applying the word "artist" to Galileo, Milton links the work of the scientist with that of the poet, emphasizing the importance of the imagination—of expectation, hypothesis, and the inductive leap—in scientific endeavor. Within its immediate context, the epithet at once designates the maker of the "optic glass" and intimates that he may be the author of its images as well. At the very least, it undermines any idea that the viewer who looks at the moon through the "optic glass" receives images passively by interposing the self-consciously designated efforts to see—the Tuscan Artist's "artistry"—between the eye and the moon. At most, it represents a criticism of this "artistic" imposition, a suggestion that the vision thus produced may be tainted.

This passage also points to certain visual difficulties associated with Galileo's earliest instruments, namely, their disruption of a celestial body's accustomed visual context, its scale and proportion with respect to other objects, and the accompanying disorientation of the viewer. The moon alone fills the instrument's field of vision; it is not seen in relation to any other body in the sky. We are told that Galileo looks at the moon "from the top of Fesole / Or in Valdarno" (1.289–90), but we have no sense of the moon's own place, the star-filled night sky that frames it. Indeed, the moon image in this passage is deracinated from the sky altogether and transported to hell, as it were, by means of the epic simile. The sense of displacement is strong, and has generally been read as an effect of the "conspicuous irrelevance" that characterizes epic simile; however, that sense of displacement also has a certain resonance with the visual displacements produced by the early telescope. The historical instrument had performed a prior deracination, showing the moon out of its "proper place," imposing new limitations on the astronomical observer's vision, preventing him from seeing bodies in relation to the stars and the sky.

The effect is disorienting when the telescope both isolates celestial objects from their visual contexts and enlarges them. The moon seen through Galileo's "optic glass" is deracinated not only because it is cut off from the rest of the sky, but also because the level of visual detail disrupts the viewer's sense of distance and scale; to be able to "descry new Lands, / Rivers or Mountains" in the moon, one should be much closer to it than Valdarno. In this sense, the moon's displacement to hell reflects a radical disorientation of the viewer, a disruption that is also reflected in the shifting size/scale of Satan in the same passage. The comparison between the Archfiend's shield and the moon viewed through the telescope tacitly evokes both the moon seen from earth with the naked eye, the size of a thumbnail in the sky, and the moon in its real dimensions, an immense (and perhaps earthlike) body. However, shifts in scale prove more problematic in the comparison that immediately follows:

> His Spear, to equal which the tallest Pine
> Hewn on *Norwegian* hills, to be the Mast
> Of some great Ammiral, were but a wand,
> He walkt with to support uneasie steps
> Over the burning Marl. (1.292–96)

This is a deceptive passage, as Stanley Fish has noted, one that reverses itself, surprises the reader, and engenders a sense of distrust in the powers of the senses and the intellect.[37] The syntax of the passage encourages the reader to assume at first that Satan's spear is the size of a ship's mast; but when we reach the end of the clause, we find that this tree is a mere "wand" in comparison with Satan's spear. Having imagined Satan to the scale of the pine tree in the first line, we are confronted with the need to revise the proportions; his spear is not the size of the tree, but many times larger than that. We are momentarily disoriented until we recalibrate the proportions between Satan and our world.

In this shifting of apparent size, the passage looks ahead to the end of

Book One, in which the demons, having built their citadel, Pandaemonium, throng the entrance and seem to shrink.

> Behold a wonder! they but now who seemd
> In bigness to surpass Earths Giant Sons
> Now less than smallest Dwarfs, in narrow room
> Throng numberless, like that Pigmean Race
> Beyond the *Indian* Mount, or Faerie Elves,
> Whose midnight Revels, by a Forrest side
> Or Fountain some belated Peasant sees,
> Or dreams he sees, while over-head the Moon
> Sits Arbitress, and neerer to the Earth
> Wheels her pale course.   (1.777–86)

Previously, the demons seemed bigger than earth's giants; now they are smaller than dwarves, more like pygmies or elves. The association between the demons and "faery elves," creatures of illusion, bewitching, and the moon, suggests that their reduction in size is only an apparent one. Does the peasant really see these tiny creatures, or does he only dream that he sees them? Are Satan and his crew larger than giants, or smaller than dwarves? The passage both echoes the reader's earlier disorientation and disrupts the previous determination of Satan's scale. It seems as if no true determination can be made, that Satan has apparent but not absolute stature. It may be, similarly, that the "optic glass" cannot reveal objects as they are in themselves, but only produce appearances, none of which is to be trusted. Certainly the disorientations associated with the instrument in the foregoing passages suggest a strong skepticism about the conditions and possibilities of human knowledge.

It is worth recalling at this point that the setting of these disorientations is hell, where little is as it seems, least of all Satan; determinations of his size and his moral stature shift throughout Book One. We are subsequently offered other points of view from which to regard him, and although clear and certain vision is never easily achieved, the possibility of a limited form of understanding begins to emerge. Indeed, in Book Three we shall see that the very form of this knowledge is limitation, and significantly, it is described by means of Galileo's instrument.

Throughout the poem the difficulties of seeking enlightenment are represented in a variety of circuitous ways that have often been termed "baroque"; the narrative is itself notorious for its wanderings, ruptures, and changes in perspective and direction, while the poem's diction and syntax are indirect, even occlusive.[38] Book Three foregrounds these problems most poignantly in the narrator's lament for his blindness and his hymn to the light that "[r]evists'st not these eyes, that rowl in vain / To find thy piercing ray, and find no dawn" (3.23–24). Milton represents the quest for enlightenment as an ascent, "hard and rare," from "the *Stygian* pool" of hell into the realm of light.

The difficulties and dangers of searching for enlightenment are further underscored by Book Three's treatment of the "optic tube." The instrument spies Satan near the end of his journey out of hell, as he lands on the sun.

> There lands the Fiend, a spot like which perhaps
> Astronomer in the Sun's lucent Orb
> Through his glaz'd Optic Tube yet never saw. (3.588–90)

Milton generally uses the word "spot" to mean a moral stain or blemish, or a site ("spot") of temptation.[39] Moreover, the association of Satan with "spots" in both this passage and the passage from Book One (in which his shield is compared to the moon's "spotty" globe) reinforces the term's pejorative connotations and suggests that there are moral dangers to the search for knowledge. The temptation and fall of Eve and Adam provide evidence that the dangers associated with the quest for knowledge are very real, dangers that Milton elaborates prior to Book Ten.

Coupled with these moral dangers of such a search are the practical difficulties of achieving a clear and certain vision, of which Milton reminds readers by referring to Galileo's work on sunspots, carried out with the help of the instrument in 1611 and 1612. The allusion to "spots" may be a glancing reference to the visual and epistemological obscurities that plagued the earliest instruments, but by 1613, when Galileo published his *Letters on Sunspots*, the grounds of the debate had shifted. Opponents of Galileo no longer questioned the veracity of the instrument's images; rather, they debated the proper interpretation of the spots the telescope revealed. Galileo interpreted them as changes on the surface of the sun itself, a theory which, like his interpretation of the irregularities on the moon's surface, was controversial because it contradicted Aristotelian suppositions about the immutability of the heavens; others interpreted the spots as clouds or planets passing in front of the sun. Thus the passage emphasizes the difficulties of vision in large part by evoking Galileo's controversial labors to construct an interpretation of what was seen through the telescope.

Milton offers another example of the limitations that circumscribe the quest for knowledge when he refers to the instrument's restricted field of vision. As in Book One, the view through the "optic tube" is local and constricted, giving readers the sun and its "spots," with no broad view of sky to augment the image. This limitation seems notably evident when contrasted with the clear, wide-ranging, and penetrating vision the sun affords Satan in a passage that follows close on the heels of the other:

> Here matter new to gaze the Devil met
> Undazl'd, farr and wide his eye commands,
> For sight no obstacle found here, nor shade,
> But all Sun-shine, as when his Beams at Noon
> Culminate from th' *Aequator,* as they now
> Shot upward still direct, whence no way round
> Shadow from body opaque can fall, and th'Air,
> No where so cleer, sharp'n'd his visual ray
> To objects distant farr.   (3.613–21)

While the astronomer has the sun in his narrow field of view and sees with a vision that may be obscured by "spots," Satan, his "visual ray" sharpened by the sun's light, sees "farr and wide," without impediment or shadow. The contrasting visual spaces suggest the depth and range that are lacking in human vision.

However, the difficulties are also charged with possibility, as Boesky argues when she reads Galileo's "spots" as both "sites of certainty, courage, and genius, and contradictorily blind spots, markers for the limits and dangers of scopic power."[40] The simile comparing Satan to a sunspot not only conveys warnings, but holds out hope as well. When we compare this passage with the previous one from Book One we notice that vision is not uprooted in the same fashion here as when the moon's "spotty Globe" is brought to hell. The sun is left in the sky, the context in which the eye is accustomed to see it. Although the "optic tube" itself does not give a broad view of the day sky, the preceding description of Satan's trajectory supplies this, and it is therefore possible to say that the sun seen through the "optic tube" is at least in the right place. Furthermore, the sun on which Satan lands is the same body against which the astronomer sees spots; there are no questions raised here about enlargement or proportion as there are in the previous passage from Book One. The limits on vision in Book Three seem not to be accompanied by the same disorientations with which similar limits are associated in Book One.

Not only does disorientation fail to attend these circumscriptions of vision, but these limits themselves constitute focus and help locate Satan in the midst of an uncertain trajectory.

> Thither his course he bends
> Through the calm Firmament; but up or down
> By centre, or eccentric, hard to tell,
> Or Longitude.   (3.573–76)

It is not clear whether he is rising, falling, or moving laterally, but the instrument fixes on Satan at one point in his flight, as he lands on the sun. While the instrument offers only limited visual orientation, its ability to locate Satan contrasts markedly with the fundamental uncertainties of the character's wandering path. To "spot" and recognize Satan is beyond even the angel Uriel, who sees Satan but mistakes him for a cherub, and aligns the instrument with Godly vision.

> For neither Man nor Angel can discern
> Hypocrisie, the only evil that walks
> Invisible, except to God alone,
> By his permissive will, through Heav'n and Earth:
> And oft though wisdom wake, suspicion sleeps
> At wisdoms Gate, and to simplicitie
> Resigns her charge, while goodness thinks no ill
> Where no ill seems: Which now for once beguil'd
> *Uriel*, though Regent of the Sun, and held
> The sharpest sighted Spirit of all in Heav'n.   (3.682–91)

Thus in Book Three the "optic tube," like the narrator's blindness, signifies a form of circumscription that can lead to knowledge. Denied his eyesight, "cut off" and "shut out" from the works of nature and society of men, the narrator prays for an inward light that will illuminate "things invisible to mortal sight" (3.55), a vision more limited but also more penetrating than physical sight. The "optic tube" helps to describe a vision that is limited to one object at a time, but which is, in this respect, able to cut through disorientation, confusion, and deception to achieve a limited understanding.

Clearly this one "spot" of certainty alone cannot obviate the many hazards of the search for knowledge, which only seem to proliferate with the approach of the temptation and Fall. These dangers are consistently figured in terms of stargazing, as temptations of vision and celestial aspiration. In the guise of serpent, Satan makes his approach to Eve in Book Nine by comparing her to a star in the firmament, admired by all creation: "Thee all things living gaze on, all things thine / By gift, and thy Celestial Beauty adore / With ravishment beheld" (9.539–41). As a heavenly creature, she should be in the heavens where all can see her "who shouldst be seen / A Goddess among Gods, ador'd and serv'd / by Angels numberless, thy daily Train" (9.546–48) rather than enclosed in a garden among beasts. This line of argument recalls Eve's dream in Book Five, where Satan's voice comes to her and bids her wake:

>   now reignes
> Full Orb'd the Moon, and with more pleasing light
> Shadowie sets off the face of things; in vain,
> If none regard; Heav'n wakes with all his eyes,

> Whom to behold but thee, Natures desire,
> In whose sight all things joy, with ravishment
> Attracted by thy beauty still to gaze.   (5.41–47)

He first exhorts Eve to open her eyes to the pleasures of the night sky, and then tempts her to see herself as the object of the stars' gaze.[41] He attempts to conflate her delight in the celestial bodies with the self-indulgent pleasure of imagining that they return her admiration. Eve's dream of the temptation to godhead culminates with her impersonation of a celestial body, when, upon eating the fruit, she ascends into the sky with her guide, "and underneath beheld / The Earth outstretcht immense, a prospect wide / And various" (5.87–89). Thus, in the temptation of Eve, the pleasures of looking at the stars gives way to the desire to *be* a celestial body, "a Goddess among Gods."

These images of temptation reinforce the suggestion, first introduced by the coupling of Satan and the instruments in Books One and Three, that the dangers associated with Galileo's instruments in *Paradise Lost* are moral as well as epistemological, that stargazing might tempt a viewer to aspire to godhead. Moreover, as we shall see, the "glass of Galileo" in Book Five seems to produce an effect similar to Eve's ascent into the sky, and her reference to the "prospect" such ascent affords echoes one of the names for the telescope in its early days: a "prospect glass." However, these images are not exclusively used to describe the illicit quest for knowledge; Raphael uses them in Book Five to recount the possibility of Adam and Eve's proper and licensed ascent to God. He describes a stratification of "one first matter all," an apportioning of substances, "Each in thir several active Sphears assign'd" according to the degree of their refinement, "Till body up to spirit work, in bounds / Propor-tion'd to each kind" (5.472, 477–79). Raphael suggests to Adam that he and Eve might one day achieve a greater refinement into spirit and ascend into the heavens.

> perhaps
> Your bodies may at last turn all to Spirit,
> Improv'd by tract of time, and wing'd ascend
> Ethereal, as wee, or may at choice
> Here or in Heav'nly Paradises dwell;
> If ye be found obedient, and retain
> Unalterably firm his love entire
> Whose progenie you are.   (5.496–503)

The implications of this distinction for Adam and Eve seem clear enough. If they obey God they may, in time, ascend like celestial bodies into the heavens, but if they eat of the forbidden fruit in the hopes of achieving such an ascent they will have sinned in aspiring to an illicit ascent. The significance of the search for knowledge in a postlapsarian world is less clear. Raphael's description of the process suggests that the impulse to improve spirit and intellect is not morally wrong, and yet the examples of Eve's dream (and her subsequent temptation and fall) seem to suggest that it is dangerous. The "glass of Galileo," introduced as Raphael stands poised at the gates of heaven, ready to undertake his errand to earth, offers some clarification on this point. Poised midway between Eve's dream and the hope offered by Raphael, the instrument points in both directions, to the hazards and the possibilities of knowledge.

The features of enhanced human vision evoked in Books One and Three —the instrument's limiting of visual field and the changes (or apparent changes) such a limitation makes in the observer's vantage point and the object's size—are reorganized in Book Five to describe a single visual axis, from Raphael's eye at the gates of heaven to the Garden of Eden on earth. The shifting sense of scale that is experienced as disorientation in this passage similarly (and paradoxically) produces a workable vision, a limited but powerful understanding that recalls Galileo's suggestion in *The Starry Messenger* that occlusions can rectify vision.

> From hence, no cloud, or, to obstruct his sight,
> Starr interpos'd, however small he sees,
> Not unconform to other shining Globes,
> Earth and the Gard'n of God, with Cedars crownd
> Above all Hills. As when by night the Glass
> Of *Galileo*, less assur'd, observes
> Imagind Lands and Regions in the Moon.   (5.257–63)

The simile that brings together Raphael and Galileo develops one of the instrument's key paradoxes, namely, that even when it is understood as bringing human vision closer to perfection, it works properly because it constitutes an "obstacle" to vision. As in the earlier passages, mechanically aided vision is compared with unaided vision, obstructed with unobstructed vision, shallow and narrow vision with broad and deep vision. The angel's glance sweeps a vast distance very quickly, from the gates of heaven to the "shining globe" of earth, to the garden itself, and its cedar trees. In apparent contrast to this astonishing breadth and penetration of vision, Galileo's "glass" is trained unswervingly on the moon, that body filling the instrument's field of vision. The visual effect is narrow and flat compared to the rich depth of the angel's whole and complete vision; once again, circumscription of the field of vision seems to constitute a judgment on the instrument's limitations. Moreover, Raphael's view of the earth from heaven is clear, and expressly lacks impediment ("no cloud, or, to obstruct his sight, / Star interpos'd"), while Galileo's observations are mediated by the instrument that strictly contrastive readings would interpret as the kind of "obstruction" the angel's view lacks, a dysfunctional instrument that only gets in the way of clear vision.

Yet the simile that structures this passage also suggests that the instrument produces a vision comparable to Raphael's. When read as prosthetic to the observer's body, the "glass of Galileo" approaches angelic sight by augmenting fallible human vision. However, when Galileo himself is read as prosthetic to the "glass," the instrument approximates Raphael's vision precisely by virtue of its "obstructive" qualities, that is, through the astronomer's attempts to construct a new vision of the sky. As we have seen, Galileo himself makes a virtue out of his instrument's self-evident mediation; in the account in *The Starry Messenger*, it is precisely because the instrument, by interposing his labors between the eye and a star in the sky, can strip away the accidental rays that make that star appear larger than it really is to the unaided eye. In a similar fashion, the "glass of Galileo" may be read as facilitating vision by obstructing it. In this case, the simile that juxtaposes it with Raphael's vision does not simply constitute a judgment that Galileo's vision was poorer than the angel's, but also points to a distinction between the ways in which vision *works* for each of them: what would obstruct the view of a celestial being are the very mechanisms of vision for the human observer.

Nevertheless, a crucial difference lies at the heart of this similarity. Raphael does not see these things as a human being would from such a vantage point, that is, as diminishing in size as they "recede" into the distance; rather, he sees them as simultaneously near and far. In this distinction we see the earlier disorientations of scale and proportion reinforced and elaborated. The viewer orders the objects by putting them into perspectival relationship with one another, but the angel does not. Raphael sees the earth at a distance, "however small," but almost at the same time spies the garden, and even the garden's cedar trees, as if the distant earth were suddenly close. For readers tracking his gaze, the proportions are skewed. The effect has been compared to the flatness of medieval painting, deficient in perspective, but it is also something like looking through a camera with a "zoom" lens; what was formerly small and far away is now large and near, and the viewer has the disorienting sense of having been instantaneously carried over a great distance.[42] Clearly the problem lies not with Raphael's gaze itself, which encompasses the earth in its distance and proximity simultaneously, but with human attempts to comprehend that gaze. The instrument offers a series of flat pictures of near and far objects, juxtaposed to create jagged "cuts" in the visual experience of space; the small and distant earth sits next to the close and detailed earth. The distance between observer and object is suddenly collapsed when the observer looks through the instrument; when the observer drops the instrument again that distance reasserts itself. A suggestion of depth can be produced by this juxtaposition of images, but the instrument cannot by itself offer any continuity between the different depths of focus or planes of space. Read as an imperfect analogue for Raphael's vision, the telescope produces disorientation in the form of an absence of scale, a series of objects that are out of all proper proportion to one another, the large and detailed set next to the small and indistinct. This sudden, almost magical visual transformation an object undergoes when it is seen through the instrument signifies that the instrument does not work, that its illusions deceive, and that it cannot even approximate the angelic visual experience. The intervening objects that would orient a human observer become obstacles when that observer tries to inhabit an angelic point of view.

Significantly, this confusion is not absolute; it happens only when the observer tries to overleap the requisite "obstacles" to human understanding. The instrument can be read as one that works, but only by renouncing aspirations to the objective "God's eye" view that encompasses all objects, near and far, at a single glance. It does not work by helping the viewer transcend physical limitations of time and place; rather, its functioning depends on the acknowledgment that, as Katherine Hayles has observed, "Instruments extend and refine human perceptions, but they do not escape the assumptions encoded within the human sensorium."[43] When the observer cedes the necessity of mediation and of situation, of objects and instruments that intervene and structure perception, and of being located in a particular "spot," the disorienting juxtapositions that attend efforts to see like an angel are neutralized, and the penetration of Galileo's gaze reads as a smooth progression.

The many complications of "telescopic" vision in *Paradise Lost* remind readers of what Galileo and his first audiences understood, that the instrument is no apparatus of godlike vision across distance, but one that embodies the difficult work of seeing and knowing, the material, pedagogical, and rhetorical craftsmanship without which knowledge is impossible. The instrument is hedged about with dangers, with possibilities of misuse; it may tempt the viewer either to despair of ever knowing the world, or to overreach proudly in the effort to grasp it. The confusion it produces in the observer's judgment seems to indicate a hopelessly limited, even solipsistic vision, while its similarities with angelic or godlike vision tempt the viewer to leap over these difficulties. Although it provides no easy access to truths about the world, it is not for this reason a faulty telescope; its occlusions are not given as reasons to shun the instrument, to refuse to look through it, or to reject scientific endeavor. Rather, they are offered as a challenge to the reader to accept limited perspective and confusion as necessary conditions of the search for knowledge, and to make of them something useful.

Le Moyne College

NOTES

1. *The Complete Prose Works of John Milton*, 8 vols., ed. Don M. Wolfe et al. (New Haven, 1953–1982), 2:538. Neil Harris, "Galileo as Symbol: The 'Tuscan Artist' in *Paradise Lost*," *Annali dell' Istituto e museo di storia della scienza di Firenze* 10 (1985): 3–29, summarizes the controversy over this visit, concluding that it probably did take place. See also *Complete Prose Works*, 2:538 n. 180 for a summary of earlier critical debate on this point.

2. Bruno Latour, *Science in Action: How to Follow Scientists and Engineers through Society* (Cambridge, 1987), 69.

3. As Latour uses it, the term "black box" signifies a complex machine about which one only knows input and output; see ibid., 2–3.

4. *OED*, citation 2.a., s.v. "instrument, *n.*"; available at http://dictionary.oed.com.

5. For sociological readings of scientific instruments, see Latour, *Science in Action*, 67–69; Steven Shapin and Simon Shaffer, *Leviathan and the Air Pump: Hobbes, Boyle, and the Experimental Life* (Princeton, NJ, 1985), 36–38; and Thomas Hankins and Robert Silverman, *Instruments and the Imagination* (Princeton, NJ, 1995), 3–13.

6. See Marjorie Hope Nicolson, *Science and Imagination* (Ithaca, NY, 1956). Galileo and his telescope offered a useful point of reference for twentieth-century scholars and critics who were interested in situating the poem within the broad intellectual and cultural networks of the period, a trend that culminated with the work of Nicolson. Other important works in this vein include E. N. S. Thompson, "A Forerunner of Milton," *Modern Language Notes* 32 (1917): 479–82; Grant McColley, "The Theory of a Plurality of Worlds as a Factor in Milton's Attitude toward the Copernican Hypothesis," *Modern Language Notes* 47 (1932): 319–25, and "The Astronomy of *Paradise Lost*," *Studies in Philology* 34 (1937): 209–47; and F. R. Johnson, *Astronomical Thought in Renaissance England* (Baltimore, 1937). After Nicolson, critical attention shifted to the poem's development of figures and ideas borrowed from cosmology. See Douglas Bush, *Science and English Poetry* (New York, 1950); E. M. W. Tillyard, *Studies in Milton* (London, 1951); Kester Svendsen, *Milton and Science* (Cambridge, MA, 1956); Walter Clyde Curry, *Milton's Ontology, Cosmogony, and Physics* (Lexington, KY, 1957); and Lawrence Babb, *The Moral Cosmos of "Paradise Lost"* (Ann Arbor, 1970). Babb argues against Nicolson's claim that the instrument was a sign for Copernican cosmology (90).

7. See Roy Flannagan, "Art, Artists, Galileo, and Concordances," *Milton Quarterly* 20 (1986): 103–5; Harris, "Galileo as Symbol."

8. Linda Gregerson, "The Limbs of Truth: Milton's Use of Simile in *Paradise Lost*," in *Milton Studies* 14, ed. James D. Simmonds (Pittsburgh, 1980), 135; Judith Scherer Herz, "'For whom this glorious sight?': Dante, Milton, and the Galileo Question," in *Milton in Italy: Contexts, Images, Contradictions*, ed. M. A. DiCesare (Binghamton, NY, 1991), 156; Donald Friedman, "Galileo and the Art of Seeing," in DiCesare, *Milton in Italy*, 166.

9. Regina Schwartz, "Through the Optic Glass: Voyeurism and *Paradise Lost*," in *Desire in the Renaissance: Psychoanalysis and Literature*, ed. Valeria Finucci and Regina Schwartz (Princeton, NJ, 1994), 150; Denise Albanese, *New Science, New World* (Durham, NC, 1996),

128; Amy Boesky, "Milton, Galileo, and Sunspots: Optics and Certainty in *Paradise Lost*," in *Milton Studies* 34, ed. Albert C. Labriola (Pittsburgh, 1996), 40.

10. Albanese, *New Science, New World*, 130.

11. Herz, " 'For whom this glorious sight?' " 156.

12. Edward Rosen, *The Naming of the Telescope* (New York, 1947), 3–5.

13. *OED*, citation 1.a, s.v. "telescope, *n.*"; available at http://dictionary.oed.com.

14. Albert Van Helden, "Telescopes and Authority from Galileo to Cassini," *Osiris* 9 (1994): 13–14.

15. Jacob Christmann. *Nodus Gordius ex doctrina sinuum explicatus. Accedit appendix observationum quae per Radium artifiiosum habitae sunt circa Saturnum, Iovem & Lucidiores stellas affixas* (Heidelberg, 1612), 41–42; quoted in Albert Van Helden, "The Telescope in the Seventeenth Century," *Isis* 65 (1974): 52.

16. Johannes Kepler, *Gesammelte Werke* (Munich 1937–) 4:322. Quoted in Albert Van Helden, *Measuring the Universe: Dimensions from Aristarchus to Halley* (Chicago, 1985), 68.

17. Vincenzo Greco, Giuseppe Molesini, and Franco Quercioli, "The Telescopes of Galileo," *Applied Optics* 32 (1993): 6224.

18. On chromatic and spherical aberration, see R. J. Charleston and L. M. Angus-Butterworth, "Glass," in *A History of Technology*, ed. Charles Singer et al. (London, 1957), 3:232–33. On the accurate theorizing of their causes, see "The Telescope," in *The Galileo Project*; available at http://es.rice.edu//ES/humsoc/Galileo/Things/telescope.html #telescope.

19. While Galileo probably knew as much as anyone about optical theory at the time, the theory of image formation was not yet advanced enough for him to construct his instrument strictly from theory. See Stillman Drake, *Galileo Studies* (Ann Arbor, 1970), 140–42; and Van Helden, "The Telescope in the Seventeenth Century," 40.

20. Stillman Drake, *Galileo at Work: His Scientific Biography* (Chicago, 1978), 148.

21. *Le opere di Galileo Galilei*, edizione nazionale, 20 vols., ed. Antonio Favaro (Florence, 1899–1909; reprint, 1929–1939, 1964–1966), 10:342–43; cited in Van Helden, "Telescopes and Authority," 11.

22. See Harold I. Brown, "Galileo on the Telescope and the Eye," *Journal of the History of Ideas* 46 (1985): 489 n. 15. Brown cites a letter from Ludovico Cigoli to Galileo, Oct. 1, 1610, in *Opere* 10:442, but points out that Cigoli attributes the report to "a friend," who is commonly assumed to be Clavius.

23. On the distinctions between mathematical and philosophical instruments, see Hankins and Silverman, *Instruments and the Imagination*, 3. On the new scientific instruments' constitution of perceptual objects, see Shapin and Shaffer, *Leviathan and the Air Pump*, 36.

24. Van Helden, "Telescopes and Authority," 8–29.

25. *Discoveries and Opinions of Galileo*, trans. Stillman Drake (New York, 1957), 28–29; hereafter cited parenthetically by page number in the text.

26. For the results of optical tests on the Galilean telescopes housed at the Florentine Istituto e Museo di Storia della Scienza, see Greco, Molesini, and Quercioli, "The Telescopes of Galileo." On the sources of Galileo's glass, see Drake, *Galileo at Work*, 142. Scholars generally cite Venice as the leader in quality glass production during this period, but Vincent Ilardi argued some years ago that the work of Galileo helped make Florence a preeminent center for the production of fine optical glass. See Vincent Ilardi, "Eyeglasses and Concave Lenses in Fifteenth-Century Florence and Milan: New Documents," *Renaissance Quarterly* 29 (1976): 341–60.

27. See Drake, *Galileo Studies*, 154; and Albert Van Helden, preface to *Sidereus Nuncius*, by Galileo Galilei (Chicago, 1989), 6.

28. An account of these techniques may be found in Charleston and Angus-Butterworth, "Glass," 3:234–37.

29. Van Helden argues in "The Telescope in the Seventeenth Century" that the role of science and scientific theory in the development of the telescope in the seventeenth century has been overestimated; with the exception of Kepler's astronomical telescope, he says, "practice preceded theory" (49). Drake, *Galileo at Work,* emphasizes the role of craftsmanship and theory equally.

30. Quoted in Drake, *Galileo at Work,* 160.

31. Albanese, *New Science, New World,* 128, 129.

32. Ibid., 127.

33. Van Helden, "Telescopes and Authority," 11. On the problem of where to visually locate the telescopic image, see Vasco Ronchi, *Optics: The Science of Vision,* trans. Edward Rosen (New York, 1957), 188–89.

34. Latour, *Science in Action,* 250. "Facts and machines have no inertia of their own . . . like kings or armies they cannot travel without their retinues or impedimenta." I use the term as one that underscores the problematic workings of the instrument; for Latour, it functions rhetorically to enhance the authority of the instrument.

35. Donald Friedman, "Galileo and the Art of Seeing," 166.

36. See Neil Harris, "Galileo as Symbol"; Roy Flannagan, "Art, Artists, Galileo, and Concordances"; and Julia Walker, "Milton and Galileo: The Art of Intellectual Canonization," in *Milton Studies* 25, ed. James D. Simmonds (Pittsburgh, 1989), 109–23.

37. Stanley Fish, *Surprised by Sin: The Reader in "Paradise Lost"* (Berkeley and Los Angeles, 1967), 22–27.

38. Classic treatments of the significance of shifting point of view and narrative discontinuity in *Paradise Lost* to the poem's structure include E. M. W. Tillyard, *Milton* (London,1930); Rosalie Colie, "Time and Eternity: Paradox and Structure in *Paradise Lost,*" in *Milton: Modern Judgments,* ed. Alan Rudrum (London, 1968), 189–204; and Isabel MacCaffrey, "The Theme of *Paradise Lost,* Book III," in *New Essays on Paradise Lost,* ed. Thomas Kranidas (Berkeley and Los Angeles, 1971), 58–85. Reader-response critics have found pedagogical significance in Milton's multiple vantage points. See Dustin Griffin, "Milton's Hell: Perspectives on the Fallen," in *Milton Studies* 13, ed. James D. Simmonds (Pittsburgh, 1979), 237–54; John Mulder, "The Lyric Dimension of *Paradise Lost,*" in *Milton Studies* 23, ed. James D. Simmonds (Pittsburgh, 1987), 145–63; Stevie Davies, "*Paradise Lost:* The Maladaptive Eye," *Milton* (New York, 1991), 95–152; and Fish, *Surprised by Sin.*

39. Boesky, "Milton, Galileo, and Sunspots," 26–27.

40. Ibid., 40.

41. See the footnote to *Paradise Lost,* 5.44 ("Heav'n wakes with all his eyes") in *John Milton: Complete Poems and Major Prose,* ed. Merritt Hughes (New York, 1957), 303.

42. On the "medievalism" of Milton's perspectival representations, see C. S. Lewis, *The Discarded Image* (Cambridge, 1964), 101.

43. N. Katherine Hayles, "Constrained Constructivism: Locating Scientific Inquiry in the Theater of Representation," *New Orleans Review* 18 (1991): 77.

MILTON'S PANDORA: EVE, SIN, AND THE MYTHOGRAPHIC TRADITION

George F. Butler

"NOT SO DILIGENTLY IS CERES, according to the Fables, said to have sought her daughter Proserpina," says Milton to Charles Diodati, "as I seek for this idea of the beautiful, as if for some glorious image, throughout all the shapes and forms of things ('for many are the shapes of things divine'); day and night I search and follow its lead eagerly as if by certain clear traces" (YP 1:326–27).[1] This passage, written in a letter dated London, September 23, 1637, points to Milton's early, ongoing, and complex use of myth. In her seminal study of Milton's Eve, Diane Kelsey McColley cites the above text and explains: "He uses pagan myth not only to contrast with Christian truth but for the traces of truth in myth itself, for its implications for the regenerative process in human lives, and in order to involve the reader in the search for the remnants of truth and beauty 'through all the forms and faces of things.'" McColley quotes Milton's letter to illuminate the poet's description of Eve in terms of several classical figures in *Paradise Lost*. Her quotation appears, appropriately, at the end of a discussion of Milton's allusion to Proserpina (*PL* 4.268–72), and it prefaces her analysis of Milton's comparison of Eve to Pandora (*PL* 4.714–19), where she observes that Milton "invites us to distinguish between the traces of truth and the parodies of truth in the myth." For McColley, "Milton elicits from us here any lurking suspicion we may have that God is the source of sin. If we believe, however, that Milton was writing to 'assert Eternal Providence,' we will notice ways in which the story of Pandora is a distorted version of the story of Eve, or the story of Eve is a rectified version of the story of Pandora."[2]

The poet's complex handling of the myth of Pandora has attracted the attention of other Miltonists. Robert Martin Adams has commented that "Satan uses Pandora (Eve) as a device to tempt Adam and succeeds in his aim," and he refers to "the countless versions of the beautiful deadly woman (Eve-Pandora), the Deity, and the serpent." John R. Knott Jr. says that at one point Eve "appears as a naive Pandora, who learns to use the power of beauty to dominate Adam." He then notes that Milton's allusions to Pandora and Circe "call sufficient attention to Eve's deceitfulness and its tragic consequences for us to see that her charm can have sinister implications." Joseph

E. Duncan has remarked that "The use of 'feign'd' myth in direct conjunction with the inspired paradise narrative in Genesis introduced some delicate problems," and that "rather strangely the heavenly choirs associate the presentation of Eve to Adam with the presentation of Pandora to Epimetheus." Margaret Justice Dean has extensively discussed the typology of Adam and Epimetheus and of Eve and Pandora. And like McColley, Stella Purce Revard has argued that Milton rewrites the Pandora myth to absolve God from the responsibility of creating evil. Revard adds that Milton's allusion to Deucalion and Pyrrha as a type of Adam and Eve (*PL* 11.1–21) relates to the myth of Pandora, since Pyrrha is the daughter of Pandora and Epimetheus. Thus, Revard notes an additional facet of Milton's providential reworking of the Pandora myth.[3]

Some critics, then, such as Adams and Knott, have interpreted Eve negatively in light of the Pandora myth. Others, such as Duncan, have been puzzled by the incongruity between Pandora and Milton's Eve. And others still, such as McColley and Revard, have considered this incongruity further and cast Eve more favorably. In reading Milton's Eve in relation to Pandora, his critics have arrived at different interpretations of his texts. The myth of Pandora, in turn, was read in various ways throughout the Renaissance, and these interpretations shaped Milton's reworking of the myth. The traditional interpretation of the Pandora myth holds that she is the deceptively beautiful source of suffering. While this interpretation agrees with a reading of Eve as the cause of the Fall, it conflicts with the more nuanced modern reading of Milton's Eve as a fallible figure of regeneration and renewal, a view reinforced by Milton's reference to "*Jesus* son of *Mary* second *Eve*" (*PL* 10.183).[4] While Eve resembles Pandora, Milton stresses that she is not identical to the classical character. But he also explores the truth behind the Pandora myth to illuminate the origin of suffering. Milton relates Pandora not only to Eve but less obviously to Sin, and he develops the recondite relationship between Sin and Pandora through a complex web of mythological associations. In doing so, he additionally demonstrates the difficulty of attaining interpretive certainty in a fallen world.

The classical myth has a convoluted history.[5] Pandora appears in the poems of Hesiod (fl. 700 BC), which were widely available during the Renaissance and among the first classical texts printed. The *Theogony* was first published in Latin by Boninus Mombritius (Ferrara, 1474), while the first printed edition of the *Works and Days* was published in Milan around 1482. The poems were later published at Venice in 1495 by Aldus Manutius, along with the works of Theocritus, in an edition that marked the first appearance of the Greek text of the *Theogony*. These were followed by numerous other editions, which included extensive commentary.[6] The *Theogony* and *Works and Days* were widely studied during the Renaissance and were central to the curriculum.[7] During his formative years as a student at Christ's College in Cambridge between 1625 and 1632, Milton was required to complete a series of academic exercises, or prolusions. He mentions Hesiod in his First and Seventh Prolusions (YP 1:223, 289), and his mythological references in those early exercises seem especially indebted to the Greek poet. In *Of Education* (1644), he lists Hesiod among the classical authors who should be studied (YP 2:394). John Aubrey notes that Milton taught Hesiod to Edward and John Phillips, and Edward Phillips similarly includes Hesiod in Milton's curriculum. So, too, Hesiod figures prominently in Milton's poetry.[8]

In the *Works and Days*, Prometheus brings fire to humanity, and Zeus decides to punish mankind with "an evil thing in which they may all be glad of heart while they embrace their own destruction" (57–58).[9] He then tells Hephaestus to create Pandora:

And he bade famous Hephaestus make haste and mix earth with water and to put in it the voice and strength of human kind, and fashion a sweet, lovely maiden-shape, like to the immortal goddesses in face; and Athene to teach her needlework and the weaving of the varied web; and golden Aphrodite to shed grace upon her head and cruel longing and cares that weary the limbs. And he charged Hermes the guide, the Slayer of Argus, to put in her a shameless mind and a deceitful nature. (60–68)

Hephaestus molds her out of clay, Athena clothes her, the Graces and Persuasion give her golden necklaces, the Hours crown her with spring flowers, and Hermes fills her with deceit and gives her the gift of speech. At Zeus's request, Hermes brings Pandora to Epimetheus. Though Prometheus had warned his brother not to accept Zeus's gifts, Epimetheus nonetheless does so. Until that time, mankind had lived in a golden age, free of sickness and hard labor. But Pandora removes the lid from a jar and releases plagues and misery into the world, leaving only Hope within the container (69–105).[10] According to Hesiod, Zeus gives Pandora her name "because all they who dwelt on Olympus gave each a gift, a plague to men who eat bread" (80–82).[11]

Hesiod tells the myth again in the *Theogony*, where his account differs. He does not name the woman sculpted by Hephaestus, nor does he mention the jar of afflictions. But he explains that from her "is the race of women and female kind: of her is the deadly race and tribe of women who live amongst mortal men to their great trouble, no helpmeets in hateful poverty, but only in wealth" (590–93). He adds that "Zeus who thunders on high made women to be an evil to mortal men, with a nature to do evil" (600–602). In the *Theogony*, Athena clothes the woman, gives her a veil, and adorns her head with garlands of flowers. She then places upon her head a golden crown, made by Hephaestus: "On it was much curious work, wonderful to see; for of the many creatures which the land and sea rear up, he put most upon it, wonderful things, like living beings with voices: and great beauty shone out from it" (581–84). He closes his account by adding that any man who avoids marriage and the sorrows brought by women is cursed to reach old age without anyone to care for him and will have his possessions divided after his death; while if a man chooses to marry, and even finds a good wife, he may be cursed with the unceasing grief caused by mischievous children (602–12).

According to the *Bibliotheca,* or *Library* of classical mythology (ca. AD 100), traditionally but mistakenly ascribed to Apollodorus, Pandora was the first woman. Deucalion, the son of Prometheus, married Pyrrha, the daughter of Pandora and Epimetheus (*Lib.* 1.7.2). So, too, the Greek geographer Pausanias (fl. AD 170) records in his *Description of Greece* that Hesiod had told of Pandora being the first woman (Paus. 1.24.7).[12] During the Middle Ages and Renaissance, the myth was retold and commented on by various authors. One of the most influential early works was the *Mythologiae* of Fabius Planciades Fulgentius, who wrote his mythography around AD 500 and influenced such medieval writers as John of Salisbury, Henry of Hereford, and Bernard of Sylvester. Fulgentius's text was first published as early as 1498 and appeared in at least a dozen editions between 1500 and 1600. Thus, it would have been available to Milton, though there is little evidence that he actually consulted it.[13] Fulgentius briefly mentions Pandora at the end of his summary of the myth of Prometheus. "Then it is told how Pandora was fashioned," he remarks, "for Pandora is the Greek for the gift of all, because the soul is universally bestowed on all."[14] Fulgentius's concern with etymology was continued by Giovanni Boccaccio in his *Genealogia Deorum Gentilium Libri,* which he began at the request of King Hugo IV of Cyprus around 1350 and continued until his death some twenty-five years later. Boccaccio's work appeared in at least twenty-seven manuscripts and in ten printed editions between 1472 and 1532, along with French, Spanish, and Italian translations. While the *Genealogia Deorum Gentilium Libri* was available to Milton, John Mulryan is skeptical of his use of it.[15] Boccaccio credits Prometheus for making Pandora. He cites Fulgentius and rejects the accepted explanation of her name as "gift to all," arguing instead that her name means that she is full of bitterness. He concludes his discussion with a reference to Job, thus linking the classical figure with the biblical exemplar of suffering.[16]

But the author probably most responsible for popularizing the Pandora myth was Desiderius Erasmus. He mentions her in his *Adages,* which first appeared at Paris in 1500 as the *Adagiorum Collectanea,* a text that included 818 proverbial sayings. This work was revised, expanded, and published in several other editions, including the *Adagiorum Chiliades* (Venice, 1508), which included 3,260 adages and an extensive commentary. The Basel, 1536 edition, published at the time of his death, included 4,151 sayings; this was the version to appear in the *Opera Omnia* of 1540.[17] A copy of the *Adages* was given to the library of St. Alban's grammar school between 1597 and 1598 and appears on a list of books at Merchant Taylors' School in 1599. Philip Melanchthon thought highly of it as a grammar school text, as did John Brinsley and John Colet, the founder of St. Paul's School, who was heavily influenced by Erasmus's educational theories.[18] Milton counts Erasmus among "the most eminent theologians" in his 1655 *Pro Se Defensio* (YP 4:725) and in that same work speaks of "the learned Erasmus, who stands in bronze at Rotterdam" (YP 4:744). In *Tetrachordon* (1645), he writes that Erasmus "for learning was the wonder of his age" (YP 2:709).[19] In his account of the adage "Malo accepto stultus sapit" [Trouble experienced makes a fool wise], Erasmus traces the saying back to Hesiod's myth of Pandora. In his retelling, he emphasizes the experiences of Prometheus and Epimetheus. After the gods endow Pandora with gifts, "Jupiter sent her to Prometheus with a box, beautiful indeed, but concealing inside it every kind of misfortune," Erasmus writes. "Prometheus refused the present, and warned his brother that if any kind of gift was brought in his absence, it must not be accepted. Back comes Pandora and, having persuaded Epimetheus, she gives him the box. As soon as he [or she] had opened it, and understood, as the diseases flew out, that Jove's 'gifts were no gifts,' he began to be wise, but too late" (*Adages* 1.1.31).[20] He mentions Pandora's box again in his discussion of "Hostium munera, non munera" [Gifts of enemies are no gifts], where he links it with the gifts of Medea and Deianira (*Adages* 1.3.35). According to Dora and Erwin Panofsky, Erasmus provided the first summary of the myth and was responsible for ascribing a "pyxis" or box to Pandora, rather than a "πίθος," or jar. In addition, Erasmus writes an ambiguous text, in which Epimetheus, not Pandora, may have opened the container.[21] Thus, he gives potential responsibility to Epimetheus, rather than clear blame to Pandora.

Erasmus's account shaped the Renaissance mythographic tradition. In his *De Deis Gentium* (1548), a particularly scholarly compendium of classical lore, Lilio Gregorio Giraldi offers a discussion of Pandora in which he cites Erasmus and other writers as authorities. Like Erasmus, he says that Pandora, after unsuccessfully attempting to persuade Prometheus, convinces Epimetheus to accept her pyxis of ills.[22] Giraldi's Basel, 1548, first edition was followed by a second (Basel, 1560), third (London, 1565), fourth (Basel, 1580), and fifth and final edition, part of the Leyden, 1696, *Opera Omnia*. Perhaps because of its scholarly nature, it was never translated into other languages. While Milton's use of *De Deis Gentium* is hard to ascertain, the

London edition probably would have been accessible to him.[23] In addition, he mentions Giraldi in his *Commonplace Book* (YP 1:469), and Carlo Dati refers to *De Deis Gentium* in a 1647 letter to Milton (YP 2:771).

The mythographic tradition culminated in Natale Conti's enormously popular *Mythologiae*, which was published in more than thirty editions during the Renaissance, from the first (Venice, 1567/8) to the last (Hanover, 1669).[24] Like Erasmus's *Adages*, it appears on a 1599 list of books at Merchant Taylors' School, and Charles Hoole recommended it as a text in his *A New Discovery of the Old Art of Teaching Schoole* (1660).[25] Dati mentions Conti's tome in his 1647 letter to Milton (YP 2:771), and Milton was almost certainly familiar with his work.[26] Conti included Pandora in his discussion of Prometheus. In Conti's account, Vulcan creates Pandora, who is so named because she is clever and has been given all arts by the gods. Jupiter sends her to Prometheus "cum omnibus malis in vasculo inclusis" [with all kinds of evil enclosed in a small vessel]. Prometheus refuses the gift, so she rushes to Epimetheus, who opens it and releases the evils into the world while leaving Hope trapped inside.[27]

Pandora also appears in the *Dictionarium Historicum, Geographicum, Poeticum* of Charles Stephanus, one of the standard Renaissance classical dictionaries. The work was first published in 1553 and was issued in at least nine editions by 1600. Later editions drew freely from Conti, Vincenzo Cartari, and other sources, so that the *Dictionarium* was perhaps the definitive work of its kind in the seventeenth century. Hoole listed it among several works that every school library should have to aid students in reading Ovid, and it was among the works available to Milton at Christ's College.[28] While Milton does not cite the *Dictionarium*, Edward Phillips drew extensively from that work in compiling his *The New World of Words: A General Dictionary* (1658), and Milton may have acquainted him with Stephanus's text. In addition, Milton probably was familiar with the *Thesaurus Linguae Latinae* (1531) of Robert Stephanus, as his early biographers note, since he apparently was creating a supplement to that work.[29] In the Geneva, 1609, edition of the *Dictionarium*, Stephanus writes as follows:

Pandora, ræ, Hesiodo fingitur prima mulier, à Vulcano Iouis iussu fabricata, quam singuli dij donis suis ornauerunt. Pallas enim sapientiæ donum ei contulit, Venus formæ, Apollo musices, Mercurius eloquentiæ. Inde dicta fuit Pandora, quasi omnium donum, vel quasi ab omnibus donata, vel omnium rerum genere dotata. Hanc postea cum pyxide clausa missam fuisse tradunt ad Epimetheum (cùm humano generi malè cupiebat Iupiter, ob promethei audaciam, qui ignem è cœlo furatus, ferulæ inclusum detulerat in terras) qui illa recepta, & pyxide aperta, cui omne malorum genus inerat, terram morbis calamitatibúsque repleuit.[30]

[Pandora, rae, is said by Hesiod to be the first woman, made by Vulcan at Jove's command, whom all the gods adorned with their gifts. Pallas for example brought her the gift of wisdom, Venus of form, Apollo of music, Mercury of eloquence. Thus she was called Pandora, either because she was endowed with all their gifts, or because she was endowed with gifts by all. Afterwards she was sent with a closed box to Epimetheus (since Jupiter yearned for vengeance against the human race, for the audacity of Prometheus, who had stolen fire from heaven and carried it hidden in a stalk down to earth), who received her, and opened the box, in which was every kind of evil, and filled the earth with diseases and calamities.]

Stephanus cites Hesiod as his source. But, like Erasmus, he says that Pandora had a pyxis, or box, and that Epimetheus opened it.

There was also an iconographic tradition featuring Pandora's box or jar. Andrea Alciato, in his *Emblemata,* which appeared in more than two hundred Renaissance editions since its initial publication in 1534, alludes to the myth of the jar in his emblem "In simulachrum Spei" [A picture of Hope], though he does not mention Pandora by name. In a pen drawing of *Pandora Opening the Box* (ca. 1540), Rosso Fiorentino illustrated the myth. The Parisian publisher Gilles Gourbin, whose business operated from 1555 to 1586, adopted Fiorentino's image as a printer's device. Around 1550, Jean Cousin painted his *Eva Prima Pandora,* which shows a nude reclining in front of shrubs, trees, and ruins. Thus Eve appeared as Pandora. The tradition was continued well into the seventeenth century and beyond by such artists as Jacques Callot, in his *Creation and Descent of Pandora* (1625). Other artists depicted Pandora in terms of Eve, substituting the infamous box for Eve's customary fig leaf.[31] Milton's knowledge of visual representations of Pandora is debatable. Roland Mushat Frye writes of "Milton's apparently limited interest in the emblem literature," but Mulryan notes the interrelatedness of Renaissance images, comments on the lack of scholarship on Milton and the emblem tradition, and questions why Milton would have referred to the books of George Wither or Francis Quarles when he could have instead consulted Alciato. In addition, Frye details Milton's exposure to art, particularly during the poet's travels in Italy.[32]

The classical myth of a lost golden age parallels the biblical myth of the loss of Eden, and the myth of Pandora neatly corresponds with the role of Eve in the fall of humanity.[33] In the Judeo-Christian tradition, the satanic serpent tempts Eve into eating the forbidden fruit. She, in turn, tempts Adam into doing the same, though both had been forewarned not to, and thus they and their offspring are cursed to a life of sickness and labor (Gen. 2–3). During late antiquity, Pandora was customarily read as a type of Eve.[34] In *The Chaplet; or, De Corona* (ca. AD 204), Tertullian says: "If there really was a Pandora, whom Hesiod mentions as the first of women, hers was the first head the graces crowned, for she received gifts from all *the gods* whence she got *her name* Pandora. But Moses, a prophet, not a poet-shepherd, shows us the first woman Eve having her loins more naturally girt about with leaves than her temples with flowers. Pandora, then, is a myth." But the church father is not entirely critical of the classical figure. In his *Against the Valentinians* (ca. AD 207), he calls the phrase "Hesiod's Pandora" a figure of speech denoting a perfect blending of all things.[35] Origen, too, commented on Pandora. In his *Against Celsus* (ca. AD 250), he debates the heathen philosopher Celsus, who had attacked Christianity in his *A True Discourse* (ca. AD 175). He notes that Celsus had criticized the biblical account of the creation of Eve and had suggested that some Jews and Christians, ashamed of the myth, had tried to give it allegorical significance. Origen responds by quoting at length the myth of Pandora from Hesiod's *Works and Days* as a classical analogue of Eve's creation and asks if the Greek poet's words "are not better fitted to excite laughter." The interpretation of Pandora as a type of Eve continued into the Renaissance. In his *Mythomystes* (1632), for instance, the English mythographer Henry Reynolds says: "What other can *Hesiod's Pandora, the first and beautifullest of all women, by whome all euils were dispersed and spred vpon the earth,* meane then *Moses* his *Eue?*"[36] Milton probably was acquainted with these works. He cites Tertullian throughout his writings, and in his *Commonplace Book* refers to Nicolaus Rigaltius's edition of Tertullian's *Opera,* which was first published at Paris in 1634 (YP 1:362). He cites Origen as an authority in *Tetrachordon* (YP 2:695), though he also refers more critically to "the erroneous *Origen*" in *Of Reformation* (1641) (YP 1:567). Milton's specific knowledge of Reynolds is more difficult to ascertain, but Reynolds's comparison of Eve to Pandora is representative of how the classical myth was read in the seventeenth century.[37]

Milton was familiar with the myth of Pandora and he alludes to it throughout his literary career. In his Second Prolusion, "On the Harmony of the Spheres," he writes: "The fact that we are unable to hear this harmony seems certainly to be due to the presumption of that thief Prometheus, which brought so many evils upon men" (YP 1:238–39). In alluding to Prometheus and the "evils" visited upon men, Milton indirectly refers to the Pandora myth.[38] He begins his Fourth Prolusion, "In the Destruction of any Substance there can be no Resolution into First Matter," by saying: "This is not the place in which to enquire too nicely whether Error escaped from Pandora's box, or from the depths of the Styx, or lastly whether he is to be accounted one of the sons of Earth who conspired against the gods" (YP 1:249).[39] In alluding to Pandora's box, rather than a jar, Milton recalls the Erasmian version of the tale, which had become a commonplace. In pointing to the difficulty of establishing the origin of Error, he suggests that Error is like one of the rebellious giants and that Pandora's box is like the classical hell. In his next sentence he remarks that Error, "like Typhon of old or Neptune's son Ephialtes," has grown so great "by imperceptible degrees" that even Truth is menaced (YP 1:249). Typhon is again the enemy of Truth in *Areopagitica* (1644), where Milton says that after the Ascension of Christ and the death of the apostles, there arose "a wicked race of deceivers, who as that story goes of the *Ægyptian Typhon* with his conspirators, how they dealt with the good *Osiris*, took the virgin Truth, hewd her lovely form into a thousand peeces, and scatter'd them to the four winds" (YP 2:549). And Typhon appears again in *Paradise Lost*, where Milton compares Satan to the classical monster. The fallen angel is

> in bulk as huge
> As whom the Fables name of monstrous size,
> *Titanian*, or *Earth-born*, that warr'd on *Jove*,
> *Briareos* or *Typhon*, whom the Den
> By ancient *Tarsus* held.[40]   (PL 1.196–200)

In his Fourth Prolusion, then, Milton begins a commentary on error, which he continues in his later writings. His exploration of error matches the intent of Erasmus's adage, since the experience of trouble making a fool wise suggests that the fool was prone to err out of ignorance. He also would have known Spenser's allegorization of Error in *The Faerie Queene* (1590), "Halfe like a serpent horribly displaide, / But th'other halfe did womans shape retaine" (1.1.14, 7–8).[41] Spenser's snaky dragon lives in the "wandring wood," which is "*Errours den*" (1.1.13, 6). And with its serpentine features, Spenser's Error is very much like Typhon, whom Milton describes in his Nativity ode (1629) as "ending in snaky twine" (226). Since Milton alludes to Typhon at length in *Areopagitica*, in which he ponders the battle of Truth and Error, and in that same work he mentions "our sage and serious Poet *Spencer*, whom I dare be known to think a better teacher then *Scotus* or *Aquinas*" (YP 2:516), the allegory of Error in *The Faerie Queene* is a likely part of the background of Milton's discussion. To err is to wander, or to stray from the truth, as the Redcrosse Knight does in Spenser's epic when he ventures into the Wandering Wood. Satan, in rebelling against God's will, committed the first error; and that error is repeated in Eden, the site of "Man's First Disobedience" (*PL* 1.1), and the place the fallen Adam and Eve must leave "with wand'ring steps and slow" (*PL* 12.648).

Later, in the 1644 second edition of *The Doctrine and Discipline of Divorce*, Milton alludes to Pandora to explain the Fall:

Whenas the doctrine of *Plato* and *Chrysippus* with their followers the *Academics* and the *Stoics*, who knew not what a consummat and most adorned *Pandora* was bestow'd

upon *Adam* to be the the the nurse and guide of his arbitrary happinesse and persever-
ance, I mean his native innocence and perfection, which might have kept him from
being our true *Epimetheus*. (YP 2:293)

In the above passage, "Pandora" does not refer to Eve, as some critics have
said, though the analogy seems natural. Instead, Milton makes clear that
"Pandora" refers to Adam's "native innocence and perfection."[42] In his focus
on Epimetheus as a type of Adam, Milton again recalls the Erasmian tradition, in which the male character is responsible for suffering. If Eve were
completely analogous with Pandora, then God, like Zeus and Hephaestus,
would be responsible for introducing suffering to humanity. But Milton aims
to show that classical and Christian myth are similar, not that they are identical. In a close reading of the above passage from *The Doctrine and Discipline
of Divorce,* Dennis H. Burden stresses that "Milton is defending his religion
from the charge that it makes God the author of sin." In not knowing what a
"consummat and most adorned *Pandora*" had been given to Adam, the
pagans, says Burden, "were ignorant about the innocence with which God
had in the beginning endowed his creatures." Because Adam had been given
the gift of innocence, he was like Epimetheus, who had been given Pandora.
But if Adam had made proper use of his gift, he would have been unlike
Epimetheus, since the gifts accompanying Pandora were punishments, while
"God's gift to Adam was a blessing, sent in order to give Adam the where-
withal to make himself very unlike Epimetheus," Burden argues.[43] Thus,
Milton uses the figure of Pandora to personify a supernatural gift. In classical
myth, that gift is a curse; in Milton's restatement of Christian lore, it is a
blessing.

    These early works by Milton demonstrate the ongoing significance of
the myth to him and the great degree of attention with which he read and
recast it. So, too, the myth of Pandora is of critical importance to *Paradise
Lost,* the culmination of Milton's theological musings and his synthesis of
classical and Christian thought. Hesiod uses the myth to explain the origin of
suffering, and in the opening invocation of *Paradise Lost,* Milton proclaims
an identical objective:

> Of Man's First Disobedience, and the Fruit
> Of that Forbidden Tree, whose mortal taste
> Brought Death into the World, and all our woe,
> With loss of *Eden,* till one greater Man
> Restore us, and regain the blissful Seat,
> Sing Heav'nly Muse.   (*PL* 1.1–6)

Much as the invocation repeats the theme of the Pandora myth, it likewise
resonates with the language of Milton's discussion of Pandora in *The Doc-*

trine and Discipline of Divorce. Immediately after he alludes to Pandora in his divorce tract, Milton says of the Academics and Stoics:

and though they taught of vertue and vice to be both the gift of *divine destiny,* they could yet find reasons not invalid, to justifie the counsels of God and Fate from the insulsity of mortall tongues: That mans own freewill self corrupted is the adequat and sufficient cause of his disobedience *besides Fate; as Homer* also wanted not to expresse both in his *Iliad* and *Odyssei.* (YP 2:293–94)

In this passage Milton reveals his desire to "justify the ways of God to men" (*PL* 1.26) and to explore "Man's First Disobedience" (*PL* 1.1), and he refers to the classical epic tradition that he will imitate in *Paradise Lost.*[44]

While the myth of the Fall is at the heart of *Paradise Lost,* and the story of Pandora is, in turn, part of the background of that myth, the classical figure is mentioned explicitly when Eve is presented to Adam. Eve is

> more adorn'd,
> More lovely than *Pandora,* whom the Gods
> Endow'd with all thir gifts, and O too like
> In sad event, when to the unwiser Son
> Of *Japhet* brought by *Hermes,* she ensnar'd
> Mankind with her fair looks, to be aveng'd
> On him who had stole *Jove's* authentic fire.   (*PL* 4.713–19)

In these lines Milton may well be synthesizing his reading of Hesiod, Fulgentius, Boccaccio, Erasmus, Conti, and other writers. Or he may simply be reflecting the widespread understanding of the Pandora myth. But the *Dictionarium Historicum, Geographicum, Poeticum* might be especially significant here. DeWitt T. Starnes and Ernest William Talbert have closely compared the relevant entry for Pandora in Stephanus's dictionary with Milton's lines from *Paradise Lost* and concluded that because of the two authors' diction, similar phrasing, and use of the active voice, "Whatever accounts of Pandora Milton had read, it looks as though that of Charles Stephanus was most vivid in his mind." Stephanus, for instance, calls Pandora the "prima mulier," or "first woman," a phrase that prompts comparison with Eve; he uses the word "ornauerunt," which resembles Milton's description of Eve as "adorn'd"; and his reference to Pandora as "quam singuli dij donis suis ornauerunt" is, according to Starnes and Talbert, "parallel in structure and meaning to 'whom the Gods Endow'd with all their gifts.' "[45]

Since Milton would have found in Pausanias (1.24.7) and Apollodorus (*Lib.* 1.7.2) references to Pandora being the first woman, Stephanus's reference to Pandora as "prima mulier" does not in itself demonstrate Milton's reliance on the *Dictionarium Historicum, Geographicum, Poeticum.* More persuasive is the similar diction and structure of Milton's "adorn'd" (*PL* 4.713) and "whom the Gods / Endow'd with all thir gifts" (*PL* 4.714–15), and Stephanus's "quam singuli dij donis suis ornauerunt." Hesiod's Greek diction and phrasing differ significantly from Milton's (*Works and Days*, 80–83; *Theog.* 573–84). So, too, the Latin accounts of Boccaccio, Erasmus, and Giraldi do not closely resemble Milton's wording (*PL* 4.713–15). None of these mythographers echo Milton's "adorn'd" (*PL* 4.713) as closely as Stephanus's "ornauerunt." Conti, however, says that Pandora "omnibus artibus à Dijs donata" [was given all arts by the gods]. His language thus resembles Milton's "whom the Gods / Endow'd with all thir gifts."[46]

Milton's remark that Eve is more adorned and lovely than Pandora echoes *The Doctrine and Discipline of Divorce*, where Adam's divine gift of "native innocence and perfection" is a "most adorned" Pandora. Philip J. Gallagher remarks, "Milton's God, unlike Hesiod's Zeus, intends Eve to rectify man's 'single imperfection' [*PL* 8.423], not to destroy him."[47] While Milton stops short of saying that Eve's beauty is beguiling, he makes clear that Pandora's "fair looks" "ensnar'd" humanity in classical myth. He suggests, too, that beauty is one of the gifts given to Pandora by the gods. The Christian truth behind the pagan myth is reinforced by Milton's reference to Japhet as the father of Epimetheus, since Japhet is the son of Noah and the father of Javan (Gen. 10:1–2), the legendary founder of the Greek people. Milton refers to Javan earlier in his poem. At the end of his catalog of demons, he says that

> The rest were long to tell, though far renown'd,
> Th' *Ionian* Gods, of *Javan's* Issue held
> Gods, yet confest later than Heav'n and Earth
> Thir boasted Parents.   (*PL* 1.507–10)

Thus, the offspring of Javan mistakenly believed that the classical gods were deities, when they really were demons.

Milton describes Eve in terms that evoke the classical representations of Pandora. When Satan first sees her in Eden,

> Shee as a veil down to the slender waist
> Her unadorned golden tresses wore
> Dishevell'd, but in wanton ringlets wav'd
> As the Vine curls her tendrils.   (*PL* 4.304–7)

Eve's hair is like a veil, an image that brings marriage to mind, along with the veil given to Pandora by Athena. Adam tells Raphael that when he first saw Eve, she was "adorn'd / With what all Earth or Heaven could bestow / To make her amiable" (*PL* 8.482–84). Adam calls God the "Giver of all things fair, but fairest this / Of all thy gifts, nor enviest" (*PL* 8.493–94). He admits to being "weak / Against the charm of Beauty's powerful glance" (*PL* 8.532–33), and he fears that perhaps Nature bestowed on Eve "Too much of Ornament, in outward show / Elaborate, of inward less exact" (*PL* 8.538–39). God, then, is a giver of gifts; he is like Zeus, who gave Pandora to humanity. And while only good things can come from God, Adam's reaction to Eve's beauty anticipates the weakness that makes him Milton's true Epimetheus. After the Fall, he calls her a "fair defect" (*PL* 10.891), a phrase that roughly translates Hesiod's description of Pandora as a "καλὸν κακὸν" (*Theog.* 585), or fair-seeming evil. When Adam first learns of Eve's transgression, he stands horrified, and "From his slack hand the Garland wreath'd for *Eve* / Down dropp'd, and all the faded Roses shed" (*PL* 9.892–93). The garland of roses recalls the flowers given to Pandora by Athena and the Hours in Hesiodic myth, and on which Tertullian had commented in his *De Corona*. But the garland "wreath'd" by Adam for Eve also recalls the appearance of Satan as an attractive, coiled serpent when he successfully tempts her: the devil "Curl'd many a wanton wreath in sight of *Eve*, / To lure her Eye" (*PL* 9.517–18). In fact, the serpent is like a piece of jewelry since his eyes are "Carbuncle" (*PL* 9.500), and his neck is "verdant Gold" (*PL* 9.501) and "enamell'd" (*PL* 9.525). With his circular form and jewel-like appearance, the serpent most closely recalls a necklace, such as those given to Pandora by the Graces and Persuasion in Hesiod's *Works and Days,* or like the golden crown made by Hephaestus and given to Pandora by Athena in the *Theogony.*

Though Milton explicitly compares Eve to Pandora and makes Hesiod's myth part of the background of the Fall, he makes clear that Eve is *not* Pandora and that there is not a point-for-point correspondence between the two. Milton's description of Eve in terms of Pandora is a matter of contrast as well as comparison. If Eve is more adorned and lovely than Pandora, then she is not the classical figure; she transcends her. As McColley notes, "both Milton's Eve and the Eve of celebratory iconography are far different from the 'sheer inescapable snare' of Hesiod and the painful dualism of allegorical interpretations."[48] Eve, for example, is "yet sinless" when the serpent tempts her (*PL* 9.659) and is thus not a divine curse. Because she is "yet sinless," she contrasts with Sin, and the birth of Sin invites comparison with the creation of Eve. When Satan meets Sin at Hell-gate, she tells him of her birth:

> All on a sudden miserable pain
> Surpris'd thee, dim thine eyes, and dizzy swum
> In darkness, while thy head flames thick and fast
> Threw forth, till on the left side op'ning wide,
> Likest to thee in shape and count'nance bright,

> Then shining heav'nly fair, a Goddess arm'd
> Out of thy head I sprung: amazement seiz'd
> All th' Host of Heav'n; back they recoil'd afraid
> At first, and call'd me *Sin,* and for a Sign
> Portentous held me; but familiar grown,
> I pleas'd, and with attractive graces won
> The most averse, thee chiefly, who full oft
> Thyself in me thy perfect image viewing
> Becam'st enamor'd, and such joy thou took'st
> With me in secret, that my womb conceiv'd
> A growing burden.   *(PL* 2.752–67)

That "growing burden," the offspring of Satan and Sin, is Death. When Sin is born, she springs from the left, or sinister, side of Satan's head, which opens wide. So, too, Adam says that God "op'n'd my left side, and took / From thence a Rib" *(PL* 8.465–66), and "wide was the wound" *(PL* 8.467). God then "form'd and fashion'd" the rib into Eve *(PL* 8.469). After the Fall, Adam condemns her as his "part siníster" *(PL* 10.886). Sin resembles Satan in appearance, and Eve resembles Adam, for she is "Manlike" *(PL* 8.471) and Adam calls her the "Best Image of myself" *(PL* 5.95). At the time of Sin's birth, Satan's appearance is still "shining heav'nly fair"; Eve is "so lovely fair, / That what seem'd fair in all the World, seem'd now / Mean" *(PL* 8.471–73). Sin is Satan's "perfect image," and he finds her so irresistibly attractive that he impregnates her. Eve likewise sees her mirror image reflected in a lake, and though she is seduced by it, she chooses to be with Adam *(PL* 4.449–91). Milton says in *Areopagitica* that he "cannot praise a fugitive and cloister'd vertue" (YP 2:515), and both Satan and Eve are tempted by their semblances. Satan yields to Sin's temptation and fathers Death. Eve initially resists temptation, turns to Adam, and becomes mother of the human race. Like Satan, though, she eventually yields to temptation, sins, and brings death into the world.

In her seduction of Satan, Sin assumes the role of Pandora and emerges as the true Miltonic original of the classical temptress. Much as Pandora brings suffering to the world of mortals, Sin potentially brings death to Satan, for she tells him that her son Death, "Save he who reigns above, none can resist" *(PL* 2.814). Milton subtly links the encounter between Sin, Death, and Satan to the meeting of Epimetheus and Pandora. Sin admonishes Satan: "I forewarn thee, shun / His deadly arrow" *(PL* 2.810–11). The verb "forewarn" indicates that Sin is giving Satan foreknowledge; that is, she is making him like forward-thinking Prometheus, which suggests that he is already like after-thinking Epimetheus. When Satan sees Eve, she is formed for "sweet attractive Grace" *(PL* 4.298), while Sin "with attractive graces won" Satan's affection (*PL* 2.762). When Satan first glimpses Eve, Milton describes her in words that contrast her with the gift-adorned Pandora, since Eve's "golden tresses" are "unadorned" (*PL* 4.305). Milton also implicitly contrasts Eve with Sin. When she stands naked, "Nor those mysterious parts were then conceal'd" (*PL* 4.312). Prelapsarian Eve's nudity does not stir thoughts of "guilty shame" (*PL* 4.313), which Milton says is "Sin-bred" (*PL* 4.315). This sin-bred shame has "troubl'd all mankind / With shows instead, mere shows of seeming pure" (*PL* 4.315–16). Milton's language recalls the woes brought by Pandora, who also seems to be pure. So, too, Sin "seem'd Woman to the waist, and fair, / But ended foul in many a scaly fold" (*PL* 2.650–51). In his description of Sin, Milton further develops the relationship between lust and Pandora's dubious gifts to humanity. He says of Sin:

> about her middle round
> A cry of Hell Hounds never ceasing bark'd
> With wide *Cerberean* mouths full loud, and rung
> A hideous Peal: yet, when they list, would creep,
> If aught disturb'd thir noise, into her womb,
> And kennel there, yet there still bark'd and howl'd
> Within unseen.   (*PL* 2.653–59)

The Hell Hounds emerge from Sin's womb, while a variety of ills fly out of Pandora's box when it is opened. Milton continues his canine imagery when Sin and Death travel to earth, thus bringing mortality and corruption to the fallen world. They are the "Dogs of Hell" (*PL* 10.616) and "Hell-hounds" (*PL* 10.630). Death is the daughter of Sin and also came out of her womb.

The obvious classical analogue of the birth of Sin is the myth of Athena springing from the head of Zeus.[49] Hephaestus, who made Pandora, plays an interesting role in some versions of that myth. According to the *Bibliotheca* ascribed to Apollodorus, when it was time for Athena to be born, "Prometheus or, as others say, Hephaestus, smote the head of Zeus with an axe, and Athena, fully armed, leaped up from the top of his head at the river Triton" (*Lib.* 1.3.6). While Zeus is Athena's father, just as Satan is the father of Sin, Hephaestus nonetheless induces her birth. And while Zeus does not engage in incest with his daughter, as Satan does with Sin, Hephaestus lusts for Athena. Apollodorus tells the myth as follows:

Athena came to Hephaestus, desirous of fashioning arms. But he, being forsaken by Aphrodite, fell in love with Athena, and began to pursue her; but she fled. When he got near her with much ado (for he was lame), he attempted to embrace her; but she, being a chaste virgin, would not submit to him, and he dropped his seed on the leg of the goddess. In disgust, she wiped off the seed with wool and threw it on the ground; and as she fled and the seed fell on the ground, Erichthonius was produced. (*Lib.* 3.14.6)

According to Apollodorus, Erichthonius was brought up by Athena, became king of Athens, erected a wooden image of Athena in the acropolis, and instituted a festival in her honor (*Lib.* 3.14.6). But the mythographer adds that Athena hid the young Erichthonius in a chest, which she gave to Pandrosos, forbidding her to open it. Her sisters nonetheless opened it out of curiosity and found a serpent coiled around the infant. Apollodorus notes that some believe the serpent destroyed Pandrosos's sisters, while others say that Athena drove them mad and prompted them to throw themselves down from the acropolis (*Lib.* 3.14.6). Ovid, too, mentions Erichthonius. Though he does not detail Erichthonius's origins, he says: "Once upon a time a child was born, named Erichthonius, a child without a mother."[50] He then explains that Pallas hid the infant in a chest, which she entrusted to Pandrosos, Herse, and Aglauros, the daughters of Crecops. In Ovid's account, Aglauros opens the box, "And within they saw a baby-boy and a snake stretched out beside him" (*Met.* 2.560–61).

The myth of Hephaestus, Athena, and Erichthonius was popular among mythographers and would have reached Milton through their works. Hyginus, in his *Fabulae* (ca. 100 BC), tells the myth and adds that "natus est puer, qui inferiorem partem draconis habuit: quem Erichthonium ideo nominarunt" [A boy was born, who had a serpent for his lower part: he was called Erichthonius]. Virgil mentions Erichthonius in the *Georgics*, where he credits the Athenian king with inventing the chariot.[51] In his commentary on the line, Servius (fl. AD 300) recounts the myth of Erichthonius's birth and explains: "inde natus est puer draconteis pedibus, qui appellatus est Erichthonius" [Thus was born a boy with serpent feet, who was called Erichthonius]. In his *Mythologiae*, Conti repeats Apollodorus and explains that Erichthonius's name "is compounded of 'strife' and 'earth.' "[52] Thus, there was a long tradition linking Erichthonius with serpents. While Ovid says that Erichthonius was found in a chest with a serpent, George Sandys provides a much fuller account in the 1632 edition of his *Ovid's Metamorphosis*, an English translation accompanied by an extensive commentary. He recounts Vulcan's attempted rape of Minerva, explains that Erichthonius's name "signifies Earth and Contention," observes that some mythographers "give *Erichthonius* the hinder parts of a dragon," and notes that Erichthonius was the fourth king of Athens. Sandys further notes that Lactantius had mentioned Erichthonius. "Were the virgins themselves, Minerva and Diana, chaste?" the church father asks in *The Epitome of the Divine Institutes* (ca. AD 315). "Whence, then, did Erichthonius arise? Did Vulcan shed his seed upon the ground, and was man born from that as a fungus?"[53]

In addition, Erichthonius was sometimes associated with Pandora. In his account of the Parthenon, the temple of Athena, Pausanias describes the statue of the goddess:

She holds a statue of Victory about four cubits high, and in the other hand a spear; at her feet lies a shield and near the spear is a serpent. This serpent would be Erichthonius. On the pedestal is the birth of Pandora in relief. Hesiod and others have sung how this Pandora was the first woman; before Pandora was born there was as yet no womankind. (Paus. 1.24.7)

But perhaps most interestingly, Fulgentius notes in his *Mythologiae* that Erichthonius had the feet of a serpent, and that Minerva had entrusted him to the two sisters, Aglauros and Pandora; he even remarks that Pandora "is called the gift of all." Thus, Fulgentius confused Pandora with Pandrosos, and in opening the basket hiding Erichthonius, Fulgentius's Pandora brings to mind the figure from Hesiodic myth.[54] Erichthonius was also associated with marriage. Sandys, for instance, remarks that he is sometimes credited "for introducing marriage among the *Athenians,* who before promiscuously coupled together."[55] The remark tenuously links Erichthonius with the first wedding, the marriage of Pandora and Epimetheus.

The myth of Erichthonius was moralized during the Renaissance. In the third edition of his *Mystagogus Poeticus; or, The Muses Interpreter* (1653), the English mythographer and churchman Alexander Ross synthesized the allegorical readings common in his day. According to Mulryan, Ross's book was highly derivative and Milton could find fuller accounts of the myths in the works of Italian mythographers such as Conti and Cartari.[56] While Mulryan is skeptical of Milton's use of the *Mystagogus Poeticus*, Ross's mythography nonetheless illustrates how the myths were allegorized in seventeenth-century England at a time when the allegorical tradition was in decline. And in the seventeenth-century manuscript for his *Directions for a Student in the Universitie,* Richard Holdsworth, master of Emmanuel College, advocates Ross's mythography over Conti's, which he says is "somewhat too large, & tedious."[57] Ross says that Erichthonius *"was a Monster, or a man with Dragons feet, begot of* Vulcans *seed shed on the ground whilst he was offering violence to* Minerva." After recounting the myth, Ross explains that Erichthonius invented the chariot to hide his deformed and serpentine feet, and "So many men goe about to hide their fowle actions, and excuse them, but not to reforme them." He then notes that Vulcan "is the elementary fire," and that in shedding his seed upon the earth, "in which are the other two elements," "of these all monsters are procreated." He reads Minerva as "the influence of heaven or of the Sun, cherished and fomented, though not at first by God produced, but since *Adams* fall, and for the punishment of sin."

The strife between Minerva and Vulcan represents the contest between virginity and the sins of the flesh, and Vulcan emerges as a symbol of lust. Sandys offers similar information in his commentary on Ovid.[58]

The serpentine feet of earth-born Erichthonius place the monster squarely within the tradition of the serpent-footed giants who rebelled against Zeus, *"Titanian, or Earth-born, that warr'd on Jove"* (PL 1.198), and the snaky Typhon of the Nativity ode and the Fourth Prolusion. Thus the monster is linked with error, or sin, and with Satan, the father of Sin and Death.[59] The association is strengthened by Ross's reading of Erichthonius as emblematic of the sinner's attempt to justify his illicit actions, and by Ross's assertion that Vulcan is the father of all monsters—a role that could be attributed to Satan. Vulcan, or Hephaestus, burns with the fire of lust in the mythographic tradition. So, too, Satan burns with lust throughout *Paradise Lost.* When he sees Adam and Eve "Imparadis't in one another's arms" (PL 4.506), he recalls the inner hell in which he dwells, "Where neither joy nor love, but fierce desire, / Among our other torments not the least, / Still unfulfill'd with pain of longing pines" (PL 4.509–11). If Starnes and Talbert are right in asserting that Stephanus's *Dictionarium Historicum, Geographicum, Poeticum* is the immediate source for Milton's comparison of Eve to Pandora in *Paradise Lost,* then there is additional reason to believe that Milton deliberately evokes the myth of Erichthonius. In the 1609 edition of the *Dictionarium,* there are two entries for Pandora. The first is for the woman from Hesiodic myth. But the second identifies her as "filia Erichthei Atheniensium regis" [the daughter of Erichtheus, king of Athens], and Erichtheus was often considered identical to Erichthonius.[60] Thus, Milton could find Pandora linked to Erichthonius immediately after the entry for the archetypal woman of classical lore.

The larger myth of Hephaestus also figures in *Paradise Lost.* When Milton describes the fallen angel Mammon, he says that "Men call'd him *Mulciber;* and how he fell / From Heav'n, they fabl'd, thrown by angry *Jove* / Sheer o'er the Crystal Battlements" (PL 1.740–42). He then recounts the fall of Mulciber onto the island of Lemnos and adds: "thus they relate, / Erring" (PL 1.746–47). Milton's tale of Mammon's fall from heaven to Lemnos evokes Homer's myth of Hephaestus's fall from Olympus (1.590–94); and as Cicero observes, "Vulcan has a different name in Italy, in Africa and in Spain."[61] Thus, Mulciber is but one of several names for the classical deity. Before he fell, Mammon was the celestial architect: "his hand was known / In Heav'n by many a Tow'red structure high, / Where Scepter'd Angels held thir residence" (PL 1.732–34). In hell, he is the chief architect and builder of Pandaemonium, for he "was headlong sent / With his industrious crew to build in hell" (PL 1.750–51). Mammon, in turn, shares his craft with humanity:

> by him first
> Men also, and by his suggestion taught,
> Ransack'd the Center, and with impious hands
> Rifl'd the bowels of thir mother Earth
> For Treasures better hid.   (*PL* 1.684–88)

Milton then describes how under Mammon's direction, the fallen angels engage in metallurgy as they refine the gold they have mined from the infernal soil (*PL* 1.700–717). The temple they build is greater than "*Babel*, and the works of *Memphian* Kings" (*PL* 1.694), and "Not *Babylon*, / Nor great *Alcairo* such magnificence / Equall'd in all thir glories" (*PL* 1.717–19). Mammon's activities are archetypal. Michael tells Adam, "behold / Th' effects which thy original crime hath wrought" (*PL* 11.423–24). After he shows Adam human history through the Great Flood, Michael tells him that a mighty hunter, who "from Rebellion shall derive his name" (*PL* 12.36),

> shall find
> The Plain, wherein a black bituminous gurge
> Boils out from under ground, the mouth of Hell;
> Of Brick, and of that stuff they cast to build
> A City and Tow'r, whose top may reach to Heav'n.   (*PL* 12.40–44)

Thus, Nimrod builds the first city and the Tower of Babel, and in doing so he replicates the construction of Pandaemonium.

In recounting the fall of Mulciber, Milton foreshadows the fall of Eve: "from Morn / To Noon he fell, from Noon to dewy Eve, / A Summer's day" (*PL* 1.742–44).[62] And in mining hell to build Pandaemonium, Mammon parodies Eve's creation: "Soon had his crew / Op'n'd into the Hill a spacious wound / And digg'd out ribs of Gold" (*PL* 1.688–90). The ribs of gold correspond with the rib of Adam, out of which Eve was made, and the anatomical imagery is reinforced by Milton's prior remark that men taught by Mammon "Rifl'd the bowels of thir mother Earth" (*PL* 1.687).[63] This creative process additionally brings to mind the creation of Pandora by Hephaestus, Mammon's classical counterpart. Indeed, the construction of Pandaemonium and Babel, and all the sins that follow in the course of history, evoke the admonition of the King James Bible (1611): "For the love of money is the root of all evil" (1 Tim. 6:10). In classical myth, Pandora—the creation of Hephaestus—is the root of all evil. In Christian teaching, the root of all evil is the love of money, the sin inspired by Mammon, the archetype of Hephaestus.

Milton's references to Pandora, then, reinforce the intricate design of *Paradise Lost*, a design that Michael Lieb has approached dialectically. In doing so, Lieb notes that Milton calls his poem "this great Argument" (*PL* 1.24), and that the dialectical opposition of contraries is a feature of Miltonic argumentation. In analyzing the poem, he proposes "to discover a common referent by which the oppositions of the poem find expression." That referent, he says, "has to do with the idea of creation in all its aspects: conception, pregnancy, birth, and offspring (both sublime and degenerate)." In the course of his study, Lieb then notes the parallels between the birth of Sin and Death and the creation of Eve, and between the creation of Eve and the construction of Pandaemonium.[64] While Lieb does not discuss Pandora in his book, she nonetheless figures as part of the larger scheme which he elucidates. Pandora emerges as the focus of Milton's counterpointing of divine and infernal creation and binds together the various mythic strands of his narrative.

Throughout his writings, Milton invites us to reassemble the scattered limbs of Truth. In his Fourth Prolusion, he links Pandora with Error, which he describes in terms of serpentine Typhon. He continues this exploration at the beginning of the 1644 edition of *The Doctrine and Discipline of Divorce*, where he writes on the hazards of blindly following custom:

To persue the Allegory, Custome being but a meer face, as Eccho is a meere voice, rests not in her unaccomplishment, untill by secret inclination, shee accorporat her selfe with error, who being a blind and Serpentine body without a head, willingly accepts what he wants, and supplies what her incompleatnesse went seeking. Hence it is, that Error supports Custome, Custome count'nances Error. (YP 2:223)

Custom, then, seduces readers into making erroneous interpretations. Milton then points to

the inveterate blots and obscurities wrought upon our mindes by the suttle insinuating of Error and Custome: Who with the numerous and vulgar train of their followers, make it their chiefe designe to envie and cry-down the industry of free reasoning, under the terms of humor, and innovation; as if the womb of teeming Truth were to be clos'd up, if shee presume to bring forth ought, that sorts not with their unchew'd notions and suppositions. (YP 2:224)

He then offers some remarks on truth:

For Truth is as impossible to be soil'd by any outward touch, as the Sun beam. Though this ill hap wait on her nativity, that shee never comes into the world, but like a Bastard, to the ignominy of him that brought her forth: till Time the Midwife rather then the mother of Truth, have washt and salted the Infant, declar'd her legitimat, and Churcht the father of his young *Minerva,* from the needlesse causes of his purgation. (YP 2:225)

Milton's comments on Pandora in *The Doctrine and Discipline of Divorce* exemplify the errors inherent in a customary and uncritical reading. Custom tells the reader to identify Pandora with Eve, as some of Milton's critics have mistakenly done, and Milton's clarification of his allusion to Pandora underscores his recognition of this customary misreading. So, too, Milton criticizes the Academics and Stoics for being ignorant of Christian truth and for falsely attributing vice to divine destiny. And because they did not know what a "consummat and most adorned *Pandora*" had been given to Adam (YP 2:293), Milton suggests that the ancients mistakenly thought a lesser Pandora had been given to him.

In his allegorical study of Custom, Error, and Truth in *The Doctrine and Discipline of Divorce,* Milton's imagery is significant. Custom is linked with Error, and Error's serpentine form recalls Spenser's allegorical monster. Spenserian Error, in turn, brings to mind Milton's later depiction of Sin in *Paradise Lost,* especially since Milton calls Sin "the Snaky Sorceress" (*PL* 2.724). In writing of the teeming womb of Truth, Milton employs an image that evokes the womb of Sin, which is teeming with hounds. And his description of Truth in terms of Minerva anticipates his account of Sin springing Minerva-like from Satan's head. Thus, Milton utilizes many of the same images in *The Doctrine and Discipline of Divorce* that he will later use in *Paradise Lost,* though he uses these images in a slightly different way in his epic.

In *Paradise Lost,* he once again leads us to equate Pandora and Eve erroneously. When Satan encounters Sin in her Pandora-like beauty, he does not recognize her for what she is. In hell, she is deceptive and deformed; in heaven, she was more enticing, so much so that she seduced him. Satan's encounter with Sin at Hell-gate corresponds with his initial glimpse of Eve, and Milton's description of Eve in terms of Pandora refers to Adam's first sight of her, "What day the genial Angel to our Sire / Brought her in naked beauty" (*PL* 4.712–13). The fallen reader here meets Eve and is tempted to mistake her for Pandora, despite Milton's explanation that she is not the classical figure. Milton's reference to Adam as "our" Sire draws the reader into the scene. In mistaking Eve for Pandora, the reader repeats the error of fallen Adam, who is too quick to call Eve a "fair defect" (*PL* 10.891), thus equating her with the woman of classical myth. The reader thus follows the tradition of the ancients, who erroneously fabricated the myth of Mulciber falling from Olympus and mistook the demons for deities. But in the act of attentively reading Milton's poem, we may eventually realize that Sin, not Eve, is Pandora's true archetype, a role that Milton reinforces through his complex web of mythological subtexts. He thus follows the mythographic and exegetical tradition in making Pandora, or Sin, the source of suffering, while he simultaneously departs from that tradition by making Eve, the false Pandora, a symbol of regeneration.

Fairfield, Connecticut

NOTES

1. Milton's prose is cited parenthetically by volume and line number from *Complete Prose Works of John Milton*, 8 vols., ed. Don M. Wolfe et al. (New Haven, 1953–1982).

2. Diane Kelsey McColley, *Milton's Eve* (Urbana, IL, 1983), 68–69.

3. Robert Martin Adams, *Ikon: John Milton and the Modern Critics* (Ithaca, NY, 1955), 47, 58; John R. Knott Jr., *Milton's Pastoral Vision: An Approach to "Paradise Lost"* (Chicago, 1971), 111; Joseph E. Duncan, *Milton's Earthly Paradise: A Historical Study of Eden* (Minneapolis, 1972), 30–31; Margaret Justice Dean, "Marriage as Unreliable Narrative in *Paradise Lost*" (Ph.D. diss., University of Kentucky, 1998), 117–20, 151–70; Stella Purce Revard, "The Troublesome Helpmate; or, How Pandora Got Her Box" (paper presented at the Modern Language Association convention, "John Milton: A General Session I," Washington, DC, December 28, 2000); Revard, "Milton and Myth," in *Reassembling Truth: Twenty-First-Century Milton*, ed. Charles W. Durham and Kristin A. Pruitt (Selinsgrove, PA, 2003), 37–44.

4. Milton's poetry is cited parenthetically from *Complete Poems and Major Prose*, ed. Merritt Y. Hughes (Indianapolis, 1957).

5. The fullest account of the myth is Dora and Erwin Panofsky, *Pandora's Box: The Changing Aspects of a Mythical Symbol*, 2nd ed. (Princeton, NJ, 1962).

6. For the publication history of Hesiod's works, see Hesiod, *Works and Days*, ed. with prolegomena and commentary by M. L. West (Oxford, 1978), 86–87; Hesiod, *Theogony*, ed. with prolegomena and commentary by M. L. West (Oxford, 1966), 61–62, 101; John Edwin Sandys, *A History of Classical Scholarship*, 3 vols. (1908–1921; reprint, Beverly Hills, 1997), 2:98, 104, 272; L. D. Reynolds and N. G. Wilson, *Scribes and Scholars: A Guide to the Transmission of Greek and Latin Literature*, 3rd ed. (Oxford, 1991), 156.

7. Harris Francis Fletcher, *The Intellectual Development of John Milton*, 2 vols. (Urbana, IL, 1956–1961), 1:254–55; Donald Lemen Clark, *John Milton at St. Paul's School: A Study of Ancient Rhetoric in English Renaissance Education* (New York, 1948), 120–21; T. W. Baldwin, *William Shakspere's Small Latine and Lesse Greeke*, 2 vols. (Urbana, IL, 1944), 1:197, 306, 310–12, 407, 412–13, 415–28, 456–57, 539–41; 2:421–22, 626, 648–53.

8. John Aubrey, "Minutes of the Life of Mr. John Milton" (ca. 1681) in *The Early Lives of Milton*, ed. Helen Darbishire (London, 1932), 12; Phillips, "The Life of Mr. John Milton" (1694), in Darbishire, *Early Lives*, 60. For Milton's use of Hesiod, see Philip J. Gallagher, "*Paradise Lost* and the Greek *Theogony*," *English Literary Renaissance* 9 (1979): 121–48; William M. Porter, *Reading the Classics and "Paradise Lost"* (Lincoln, NE, 1993), 53–67; Stella P. Revard, *The War in Heaven: "Paradise Lost" and the Tradition of Satan's Rebellion* (Ithaca, NY, 1980), 148–52, 192–94.

9. Hesiod's poetry is cited by line number from *Hesiod, the Homeric Hymns, and Homerica*, trans. Hugh G. Evelyn-White (Cambridge, MA, 1914).

10. The meaning of ἐλπὶς, or "hope" (*Works and Days*, line 96), has been debated. See the gloss on the line in West's edition.

11. The meaning of Pandora's name is unclear. Evelyn-White, *Hesiod*, glosses her name as "The All-endowed" (line 81) and says in a note on line 94 that Pandora's jar "contained the gifts of the gods mentioned in l. 82." After noting Pandora's possible relation to an Earth goddess (gloss on line 81), West notes that Hesiod's "δῶρον ἐδώρησαν" (line 82) could mean either that the gods gave her a gift, or that they gave her as a gift, since "Zeus" and "all the gods" were sometimes interchangeable. Thus Zeus may have given her as a gift to Epimetheus, or all the gods may have given their various gifts to Pandora, making her a gift to Epimetheus from all of them.

12. Apollodorus is cited parenthetically by book, chapter, and section number from *The Library*, 2 vols., trans. James George Frazer (Cambridge, MA, 1921). Pausanias is cited paren-

thetically by book, chapter, and section number from *Description of Greece*, 5 vols., trans. W. H. S. Jones (Cambridge, MA, 1918–1935).

13. Don Cameron Allen, *Mysteriously Meant: The Rediscovery of Pagan Symbolism and Allegorical Interpretation in the Renaissance* (Baltimore, 1970), 137, 210–12. For the influence of Fulgentius, see Jean Seznec, *The Survival of the Pagan Gods: The Mythological Tradition and Its Place in Renaissance Humanism and Art*, trans. Barbara F. Sessions (Princeton, NJ, 1953), 104, 172, 175, 228, 234–36, 306; Jane Chance, *Medieval Mythography: From Roman North Africa to the School of Chartres, A.D. 433–1177* (Gainesville, FL, 1994), 93–128, 165–66, 245–46, 301; Chance, *Medieval Mythography: From the School of Chartres to the Court at Avignon, 1177–1350* (Gainesville, FL, 2000), 70, 98–101, 147, 165–67, 228–29, 342–44. Fulgentius is not among the authors listed in Jackson Campbell Boswell, *Milton's Library: A Catalogue of the Remains of John Milton's Library and an Annotated Reconstruction of Milton's Library and Ancillary Readings* (New York, 1975). John Mulryan, *"Through a Glass Darkly": Milton's Reinvention of the Mythological Tradition* (Pittsburgh, 1996), 201–2, briefly discusses Fulgentius but does not point to the Latin mythographer as one of Milton's principal sources. Fletcher, *The Intellectual Development of John Milton*, 2:131–32, notes that Fulgentius was anthologized in a mythography edited by Iacobus Micyllus (Paris, 1578) and argues that the book "would have been almost indispensable as a reference work" for college students.

14. Fulgentius, *The Mythologies*, in *Fulgentius the Mythographer*, trans. and ed. Leslie George Whitbread (Columbus, 1971), book 2, chap. 6, p. 72.

15. Mulryan, *"Through a Glass Darkly,"* 204–6; Seznec, *The Survival of the Pagan Gods*, 220–24; Allen, *Mysteriously Meant*, 214–18.

16. Boccaccio, *Genealogie Deorum Gentilium Libri*, 2 vols., ed. Vincenzo Romano (Bari, 1951), book 4, chap. 45, p. 202; *Della Geneologia de gli dei di M. Giovanni Boccaccio libri quindeci*, trans. Giuseppe Betussi (Venice, 1606), book 4, p. 73v.

17. For the history of the *Adages*, see Margaret Mann Phillips, *The Adages of Erasmus* (New York, 1964).

18. Baldwin, *William Shakspere's Small Latine and Lesse Greeke*, 1:394, 421; 2:32; Clark, *John Milton at St. Paul's School*, 100–130, 218–19.

19. For an overview of Erasmus's influence on Milton, see Rosemary Masek, "Erasmus, Desiderius," in *A Milton Encyclopedia*, 9 vols., ed. William B. Hunter Jr. et al. (Lewisburg, PA, 1978–1983), 3:65–68.

20. Erasmus is cited parenthetically from *Adages*, trans. Margaret Mann Phillips, annotated by R. A. B. Mynors, vols. 30–36, *Collected Works of Erasmus* (Toronto, 1974–).

21. Panofsky and Panofsky, *Pandora's Box*, 17. In his discussion of "Malo accepto stultus sapit," Erasmus, *Adagiorum Chiliades Tres* (Venice, 1508), writes: "Redit Pandora, persuasoque Epimetheo pyxidem donat. Eam simul ac aperuisset, evolantibusque morbis, sensisset Iovis ἄδορα δῶρα, sero nimirum sapere coepit" (fol. 12r–v, cited in Panofsky and Panofsky, *Pandora's Box*, 16). Panofsky and Panofsky note that the sentence is grammatically ambiguous, suggesting that Epimetheus rather than Pandora may have opened the box (17). In a note on Hesiod's *Works and Days*, line 94, West explains that πίθου refers to a "pithos," or large storage jar, not a box. He traces to Erasmus the popular notion that Pandora opened a box, and he suggests that Erasmus was probably thinking of the box that Psyche opens, though she had been told not to. The myth of Psyche appears in Apuleius, *Metamorphoses*, 2 vols., trans. J. Arthur Hanson (Cambridge, MA, 1989), 6.19–21. Apuleius uses the word "pyxidem" or "pyxis" to refer to the container, and Hanson translates this as "jar" rather than the more customary "box."

22. Giraldi, *De Deis Gentium* (Basel, 1548), syntagma 13, pp. 571–72.

23. Mulryan, *"Through a Glass Darkly,"* 207–9; Allen, *Mysteriously Meant*, 221–25; Seznec, *The Survival of the Pagan Gods*, 230–33.

24. Seznec, *The Survival of the Pagan Gods*, 279; Allen, *Mysteriously Meant*, 225–28; Mulryan, *"Through a Glass Darkly,"* 213; Mulryan, "Mythographers," in *The Spenser Encyclopedia*, ed. A. C. Hamilton (Toronto, 1990), 493; Mulryan, "Translations and Adaptations of Vincenzo Cartari's *Imagini* and Natale Conti's *Mythologiae:* The Mythographic Tradition in the Renaissance," *Canadian Review of Comparative Literature* 8 (1981): 272–83. Mulryan, *"Through a Glass Darkly,"* 213, notes that an error traceable to eighteenth-century bibliographies created a Venice, 1551, ghost edition of Conti's work.

25. Baldwin, *William Shakspere's Small Latine and Lesse Greeke*, 1:421–22; 2:291, 396; DeWitt T. Starnes and Ernest William Talbert, *Classical Myth and Legend in Renaissance Dictionaries: A Study of Renaissance Dictionaries in Their Relation to the Classical Learning of Contemporary English Writers* (Chapel Hill, NC, 1955), 25–26; Charles Hoole, *A New Discovery of the Old Art of Teaching Schoole* (1660), 181–86.

26. For Milton's likely familiarity with Conti, see Mulryan, *"Through a Glass Darkly,"* 229–86; George F. Butler, "Milton's Briareos, Satan's Rebellion, and the Primacy of Natale Conti's *Mythologiae* in *Paradise Lost*," *Notes and Queries* n.s. 46 (1999): 330–32.

27. Conti, *Natalis Comitis Mythologiae, sive Explicationum Fabularum, Libri Decem* (Frankfurt, 1581), book 4, chap. 6, pp. 316–18.

28. Starnes and Talbert, *Classical Myth and Legend*, 8–9, 25–26; Mulryan, *"Through a Glass Darkly,"* 179; Hoole, *New Discovery*, 162–63; Baldwin, *William Shakspere's Small Latine and Lesse Greeke*, 1:421–22, 2:396.

29. Starnes and Talbert, *Classical Myth and Legend*, 227; Anthony à Wood, "*Fasti Oxonienses;* or, *Annals* of the University of Oxford" (1691), in Darbishire, *Early Lives of Milton*, 45–46; Phillips, "The Life of Mr. John Milton" (1694), in Darbishire, *Early Lives of Milton*, 72; John Tolland, "The Life of John Milton" (1698), in Darbishire, *Early Lives of Milton*, 192.

30. Stephanus, *Dictionarium Historicum, Geographicum, Poeticum* ([Geneva], 1609), 333v.

31. Alciato, *Emblemata: Lyons, 1550*, trans. and ed. Betty I. Knott (Brookfield, VT, 1996), 51–52; Panofsky and Panofsky, *Pandora's Box*, 34–78; Diane Kelsey McColley, *A Gust for Paradise: Milton's Eden and the Visual Arts* (Urbana, IL, 1993), 33–34; Roland Mushat Frye, *Milton's Imagery and the Visual Arts: Iconographic Tradition in the Epic Poems* (Princeton, NJ, 1978), 277–78; J. B. Trapp, "The Iconography of the Fall of Man," in *Approaches to "Paradise Lost": The York Tercentenary Lectures*, ed. C. A. Patrides (Toronto, 1968), 260–61.

32. Frye, *Milton's Imagery and the Visual Arts*, 18, 20–39; Mulryan, *"Through a Glass Darkly,"* 114. See also Michael O'Connell, "Milton and the Art of Italy: A Revisionist View," in *Milton in Italy: Contexts, Images, Contradictions*, ed. Mario A. DiCesare (Binghamton, NY, 1991), 215–36.

33. Duncan, *Milton's Earthly Paradise*, 21; J. M. Evans, *"Paradise Lost" and the Genesis Tradition* (Oxford, 1968), 114–42; A. Bartlett Giamatti, *The Earthly Paradise and the Renaissance Epic* (Princeton, NJ, 1966), 11–86; Jean Delumeau, *History of Paradise: The Garden of Eden in Myth and Tradition*, trans. Matthew O'Connell (New York, 1995), 3–21.

34. John A. Phillips, *Eve: The History of an Idea* (New York, 1984), 22–23.

35. Tertullian, *The Chaplet; or, De Corona*, trans. S. Thelwall, in *Ante-Nicene Fathers: The Writings of the Fathers Down to A.D. 325*, 10 vols., ed. Alexander Roberts and James Donaldson (1885; reprint, Peabody, MA, 1994), vol. 3, chap. 7, p. 97; Tertullian, *Against the Valentinians*, trans. Roberts, in Roberts and Donaldson, *Ante-Nicene Fathers*, vol. 3, chap. 12, p. 510.

36. Origen, *Origen against Celsus*, trans. Frederick Crombie, in Roberts and Donaldson, *Ante-Nicene Fathers*, vol. 4, book 4, chap. 38, p. 514; Henry Reynolds, *Mythomystes, wherein a short survay is taken of the natvre and valve of trvw poesy and depth of the ancients above ovr moderne poets*, in *Critical Essays of the Seventeenth Century*, 3 vols., ed. J. E. Spingarn (Bloomington, IN, 1957), 1:175; Allen, *Mysteriously Meant*, 11–12.

37. For Milton and Origen, see Harry F. Robins, *If This Be Heresy: A Study of Milton and Origen* (Urbana, IL, 1963). Mulryan, *"Through a Glass Darkly,"* 223–25, briefly summarizes Reynolds's work.

38. Kathryn A. McEuen agrees with this in her note on the passage (YP 1:239 n. 15).

39. In the Latin text appearing in *The Works of John Milton,* ed. Frank Allen Patterson, 18 vols. in 23 (New York, 1931–1940), Milton writes: "Error an *è Pandoræ* pixide, an ex penitissimo eruperit *Styge,* an denique unus ex Terræ filiis in cœlites conjuraverit, non est hujus loci accuratius disquirere" (12:172).

40. For the background of Milton's Typhon, see George F. Butler, "Milton's Typhon: Typhaon and Typhoeus in the Nativity Ode and *Paradise Lost,*" *Seventeenth-Century News* 55 (1997): 1–5.

41. Spenser's poetry is cited by book, canto, stanza, and line number from *The Faerie Queene,* 2nd ed., ed. A. C. Hamilton, Hiroshi Yamashita, and Toshiyuki Suzuki (New York, 2001).

42. The point is made forcefully by Philip J. Gallagher, *Milton, the Bible, and Misogyny,* ed. Eugene R. Cunnar and Gail L. Mortimer (Columbia, MO, 1990), 65 n. 35: "Milton is not identifying *Pandora* (Greek *all-gifted*) with Eve in this passage, because only in the fall does she become in any sense Adam's 'nurse and guide,' and even then the '[*un*]happiness' to which she seduces him is still his own arbitrary choice." Dean, "Marriage as Unreliable Narrative," 194 n. 49, generally agrees with Gallagher's assertion. Some critics have erred on this point, including Starnes and Talbert, *Classical Myth and Legend,* 270; and Giamatti, *The Earthly Paradise,* 326. Hughes's gloss on Pandora in *Paradise Lost,* Book Four, lines 714–19, quotes the passage from *The Doctrine and Discipline of Divorce* but is misleading because it omits several words.

43. Dennis H. Burden, *The Logical Epic: A Study of the Argument of "Paradise Lost"* (London, 1967), 69–70.

44. See John T. Shawcross, *John Milton: The Self and the World* (Lexington, KY, 1993), 289–94, for a discussion of Milton's work on *Paradise Lost* in the Trinity manuscript between 1640 and 1642, a period roughly contemporaneous with *The Doctrine and Discipline of Divorce.*

45. Talbert and Starnes, *Classical Myth and Legend,* 270; Stephanus, *Dictionarium Historicum, Geographicum, Poeticum,* 333v.

46. Boccaccio, *Genealogie Deorum Gentilium Libri,* book 4, chap. 45, p. 202; Erasmus, *Adagiorum Chiliades Tres,* fol. 12r–v, cited in Panofsky and Panofsky, *Pandora's Box,* 16; Giraldi, *De Deis Gentium,* syntagma 13, pp. 571–72; Conti, *Natalis Comitis Mythologiae,* book 4, chap. 6, pp. 316–18; Stephanus, *Dictionarium Historicum, Geographicum, Poeticum,* 333v.

47. Gallagher, *Milton, the Bible, and Misogyny,* 144.

48. McColley, *A Gust for Paradise,* 34.

49. The point is generally noted by Milton's editors. Mulryan, *"Through a Glass Darkly,"* 236–39, discusses Milton's use of the myth as it was related by Conti, *Natalis Comitis Mythologiae,* book 2, chap. 1, pp. 111–12, and Vincenzo Cartari, *Le Imagini de idei de gliantichi* (Venice, 1571), 358–60.

50. *Metamorphoses,* 2.552–53. Ovid is cited parenthetically by book and line number from *Metamorphoses,* 3rd ed., 2 vols., trans. Frank Justus Miller (Cambridge, MA, 1977).

51. Virgil, *Georgics* 3.113, in *Virgil,* rev. ed., 2 vols., trans. H. Rushton Fairclough (Cambridge, MA, 1934–1935), 1:79–237.

52. Hyginus, *Hygini: Quae hodie extant, adcurante Joanne Scheffero . . . Accedunt Thomae Munckeri in fabulas Hygini annotationes* (Hamburg, 1674), fab. 166, pp. 140–41; *P. Virgilli Maronis cum veterum omnium commentariis et selectis recentiorum notis nova editio,* ed. Gualtero Valkenier (Amsterdam, 1646), 164; *Natale Conti's Mythologies: A Select Translation,* ed. and trans. Anthony DiMatteo (New York, 1994), book 4, chap. 5, p. 196. For a review of the

medieval exegesis of the myth of Erichthonius, see Chance, *Medieval Mythography: From Roman North Africa to the School of Chartres*, A.D. 433–1177, 320–21; Chance, *Medieval Mythography: From the School of Chartres to the Court at Avignon, 1177–1350,* 368.

53. Sandys, *Ovid's Metamorphosis Englished, Mythologized, and Represented in Figures,* ed. Karl K. Hulley and Stanley T. Vandersall (Lincoln, NE, 1970), 114–15; Lactantius, *The Epitome of the Divine Institutes,* trans. William Fletcher, in Roberts and Donaldson, *Ante-Nicene Fathers,* vol. 7, chap. 9, p. 227.

54. Fulgentius, *The Mythologies,* book 2, chap. 11, pp. 75–76. Fulgentius's departure from Apollodorus was duly noted by the Renaissance mythographers. In his *Notae ac Emendationes in Hygini Fabulas* (Hamburg, 1674), note on fab. 166, p. 44, Thomas Munckerus remarks that Fulgentius mentions Pandora, while Pandrosos is customary.

55. Sandys, *Ovid's Metamorphosis,* 114.

56. Mulryan, "Through a Glass Darkly," 226–27.

57. Holdsworth, 25, quoted in Fletcher, *The Intellectual Development of John Milton,* 2:639.

58. Ross, *Mystagogus Poeticus; or, The Muses Interpreter, explaining the historicall Mysteries, and mysticall Histories of the ancient Greek and Latine Poets,* 3rd ed. (London, 1653), 113–14; Sandys, *Ovid's Metamorphosis,* 114–15.

59. For Erichthonius as a classical analogue of Milton's Sin, see Timothy J. O'Keeffe, "An Analogue to Milton's 'Sin' and More on the Tradition," *Milton Quarterly* 5 (1971): 74–77; John M. Steadman, *Nature into Myth: Medieval and Renaissance Moral Symbols* (Pittsburgh, 1979), 175, 179.

60. Stephanus, *Dictionarium Historicum, Geographicum, Poeticum,* 333v. In his entry for Erichthonius, 201r, Stephanus writes: "qui etiam Erichtheus dictus est" [who was likewise called Erichtheus].

61. Cicero, *De Natura Deorum,* 1.30. Homer's poetry is cited parenthetically by book and line number from *The Iliad,* 2 vols., trans. A. T. Murray (Cambridge, MA, 1924–1925); Cicero is cited parenthetically by book and chapter number from *De Natura Deorum,* in *De Natura Deorum Academica,* trans. H. Rackham (Cambridge, MA, 1933). For Mulciber as a name for Vulcan, see Stephanus, *Dictionarium Historicum, Geographicum, Poeticum,* 308r–v; Giraldi, *De Deis Gentium,* syntagma 13, p. 569. Starnes and Talbert, *Classical Myth and Legend,* 284, note that Mulciber appears often in Ovid and cite Stephanus as a possible source for Milton's account. In Giraldi's mythography, the discussion of Pandora is a subentry under "Vulcan."

62. Christopher Collins, "Milton's Early Cosmos and the Fall of Mulciber," in *Milton Studies* 19, *Urbane Milton: The Latin Poetry,* ed. James A. Freeman and Anthony Low (Pittsburgh, 1984), 50, links the fall of Mulciber with the fall of Adam.

63. Richard J. DuRocher, *Milton among the Romans: The Pedagogy and Influence of Milton's Latin Curriculum* (Pittsburgh, 2001), 130–38, relates the wounding of the earth to the creation of Eve and the wounding of Christ on the cross. See also DuRocher, "The Wounded Earth in *Paradise Lost,*" *Studies in Philology* 93 (1996): 93–115. Ken Hiltner, "The Portrayal of Eve in *Paradise Lost:* Genius at Work," in *Milton Studies* 40, ed. Albert C. Labriola (Pittsburgh, 2001), 73–75, discusses and expands DuRocher's remarks on this subject.

64. Michael Lieb, *The Dialectics of Creation: Patterns of Birth and Regeneration in "Paradise Lost"* (Amherst, 1970), 7, 142–60, 242.

DISCONTINUOUS WOUND:
MILTON AND DEISM

Abraham Stoll

WHEN JOHN TOLAND BRIEFLY doubted the contours of the New Testament canon in his *Life of Milton* (1698), public outrage led him to defend his skeptical approach. So we are left with the fascinating accident that an important deist questioning of revealed authority is named *Amyntor; or, Defense of the Life of Milton* (1699).[1] That a key text in the deist controversy should at least in title be a defense of Milton may be more appropriate, however, than criticism has so far recognized. For Milton's early reception includes a number of readings that assume an association between Milton and deism.

In the *Life*, Toland circumscribes Milton's thought within a decidedly deistic space:

> but in the latter part of his Life, he was not a profest Member of any particular Sect among Christians, he frequented none of their Assemblies, nor made use of their peculiar Rites in his Family. Whether this proceded from a dislike of their uncharitable and endless Disputes, and that Love of Dominion, or Inclination to Persecution, which, he said, was a piece of Popery inseparable from all Churches; or whether he thought one might be a good Man, without subscribing to any Party; and that they had all in som things corrupted the Institutions of Jesus Christ, I will by no means adventure to determin.[2]

These innuendoes powerfully gloss Milton's invocation to the spirit "that dost prefer / Before all temples the upright heart and pure."[3] For as Toland remarks, *Paradise Lost* widely excited charges of heresy in the late seventeenth century, although in Toland's mind these readings actually validate Milton's accuracy and truthfulness:

> As to the choice of his Subject, or the Particulars of his Story, I shall say nothing in defence of them against those People who brand 'em with Heresy and Impiety: for to incur the Displeasure of certain ignorant and supercilious Critics, argues free thinking, accurat Writing, and a generous Profession of Truth.[4]

John Shawcross refers to "the continued antagonism which Toland's view of religion raised and which was usually transferred uncritically to Milton." Milton's name itself became a marker for general impiety, and readers then and now have branded him with such heresies as Mortalism, Arianism, and Socinianism.[5] But Toland names Milton a free thinker, and so directs us toward deism: the phrase "free thinking" as a synonym, even euphemism, for deism gains enduring force with the publication of *A Discourse of Free Thinking* (1713), by Toland's friend Anthony Collins. There Collins constructs a genealogy that includes Milton in a list of free thinkers. And late in the controversy, when David Hume takes deism apart in *The Natural History of Religion* (1757), a first target is *Paradise Lost*. Arguing that mankind could not exercise sufficient reason to know God merely through the study of nature, he contests Adam's awakening in Book Eight. Hume recognizes how near that passage is to dramatizing the core tenet of deism's natural religion, that God can be known from the study of nature and without specific revelation.[6]

Deism's main political manifestation is the shaking of "priestcraft," and Milton's anti-prelatical writings, his republicanism, his toleration of free speech and Independency, as well as his apparent habits of worship, won the respect of deists.[7] But deism is first a theological revolution, best understood as the period's most forceful challenge to miracle and religious mystery—a challenge that centers on the subversion of revelation. As John Leland, deism's most complete chronicler, explains, deism had "one main end, viz. to set aside revelation, and to substitute mere natural religion, or, which seems to have been the intention of some of them, no religion at all in its room."[8] Deism questions local revelations, in the forms of miracles or angelic visitations. And it radically extends its questioning by leveling a skeptical gaze on the revealed authority of sacred scripture, and, as Leland suggests, even the Judeo-Christian revelation itself. *De Doctrina Christiana* suggests, despite Hume's reading, that Milton did not reject revealed religion, and so was not in doctrine a deist: "No one, however, can form correct ideas about God guided by nature or reason alone, without the word or message of God."[9] But the fact of Milton's deist reception should not be taken as mere misreading. Rather, that *Paradise Lost* was often read as deist indicates Milton's proximity to the radical theology that gains publicity at the same time as his late poetry.[10]

A few modern critics have noticed the proximity. Joseph Frank surveys Milton's anti-prelatical and divorce tracts, and his late poetry, and persuasively, if cursorily, evokes Milton's "movement towards deism." J. B. Broadbent suggestively finds an affinity between the God of Book Three and the abstract godhead of deism, but does not develop the insight. Only William Kolbrenner pursues the connection at length, arguing that Richard Bentley's "emendations to *Paradise Lost* represent an attempt to distinguish Milton's metaphysics from those of the free-thinkers, republicans and Deists who claimed him for their cause."[11] Intersecting Kolbrenner's work, this essay finds a stronger basis for explaining Milton's deist reception by focusing on the central issue of revelation and its poetic manifestation: epic machinery. Such a focus recovers what concerned many of Milton's early readers, particularly John Dennis. *The Advancement and Reformation of Modern Poetry* (1701), which is the first extended critical response to *Paradise Lost*, argues for identifying machinery with the workings of revealed religion:

> Now the passages of the Ancient Poets, which seem to have most Religion in them, are either those Addresses by which Men approach'd the Gods, as Invocations, Apostrophes and the like: or those Condescensions, by which the Gods communicated themselves to Men, as Revelations, Machines, etc. the First of which are Duties that belong to universal Natural Religion, the Second to Religion which is Reveal'd, Extraordinary and Miraculous.[12]

Milton's machinery, particularly in the war in heaven, has proven to be so vexed as to imply doubt for readers in the early reception, in the workings of revealed religion.

Milton's skeptical machinery need not be read as deistic—in fact, monotheistic will prove to be a better characterization—but it nevertheless was taken as such by thinkers on both sides of the deist controversy. For heretical readers, such as Toland and Collins, as well as for the more orthodox, such as Charles Leslie and Daniel Defoe, the war in heaven became an important locus for debate. Deep uncertainty over Milton's machinery in the war reflects what can be called its deist potential. This potential in the war is felt most acutely by Dennis, who can justify Milton's machinery only after forty-two octavo pages of *The Advancement* are devoted to a polemic against deism.[13] For Dennis and Milton's other readers, it is especially the war in heaven's tendency to slip suddenly from the sublime into bathos that threatens to make *Paradise Lost* into a deist document.

Alexander Pope, in *Peri Bathous,* recommends Milton's devils as an aid to "the art of sinking in poetry."[14] And, in what Edward Le Comte calls "the most devastating comment ever made on VI," Pope teases Milton for his machinery in *The Rape of the Lock:*

> The Peer now spreads the glitt'ring *Forfex* wide,
> T'inclose the Lock, now joins it, to divide.
> Ev'n then, before the fatal Engine clos'd,
> A wretched *Sylph* too fondly interpos'd;
> Fate urg'd the Sheers, and cut the *Sylph* in twain,
> (But Airy Substance soon unites again).   (3.147–52)[15]

What Pope mocks is the narrative absurdity of staging a duel between Michael and Satan in which the combatants instantly heal up: "So sore / The griding sword with discontinuous wound / Passed through him, but the ethereal substance closed / Not long divisible" (6.328–31). Pope's humor raises the questions: How can the sword fight matter if there is such a short-lived effect? And how can the sublime strain, built upon the severing of flesh, be maintained when that flesh heals itself into oblivion in the following line? The contradiction of "Not long divisible" renders Satan's "discontinuous wound" narratively inert, and the war plummets, momentarily, into bathos.

Less willing than Pope to view Milton's infelicity as a mistake, Arnold Stein argues that the war in heaven is an intentional burlesque. He likens Michael's wounding of Satan to hitting "a man proud of his bearing and composure with a custard pie."[16] By blunting Michael's "griding sword" into custard, the incision and its subsequent healing are covered over. Accentuating the bathos, Stein saves Milton from Pope's mockery—Milton meant to be funny. In contradiction with both Stein and Pope, however, the early reception also regularly lauds Book Six as a high point of the poem, and not at all funny. Samuel Barrow and the Earl of Roscommon both use the war to stand for the greatness of the whole poem, while Dennis and Addison list Books One, Two, and Six as the poem's most sublime.[17] Reading the war as consistently elevated, though, requires overlooking that Satan's wound is "not long divisible," as well as many other moments of absurdity.[18] Indeed, Addison locates the sublime only by laboring against readings that, like Pope's, have been filled with laughter: "It required great Pregnancy of Invention, and Strength of Imagination, to fill this Battel with such circumstances as should raise and astonish the mind of the Reader; and, at the same time, an Exactness of Judgement to avoid everything that might appear light or trivial."[19] Only by expunging the light and trivial can Addison portray a war that, in a sublime manner, astonishes the mind.

There is great reason for eliding such laughter, which, after all, is raillery aimed at angels and the sacred history of angelic war. For by pointing to the bathetic, Pope raises a kind of laughter that sounds very much like the skeptical laughter advocated by Shaftesbury, for whom ridicule represents the best test of truth: "For nothing is ridiculous except what is deformed, nor is anything proof against raillery except what is handsome and just."[20] The contradictory presence of the sublime and the bathetic together in the deformed narrative of the discontinuous wound, like much of Book Six, cannot stand up to Shaftesbury's proof. Shaftesbury's philosophy of ridicule so neatly describes the deists' own habit of raillery that many consider him a deist. Indeed, outright deists such as Collins and Thomas Woolston regularly make strategic use of ridicule against the truths of revealed Christianity, making humor "the principal weapon employed to discredit Christian miracles."[21] Parody is a devastating weapon against revealed religion in particular since revelations combine the potential outlandishness of miracle with a thoroughly serious insistence on authority. So as Lord Bolingbroke reads *The Rape of the Lock* in a letter to Pope, mockery makes the machinery of *Paradise Lost* indistinguishable from pagan superstition:

(Homer) meant to flatter his countrymen, by recording the feats of their ancestors, the valor of some, and the prudence of others; and he employed for the machinery of his poem the theology of his age, as Tasso and Milton have employed that of theirs. Had Arnobius, and much more such a weak philosopher as Justin, or such a warm rhetor as Tertullian, lived in our days, you would have been attacked in your turn, and have been made the father of rosycrusianism, and of all the silly doctrines about sylphs and gnomes; just as reasonably as Homer has been attacked, by the zeal of Christian writers, for teaching polytheism and idolatry.[22]

Milton's machinery is grouped with that of Homer and Pope: all such revelation is superstition and polytheism to Bolingbroke the deist.[23] Reading Milton and Pope's machinery as identically ridiculous, Bolingbroke not only undermines the local revelations of angels, but by extension rejects the Judeo-Christian revelation, which would separate Christian angels from the mythology of Homer and Pope. The deism is explicit in Bolingbroke's reading and is implicit in Pope's parody—but it is also part of Milton's poem, for a silly war in heaven threatens to become a deist war in heaven.

It is just such a perceived lack of seriousness in the war that touches off the early reception's most virulent attack on *Paradise Lost,* Charles Leslie's *The History of Sin and Heresie* (1698). Toland's dismissal of "those People who brand 'em (Milton's subject and story) with Heresy and Impiety" may be in dialogue with the orthodox polemicist, who published *Sin and Heresie* in the same year as Toland's *Life.* Meditating on the feast of Saint Michael, Leslie takes as his text Revelations 12:7, "There was War in Heaven," but endeavors "to give a more *Serious* Representation of that *War in Heaven,*" than Milton.[24] What makes Milton's war heretical is that:

The Gravity and Seriousness with which the Subject ought to be treated, has not been Regarded in the Adventurous Flight of Poets, who have Dress'd Angels in Armor, and put Swords and Guns into their Hands, to Form Romantick Battles in the Plains of Heaven, a Scene of Licentious Fancy. (*Sin and Heresie*, A2r)

Leslie's great anxiety is that Milton's literal and material narrative, in making the war in heaven too common a subject, has opened up the sacred event to subsequent degradation among wits: "but the Truth has been Greatly Hurt thereby, and Degraded at last, even into a Play, which was Design'd to have been Acted upon the Stage: And tho once happily Prevented, yet has Pass'd the Press, and become the Entertainment of Prophane Raillery" (*Sin and Heresie,* A2r–2v).

Shaftesbury may make a virtue of raillery, but Leslie is, in Shaftesbury's terms, a melancholy divine. He sees Milton's war as pure debasement. Leslie's fear that a material reading of Revelation 12:7 could serve profane raillery in fact proves well founded. Collins, as Richard Bentley recognizes, smirks at the biblical war in heaven in *A Discourse of Free Thinking* (1713). Demonstrating that Socrates was a freethinker, Collins lauds him because he "disbeliev'd the Gods of his Country, and the common Creeds about them, and declar'd his Dislike, when he heard Men attribute Repentance, Anger, and other Passions to the Gods, and talk of Wars and Battels in Heaven, and of the Gods getting Women with Child, and such-like fabulous and blasphemous Storys." Socrates is proven a freethinker—that is, a deist—for disbelieving such superstitious details. In his *Remarks upon a Late Discourse of Free-Thinking* (1713), Bentley recognizes Collins's "talk of Wars and Battels in Heaven" as "pointed against" Revelation 12:7, complaining, "Now where has this Writer liv'd, or what Idiot Evangelist was he bred under; not to know that This is all Vision and Allegory, and not propos'd as literal truth." Kolbrenner finds it "irresistible to speculate that Bentley was thinking here also of Milton's 'war in heaven.' "[25] Since Collins lists Milton as a freethinker, it is also possible that his "Wars and Battels in Heaven" derives from *Paradise Lost.* In that case, the "Idiot Evangelist" who Bentley says bred Collins and his deist raillery would be Milton.

If, as Leslie claims, Milton's war in heaven enables heresy, it is the literalness and materiality of the fighting that is to blame. Just as Bentley complains that Collins ought to know that the war is "all vision and allegory" and "not literal truth," so for Leslie the gravity and seriousness of the narrative are compromised by the literal presence of armor, swords, and guns. Milton's excessive materiality, however, is not threatening in itself but for the way it can be read. Leslie fears that literal bodies lead to contradiction and absurdity in the war in heaven, and so potentially to heresy.

As a corrective to *Paradise Lost,* Leslie offers his own narrative of the war in heaven. Like Milton, Leslie locates the origin of sin and heresy in the angelic revolt. But he takes issue with Milton for linking the revolt not to the incarnation but to the Son's begetting, an attack on Milton's Arianism (*Sin and Heresie,* A2v).[26] He then offers a midrashic alternative, imagining as the beginning of the war an argument between Michael and Satan over the Incarnation. The argument is set in notably current theological terms, dramatizing how a thoroughly abstract godhead leads to a dismissal of revelation.

In Leslie's version, Satan contends that God could not debase himself by taking on the form of a human, and revolts because his reason cannot reconcile God's omnipotence with the Incarnation. At the heart of Satan's objection is his rational conviction that God is utterly transcendent and omnipotent: Michael and Satan's argument, according to Leslie, "proceeded from the Different Notions they had of God" (*Sin and Heresie*, 11). Satan insists upon an absolutely perfect and omnipotent godhead, and logic therefore leads him to deny the possibility that "God shou'd be a *Man*, Subject to Infirmities and Death" (*Sin and Heresie*, 11). The godhead conceived of as utterly abstract is a position common to both Socinians and deists—one of the ways in which they overlap.[27] In general, such an exaltation of God may seem unimpeachable. But it is heretical when, like Leslie's Satan, the logic of God's abstraction undermines the divinity of Christ. When this skeptical attitude extends also to the angels of the war in heaven, the rational impulse turns to a rejection of revealed religion.

In response to Satan, Leslie's Michael argues for a mysterious rather than literal reading of both Christ and the war. God can be both omnipotent and incarnate because "the ways were Unsearchable, by which God did Communicate Himself to His Creatures" (*Sin and Heresie*, 11). Similarly, regarding Satan's revolt: Revelation 12:7, Leslie says, is "a Great *Mystery*," and therefore "our Inquiries must be with Reverence and profound Humility. Why else are they Mysteries?" (*Sin and Heresie*, 1). In a frequent orthodox gesture against deism, similar to Bentley insisting on an allegorical reading, Michael's mystery turns away the skeptical gaze that has settled on the materiality of revelation. Mystery dissolves (rather than solves) Satan's rational argument. Mystery, furthermore, removes the war from the material space that allows for representation and extension in plot: Leslie's war has no armor or guns, no bodies or wounds—in fact, is no representation at all. After Satan and Michael's argument, Leslie's narrative merely states that "Michael fought" and goes on to lavish praise on his victory (*Sin and Heresie*, 11–14). While this may be a perfectly tenable move in a sermon, it is deeply destructive of a poem that depends upon narrative. Leslie's reimagining of the war in heaven casts Milton as the argumentative Satan—that is, as a deist—and then censors him.

Leslie corrects Milton into silence in order to avoid a poetic materiality that draws near to deism. And here we arrive at a key reversal of expectations. Leslie's antideist stance does not seek to revivify a stripped-down and austere version of religion, but rather seeks to control the proliferation of Christian machinery. In its rejection of revelation, deism generally pushes toward a rational religious economy free from what Bolingbroke calls "pneumatical madness."[28] And yet Milton is received as deistic not because he has constructed a cosmos devoid of the visible Christian agents of revelation, but rather because he has so accentuated them.

Indeed, it is Milton's shaping of the Christian supernatural into actual beings, with bodies, personalities, and histories, that threatens to become deism in Daniel Defoe's response to *Paradise Lost, The Political History of the Devil* (1726). Maximillian Novak has characterized Defoe's occult writings of 1726–1727 as part of his long-standing aversion to such deists as Toland and Collins.[29] While Defoe praises Milton's poetic powers, he is concerned, like Leslie, to prevent *Paradise Lost* from being read as literal theology. The problem is that Milton has given sacred history such particularity and materiality that the Bible as a whole can be questioned. Speaking of the angelic rebellion, Defoe makes *Paradise Lost* a catalyst for the rejection of the entire revelation:

Mr. Milton here takes it upon him to give the History of it as particularly as if he had been born there, and came down hither on purpose to give us an account of it; (I hope he is better inform'd by this time;) but this he does in such a manner, as jostles with Religion, and shocks our Faith in so many points necessary to be believ'd, that we must forbear to give up to Milton, or must set aside part of the Sacred Text, in such a manner, as will assist some people to set it aside all.[30]

Aware of the deist strategy of using local contradictions to invalidate the entirety of Scripture, Defoe fears that the jostling of Milton's "history" assists in marginalizing the Bible. In *A Short and Easie Method with the Deists* (1697), Leslie makes the same observation about deists, who believe that "if things be not as they are told in any relation, that Relation must be false. And if false in Part, we cannot Trust to it, either in whole, or in Part. . . . We must receive all, or Reject all. I mean in any Book that pretends to be written from the mouth of God. For in other common Histories, we may believe Part and reject part, as we see Cause."[31]

Accordingly, Defoe ironizes the idea of a history of the devil, making references to the devil as "historian," "chronologist," and "antiquarian" (*The Political History*, 12, 13). He gives ironic credit for such a personal version of Satan to Milton (27). Defoe also denies the devil his traditional iconography, such as the cloven foot, as well as the materiality of the Miltonic hell (27, 36, 77, 208). The cloven foot, like all material and personal conceptions of the devil, is actually a stratagem to make Christianity seem superstitious: "he finds it his Interest to foster the cheat, and serve himself of the Consequence" (265). This diabolical consequence is disbelief in the revealed specifics of Christianity. And so, while deism skeptically strips away miracle and revelation in constructing an abstract and rational religion, paradoxically Defoe strips Milton's Satan of personality and attributes as a means of combating deism. Defoe and Leslie read the profusion of literal detail in *Paradise Lost* with the same anxiety: that it provides an opening for skepticism, and so is potentially deist.

However, the mere presence of material angels in *Paradise Lost* is not what excites a deistic response. Henry More's insistence on material spirits, often compared to Milton's, in contrast supports revelation against protodeist skepticism. Rather, it is the presence of a deeply vexed materiality, Milton's inconsistent system of blending materiality and immateriality, that, as Samuel Johnson says, "perplexed his poetry."[32] Both material and not, Milton's angelic machinery puts the reader in unstable interpretive positions—in positions of doubt requiring ontological calculation. Such moments of discursivity undercut the forward momentum of the narrative, bathetically knocking it from its sublime pitch. And such discursivity establishes in the poetry the kind of rational and skeptical thought processes about revelation that invite deism.

It is in the strange narrative of the discontinuous wound that materiality most interestingly perplexes poetry. The duel is so terribly visceral, and the wound is felt so literally, that its subsequent healing becomes deeply incongruous. Michael's sword

>   met
> The sword of Satan with steep force to smite
> Descending, and in half cut sheer, nor stayed,
> But with swift wheel reverse, deep entering shared
> All his right side; then Satan first knew pain,
> And writhed him to and fro convolved; so sore
> The griding sword with discontinuous wound
> Passed through him, but the ethereal substance closed
> Not long divisible.   (6.323–31)

Striving toward the epic pitch of battle, the dazzling movements of Michael's sword are physically enacted in the enjambment of "steep force to smite / Descending," and in the additional thrust of the "swift wheel reverse." And the consequence of Michael's swordsmanship, Satan's wound, is fleshed out for the reader by "deep entering," and "griding." But for all that, the incision barely stays open. The difficult modifier of the wound, "discontinuous," is itself busy reknitting Satan's body even as it is cut. A wound, by definition, is already a break in the flesh, and a discontinuous wound may be one that does not maintain its incision throughout: with "discontinuous" coming first in the progression of the narrative, the wound is healing even as it comes into being.

Behind the perplexing discontinuity of the wound narrative is the problem of whether or not Satan's hurt actually matters. Like the coyote who goes over a cliff only to return with a Band-Aid, the wound becomes absurd as it implies that these bodies and their actions lack consequence. This is what Pope's sylph lays bare: the duel is inconsequential. But additionally, and contradictorily, the poetry asserts that the fight is of surpassing consequence. Just before the duel, as Michael and Satan address to fight, Raphael claims that "Stood they or moved, in stature, motion, arms / Fit to decide the empire of great heaven" (6.302–3). The duel is decisive—at least until the cut is suddenly undone. The incongruity of the discontinuous wound is part of a contradictory tendency in Book Six to vacillate between a sense that local action is critically important and utterly inconsequential. I argue in this section that this pattern is symptomatic of a structural disjunction between the war narrative's need for important action, and the poem's doctrinal need for an absolutely transcendent—omniscient and omnipotent—God. Milton: (1) forgets God's totalizing influence in order to give the war narrative consequence and so sublimity; and (2) punctures the sense of consequentiality and, with the bathos of local insignificance, reinserts God into the narrative.

Book Six begins with little Abdiel heroically flying "Through heaven's wide champaign" to report to God Satan's plans for war. As the lone just angel to emerge from Satan's Book Five colloquy, Abdiel in his flight carries the doctrinal weight of free will, and the dramatic import of the commencement of the war in heaven. Flying all night, "till morn, / Waked by the circling hours, with rosy hand / Unbarred the gates of light" (6.2–4), Abdiel's journey is a rousing opening scene. But when he arrives, he suddenly gets a view of the angelic troops: "War he perceived, war in procinct, and found / Already known what he for news had thought / To have reported" (6.19–21). As with Satan's wound, the narrative grinds to a bathetic halt, with Abdiel's heroism laid bare as entirely unnecessary. Abdiel's knowledge is not new because, of course, God is omniscient.[33]

The sophisticated play between the words "known" and "news" points out the disjunction between omniscience and narrative that underlies this passage. "News" is knowledge, but knowledge that must be new—news is knowledge that has a position in time and (given Abdiel's flight) also in space. But omniscience, in its infinite reach, must transcend time and space. It has an always-already logic that resists such things as a messenger, a messenger's flight, and, indeed, all plot events, which must unfold within time and space. The two radically separate time frames of God and narrative cannot be integrated. Instead, the heroic press of the narrative—the suspenseful march of time that is wrapped up in a good story—must be interrupted, and undercut, by God's abstracting omniscience.

Similarly, as the narrative turns to action the poet must confront God's omnipotence. When the war begins, it is precisely God's unlimited power that must be forgotten. In the first press of battle, "each on himself relied, / As only in his arm the moment lay / Of victory" (6.238–40). Each angelic arm recalls—in order to set aside—the totalizing arm of God. "Moment," as Fowler glosses it, primarily means "determining influence"—each angel fights as if he, rather than God, controlled the outcome. But the enjambment separates "moment" from "Of victory," suggesting that we first read "moment" for its temporal meaning. In the littleness in time that is a moment, however, time dwindles as the word is recast to mean consequence. As the less obvious meaning becomes primary, we feel a forcing of perspective, a deliberate narrowing, until we are so focused on the angelic arms that they actually do seem to matter. But the poetry makes clear that before the stirring sense of consequentiality can enter, before each angel can imagine that in his actions lie the outcome, temporal limits must be erased. For each angel to fight as if victory really depended upon his arm, which is to say for the battle narrative to matter, angelic action must seize our attention to the point that God is forgotten.

To the extent that the war in heaven reads as heroic poetry, God's omnipotence and omniscience must be fenced out of each moment of battle. The very possibility of a war narrative, in fact, depends on God's own self-limiting, for if God were to exert his full omnipotence, not only would there be no war, there would also be no war narrative. Much as Leslie censors Milton's war in heaven, logical consistency with the omniscient and omnipotent godhead would silence Book Six. And so God "suffered" the battle to continue, he tells the Son,

> that the glory may be thine
> Of ending this great war, since none but thou
> Can end it. Into thee such virtue and grace
> Immense I have transfused, that all may know
> In heaven and hell thy power above compare,
> And this perverse commotion governed thus,
> To manifest thee worthiest to be heir
> Of all things.   (6.701–8)

God has governed the war in heaven in order to "manifest" the Son—that is to make the Son's glory narratable. The Son's manifestation in his chariot is immediately for the sake of the warring angels. But it is soon a narrative for Raphael to pass on to Adam—and for Milton his readers. If a fully transcendent God denies the possibility of meaningful action, then Milton's sudden movements from consequential to inconsequential action may be seen as a necessary strategic solution to the disjunction between God and narrative. Were Satan to be permanently injured, Michael might indeed decide events.

His "griding sword" would then encourage the reader, in the heat of the narrative, to forget God's role. But the closing of the wound, by rendering the duel inconsequential, reminds us of God and of the vast provenance of his knowledge and power. It is precisely by means of puncturing the epic pitch that Milton reinserts what the sublime narrative forgets: God's omnipotence and omniscience.

And yet as Milton bridges the disjunction between the war narrative and God's omnipotence and omniscience, it is remarkable how uninterested he seems in finesse. Milton goes out of his way to make clear how contradictory his narrative is. Just ten lines before "each on himself relied, / As only in his arm the moment lay / Of victory," Milton announces God's omnipotence and claims that God is containing angelic action: "the eternal king omnipotent / From his strong hold of heaven high overruled / And limited their might" (6.227–29). Victory does not lie in angelic arms, and it only can if we turn God's gesture back on him and limit his might by forgetting what we read a few lines earlier. Even more broadly, as Abdiel steps in front of the armies to confront Satan, just before the initial blow, Abdiel pronounces the war absurd:

> fool, not to think how vain
> Against the omnipotent to rise in arms;
> Who out of smallest things could without end
> Have raised incessant armies to defeat
> Thy folly; or with solitary hand
> Reaching beyond all limit at one blow
> Unaided could have finished thee, and whelmed
> Thy legions under darkness.   (6.135–42)

It is not the angelic arms that will decide events, but God's solitary hand, and it is foolish to think otherwise. Abdiel's words not only charge Satan, but also Milton himself, with folly. They begin the war in heaven by overtly parodying the sublime claims upon which Milton's narrative will depend. The poet intends no trickery. He is not trying to catch his reader in error, but rather is making entirely clear what he is doing.[34]

Although he is forthright about it, what Milton is doing *is* impossibly contradictory. "Discontinuous" may be said to modify not only Satan's wound, but the entire topos of wounding, emphasizing that the very idea of a war in heaven cannot work. The rigorous illogic of Satan's wound cuts its own kind of hole in the fabric of the narrative, leading to what Johnson says about the war in heaven: "The confusion of spirit and matter which pervades the whole narration of the war of heaven fills it with incongruity; and the book in which it is related is, I believe, the favourite of children and gradually neglected as knowledge is increased."³⁵ Incongruity leads to a sense that the text itself is childish, or, as with Stein's custard pie, that the poem is cartoonish. The many moments of illogic send the war in heaven plummeting from the sublime to the bathetic, deforming the narrative into absurdity and laughter.

And laughter and ridicule, as Shaftesbury argues, are powerfully discursive tools, sorting what in religion is reasonable and what not. Laughter in the war in heaven functions as a sharply skeptical device, challenging the reader to consider carefully epic machinery. When the wound heals so suddenly, the possibility of representing divine matters in spatial and temporal terms, the possibility of a divine narrative based on visible beings and consequential actions, becomes a subject of the poetry—and an object of doubt. The poem's sudden moves from sublimity to bathos place machinery, and so revelation, within an anxious calculus that is congruent with the rational skepticism toward miracle and revelation that drives deism. This quality is the key to understanding Milton's deist reception. Milton offers a puppet show but insists on exposing the strings—machinery is revealed as illusion, and so the epic reads as skepticism.

But mindful that Milton did not endorse a rejection of all revelation, I suggest reading even the most absurd incongruities of the war not as deistic but as monotheistic. The discontinuous wound and similar moments operate very like a particular kind of skepticism: iconoclasm. First putting forward a narrative that is exciting but doctrinally questionable, and then recovering the doctrine by undoing the narrative, these moments actually portray God by demonstrating what he and his cosmos are not. Lenn Evan Goodman explains that

The absolute transcendent perfection of God as understood in the integrated concept of divinity precludes the penetration of the human analytical intelligence, which is finite and can know nothing of the infinitude save only its direction—symbolically represented as upward, that is towards perfection but transcending all humanly conceptualized and so delimited notions of the perfect. It was the recognition of this fact which was expressed in the Mosaic iconoclasm.³⁶

Like the monotheistic breaking of images, Milton's machinery points, by staging its rejection of visible and material divinity, toward God's transcendence. We not only get the story acted by the puppets, but we also learn of the puppeteer's art, and of the puppeteer himself. Contradictions and absurdities such as the discontinuous wound enable narrative, and so are constitutive of the abstract God of monotheism. Furthermore, a text that elicits discursivity and ontological calculation brings the reader into a typically monotheistic space. Unlike polytheism, monotheism must carefully monitor all revelations and all forms of the supernatural. Such a rigorous defense of its ontological borders leads Aryeh Botwinick to identify monotheism with skepticism. Skepticism "has at least two 'runs' in Western intellectual history: first as monotheism and then, more explicitly, and self-consciously, as skepticism."[37] Monotheistic discursiveness creates, and depends upon, narratives that are disrupted and discontinuous. The bathos of the war in heaven can thus be seen as a version of the "background" or "gaps" that such critics as Erich Auerbach, Robert Altar, and Meir Sternberg have associated with biblical narrative.[38]

But even if it is best viewed as a feature of Milton's monotheistic narrative, the problem of bathos, with its insertion of discursivity into the war, may also be read as deistic. The period's deism may be seen as an extreme but logical result of monotheism's skepticism.[39] And so while Milton may not be a deist, his monotheism was taken by many, notably John Dennis, as potential deism.

The most thorough rebuttal of the deistic reception of Milton, coming three years after Toland's *Life*, is Dennis's *The Advancement and Reformation of Modern Poetry*. Arguing for the truth of revealed religion and its value to poetry, Dennis justifies Milton's machinery by means of a rejection of deism. He embarks on his lengthy polemic against deism in order to rescue Milton's machinery from the kind of skeptical equivocation that Leslie and Defoe both fear. The text's anxiety clearly demonstrates the potential for a deist reading of *Paradise Lost*, as well as the necessity, for the sake of orthodox Christianity, of suppressing such a reading. This suppression takes the form of elision, in *The Advancement* and throughout Dennis's writings on *Paradise Lost*, as Dennis is forced to misread Milton's machinery to preserve the orthodoxy of the war in heaven.

In addition to clarifying the association between Milton and deism, Dennis's criticism also reveals how hard Milton's early readers worked to read *Paradise Lost* as sublime, and the serious stakes in the construction of the eighteenth century's sublime Milton. Dennis is read usually as an early champion of Milton as sublime.[40] His readings of the war in heaven suggest that the emergence of the sublime Milton was a reception bound up in the denial of a deist Milton.

The problem of Milton's material representation of the war in heaven is, in neoclassical terms, a problem with Christian machinery. On one side of the lengthy debate, René Le Bossu insists upon machinery in epic, but argues that all such machinery is allegorical.[41] Freeing it from the literal, Le Bossu's allegory, like Leslie's mystery, implies that true divinity exists and functions in a plane other than that of the narrative—epic machinery is not idolatrous because it allegorically figures religious truth. Dryden expresses a common-sensical middle ground by simply allowing angels, which are authorized by Scripture, to be epic machinery.[42] Boileau, however, insists that Christianity must not be mingled with the visible figures of epic poetry. Dennis translates Boileau's famous verses from *L'art Poetique*, where "ornaments" should be understood as machines: "The terrible mysteries of the Christian Faith are not capable of delightful Ornaments; that the Gospel offers nothing to our View, but Repentance on the one side, and eternal Torments on the other; and that the criminal Mixture of Poetical Fictions, gave a fabulous Air even to its most Sacred Truths" (*Critical Works*, 1:252). For Boileau there is no place for epic machinery in Christianity because "the Gospel offers nothing to our View"—Christianity denies a visible religious economy. Boileau offers a rigorously monotheistic version of religion, so that, recalling the second commandment, machinery in a Christian epic is criminal. Milton, clearly, does not agree with Boileau's austere Christianity. But the deep equivocation that marks Milton's machinery demonstrates that he also does not, like Le Bossu, simply invoke allegory or mystery and call it good. Rather, Milton writes Boileau's skepticism into his machinery, even as he, contradictorily, continues to proliferate it. The fundamental illogic of his machinery may be iconoclastic, and so represent Milton's monotheism. But it readily can be received as deistic, and so causes Dennis significant problems.

Dennis's troubles are first visible in *Remarks upon a Book Entituled Prince Arthur* (1696), his earliest statement on epic. There Dennis quotes approvingly Boileau's rejection of Christian machinery and says that Blackmore's machinery cannot be pleasing because "Christian Machines are quite out of Nature, and consequently cannot delight" (*Critical Works*, 1:53, 105). Immediately after, however, he must admit that Milton's machinery could be censured for the same reason. He defends *Paradise Lost* with an argument about the fallen angels' goodness, but the defense is weakly beside the point —following Boileau gets Dennis into trouble with *Paradise Lost* (*Critical Works*, 1:106–8). And so in *The Advancement*, Dennis changes his mind. Dennis revisits the Boileau passage, only here he hedges his statement:

we only made use of this Passage in the foremention'd Treatise, to shew, That the Mysteries of the Christian Religion were not to be mix'd with Fiction, and consequently, that it would be a hard matter to contrive Machines for an Epick Poem, upon a Modern Christian Subject; and if Boileau means any thing more by the foremention'd Passage, I shall endeavour to shew that he is mistaken and that there may not only be most exalted Poetry upon a Christian Subject, without Machines, and without Fiction, but that the True Religion, is more favourable to Poetry than Paganism, or Philosophy or Deism. (*Critical Works*, 1.252)

Dennis wants to prove that Christianity is consistent with poetry, and this is identical with an advocacy of Milton: his argument that a Christian subject will elevate modern poetry above the ancients is largely defended with passages from *Paradise Lost*. The main clog, though, is machinery, and Dennis captures perfectly the narratological difficulty that permeates the war in heaven when he says that contriving machinery for a Christian epic is a "hard matter."

Because of such difficulty, Dennis's justification of Christian machinery in poetry is not by positive assertion but comparative statement: Dennis does not say that true religion can use machinery, but that it is "more favourable" to poetry than other religions. The acceptability of Christian machinery therefore rests upon the rejection of the heretical extremes of "Paganism, or Philosophy or Deism." In the following chapter, *Paradise Lost* is compared to Virgil's pagan machinery. But before Dennis proceeds to this evidence, he gives a full forty-two pages to disposing of philosophy and deism. He takes philosophy as the general elevation of reason over passion and uses it mostly as an entrance into his discussion of deism. Dennis's argument for Christian machinery, therefore, proceeds via deism—it is only after deism is rejected, in fact only by means of that rejection, that Christian, and specifically Milton's, machinery can be defended.

Proving that Christianity is favorable to poetry, Dennis argues that passion is the true end of poetry, and that religion, whether pagan or Christian, is the most valuable subject of poetry because it raises the highest form of passion, "enthusiasm." In contrast, deism, lacking revelation, combats the passions and offers proof only to human reason. Dennis argues that the masses are incapable of understanding such purely rational proofs:

all are capable of the Proofs of Revealed Religion: For, by proving the Divinity of the Revelation, the Doctrine is proved in course. But Miracles are Proofs of which all Men are capable, because they speak to the Passions, and appeal to the Senses. Since therefore, the True Religion must be design'd for all; and all Men are capable of the Proofs of Reveal'd Religion, whereas not one in Forty is capable of the Proofs of Deism, it follows, that a Religion that is not Reveal'd, cannot be the True Religion. (*Critical Works*, 1:259)

Deism is rejected because, in denying miracles and revelation, it cannot offer sufficiently passionate, and therefore convincing, evidence of the divine. Christian revelation is more passionate than deist argument, and, Dennis insists, it also harmonizes passion and reason. Such harmony between passion and reason —which is absent in deism—makes Christianity less open to ambiguity:

For, after that Christianity has gain'd its Professors, by proving after the most plain and simple manner, all that is necessary to be believ'd in it; that is, by Miracles, attested by the unexceptionable Witnesses, it gains its End, which is the Happiness of its Believers, in so plain, so sure, and so short a Way, that the Way to Happiness, and the End, is but one and the same Thing. (*Critical Works*, 1:260)

There is no equivocation in revealed religion: miracles and revelation convince totally and immediately, so that the "way" and the "end" are the same. Deism fails, in contrast, because rational argument requires a process that must engage and logically overcome potential moments of contradiction. Deism gets caught in the labyrinths of thought, of argument and counterargument, and thus proves itself in dilatory time. Without revelation and its recourse to mystery for explanation, deism offers only the kind of rational and discursive evidence of the divine that, in its lack of immediacy and passion, loses most people: "Thus the Proofs of Christianity are short and plain, and its Doctrine that leads to Felicity, admirably short and unperplexed, whereas the Proofs of Deism are abstruse" (*Critical Works*, 1:261).

It is against this sense of discursiveness and perplexity that Dennis justifies Christian machinery. Deism, and therefore deist poetry, entangles one in the mazes of ratiocination. Without revelation and its poetic equivalent, machinery, deism struggles to prove the divine and succeeds mostly in creating a morass of discursive and rational argument. In contrast, Christianity and Christian poetry easily secure happiness through harmonizing reason and passion. Stressing the necessity of decorum, Dennis ejects "discord"—that is, the kind of perplexity and discursiveness that he has associated with deism (*Critical Works*, 1:263–64). The harmony and continuity of decorous poetry, moreover, are specifically associated with Christian machinery. The key to this kind of decorum, passion, is represented as an angel: "the Passions, as it were, in a fiery Vehicle, transport the Reason above Mortality, which mounting, soars to the Heaven of Heavens" (1:261). In "fiery vehicle," Dennis uses a common term for angelic beings, aligning the success of Christian poetry with the literal functioning of angels. Dennis then provides a vision of the successful poem that is nothing less than a profusion of angelic beings and miraculous revelations: "he who is entertain'd with an accomplish'd Poem, is, for a time, at least, restored to Paradise. That happy Man converses boldly with Immortal Beings. Transported, he beholds the Gods ascending and descending, and every Passion, in its Turn, is charm'd, while his Reason is supremely satisfied" (1:264). In this vision of a supernatural cosmos, angels represent Dennis's hopes for Christian poetry: the harmony of passion and reason, and the easy commerce between the human and heavenly worlds. Coming just after his polemic against deism, the vision secures machinery and revelation as essential to Christian poetry.

This vision, furthermore, is of *Paradise Lost*. Dennis's idea of an "accomplish'd Poem" repeatedly echoes Milton's: in a restoration to paradise (1.5); in its "happy" man, picking up Milton's favorite modifier of the prelapsarian state (1.29, 3.66, 5.234, 12.642, and so on); in the frequent ascent and descent of angels; and in the bold conversation with immortal beings (3.13, 5.358, 8.367). Dennis makes *Paradise Lost* his main example of Christian poetry—the proof for all his arguments—and it is particularly Milton's machinery that characterizes this vision of the perfect poem. It is only after deism is dismissed, therefore, that Milton's machinery can be appreciated.

Like Leslie and Defoe, Dennis recognizes the deist potential in Milton. But he fights for Milton by insisting on his clear distance from deism. This is, in fact, a reinvention of Milton—and one that depends upon a thorough misreading of *Paradise Lost*. Milton's accomplished poem is complete and decorously without discontinuous wounds: Dennis blinds himself to Milton's bathos.

While *The Advancement*, through its polemic against deism, establishes machinery as necessary to religious proof, when Dennis turns to *Paradise Lost* he curiously offers no examples of machinery. Rather, he focuses only on the Creation—a sublime narrative, but one that, with the abstraction of the divine fiat as its crux, shies away from machinery. At the end Dennis gestures toward those parts of Milton's poem that do involve machinery:

I thought to have proceeded, and to have compar'd the Councils and Fights of Virgil and Milton; and above all, their Description of Hell and its Torments; in which both those great Poets seem to have exerted all their Strength. But I am afraid I have already run into Length, and there is Matter remaining for an intire Volume. (*Critical Works*, 1:278)

If revealed Christianity is truly favorable to poetry, even in the hard matter of machinery, then councils, wars, and the underworld would seem to be the obvious places to prove it. Dennis dodges these, and any reading of machinery, citing lack of space. Yet in his next volume, *The Grounds of Criticism in Poetry* (1704), which is explicitly a continuation of *The Advancement*, Dennis mostly discusses the invocations and hymns in *Paradise Lost*, again avoiding machinery. His one approach to the matter of machinery is his praise of Raphael's descent (5.266–87), a passage that, in its untroubled and evocative presentation of angelic visitation, resembles Dennis's vision of an "accomplish'd Poem."

This notable avoidance of Milton's machinery continues until *Letters on Milton and Wycherley* (1721–1722). There Dennis finally turns to the war in heaven, but Milton's machinery continues to perplex, creating in Dennis's criticism disturbing holes. Finally reading the machinery, Dennis simply excises the bathos. Chastising Addison for failing to exalt Milton over Homer, Dennis insists that the war in heaven, because it is so much more exalted than

Homer's subject matter, must be more sublime. To prove it, Dennis quotes at length from the beginning of the battle (6.203–23). This passage ends with Milton's flight into the heroic strain:

> Millions of fierce encountering angels fought
> On either side, the least of whom could wield
> These elements, and arm him with the force
> Of all their regions. (6.220–23)

He argues that if the least angel has so much power, then millions will have sublimely unutterable power. And then Dennis moves on to another image of angelic self-sufficiency, the familiar "each on himself relied, / As only on his arm the moment lay / Of victory" (6.238–40). In demonstrating Milton's sublimity, Dennis accentuates the power and consequence of the fighting angels. But Dennis here elides what I have suggested is the crucial quality of Milton's war, the sudden and contradictory descent from the heroic strain into the bathos created by God's omnipotence. In moving from line 223 to line 238, Dennis jumps over the detail that, "the eternal king omnipotent / From his strong hold of heaven high overruled / And limited their might" (6.227–29). While Milton insists on the contradiction between God's omnipotence and the consequence—"moment"—of each angelic arm, Dennis effaces it.

Dennis goes on to quote "The least of whom could wield these Elements / And arm him with the Force of all their Regions" (changing the enjambment, as if to bring it nearer to the heroic couplet) three more times as he builds up to Michael and Satan's duel. Finally, he gets to the "transcendentally Sublime" (*Critical Works*, 2:227): "Together both with next to almighty arm / Uplifted imminent one stroke they aimed, / That might determine, and not need repeat, / As not of power, at once" (6.316–19). The heroic sense of power and of its consequentiality, the sense that the strokes that Michael and Satan aim matter, form the foundation of Dennis's argument. But having drawn our attention to this sublime moment of Christian machinery, Dennis suddenly gives up on Book Six, and, to finish his letter, turns to the image of Satan adjourning the council of Book Two (2.506–9). The sublimity of the duel reminds Dennis of the sublimity of Satan, another example of machinery. But when Dennis leaves Michael and Satan with their arms upraised, he again turns away at the very height of consequentiality: just as the "moment" of victory lays in each angelic arm, so "with next to Almighty Arm" Michael and Satan aim blows that will "determine." Based upon the apparent power of the angelic combatants, the duel seems really to be consequential. Opportunistically quoting, Dennis establishes sublimity of machinery and then runs before it is put to the Miltonic test. For in cutting away from Michael and Satan, leaving them frozen like Pyrrhus, Dennis edits out the influence of God. In the four lines after Dennis stops quoting, Milton describes Michael's sword, given "from the armoury of God"—God returns to the narrative, reminding us that the heroic and sublime pitch of the duel depended upon God's exclusion. And then Dennis leaves out what necessarily follows from the reminder of God, the contradiction and bathos of Satan's discontinuous wound. Michael's sword meets Satan's "with steep force to smite / Descending," and sheers Satan's right side, cutting with "griding sword" Satan's "discontinuous wound"—"but the ethereal substance closed / Not long divisible." Milton carefully makes bathos as prominent as the sublime, a crucial reminder that true power rests not in angelic arms but in the omnipotence of the monotheistic God. But for the sake of his defense of Milton's machinery—in order to show its sublimity—Dennis studiously ignores the bathos.

According to Dennis, Christian revelation proves itself "in so plain, so sure, and so short a Way, that the Way to Happiness, and the End, is but one and the same Thing." But deism, by becoming involved in rational argument, does not convince easily or immediately. As long as the war in heaven is read only for sublimity—as long as Michael and Satan are frozen with the "next to almighty arms"—Milton and his machinery demonstrate the efficacy of Christian poetry and Christianity itself. But as soon as the arms come down, the moment, in both senses of the word, stops being single and immediate. The healing wound opens up the labyrinths of equivocation; contradiction undermines decorum; bathos threatens the efficacy of sublimity; and revelation undergoes skeptical appraisal. The reader is suddenly thrown back upon the skeptical calculation that characterizes Milton's monotheistic narrative, and which creates the text's deistic potential. While Dennis sometimes was willing to recognize Milton's heresies—he associates him with Socinianism in *The Grounds* (*Critical Works,* 1:345)—his determination to ignore bathos makes clear how radical a move it would be to actually notice it.

Dennis's last misreading of the discontinuous wound itself reaches absurdity in its remarkable effort to ignore. In *Remarks upon Mr. Pope's Rape of the Lock* (1728), Dennis criticizes Pope for deploying inconsequential machinery: "for what he calls his machinery has no Manner of Influence upon what he calls his poem, not in the least promoting, or preventing, or retarding the Action of it" (*Critical Works,* 2:328). Pope's machines, Dennis goes on, "do not in the least influence that Action; they neither prevent the danger of Belinda, nor promote it, nor retard it, unless, perhaps, it may be said, for one Moment, which is ridiculous" (2:337). This one "moment" of consequentiality, of course, is Pope's version of the discontinuous wound, where "A wretched *Sylph* too fondly interpos'd; / Fate urg'd the Sheers, and cut the

Sylph in twain, / (But Airy Substance soon unites again)." As Geoffrey Tillotson has noted, Dennis often fails to realize that the poem is mock epic.[43] Absurdly, Dennis neglects the satire altogether, and taxes Pope for ridiculousness that clearly originates in Milton. Dennis insists upon finding nothing funny in the war in heaven, and so preserves, however forcibly, his lasting judgment that Book Six is "transcendentally sublime." This is a judgment with an orthodox motive. For deism is the party of bathos, and a sublime Milton is a Milton liberated from deism.

Looking back on Dennis and his argument for Christian machinery, Isaac Watts suggests that "if his proposal of criticism had been encouraged and pursued, the nation might have been secured from the danger of deism."[44] It did not work on the eighteenth century as a whole. But Dennis's criticism, by constructing the sublime Milton, did help secure Milton's reputation from the taint of deism. And so, as Milton studies work to recover the early reception's strong sense of Milton's heretical leanings, we do well to return to Dennis's opponent, Alexander Pope. His *Essay on Man,* addressed to Lord Bolingbroke, recognizes that laughter is unavoidable in Milton's theodicy: "Laugh where we must, be candid where we can; / But vindicate the ways of God to Man" (1.17). Pope's more honest, bathetic reading of *Paradise Lost* suggests that Milton was of the deist's party, although perhaps without knowing it.

University of San Diego

NOTES

This essay grew from conversations with Jonathan Lamb, and with the generous guidance of Victoria Kahn. Thanks are also due to Richard McCoy, Denise Gigante, Erik Gray, Christopher Rovee, Nigel Smith, and Michael Lieb.

1. Henning Graf Reventlow, *The Authority of the Bible and the Rise of the Modern World,* trans. John Bowden (Philadelphia, 198), notes, "Though he does not raise any objections against parts of the canon itself, Toland's references are still effective in the way in which they radically question the certainty with which all parties felt that they could refer to the New Testament as a fixed entity. This, however, is to attack at a central point the scriptural faith dominant in Humanist Protestantism of a Calvinist stamp, above all among the Puritans" (308).

2. John Toland, *Life of Milton,* in *The Early Lives of Milton,* ed. Helen Darbishire (London, 1932), 195.

3. *Paradise Lost* 1.17–18, from *Paradise Lost,* ed. Alastair Fowler (New York, 1971); hereafter cited parenthetically in the text.

4. Toland, *The Life of Milton,* 178–79.

5. John T. Shawcross, *Milton: The Critical Heritage, 1732–1801* (London, 1972), 89. Sharon Achinstein, "Milton's Spectre in the Restoration: Marvell, Dryden and Literary Enthusiasm," in

Huntington Library Quarterly 59 (1997): 1–29. For Milton's heretical opinions, see Christopher Hill, *Milton and the English Revolution* (New York, 1978); and *Milton and Heresy*, ed. Stephen B. Dobranski and John P. Rumrich (Cambridge, 1998).

6. Anthony Collins, *A Discourse of Free-Thinking* (London, 1713), 177, lists "Erasmus, Father Paul, Joseph Scaliger, Cartesius, Gassendus, Grotius, Hooker, Chillingworth, Lord Falkland, Lord Herbert of Cherbury, Selden, Hales, Milton, Wilkins, Marsham, Spenser, Whitchcot, Cudworth, More, Sir W. Temple, and Locke."

David Hume, *The Natural History of Religion*, ed. H. E. Root (Palo Alto, CA, 1956), remarks: "ADAM, rising at once, in paradise, and in the full perfection of his faculties, would naturally, as represented by MILTON, be astonished at the glorious appearances of nature, the heavens, the air, the earth, his own organs and members; and would be led to ask whence this wonderful scene arose. But a barbarous, necessitous animal (such as a man is on the first origin of society), pressed by such numerous wants and passions, has no leisure to admire the regular face of nature, or make inquiries concerning the cause of those objects, to which from his infancy he has been gradually accustomed" (24).

7. Charles Blount's *A Just Vindication of Learning* (1679) and the beginning of John Toland's *Christianity Not Mysterious* (1697) owe a clear debt to *Areopagitica*. For deism's role in the rise of anticlericalism, see J. A. I. Champion, *The Pillars of Priestcraft Shaken* (Cambridge, 1992).

8. John Leland, *A View of the Principal Deistic Writers*, vol. 1 (Edinburgh, 1807), ii.

9. *De Doctrina Christiana*, in *Complete Prose Works of John Milton*, 8 vols., gen. ed. Don M. Wolfe et al. (New Haven, 1953–1982), 6:132.

10. English deism is rooted in the writing of Edward, Lord Herbert of Cherbury, especially *De Veritate* (1624) and *De Religione Gentilium* (1663). But Charles Blount initiates the polemic in *Anima Mundi* (1679), and names himself Cherbury's disciple in *Religio Laici* (1682). Two years before the *Life of Milton*, Toland's *Christianity Not Mysterious* (1696) broadened the controversy.

11. Joseph Frank, "Milton's Movement toward Deism," *The Journal of British Studies* 1 (1961): 38–51; J. B. Broadbent, *Some Graver Subject: An Essay on "Paradise Lost"* (London, 1960), 143; William Kolbrenner, *Milton's Warring Angels* (Cambridge, 1997), 118.

12. John Dennis, *The Advancement and Reformation of Modern Poetry*, in *The Critical Works of John Dennis*, vol. 1, ed. Edward Niles Hooker (Baltimore, 1939), 229; hereafter cited parenthetically in the text.

13. Dennis's clear opposition to deism in *The Advancement* is interestingly complicated by his own anticlerical statements a year later in *The Danger of Priestcraft to Religion and Government* (1702), which occasioned a response by Charles Leslie, *The New Association* (1702).

14. Alexander Pope, *Peri Bathous*, in *Poetry and Prose of Alexander Pope*, ed. Aubrey Williams (Boston, 1969), 434; hereafter cited parenthetically in the text.

15. Edward Le Comte, "Dubious Battle: Saving the Appearances," *English Language Notes* 19 (1982): 183.

16. Arnold Stein, *Answerable Style: Essays on "Paradise Lost"* (Minneapolis, 1953), 22.

17. Samuel Barrow, "In Paradisum Amissam Summi Poetae Johannis Miltoni," in *The Riverside Milton*, ed. Roy Flannagan (Boston, 1998), 349; *Milton: The Critical Heritage*, ed. John T. Shawcross (London, 1970), 92, 99, 156.

18. For a recent account of Milton's polemical humor in Book Six and throughout the poem, see John King, *Milton and Religious Controversy: Satire and Polemic in "Paradise Lost"* (Cambridge, 2000).

19. Shawcross, *Milton: The Critical Heritage*, 191.

20. Shaftesbury, Anthony Ashley Cooper, *Characteristics of Men, Manners, Opinions, Times*, ed. Lawrence E. Klein (Cambridge, 1999), 59.

21. James A. Herrick, *The Radical Rhetoric of the English Deists: The Discourse of Skepticism, 1680–1750* (Columbia, SC, 1997), 54. Also see John Redwood, *Reason, Ridicule, and Religion: The Age of Enlightenment in England, 1660–1750* (London, 1976).

22. Henry St. John, Lord Viscount Bolingbroke, *The Works*, vol. 3 (New York, 1967), 235–36.

23. Leland devotes a large portion of his study to Bolingbroke. "Any one that reads Lord Bolingbroke's work with attention, must be convinced, that one principal design he had in view, was to destroy the authority of the divine revelation in general, and the Jewish and Christian in particular." See Leland, *A View of the Principal Deistic Writers*, vol. 2, 46.

24. Charles Leslie, preface to *The History of Sin and Heresie* (London, 1697), A2v; hereafter cited parenthetically as *Sin and Heresie* in the text.

25. Collins, *A Discourse of Free-Thinking*, 123–24; Richard Bentley, *Remarks upon a Late Discourse of Free-Thinking, Part the Second*, 6th ed. (Cambridge, 1725), 31–32; Kolbrenner, *Milton's Warring Angels*, 122.

26. For the importance to Arianism of emphasizing the Son's begetting over his Incarnation, see Michael Bauman, *Milton's Arianism* (Frankfurt am Main, 1986), 95–99.

27. While Leslie's declared opponents are Socinians and Arians (*Sin and Heresie*, 17), his concentration on the abstraction and omnipotence of God focuses on that point at which these two heresies intersect with deism. Socinian and deist were in many ways synonymous accusations. But for Charles Blount and Charles Gildon, *The Oracles of Reason* (London, 1693), the abstract godhead and the polytheistic threat to that godhead by Jesus Christ mark the difference between Socinianism and the even purer aniconism of deism: "The Jew and the Mahometan accuse the Christian of Idolatry, the Reform'd Churches, the Roman, the Socinian the other Reformed Churches, the Deists the Socinian, for his *Deus factus;* but none can accuse the Deist of Idolatry, for he only acknowledges one Supream, Everlasting God, and thinks magnificently of him" (91).

28. Bolingbroke, *The Works*, vol. 3, 532.

29. Maximillian E. Novak, "Defoe, the Occult, and the Deist Offensive during the Reign of George I," in *Deism, Masonry and the Enlightenment: Essays Honoring Alfred Owen Aldridge,* ed. J. A. Leo Lemay (Newark, 1987), 93–94.

30. Daniel Defoe, *The Political History of the Devil* (London, 1726), 73; hereafter cited parenthetically in the text.

31. Charles Leslie, *A Short and Easie Method with the Deists* (London, 1697), 16.

32. Samuel Johnson, "Life of Milton," in *Lives of the Poets*, ed. George Birkbeck Hill (Oxford, 1905), writes,

> Another inconvenience of Milton's design is that it requires the description of what cannot be described, the agency of spirits. He saw that immateriality supplied no images, and that he could not show angels acting but by instruments of action; he therefore invested them with form and matter. This being necessary was therefore defensible; and he should have secured the consistency of his system by keeping immateriality out of sight, and enticing his reader to drop it from his thoughts. But he has unhappily perplexed his poetry with his philosophy. His infernal and celestial powers are sometimes pure spirit and sometimes animated body. (184)

33. Noticing the problem, Patrick Hume, *Annotations on Milton's "Paradise Lost"* (London, 1695), observes that these lines are said "after the manner of Men, for it is unconceivable that an Angel (a Spirit of more pure and enlighten'd Perfection than Mankind is) should be a stranger to the *Omniscience of GOD Almighty*" (193).

34. Such clarity belies the deviousness of Stanley Fish's paradigm of readerly temptation in *Surprised by Sin: The Reader in "Paradise Lost"* (Berkeley and Los Angeles, 1971), and in *How Milton Works* (Cambridge, MA, 2001). While Fish contributes to modern readings a crucial

awareness of the contradictory texture of Milton's verse, at least in the war in heaven self-conscious parody—the presence of the comic—undercuts the seriousness of Fish's version of authorial intent. Neither a sternly puritanical image of Milton nor the chastened reader of Fish's paradigm can survive the kind of laugh elicited by a custard pie. Ridicule, Shaftesbury, *Characteristics,* contends, is the best defense against the "melancholy way" of religion (18)—just as the humor in Book Six denies Fish's melancholy version of *Paradise Lost.*

    35. Johnson, *Lives of the Poets,* 185. Robert H. West discusses Johnson's critique in *Milton and the Angels* (Athens, GA, 1955), 108–12.

    36. Lenn Evan Goodman, *Monotheism: A Philosophical Inquiry into the Foundations of Theology and Ethics* (Totawa, NJ, 1981), 22. James Noggle, *The Skeptical Sublime: Aesthetic Ideology in Pope and the Tory Satirists* (Oxford, 2001), 104, associates Pope's blending of the sublime and the bathetic in *Peri Bathous* with Kant's later claim that the second commandment is the most sublime passage of Jewish Law.

    37. Aryeh Botwinick, *Skepticism, Belief, and the Modern: Maimonides to Nietzsche* (Ithaca, NY, 1997), 7.

    38. Erich Auerbach, *Mimesis,* trans. Willard Trask (Garden City, NJ, 1957), 1–20; Robert Alter, *The Art of Biblical Narrative* (New York, 1981); Meir Sternberg, *The Poetics of Biblical Narrative* (Bloomington, IN, 1985). Alter draws the connection between monotheism and the disjunctions of biblical narrative:

> The monotheistic revolution of biblical Israel was a continuing and disquieting one. It left little margin for neat and confident views about God, the created world, history, and man as political animal or moral agent, for it repeatedly had to make sense of the intersection of incompatibles—the relative and the absolute, human imperfection and divine perfection, the brawling chaos of historical experience and God's promise to fulfill a design in history. The biblical outlook is informed, I think, by a sense of stubborn contradiction, of a profound and ineradicable untidiness in the nature of things, and it is toward the expression of such a sense of moral and historical reality the composite artistry of the Bible is directed. (154)

    39. Bolingbroke's deist writings include the first extended study of monotheism per se: "Farther Reflections on the Rise and Progress of Monotheism" (1745); *Theologische Realenzyklopädie,* 1994, s.v. "Monotheismus."

    40. See, for example, David B. Morris, *The Religious Sublime: Christian Poetry and Critical Tradition in Eighteenth-Century England* (Lexington, KY, 1972); and Leslie E. Moore, *Beautiful Sublime: The Making of "Paradise Lost," 1701–1734* (Palo Alto, CA, 1990).

    41. René Le Bossu, *Treatise of the Epick Poem,* trans. W. J. (London, 1695), reprinted in *Le Bossu and Voltaire on the Epic,* ed. Stuart Curran (Gainesville, 1970), states, "He therefore that would be a Poet, must leave Historians to write, that a Fleet was shattered by a storm and cast upon a strange coast: And must say with Virgil, that Juno went to Aeolus, and that this God upon her instance unkennel'd the wind against Aeneas" (225).

    42. John Dryden, *Discourse concerning the Original and Progress of Satire,* in *The Works of John Dryden,* gen. eds. Edward Niles Hooker and H. T. Swedenberg (Berkeley and Los Angeles, 1956–1987), vol. 4, writes, "Christian Poets have not hitherto been acquainted with their own Strength. If they had search'd the Old Testament as they ought, they might there have found the Machines which are proper for their Work" (19).

    43. *The Rape of the Lock and Other Poems,* ed. Geoffrey Tillotson (New Haven, 1962), 343.

    44. Isaac Watts, preface to *Horae Lyricae,* in *The Works of The Rev. Isaac Watts,* vol. 9 (London, 1813), 222; quoted in A. F. B. Clark, *Boileau and the French Classical Critics in England* (New York, 1965), 314.

MILTON'S VIEW OF IRELAND: REFORM, REDUCTION, AND NATIONALIST POLITY

Mary C. Fenton

THE JOHN MILTON WHO WROTE *The Tenure of Kings and Magistrates* in February 1649, declaring "there is a mutual bond of amity and brother-hood between man and man over all the World" (YP 3:214),[1] also wrote *Observations upon the Articles of Peace* just months later, proclaiming that the Irish people are "justly made . . . vassalls" of the English nation (YP 3:302). While Milton sees his own Puritan cause against the monarchy during the 1640s as noble, indeed morally imperative and driven by hope for a changed, bettered world, he sees the 1641–1649 Irish Catholic rebellions against English religious and political hegemony as merely barbarous and seditious. Milton's views of Ireland expose a significant moral contradiction for the modern reader: Milton, the rational, liberal advocate for individual, civil, and domestic liberty and religious tolerance seems to be, concurrently, Milton the apologist for Cromwell's devastating hegemonic policies against the Irish. But being consistent and being truthful are not synonymous, and the truth is that Milton did, in fact, feel great antipathy toward the Irish by the time he wrote for the Commonwealth in 1649. Miltonists have focused primarily on the 1649 *Observations upon the Articles of Peace* and *Eikonoklastes* to determine the limits of Milton's liberalism, the bounds of his radicalism, and the perimeters of his tolerance.[2] Milton's attitudes about the Irish, however, had been emerging for nearly a decade before he served Cromwell, and by limiting the focus to 1649 Miltonists have often overlooked the significant ways in which Milton's ideology about Ireland reveals the depth of his English nationalism, his long-standing justification of hegemony in the cause of Protestant reform and, later, the boundaries of his republicanism.

This essay will provide the much-needed wider context for considering Milton's views on Ireland, first by focusing on Milton's tracts of the early 1640s, *Of Reformation*, *The Reason of Church-Government*, and *An Apology against a Pamphlet*. These tracts reveal that Milton's early views about Ireland are grounded in his larger overriding political agenda to achieve a unified British polity that would include Ireland. Second, this essay offers examples of contemporary pamphlets and tracts of the 1640s to demonstrate that although Milton exploited the virulent anti-Irish sentiment that saturated English culture, his pre-1649 discourse differs substantially from the prevalent popular anti-Irish discourse; his 1649 tracts, *Observations* and *Eikonoklastes*, however, absorb and utilize the popular discourse to promote the new republican government. Finally, the essay argues that Milton remained largely in agreement with Cromwell that "reducing" Ireland was necessary, just, and providentially sanctioned. By mapping out the larger trajectory of Milton's thought instead of focusing mainly on his 1649 writings, this essay concludes that Milton's English nationalism and his desire to perpetuate Protestant reforms exceed any moral uncertainties he had, or that modern readers might wish he would have had, about the Commonwealth's policies in Ireland.

IRISH CATHOLICISM SERVING THE CAUSE OF PROTESTANT REFORM

Neither *Of Reformation* (May 1641) nor *The Reason of Church-Government* (January or February 1642) advocates violence as the way to manage England's relations with Ireland. Both tracts assert that Ireland should be incorporated in the emerging *"Britannick Empire"* (YP 1:614), but both tracts insist, moreover, on ecclesiastical reform. Published after the Catholic rebellions began in Ulster on October 23, 1641, *Reason* does not advocate legal or military retaliation for the Irish rebellions, but simply "a speedy redresse" to the Irish Catholic uprisings because any resurgence of Catholicism might interfere with the progress of Protestant reform, and such reform is Milton's predominant goal. Both *Of Reformation* and *Reason* are unquestionably anti-Catholic and also perpetuate anti-Irish stereotypes, but neither tract participates in the widespread discourse of atrocity that characterized popular accounts of the Irish Catholic rebellions. Ultimately, Milton's concern in the early 1640s was instead for protecting the "true religion" of Protestantism and for creating a united realm. Perhaps such an agenda is just one degree of separation from the hegemony and ethnonationalism of *Observations*, but Milton's early tracts initiate his discourse of ecclesiastical and cultural reform —some of which would persist, some of which would dissolve.

Even before the October 1641 rebellions in Ireland, Milton had espoused a colonialist agenda akin to that of the Elizabethan and Jacobean planters. Milton's views about the Irish before the rebellions were formed primarily by early pro-Protestant, nationalist apologists, such as Sir John Davies, Barnaby Rich, and Edmund Spenser, none of whom were at all positive about Irish culture, Irish landscape, or Irish religion and politics.[3] Sir John Davies's 1612 *Discoveries* had represented the Irish nation as "a field being prepared for husbandry" (218–19), and Spenser's descriptions of the land and people of Ireland in *A View* and in *The Faerie Queene* were notoriously disparaging, helping to establish stereotypes of Irish incivility and barbarity.[4] Though not referring directly or specifically to Ireland, Milton's *Of Reformation* nonetheless presents a suggestive metaphor that implies the wild, dangerous, and menacing interior geography of Ireland to describe the Catholic adversaries of true religion:

> [The adversaries of reform] feare the plain field of the Scriptures, the chase is too hot; they seek the dark, the bushie, the tangled Forrest, they would imbosk: they feel themselvs strook in the transparent streams of divine Truth, they would plunge, and tumble, and thinke to ly hid in the foul weeds, and muddy waters, where no plummet can reach the bottome. (YP 1:569)

While certainly a generalized metaphor for any hostile moral, political, or civil landscape, Milton's images also more directly recall the stereotypical English view of an Irish geography so prevalent in Davies and Spenser. In "Savage Landscapes: Ireland and the Irish Rebels," Joan Fitzpatrick says that "comments on the impassability of the Irish landscape, because of geographical impediments and dangerous inhabitants are common in English colonial writings on Ireland" (79).[5] *Of Reformation's* description of "the bushie, the tangled Forrest" insinuates the wild gorse and rhododendrons in west Ireland's Connemara, County Clare, and the Burren, as well as the Irish forests that had long been considered by the English as not only wasteland but as a warren of the corrupt. According to *A Natural History of Ireland* (1726), the English had been destroying Irish woods as far back as Henry II's reign, "partly [to] deprive the thieves and rogues, who used to lurk in the woods in great numbers, of their refuge and starting-holes" (67).[6]

Furthermore, Milton's reference to the "foul weeds" brings to mind the river weeds and coarse straw that Irish peasants used to thatch the roofs of their turf or wattle cottages, habitations considered primitive by English architectural and cultural standards. Additionally, the "foul weeds" evoke an important connection to Spenser, which Joan Fitzpatrick has pointed out: Book Four of *The Faerie Queene* uses "wicked weeds" sown by Ate, Duessa's malevolent companion, to suggest Roman Catholic sedition (86). The "muddy waters" into which Milton's adversaries of reform plunge suggest both the famously dirty River Liffey in Dublin (Gaelic *Dubhlinn,* meaning "dark pool") and the turbulent Shannon River in west Ireland. "Muddy waters" also suggest Ireland's infamous bogs, and as Eileen McKracken notes, "the Irish had resisted the invaders from the shelter of the bogs and woods whenever possible," and such features of the Irish landscape "had been a serious obstacle to the Tudor conquest and colonization of Ireland" (287).[7]

Descriptions of landscape fused with insinuations about the land's inhabitants had become common in writings about Ireland. In addition to Davies's and Spenser's more famous examples, even the relatively minor 1642 text, *A Geographicall Description of the Kingdome of Ireland,* states overtly that "The Irish for the most part are proud & haughty, cruell and barbarous, variable and inconstant in disposition, apt and forward to Tumults, rebellious of Government, false and hollow-hearted, more ready in promise then performance, the meaner lazie, idle, and sluggish especially the wild Irish, and the English Irish much degenerated" (25).[8] Milton seems likewise to have perpetuated the popular perceptions of Ireland's "hostile" geographical landscape and decadent inhabitants in order to implicate moral (that is, Catholic) impediments and aberrations that would clash with the pure, "plain field" of scriptural (that is, Protestant) truth. Rather than simply whipping up a froth of ethnic bigotry against the Irish per se, however, Milton alluded to stereotypes and established prejudices in order to advance his more general cause of anti-Catholicism and the need for Protestant reform.

To this end, Milton also attacks the subversive intentions of Catholics because, he argues, papists had long seen Ireland as a stronghold from which to undermine Protestantism and British unity. *Of Reformation* argues that papists had attempted to instigate "an abhorred, a cursed, a Fraternall *Warre*" among the members of the British realm, and the Catholic presence in Ireland was "a piece of Service that the *Pope* and all his Factors have beene compassing to doe ever since the *Reformation*" (YP 1:596). Although Aiden Clark asserts that it was only *after* the 1641 rebellions that the English considered Catholicism as "a papally directed international monolith ceaselessly plotting the overthrow of Protestantism," *Of Reformation* clearly indicates that Milton recognized the threat well before the rebellions.[9] Further, as Paul Stevens argues, Milton emphasizes preserving control over Ireland because of her strategic proximity to England and his long-standing fear of Catholic aggression there fueled by Spanish imperialism.[10] Milton agreed with the well-established English policies of subduing Irish Catholicism because it was both a political detriment and a demographic deterrent to English Protestantism.

Of Reformation also designates the Irish as alien or foreign, though technically Ireland was one of the king's three kingdoms. Where Milton sees "ENGLAND and SCOTLAND dearest Brothers both in *Nature,* and in CHRIST," he identifies Ireland as merely "our free Denizon upon the back of us both" (YP 1:596). Ireland would of course be part of the realm, and yet a "denizon" is not equal to a "Brother." A denizen is a citizen, "By restriction: One who lives habitually in a country but is not a native-born citizen; a foreigner admitted to residence and certain rights in a country; in the law of Great Britain, an alien admitted to citizenship by royal letters patent, but incapable of inheriting, or holding any public office" (*OED*, def. 2). Milton's use of "denizon" encapsulates two different components of his complex and contradictory notion about Ireland's role: he includes Ireland in the emerging British polity because Catholicism and its threat to English Protestantism need to be eradicated and ecclesiastical reforms need to be enacted there. However, he excludes the Irish from the legal and financial privileges of full citizenship for the sake of maintaining political and legal supremacy over them. Milton instead adheres to the tradition of *ius soli*, "the law of the soil," which had long determined legal conceptions of subjecthood based on the notion that a person born on the monarch's territory owed allegiance to the monarch. As historians state, "The main rule is very simple. The place of birth is all-important."[11] Though the Irish were expected to behave as loyal subjects of the crown, they were still just denizens, "upon the back of us," as both a burden and a commodity. What Milton gives with one hand, he takes away with the other: the benefits of reform would be spiritual, not necessarily legal or financial. As the 1642 Adventurer's Act and the later Cromwell Land Settlement would evince, those benefits were to be enjoyed by English Independents, English Adventurers, and soldiers loyal to Cromwell.

Further, Milton follows in the English tradition that had long perceived Ireland as her "internal colony,"[12] simply one of the "Daughter Ilands" (YP 1:614) of the *Britannick Empire* whose mission is the "Divinely-warranted *Reformation*" (YP 1:602). England was to be "the new Lampe of *saving light* to all Christendome" (YP 1:525), and England had the God-given "*Precedencie . . .* to be the first *Restorer* of *buried Truth*" (YP 1:526). At this point in 1641, Milton seems to believe that this Irish "Other" is politically malleable, their Catholicism a matter of wrong reasoning and improper socialization. Milton can argue, therefore, that "a Commonwelth ought to be but as one huge Christian personage, one mighty growth, and stature of an honest man, as big, and compact in vertue as in body; for looke what the grounds, and causes are of single happines to one man, the same yee shall find them to a whole state" (YP 1:572). But the state to which Milton refers is an English polity, and he clearly speaks as an English nationalist who does not see beyond the borders of his nationalism, and so would not respect Irish nationalists who would, just like him, fight for the "single happiness" of *their* own "personage." But Ireland was not yet the direct and considerable problem it would become to the English after October 1641, so in May 1641 Milton simply emphasizes the foremost political fact that Catholicism still exists as a threatening and competing presence that could potentially damage or deter the paramount cause of emerging Protestant reforms.[13]

When Milton next writes about Ireland in *The Reason of Church-Government*, published in January or February 1642, the Irish rebellions were three months old and raging. David Loewenstein emphasizes that the rebellions were "unusually alarming to Milton and his Protestant contemporaries, who saw their world and its conflicts in fiercely eschatological terms. In their eyes, this was no war of national liberation or resistance, but a monstrous Antichristian threat."[14] The "peace of the [Protestant] Church" for which Milton argues in *Reason* is contingent upon suppressing Irish Catholic claims to national authenticity and upon subjugating Catholic claims to power. *Reason,* like *Of Reformation,* also foregrounds the inclusion of Ireland in a polity designed to protect and promote "true religion" and individual liberty of conscience. At this point, Ireland should assume its position as an ideological and ecclesiastical extension of Protestant reforms in England begun with the plantations of Elizabeth and James I.

The thrust of *Reason* is, therefore, to explain the difference between rebellion and reformation in order to show that where the English use civil and ecclesiastical renovations to preserve true religion, the Irish lack the integrity of a valid, lawful, or legitimately moral cause. As Anthony Low says, "although the proper exercise of freedom entails the overthrow of authority, Milton everywhere insists that freedom is not something that the individual seizes in rebellion against the natural order, but a free gift to all persons from God himself."[15] *Reason* therefore does not respond directly to the Irish rebels' issues and demands, one of which was the freedom to practice their Catholic religion openly and without persecution. Milton's apparent indifference does not indicate his ignorance of their demands but instead his deliberate desire *not* to credit their cause as even worthy of address or consideration. He denigrates the validity of the Catholic cause simply by not acknowledging it. The rebels' desire to protect their Catholicism is nothing more than, in Milton's mind, an odious regression, the antithesis of a just cause, a misguided sedition, a kind of antireformation and "sliding back to *Rome*" (YP 1:527). To Milton, Catholics therefore merit their own suppression because the light they follow is not "the sacred Bible" but the self-serving institution of the Catholic Church and the Antichrist pope. Catholicism renders itself the antithesis of a just cause. Further, Milton insists that rebellion warrants correction, a position Cromwell would later make explicit in his 1650 *Declaration to the Irish Prelates:* "We come to break the powere of a company of lawless rebels, who having cast off the authority of England, live as enemies to human society; whose principles (the world hath experience of) are, to destroy and subjugate all men not complying with them" (205).[16]

Instead of vilifying the Irish rebels for the alleged barbarities, however, Milton argues that their rebellions result from the English government's and the English church's failure to control, convert, or reform potential rebels in the first place. Therefore, *Reason* lays the initial blame for the Irish rebellions upon the Church of England's bishops, who had long "famished" the souls of the Irish: "What can the Irish subject do lesse in Gods just displeasure against us, then revenge upon English bodies the little care that our Prelats have had of their souls. Nor hath their negligence been new in that Iland"(YP 1:798). Milton had already written on the *"Depravities* of the *Church"* at consider-able length in *Of Reformation* (YP 1:524), and *Reason* again accuses the bishops of even more failures, this time in Ireland, because they did not adequately "represse heresie and idolatry" (YP 1:798).[17] Thus can Milton construe the rebellions as a political expedient for reform: "neither the feare of sects no nor of rebellion can be a fit plea to stay reformation, but rather to push it forward with all possible diligence and speed" (YP 1:800); *"That those many Sects and Schismes by some suppos'd to be among us, and that rebellion in* Ireland, *ought not to be a hindrance, but a hastning of reformation"* (YP 1:794); "Tis not rebellion that ought to be the hindrance of reformation, but it is the want of this which is the cause of that" (YP 1:798).

However, *Reason* also recognizes that "the reformation is a long work, and the miseries of *Ireland* are urgent of a speedy redresse" (YP 1:799).[18] Milton's empathy for "the miseries of *Ireland"* was not of course with the Irish, but with the persecuted Protestants who were allegedly being slaugh-tered and brutalized by Irish Catholics. And although Milton's concern was evident from the fact that he donated £4 to the relief of the Irish Protestants on June 2, 1642,[19] Milton's deeper desire was to resolve the Irish issues so they would not impede or distract from the formation of a united Protestant polity.[20] Book One of *Reason* begins graphically, almost bathetically, by align-ing the urgency of reformation with the urgency of relief for the besieged Protestants in Ireland, but Milton plays the humanitarian card in order to trump it with the "urgent need for reform" card:

and how speedy we are, the poore afflicted remnant of our martyr'd countrymen that sit there on the Sea-shore, counting the houres of our delay with their sighs, and the minuts with their falling teares, perhaps with the destilling of their bloody wounds, if they have not quite by this time cast off, and almost curst the vain hope of our founder'd ships, and aids, can best judge how speedy we are to their reliefe. But let their succors be hasted, as all need and reason is, and let not therefore the reformation which is chiefest cause of successe and victory be still procrastinated. (YP 1:799)

A couple of months later, in *An Apology against a Pamphlet* (April 1642), Milton articulates what would also become one of Cromwell's con-stant, adamant rationales for the reduction of Ireland: providential sanction. In *An Apology,* Milton argues that the recent rebellions in Ireland should be interpreted as an opportunity to renew God's covenant with England:[21]

Therefore the more they seeke to humble themselves, the more does God by manifest signes and testimonies visibly honour their proceedings; and sets them as the mediators of this his cov'nant which he offers us to renew. Wicked men daily conspire their hurt, and it comes to nothing, rebellion rages in our Irish Province, but with miraculous and losselesse victories of few against many is daily discomfited and broken; if we neglect not this early pledge of Gods inclining toward us, by the slacknesse of our needful aids. (YP 1:927)

Milton warns not to disregard "Divine providence" and "what is it when God himselfe condescends, and workes with his owne hands to fulfill the requests of men" (YP 1:927). Cromwell's later letters and state papers reiterate such claims of providential endorsement of the new polity, for example, when he admonishes the Irish Prelates in 1650: "But as for those who . . . persist and continue in arms, they must expect what the Providence of God (in that which is falsely called the chance of war) will cast upon them."[22] What becomes clear in Milton's early tracts of the 1640s is that his thinking about the Irish situation adheres to long-standing attitudes and policies that would sanction violence to serve the cause of Protestant reformation. With Cromwell in charge in the future, Milton would put even more pressure on the providential legitimacy and necessity of reform.

The Discourse of Atrocity versus Milton's Apologies for Reform

Reason and *An Apology*'s emphasis is clearly on gaining political support for Protestant reforms, yet the tracts do not imitate traits of the contemporary rhetoric about the Irish rebellions that could have additionally, and probably effectively, served Milton's anti-Catholic cause. More than two hundred news reports and pamphlets were issued from October 1641 to April 1642, and the majority of them were openly vicious in their anti-Irish, anti-Catholic stance. With only very few exceptions, the reports of ongoing events in Ireland were saturated with shock, disgust, and explosive fury, and—as historians have now proven—immense distortion and exaggeration.[23] While Milton does indeed berate and deride the Irish, calling them for example, "these murdrous Irish the enemies of God and mankind" (YP 1:798), his early tracts do not reflect the predominant racist discourse nor the discourse of atrocity that came to characterize accounts and assessments of the rebellions. Milton does play to febrile anti-Irish sentiment, but his discourse largely eschews the discourse of atrocity. Perhaps Milton did not want to participate in the lowbrow bigotry of the "rabble," but more likely, maligning the Irish in the style of the broadsides and pamphlets simply would not have been the most effective way for Milton to articulate and advance his ideology of reform.

What becomes clear, regardless of the actual truth that might never be known about the Irish rebellions of the 1640s, is that Protestant voices dominated and eventually controlled the discourse,[24] and as far as we know, Milton was not reading contemporary Irish Catholic voices that would have presented alternative views of the rebellions, such as the letters of confederate warrior and leader Owen Roe O'Neill, Sir Richard Belling's *History of the Irish Confederation and the War in Ireland* (1641–1643), or the later *Aphorismical Discoveries*, written by an Irish priest who acted in the capacity of secretary to Owen Roe, which chronicled the rebellion. Milton's view of the Irish situation was likely to have been restricted to the accounts saturated with rhetoric that had almost instantly congealed into clichés not only vilifying but demonizing the Irish Catholics.[25]

From the very first days after the initial rebellions in Ulster on October 23, 1641, news reports and pamphlets unwaveringly insisted upon the authenticity of their accounts—either because the events they reported were actually so ghastly as to seem almost incredulous, or because the reports were actually spurious but needed to be convincingly misrepresented in order to incite or increase anti-Irish, anti-Catholic sentiment. One of the very early accounts, for example, republished several times in subsequent days after October 23, offers the first glimpse of the emerging discourse. The pamphlet's title page is purposefully incendiary: "A TRUE AND FULL RELATION of the horrible and hellish Plot of the Jesuites Papist Priests and other Papists in Ireland, for the Massacring of the two chiefe Justices, and all the Privie Councell and Protestants in that Kingdome."[26] The contents, however, are nonetheless surprisingly straightforward and factual, opening with a report of the rebels' demands:

1. First, to have their Crowne not to bee dependant upon *England,* nor to be a conquered Nation.
2. Secondly, to have their *Irish* Lawes established, and such as should be made hereafter.
3. Thirdly, to have free liberty of the exercise of their Relegion. (1)

Though this very early pamphlet offers an unembellished account of the rebels' failure in the siege on Dublin castle (3–5), pamphlets just two weeks later would begin to omit the demands of the rebels and instead post lurid accounts of the rebels' alleged atrocities.

Pamphlets asserted the veracity of their reports by consistently juxtaposing "true" with "barbarous" and "Papists," as in, "A Late and True Relation from Ireland: Of the Warlike and bloody Proceedings of the Rebellious Papists in that Kingdome . . . Wherein is declared their barbarous and cruell Actions, the great and many outrages and Robberies committed by them in divers Provinces of that Kingdome" (November 1641); and "LATE And Lamentable News FROM IRELAND, Wherein are truly related, the Rebellious, and Cruel proceedings of the Papists there" (November 16, 1641).[27]

As the following examples demonstrate, discourse about the events in Ireland would also quickly solidify into sensationally graphic horrors: "BLOUDY NEWES FROM IRELAND, OR The barbarous Crueltie BY the Papists used in that KINGDOME. By putting men to the sword, deflowering Women, and dragging them up and downe the Streets, and cruelly murdering them, and thrusting their Speeres through their little Infants before their eyes, and carrying them up and down on Pike-points, in great reproach, and hanging Mens quarters on their Gates in the Street" (December 1, 1641), and "A BLOODY BATTELL: OR THE REBELS OVERTHROW And Protestants Victorie. Being a True Relation of a great skirmish . . . Also of a creull and detestable Murther committed by 7. Soldiers on the body of Mr. Atkins, his Wife, and young Child. In what a horrid manner they Ript up his Wives wombe being great with Child, and afterward burnt her and her Child in most lamentable manner" (December 2, 1641).[28] These chronicles immediately following the October rebellions were not, however, as disproportionately exploitative and sensationalized as they would become in the years after 1641, but they were horrific enough to ignite the already volatile English relations with the Irish.[29]

Although *Reason* does not address the Irish rebellions in the same manner as these contemporary pamphlets and broadsides, Milton certainly took advantage of the effect that this discourse was having on the English populace. For instance, that the Irish Catholics were savage, uncivilized barbarians was an already well-established stereotype in the English mind, so Milton added another dimension to this portrait of the Irish. The Irish were barbarians without a cause. The Irish Catholic cause was neither worthy nor formidable enough to interrupt the "chiefest cause" of *true* reformation:

And we for our parts a populous and mighty nation must needs be faln into a strange plight either of effeminacy, or confusion, if *Ireland* that was once the conquest of one single Earle with his privat forces, and the small assistance of a petty Kernish Prince, should now take up all the wisdome and prowesse of this potent Monarchy to quell a barbarous crew of rebels, whom if we take but the right course to subdue, that is beginning at the reformation of our Church, their own horrid murders and rapes will so fight against them, that the very sutlers and horse boyes of the Campe will be able to rout and chase them without the staining of any Noble sword. (YP 1:799–800)

Milton renders the Irish cause so weak and so appalling as to be not even a daunting opponent to the providential English goals and power. Rather than emphasize Irish barbarism, which was being almost daily proclaimed by the pamphlets and news reports anyway, Milton transforms the Irish rebels into agents for Protestant reform: their actions simply confirm that reformation is sorely and urgently needed to preclude just such rebellion against true religion in the future.

1649: THE RHETORIC OF HEGEMONY

By the mid-1640s, Milton still urged "a speedy redresse" to the Irish problem, and prompt resolution was still a recurring objective for Milton and for politicians dealing with Ireland, even as the increasing complexity of the situation in Ireland made it clear that swift resolution was unlikely. Although Milton grew increasingly impatient with the politics of the Irish situation throughout the decade, and his hope for a peaceful solution ran thin at times, his hope never entirely dried up, and he never participated in the prurient racism that characterized so much of the popular literature of the early and mid-1640s. By 1649, however, Milton's writings engaged in what Thomas Corns has called the "new republican rhetoric," which for Milton was also the rhetoric of hegemony and nationalist exclusion.[30]

Milton's 1648 translations of the Psalms reveal that by the end of the 1640s Milton had come to consider violence as a potentially justifiable means to ensure reform, and that "wrong causes" require suppression or correction. His translations deal with violence and safety (Psalm 80), slavery (Psalm 81), order (Psalm 82), shame and violence (Psalm 83). They were written, John Shawcross reminds us, "in the midst of the Civil Wars," and they reflect Milton's "dejection caused by his pusillanimous fellow countrymen and . . . the hope for enlightened leadership."[31] However, the translations were, significantly, written at a time when Puritan intolerance of the Irish situation was approaching its nadir and policies increasingly favored violent solutions to the ongoing "complication of interests" there.

When the new government took over in England in early 1649, the images, stories, and reports of Irish rebellions were still rampant, aided in no small part by popular texts like the Bishop of Clogher, Henry Jones's *Remonstrance of Divers Remarkable Passages Concerning the Church and Kingdom of Ireland* (1642), and Sir John Temple's 1646 *Irish Rebellion,* which had tallied Protestant deaths during the rebellions at 300,000, though in 1641 fewer than 100,000 Protestants inhabited Ireland.[32] John Dillingham's weekly newsbook, *The Modern Intelligencer,* resolutely defended the Commonwealth, making statements to the effect that Irish barbarism alone was sufficient to justify English conquest, "had they never been in any kinde so cruell and bloudy to the English."[33] A decade's worth of such widespread discourse only added to the political and financial rationale of the new government's "civilizing mission." On March 30, 1649, when Cromwell accepted the Council of State's request to command an Irish expedition, public support in England was at least in part the result of the popular anti-Catholic discourse, anti-Irish bigotry, and extremist Protestant nationalism. The Committee for Irish Affairs would readily request Cromwell's military leadership for "the reduction of Ireland."

"Reduction" became a principal word to describe the policy for dealing with Ireland. The Latin *reducere* means to bring back or restore, as well as to "lead back from an error in action, conduct or belief especially in matters of morality or religion; to restore to the truth and right faith" (*OED*, def. 2.8a). This was a common usage in the sixteenth and seventeenth centuries, as for example, when Milton says in *Of Prelatical Episcopacy*, "it came into my thoughts . . . that I could do Religion, and my Country no better service . . . [than] to reduce them to their firme stations under the standard of the Gospell" (YP 1:627).[34] "Reduction" also had the additional meaning of bringing order by constraint or compulsion, and Cromwell used the word frequently in his summons to surrender, for example, to Arthur Aston, governor of Drogheda: "Having brought the army belonging to the Parliament of England before this place, to reduce it to obedience" (September 10, 1649). And likewise later to the governor of Kilkenny: "My coming hither is to endeavor, if God so please to bless me, the reduction of the city of Kilkenny to their obedience to the State of England" (March 22, 1650), and "I tell you my business is to reduce you from arms, and the country to quietness and their due subjection" (March 26, 1650).[35] "Reduction" was used officially to combine theological justification with political expediency.

Writing for the Commonwealth in 1649, Milton defends this reduction as well as registers increasingly virulent views toward Ireland. In *Observations upon the Articles of Peace* (May 1649), when he states that the Irish deserve only to be "govern'd by Edicts and Garrisons" (YP 3:303), Milton's view is, in part, a response to the popular accounts of the rebellions that permeated the culture and fed an already fervent antipathy. Milton reiterates the popular assessment of the Irish as both treacherous and detestable, their rebellion having involved "the mercilesse and barbarous Massacre of so many thousand *English*" (YP 3:301). *Observations* does not characterize the New English, those Protestant settlers from the earlier plantation projects, as having oppressed the Irish, but instead as their just Conquerers, "who had us'd their right and title to that Countrey with such tendernesse and moderation, and might otherwise have secur'd themselvs with ease against their Treachery" (YP 3:301). In Milton's mind, the English have rights over the Irish because, as subjects of the realm, the Irish ought to know the limits of their freedom, as all subjects would, and should neither hope for nor attempt a different level or kind of freedom. Therefore, "by their own foregoing demerits and provocations [are] justly made our vassalls" (YP 3:302).

The Irish request to repeal Poynings Act, the 1494 law established to prohibit an independent Irish Parliament is untenable because, Milton argues, the Irish have exploited their freedom, dissociating it from obedience: "The recalling of which Act, tends openly to invest them with a law-giving power of their own, enables them by degrees to throw off all subjection to this Realme, and renders them who by their endlesse treasons and revolts have deserv'd to hold no Parlament at all" (YP 3:303). The Irish do not deserve the privilege of governing themselves independently because they have traditionally shown themselves neither able nor willing to follow English law. Besides, from the Anglocentric standpoint, Poyning's Law represents "the civillest and most moderate acknowledgement impos'd of their dependance on the Crown of *England*" (YP 3:303).

Milton sees England as offering the Irish a kind of freedom, the benefit and privilege of being an obedient subject of the British realm, which the Irish *should* have desired. But the Irish have been "indocible and averse from all Civility and amendment, and what hopes they give for the future . . . [and] preferre their own absurd and savage Customes before the most convincing evidence of reason and demonstration" (YP 3:304). While Milton here directly refers to the Gaelic tillage and harvesting methods, which the English considered primitive, he sees their "rejecting the ingenuity of all other Nations to improve and waxe more civill by a civilizing Conquest" as a testimony not of admirable Irish nationalism, but of "their true Barbarisme and obdurate wilfulnesse" (YP 3:304). From his presumed position of cultural superiority, it is beyond reason and common sense that the Irish would not want what so clearly would profit them, that they would not want the same customs and values as the English, but would instead rebel against the very "amendments" that could correct and improve them. Their recalcitrance baffles and exasperates him. Additionally, Paul Stevens argues that Milton's ability for "ethnic hatred" is part of his Janus-faced, "contro-versial" nationalism that at once is "both terrible and enabling" (268).[36]

In October 1649, when Milton next speaks of the Irish situation in *Eikonoklastes,* he flaunts the terrible righteousness of the newly enabled: Cromwell had already felled Drogheda and Wexford, New Ross would soon surrender, and a treaty between Ormond and Owen Roe was pending. At Wexford alone, Cromwell's army had killed approximately 2,000 Irish, and at Drogheda a garrison of approximately 2,500 rebels was given no quarter. At home in England, the Commonwealth had been officially established in March, and the Council of State had full executive powers, so republican goals must have seemed more viable than ever. Further, Cromwell's own persuasive insistence on providential justification incites some of this confident rhetoric. In his letter to Parliament describing the siege on Drogheda, for example, Cromwell would claim that he was "persuaded that this is a righteous judgment of God upon these barbarous wretches, who have imbrued their hands in so much innocent blood" (127).[37] Cromwell would reiterate this claim many times throughout the Irish campaign, and Milton would continue to endorse it later in *The First Defense* when he says that Cromwell conquered Ireland in "full accordance with the will of God" (YP 4:1.458).[38]

Because *Eikonoklastes* is at least in part aimed at an English audience faltering in their support for the new government, and the tract is designed to offset any residual power or sympathy for Charles that was being stirred by *Eikon Basilike,* the greatest weight of Milton's argument about the Irish, especially in chapter 12, "Upon the Rebellion in *Ireland,*" is devoted more to undermining Charles, his alleged book and its influence, than to justifying or defending Cromwell's ongoing military action in Ireland. Milton recalls Charles's own denunciation of the Irish as "wicked and detestable Rebells, odious to God and all good Men" (YP 3:580), and when he accuses Charles of allowing the slaughter of his subjects and then asking that mercy be shown to the murderous Irish rebels. Milton vindicates Cromwell's "justice to retaliat" (YP 3:481). That is, Milton offers biblical precedent for "a Nation by just Warr and execution to slay whole Families of them who so barbarously had slaine whole Families before," though he qualifies this by saying, "I speak not this that such measure should be meted rigorously to all the Irish" (YP 3:482).[39] Milton additionally connects the inflated statistic of 154,000 English Protestant deaths caused by Catholic rebels in Ulster alone (he had claimed 200,000 total Protestant deaths in *Observations*)[40] with the clichéd assessment of Irish barbarism *"so sudden, and so violent,* as at first to amaze all men that were not accessory" (YP 3:470), as a way to accentuate Charles's culpability.

Milton argues that Parliament's justice and wisdom were Charles's true enemies, and he further argues that Parliament would have guided Charles down the right path in his dealing with the Irish had he only heeded Parliament's counsel. But Charles had feared and disrespected the Puritan Parliament, Milton says, which led only to disaster in the Irish situation: "without advice of Parlament, to whom he himself had committed the mannaging of that Warr, makes a Cessation; in pretence to releive the Protestants, *overborne there with numbers,* but as the event prov'd, to support the Papists, by diverting and drawing over the English Army there, to his own service heer against the Parlament" (YP 3:483). Parliament acted rightly in supporting the English Protestants against the papist rebels, and Charles undermined that support, for "why did he stop and waylay both by Land and Sea, to his utmost power, those Provisions and Supplies which were sent by the Parlament?"(YP 3:483). Milton indicts Charles at the same time that he advances the legitimacy of the new Commonwealth by calling attention to Parliament's crucial role in domestic and foreign politics.[41]

While Milton lays the blame for the Irish rebellions squarely on Charles and his Catholic inclinations, unlike *Observations,* which accentuates Irish barbarism, *Eikonoklastes* mainly portrays the Irish as too stupid and too inept to have organized and accomplished their rebellion without some kind of underground support from Charles. It defies reason and common sense, Milton says, that the Irish, "as not supported with other strength then thir own, to begin a Warr so desperate and irreconcileable against both England and Scotland at once" (YP 3:471). Milton concludes that it was promises of assistance from Charles (as well as from "*Italian* heads of the Romish party") that facilitated and sponsored the Irish undertaking: "It remaines then that either some autoritie or som great assistance promis'd them from England, was that wheron they cheifly trusted" (YP 3:470, 471).[42] *Eikonoklastes* casts Charles as simultaneously betraying the English and duping the Irish. Milton's vituperation is clearly aimed more at Charles than at the rebelling Irish, for whom he reserves his condescension and righteous defense of Cromwell's ongoing "resolution," which had proven, just at Drogheda and Wexford alone, devastatingly effective.

Nonetheless, England's means of resolving the "complication of interests" in Ireland had paradoxically become an imitation of the Irish methods that the English had found so barbaric. Milton played a part in the English policies to resolve the rebellions and ensure reform.[43] As Cromwell's polemicist, Milton had the multiple tasks of presenting the situation, interpreting it for an audience he felt needed help with "right reading," and continuing to enforce the new republican rhetoric.[44] It is also clear that Milton's attitudes toward the Irish had long been evolving, and by 1649 his views were largely aligned with Cromwell's: both agreed that violence was justified and that the reduction of Ireland was divinely sanctioned. Finally, the values of a republic that Milton advocated would not apply to the Irish, and any earlier hopes of including Ireland in a unified polity would revert instead to reducing them with hegemony.

THE RECONFIGURATION OF NATIONALISM: AN ENGLISH REPUBLIC VERSUS A "BRITTANICK EMPIRE"

In 1651, ten years after Milton's first statements about "a speedy redresse" to the Irish situation, *The First Defense* asserts some of his most concisely caustic accusations against the Irish. He typifies the Irish as "our most savage and inhuman enemies," and hyperbolically states that the Irish Catholics caused the deaths, "with most exquisite torments" of 500,000 English Protestants, a claim that exceeds his already excessive declarations in *Observations* and *Eikonoklastes*. Milton may not have sensationalized the details of the alleged massacres in Ireland, but his numbers are accusations, and they artificially amplify Irish destructiveness and barbarity. He seemed to know that the gravity of statistics is often as effective as graphic description, and ten years after he had first written about the Irish his once hopeful views had congealed instead into succinct vituperation.

Milton's writings after 1649 while he still served Cromwell do not reveal any significant ambivalence about Cromwell's role in the Irish campaign, which lasted until 1653, though Cromwell left Ireland in May 1650 to lead forces against the Scots and never returned to Ireland. However, Milton's May 1652 *Sonnet XVI*, "To the Lord Generall Cromwell," does reveal significant awareness of the complexity of hegemony. That is, Milton simultaneously praises the effectiveness of violence as well as the desirability and nobility of peace. His sonnet is consistent with his earlier assertions that there are causes and boundaries that not only guide people, but also into which can rightly coerce and restrict people. If promoting and preserving truth are the goals of reform, sometimes violent means to this end are justified. Of Cromwell, however, Milton says that "To peace & truth thy glorious way hast plough'd" (4).[45] Perhaps "plough" is meant to connote something about readying the Irish land for English husbandry and more Protestant plantations, but the word also alludes to the facts that Milton would have known: Cromwell and the New Model Army began on the east coast at Drogheda and Wexford and literally cut a swathe through to the south and eventually to the west, killing thousands of Irish on the way and destroying churches, castles, monasteries, and villages full of men, women, and children. Cromwell's actions there from August until May 1650 served to "break the backbone of Irish resistance" and establish a sense of terror, as one historian has put it.[46] In early 1652, a standing army of about 30,000 English troops were in Ireland, and in August 1652, England had passed the Act for the Settling of Ireland, which would legally enable the English to confiscate Irish lands according to an Irish subject's degree of loyalty or "affection" to England during the previous decade. Milton's use of "plough" in 1652 should, then, be read for its complexity since it suggests that he both admires Cromwell's victories as well as recognizes that the military tore up, rooted out, and gashed their way to success. Though by 1652 the Irish and Scottish threats abroad had been overcome, and the Levellers suppressed at home in England, Milton also still insists that "much remaines / To conquer still . . . new foes aries [*sic*]" (9–11). Again, however, Milton also elevates the stature of peace, which "hath her victories / No less renownd then warr" (10–11).

Nonetheless, Milton's 1653 translations of Psalms 1 and 2 revisit the righteousness of correcting those who are not wise enough *not* to "revolt when truth would set them free." Written after England's military campaign in Ireland had officially concluded, but while the land settlement[47] was still ongoing, Psalm 1 states, "For the Lord knows th' upright way of the just, / And the way of bad men to ruine must" (15–16). Psalm 2, translated August 8, 1653, states God's commission to the Son:

> As thy possession I on thee bestow
> Th' Heathen, and as thy conquest to be sway'd
> Earths utmost bounds: them shalt thou bring full low
> With Iron Scepter bruis'd, and them disperse
> Like to a potters vessel shiver'd so.   (17–21)[48]

The violent images of the messianic deliverer using an "Iron scepter" (perhaps Ironsides?) to bruise and scatter his enemy like the shards of a disintegrated ceramic pot illustrate the simultaneously destructive yet potentially redemptive role of violence. And Milton probably did consider that, in fact, Cromwell's early and terrifying violence may have brought about the relatively swift end of Catholic violence against Protestants, enabling the subsequent victories of the New Model Army led by Ireton. Following the execution of Sir Phelim O'Neil in March 1653, which both symbolically and effectively marked the end of Irish rebellions, the surrender of Cloughoughter in April 1653 completed the English conquest of Ireland, just three short years after it had begun. In May 1653, the order was given for the transplantation of the Ulster Presbyterians, and in July both the order for transplantation of vagrants to America and the order for transplantation of native Irish to Connacht or Clare were issued. Certainly there is scriptural precedent warranting such violence and displacement, and in 1653 England had gained the kind of foothold for reform in Ireland that even Milton had hoped for, even if, as it turns out, it was only territorial. If the goal had once been for ecclesiastical and moral reform in Ireland, to the Irish it was neither geographically nor legally configured that way. To the Irish, reform would signify "reduction," "extirpation," subjugation, and rapacious confiscation and redistribution of their land. To the English, reform meant that Protestantism might once more be safely planted because the English would confiscate the best lands in north and east Ireland, and the threat of Catholic support for the monarchy was suppressed—though only temporarily. As Terry Eagleton states, "the real test of hegemony is whether the ruling class is able to impose its spiritual authority on its underlings, lend them moral and political leadership, and persuade them of its own vision of the world. And on all these counts . . . the Anglo-Irish must be reckoned an egregious failure" (30).[49]

Milton would continue to praise Cromwell's military prowess in Ireland, proclaiming in *The Second Defense* (1654) that, "When all Ireland was lost, but for a single city, you [Cromwell] transported the army and in one battle instantly broke the power of Hibernia" (YP 4:1.670). Clearly this is a eulogistic oversimplification of the facts, disregarding, for instance, the essential role that Colonel Michael Jones played in defeating Ormond at the Battle of Rathmine before Cromwell even arrived in Ireland, as well as the real difficulties Cromwell had at the siege of Clonmel.[50] If Milton's misrepresentation is intentional, then, it reflects his unequivocal praise for Cromwell's military action and the result Milton perceived it to have had: Ireland was "reduced." However, it is also possible that Milton's statements reflect the fact that there still remains some question about exactly what Milton did precisely and accurately know, even serving as secretary of foreign tongues to the Council of State. That is, the Council of State papers to which Milton would have had access would, of course, offer factual and numerical accounts, proclamations, and so on, but these papers sanitize the brutality of some of Cromwell's measures in Ireland by translating the results into military terms of "conquest" and "victory." Other publications simplified Cromwell's military prowess in subduing the Irish "enemy,"[51] and perhaps most significantly Cromwell himself was rarely forthcoming with the facts. Wilbur Abbott, editor of *The Writings and Speeches of Oliver Cromwell*, quotes Cromwell's anonymous biographer as saying, "Privacy and Silence in his Managements were to him Assistance beyond all Arts and Sciences" (542). Abbot argues that Cromwell distorted the facts of the campaign and his role in it, and that Milton's statements in *The Second Defense* about Cromwell may reflect such distortion. As Abbot says, "It would be difficult to compress more misinformation, conscious or unconscious, into a single sentence than this description of Cromwell's activities in Ireland. Yet it may also serve to represent something of the impression on the English mind of Cromwell's share in that conquest" (258–59).

Regardless of the accuracy of actual facts that Milton did or did not know, *The Second Defense* celebrates Cromwell's success in Ireland even while it raises questions about Cromwell's desire and ability to maintain pious and just governance over an increasingly difficult situation at home in England. Milton's tract urges the English people to redeem their integrity and resolve, as Sharon Achinstein has emphasized in *Milton and the Revolutionary Reader*, but Milton likewise exhorts Cromwell to "revere" the country's expectations that he be, truly, the protector of liberty. While Milton praises Cromwell's military prowess and victories over the Scots and the Irish, he also cautions Cromwell not to succumb to the temptations and corruptions of power and glory, reminding him that "Many men has war made great whom peace makes small" (YP 4:1.680), a statement that reiterates his sonnet to Cromwell on the challenges that governing in peacetime presents. Thus, while on the one hand Milton clearly disrespected the Irish Catholics and their cause, and though he was clearly intolerant of their "obdurate willfulness," on the other hand he also clearly admired Cromwell because he was not favoring the Catholics in the manner of Charles and his foreign policy was grounded in the desire to accomplish England's providential role (YP 1:526).

Whatever ambivalence he may have had about Cromwell's centralizing of executive power, Milton registers no condemnation of Cromwell's policies in Ireland.[52] Because Milton openly continued to support Cromwell's "victories" in Ireland and did not oppose the hegemonic boundaries drawn around the Irish in the campaign, Milton may be perceived as someone who drew national borders around his version of republicanism. By *not* denouncing Cromwell's violent military campaign in Ireland or the subsequent economic exploitation of the land settlement, Milton implies that the privileges and advantages of republicanism—civic, domestic, and ecclesiastical liberties accompanied by liberty of conscience—should belong exclusively to the English populace. Milton's continued support of Cromwell's actions in Ireland, in contrast to his statements about Cromwell's leadership of the new Commonwealth, reveals that national borders confined Milton's republican aims in the early 1650s.

It is not surprising, then, that although there should have been plenty left to say about Ireland, Milton would say little more after Cromwell became lord protector.[53] Though Milton would never fully relinquish all hope for a reformed, changed world, he turned his attention homeward to the care of the English citizenry as internal tensions increased during the 1650s and the Commonwealth was becoming less of what he had idealistically envisioned and Cromwell was becoming more of a quasi-monarchical lord protector than a true Reformer. Nonetheless, Milton's *The First Defense* (which he actively revised until 1658) continued to support Cromwell's action in Ireland as divinely sanctioned, and Milton continued to write with passion about his belief in the preeminence of liberty of conscience in *A Treatise of Civil Power* (1659). He would continue to be a spokesperson for the Commonwealth in *The Readie and Easie Way* (1660) and mentions "the *Irish* massacre" only to stress Charles's "fomenting and arming the rebellion" (YP 7:410).[54] Even though at the time of Charles II's restoration Catholics were left with just over 20 percent of Irish land, compared with the almost 60 percent they held in 1641, Irish Catholics would place new hope in the restored British monarchy, another action that surely would have rendered the Irish unworthy of belonging in any version of Milton's envisioned republic, whether it could be revived in the future or not. In 1661, the "loyal formulary of Irish remonstrance" was put forth, stating that Irish Catholics acknowledged Charles II as their lawful king, "to be obeyed under pain of sin, any papal claims to the contrary notwithstanding."[55] Milton knew of these reversals, but he would never directly address the Irish situation again, though he would continue to rail against Catholicism in *Of True Religion* (1673) until very near the time of his own death.

Milton's desire for Protestant reform began with the belief that Ireland could and should be part of a united "British" polity. Yet in the end Milton simply asserted English nationalism of the sort that enabled him to justify imperialist hegemony instead of inclusive republicanism. Milton's views of Ireland reveal that his republican values were ultimately limited to an English polity, and if England were indeed to forge a *"Britannick Empire,"* some would be citizens of an English republic, and others would be merely denizens upon its back or under its plough.

Western Carolina University

NOTES

I am grateful to John T. Shawcross and Paul Stevens for their generous assistance during the composition of this essay.

1. All references to Milton's prose are from *The Complete Prose Works of John Milton,* 8 vols., ed. Don M. Wolfe et al. (New Haven, 1953–1982). All quotations are from this edition, and subsequent volume and page references, will appear in the text and in these notes as YP.

2. Several excellent studies about Milton's response to the Irish have been published in recent years, most notable of which are: Paul Stevens, "Milton's Janus-Faced Nationalism: Soliloquy, Subject, and the Modern Nation State," *Journal of English and Germanic Philology* 100 (2001): 247–68; Paul Stevens, "Milton's 'Renunciation' of Cromwell: The Problem of Raleigh's Cabinet-Council," *Modern Philology* 98 (2001): 363–93; Paul Stevens, *"Paradise Lost* and the Colonial Imperative," in *Milton Studies* 34, ed. Albert C. Labriola (Pittsburgh, 1996), 3–22; Paul Stevens, "Spenser and Milton on Ireland: Civility, Exclusion, and the Politics of Wisdom," *ARIEL: A Review of International English Literature* 26 (1995): 151–67; Willy Maley, "Rebels and Redshanks: Milton and the British Problem," *Irish Studies Review* 6 (1994): 7–11; Willy Maley, "How Milton and Some Contemporaries Read Spenser's *View,*" in *Representing Ireland: Literature and the Origins of Conflict, 1534–1660,* ed. Brendan Bradshaw, Andrew Hadfield, and Willy Maley (Cambridge, 1993), 191–208; Willy Maley, "Milton and 'the complication of interests' in Early Modern Ireland," in *Milton and the Imperial Vision,* ed. Balachandra Rajan and Elizabeth Sauer (Pittsburgh, 1999), 155–68; Linda Gregerson, "Colonials Write the Nation: Spenser, Milton, and England on the Margins," in Rajan and Sauer, *Milton and the Imperial Vision,* 169–90; Norah Carlin, "Extreme or Mainstream?: The English Independents and the

Cromwellian Reconquest of Ireland, 1649–51," in Bradshaw, Hadfield, and Maley, *Representing Ireland*, 209–26; Joan Fitzpatrick, *Irish Demons: English Writings on Ireland, the Irish, and Gender by Spenser and His Contemporaries* (Lanham, MD, 2000); Jim Daems, "Dividing Conjunctions: Milton's *Observations upon the Articles of Peace,*" *Milton Quarterly* 33 (1999): 51–55; Catherine Canino, "The Discourse of Hell: *Paradise Lost* and the Irish Rebellion," *Milton Quarterly* 32 (1998): 15–23; Thomas Corns, "Milton's *Observations upon the Articles of Peace:* Ireland under English Eyes," in *Politics, Poetics, and Hermeneutics in Milton's Prose,* ed. David Loewenstein and James Grantham Turner (Cambridge, 1990), 123–34. General studies that discuss Milton and Ireland are David Loewenstein, *Representing Revolution in Milton and His Contemporaries: Religion, Politics, and Polemics in Radical Puritanism* (Cambridge, 2001); David Norbrook, *Writing the English Republic: Poetry, Rhetoric, and Politics, 1627–1660* (Cambridge, 1999); Walter Lim, *The Arts of Empire: The Poetics of Colonialism from Ralegh to Milton* (Newark, 1998).

3. On national apologists, see Sheila T. Cavanagh, " 'The fatal destiny of that land': Elizabethan Views of Ireland," in Bradshaw, Hadfield, and Maley, *Representing Ireland*, 116–31. The author traces the pervasive English Protestant views toward Ireland and Irish culture. Sir John Davies was James I's Irish solicitor-general (1603–1609) and attorney general (1606–1619). His *Discovery of the True Causes Why Ireland Was Never Entirely Subdued* (1612) praises the role of English common law in Ireland, but various scholars have asserted that Davies had self-serving interests and influence in the Ulster plantation project. Barnaby Rich wrote *A Short Survey of Ireland Truly Discovering Who Hath Armed That People with Disobedience* (1609) and *A New Description of Ireland: Wherein Is Described the Disposition of the Irish* (1610). Though it cannot come within the scope of this article, there are excellent studies that have addressed other major English voices commenting on Ireland. See Joan Fitzpatrick, *Irish Demons: English Writings on Ireland, the Irish, and Gender by Spenser and His Contemporaries,* and Willy Maley, "How Milton and Some of His Contemporaries," 191–208. About Spenser's *View* (1598/1633), Stephen Greenblatt argues that in establishing the cult of Gloriana in *The Faerie Queene,* Spenser depends upon "a perception of the not-self, of all that lies outside, or resists, or threatens identity." See Greenblatt, *Renaissance Self-Fashioning: From More to Shakespeare* (Chicago, 1980), 177.

4. Entries in Milton's *Commonplace Book* in 1641–1642 address Spenser's *View of the Present State of Ireland* and show Milton's familiarity with it. Also, there are several excellent analyses of Spenser's views of Ireland, but Bruce McLeod's chapter, "Thinking Territorially: Spenser, Ireland, and the English Nation-State," in *The Geography of Empire in English Literature, 1580–1745* (Cambridge, 1999), 32–75, is most pertinent and insightful. The 1594 text, *Solon His Follie; or, A Politique Discourse Touching The Reformation of common-weals conquered, declined, or corrupted,* by Richard Beacon, attorney general for the Province of Munster from 1586–1591, should have counteracted some of the effect of Spenser's *View,* but it did not. Beacon "eschewed this demonization of the Irish and struck a balance between Old English legal reform and New English military conquest." See *Renaissance English Text Society,* ed. and annotated by Clare Carroll and Vincent Carey, 7th series, vol. 18 for 1993 (Binghamton, NY, 1996), xxvii. Additionally, Milton may also have been familiar with descriptions of Ireland by interactions with friends and family, for example, through letters between Milton and Arthur Jones, who was Milton's student during the 1650s. Jones was the second viscount, and father of Richard, who was the First Earl of Ranlagh. Lady Catherine Ranlagh (née Boyle) was a friend of Milton's. Also, Milton's daughter Deborah went to Ireland before 1672 though she did not return until after 1688, apparently by 1697. Milton's nephew Richard was in Ireland much later (1688–1713). This information was communicated to me by John T. Shawcross on April 26, 2002.

5. Joan Fitzpatrick also offers extensive review and analysis of Spenser's Fairyland, which she says is "a fictitious and mythical landscape which harbors all kinds of monsters, [and] is perhaps not so far removed from those parts of early modern Ireland that presented such a challenge to the English colonists." See Fitzpatrick, *Irish Demons*, 80.

6. *A Natural History of Ireland in Three Parts, by Several Hands (Dublin: 1726), Chapter 15 Of the Woods in Ireland,* sec. 1, 66, also notes that woods in Ireland were considered barren land because they were not arable, a condition attributable to excessive moisture in the ground.

7. Eileen McKracken, "The Woodlands of Ireland circa 1600," *Irish Historical Studies* 11 (1959): 271–96. *A Natural History of Ireland* also offers relevant descriptions of Ireland's "hostile" terrain in the sixteenth and seventeenth centuries, indicating that there were few navigable rivers because of impediments such as fords, cataracts, and *weres* (large stones located so closely together that they block the flow of water, leaving only a hole that can be used as a place to put a basket to catch fish or to mill). See also chap. 8, "Of the Rivers of Ireland"; section 1, "Of the Shannon," and section 3, "Of the Liffey and the Boyn," 36–37, and chapter 13, "Of the Heaths and Moors or Bogs," 59–62.

8. *A Geographicall Description of the Kingdome of Ireland,* by G. N., printed by I. R. for Godfrey Emerson (London, June 1642) (Thomason tract E149 [11]).

9. Aiden Clark, "The 1641 Rebellion and Anti-Popery in Ireland," in *Ulster 1641: Aspects of the Rising,* ed. Brian Mac Cuarta, S.J. (Belfast, 1993), 139.

10. Paul Stevens discusses in detail Milton's aversion to Spanish imperialism and his admiration for Cromwell's foreign policy, which attempted to keep the Catholic powers of France and Spain apart because of their potential threat to Protestant England. See Stevens, "Milton's 'Renunciation' of Cromwell," 363–93.

11. See F. Pollock and F. Maitland, *History of English Law,* 2nd ed., vol. 1. (Cambridge, 1952), 458. See also Ann Dummett and Andrew Nicol, *Subjects, Citizens, Aliens and Others: Nationality and Immigration Law* (London, 1990), 21–39; Linda Colley, *Britons: Forging the Nation, 1707–1837* (New Haven, CT, 1992).

12. See M. Hechter, *Internal Colonialism: The Celtic Fringe in British National Development, 1536–1966* (Berkeley and Los Angeles, 1975).

13. For centuries, prior to October 1641, English relations with Ireland had been based predominantly on economic and legal oppression as well as territorial confiscation. Ireland had long been problematic for the English, but not an imminent threat or destructive force. See Nicholas Canny, *Making Ireland British, 1580–1650* (Oxford, 2001), and *Oliver Cromwell and the English Revolution,* ed. John Morrill (New York, 1990), for further discussion of English policies and attitudes.

14. Loewenstein, *Representing Revolution,* 192.

15. Anthony Low, "'Umpire Conscience': Freedom, Obedience, and the Cartesian Flight from Calvin in *Paradise Lost,*" *Studies in Philology* 96 (1999): 349.

16. *A Declaration of the Lord Lieutenant of Ireland, For the Undeceiving of deluded and seduced People: which may be satisfactory to all that doe not willfully shut their eyes against the light. In answer to certain late Declarations and Acts, framed by the Irish Popist Prelates and Clergy, in a Conventicle at Clonmacnoise,* March 21, 1650. Reprinted in *The Writings and Speeches of Oliver Cromwell,* vol. 2: *The Commonwealth,* ed. Wilbur Cortez Abbott (New York, 1939), 196–205. Cromwell's *Declaration* was a rebuttal to Irish prelates who had convened in December 4, 1649, at Clonmacnoise issuing their own declaration which contended that Cromwell intended to extirpate Catholicism in Ireland via extermination, banishment, transportation, and confiscation of land.

17. Under the heading, "POLITICAL ADROITNESS," in his *Commonplace Book,* Milton comments upon Spenser's *View:* "The wicked policies of divers deputies & governours in Ireland

see Spenser dialogue of Ireland," referring to Spenser's assessment that self-serving governors in Ireland did not do enough to quell the rebellious factions. See YP 1:465. Milton claims that the "wicked policies" made the English vulnerable and thereby set the historical stage for the major uprisings in the 1640s. Ruth Mohl cites this entry on Spenser as having been written by Milton, in English, "sometime between 1642–44(?)." See YP 1:465 n. 7.

18. David Loewenstein, *Milton and the Drama of History: Historical Vision, Iconoclasm, and the Literary Imagination* (Cambridge, 1990), states that Milton's early prose tracts "reveal his remarkable sensitivity to the historical process" and a recognition that reformation is an "exceptionally turbulent and dynamic process" (8, 15). It is interesting to note that much of the discourse concerning the Irish indicates that the English in some way continually underestimated the vigor and power of their Irish opponent. In 1641, Milton urged "speedy redresse" of the situation as an important part of the solution, a request that would be continually echoed, even by Cromwell himself in letters requesting additional support and funding. As late as 1649, in a February 25 letter to Parliament, Cromwell states, "Sir, [William Lenthall, speaker of the Parliament] I desire the charge of *England,* as to this War, may be abated as much as may be, and as we know you do desire out of your care to the Commonwealth; but if you expect your work to be done (if the marching Army be not constantly paid, and the course taken that hath been humbly presented) indeed it will not be for the thrift of *England,* as far as *England* is concerned in the speedy reduction of *Ireland,*" and then Cromwell "gives hopes of a speedy issue to this business." See "A LETTER From the Lord Lieutenant of IRELAND to The Honorable William Lenthall, esp.; Speaker of the Parliament of England, Relating the good Successes God hath lately given to The Parliament Forces there. Die Lunae 25 Februarii, 1649" (London, 1649), 7, 8.

19. The document concerning this contribution is Public Record Office MS E179/252/14, and it also indicates that Milton was then living in St. Botolph's Street (Aldersgate area). I am indebted to John T. Shawcross for this information (e-mail with the author, June 12, 2001).

20. Also, Milton is implicating Charles for not swiftly and adequately supporting the besieged Protestants and for not forcefully suppressing and punishing the rebels, accusations that would resurface throughout the decade and fuel antiroyalist fires.

21. For a full discussion of what Milton meant by this federal covenant, see John T. Shawcross, *John Milton: Self and World* (Lexington, KY, 1993), 128–42.

22. Abbott, *Writings and Speeches of Oliver Cromwell,* 205.

23. During the late nineteenth century, inflamed by oppressive British policies that failed to alleviate the horrors of the potato famine, and arguably even exacerbated the famine's devastation, Irish historians renewed their interest in the 1640 rebellions, bringing to the forefront the discrepancies regarding the accounts of the alleged massacres associated with the rebellions. "The Depositions," approximately 19,000 pages (in thirty-three volumes), have been housed in Trinity College Library in Dublin since 1741; they have served as the main source of information about the rebellions because they were allegedly given by witnesses to the rebellions, but their authenticity and reliability have come under scrutiny and suspicion. In 1868, an Irish Catholic scholar called into question not only the validity of the depositions, but declared, "That there was no regular or indiscriminate massacre of Protestants by Catholics at this period appears to be proved beyond question by the fact, that no mention of such an outrage was made in any of the letters of the Lords Justice to the Privy Council," though she admits that "it is probable, however, that the Catholics did rise up in different places, to attack those by whom they had been so severely oppressed." See Mary Frances Cusack, *An Illustrated History of Ireland: From A.D. 400 to 1800* (1868; reprint, Middlesex, 1998), 480. In 1879, John T. Gilbert's pro-Protestant work attempted to counter these and other such accusations. See Gilbert, *A Contemporary History of Affairs in Ireland from 1644 to 1652. Now for the first time published with an Appendix of*

Original Letters and Documents, vol. 1, pt. 1 (Dublin, 1879). For other illustrations of the various interpretations of the depositions, see John P. Prendergast, *The Cromwellian Settlement of Ireland,* 2nd ed. (London, 1870); Mary Hickson, *Ireland in the Seventeenth Century or the Irish Massacres of 1641–2 Their Causes and Results,* 2 vols., preface by J. A. Froude (London, 1884); Patrick Francis Moran, *Historical Sketch of the Persecutions Suffered by the Catholics of Ireland under the Rule of Cromwell and the Puritans* (Dublin, 1884); Thomas Fitzpatrick, "Sir Phelim O'Neill's Rebellion," in *The Bloody Bridge and Other Papers Relating to the Insurrection of 1641* (Dublin, 1903).

24. Again, from almost the very start there has been enormous controversy over the authenticity of depositions and accounts, and almost all scholars now agree that the documents are not entirely reliable sources for accurate information about and numbers of those allegedly killed in the rebellions, nor the manner in which so many were allegedly slaughtered. See Toby Barnard, "1641: A Bibliographical Essay," in Mac Cuarta, *Ulster 1641,* 176–77, about the debate regarding the authenticity of the depositions. See also Aiden Clark, "Anti-Popery," in Mac Cuarta, *Ulster 1641,* 149–50. Also compare Protestant information about the Catholic depositions presented in Cusack, appendix to *An Illustrated History of Ireland,* 658.

25. For an alternative view of the rebellions, see Russell K. Alspach, *Irish Poetry from the English Invasion to 1798* (Philadelphia, 1959), 37–48; Marc Caball, *Poets and Politics: Continuity and Reaction in Irish Poetry, 1558–1625* (Notre Dame, 1998). See also Michelle O Riordan, "'Political' Poems in the Mid-Seventeenth-Century Crisis," in *Ireland from Independence to Occupation 1641–1660,* ed. Jane H. Ohlmeyer (Cambridge, 1995), 112–27. O Riordan analyzes three categories of Gaelic political poems that help to identify and "highlight the divisions inherent in Irish politics and society prior to Rinuccini's arrival [the papal nuncio arrived in Ireland in 1646] and long after his departure" (115).

Sir Richard Bellings (1613–1677), *History of the Irish Confederation and the War in Ireland, 1641–43, containing a narrative of affairs of Ireland . . . With correspondence and documents of the confederation and of the administrators of the English government in Ireland, contemporary personal statements, memoirs, etc.,* ed. John T. Gilbert (Dublin, 1882–1891). Bellings was vice president of the Supreme Council of Confederate Catholics, and in March 1645 set out to bring a papal nuncio to unite all the contending powers in Ireland. This nuncio was Giovanni Rinuccini.

An Aphorismical Discovery of Treasonable Faction (written sometime between 1652 and 1660) is presented and analyzed carefully in Gilbert, *A Contemporary History,* vol. 1, i–xv, in which Gilbert gives a thorough description of the text and its value and then reprints it in full. On Milton's view of the Irish situation, see Canino, "The Discourse of Hell," 15–23, for an excellent discussion about the demonizing versus mere vilifying of the Irish *after* the 1641 rebellion.

26. "A TRUE AND FULL RELATION," Thomason Tract E173 (30).

27. "A Late and True Relation . . ." (London, 1641); "LATE And Lamentable News FROM IRELAND, Thomason Tract E179(13). An additional example: "The last and best newes from IRELAND: Declaring First the warlike and cruell proceeding of the Rebels who are all papists and Jesuits of that Kingdome . . ." (November 3, 1641), Thomason Tract E177 (10).

28. "BLOUDY NEWES FROM IRELAND," Thomason Tract E179 (9); "A BLOODY BATTELL," Thomason Tract E180 (7). An additional example includes *An Exact and True Relation of the late Plots which were contrived and hatched in Ireland* (November 1641), which typifies the vituperation and demonizing of the Irish that would become standard in English discourse about the Irish. This pamphlet contains, among other things, *The true Coppy of a Letter written from a Gentleman in Ireland, to his friend in England,* which claims the Irish Catholics had "as much liberty as wee have had, if not more; but their father the Divell hath set them upon this damnable act I hope to their utter ruine in this Kingdome." See Thomason Tract E173 (30), 2.

29. Predictably, few voices representing the Catholic viewpoint would be heard. Published on October 30, 1641, a week after the first day of the rebellion at Drogheda, an atypical pamphlet exemplifies one of the small number of Catholic articulations in England about the rebellions. It is an emboldened Catholic plea written by a priest, friar, and two "soldiers," one of whom was Patrick O'Neal, the chief commander of the rebels and "the high Sheriff of a County in *Ireland*" (6). Its title is noninflammatory, promising an objective reporting of the incidents: "AN EXACT RELATION OF a Battell fought by the Lord *Moore*, against the Rebels in *Ireland*; with the number that were slain on both sides." Its contents foreground the Catholic rebels' three main demands but, significantly, these are also followed by an impassioned vindication and a call to action: "therefore, it is high time to stirre, since it is of so great a consequence; therefore all that wish well to the Catholique Faith, let them now betake themselves to their Arms, and come now and assist us who are now in the field, to defend the Religion with our swords." See Thomason Tract E175 (8), 7.

30. Thomas Corns, "Milton's *Observations upon the Articles of Peace:* Ireland under English Eyes," in Loewenstein and Turner, *Politics, Poetics, and Hermeneutics*, 123.

31. Shawcross, *John Milton*, 164.

32. Henry Jones's *Remonstrance* (London, 1642) offers graphic accounts of alleged barbarities—women and children being slaughtered, as well as an extended discussion of how the Irish expected support for their rebellions from the Spanish, Scots, and French. Master of the Irish Rolls, Sir John Temple, wrote the 1646 *Irish Rebellion*, which epitomized anti-Irish sentiment and stereotypes for decades, even centuries, to come. *Irish Rebellion* was, as Toby Barnard, "A Bibliographical Essay," in Mac Cuarta, *Ulster 1641*, contends, "the book which had most authoritatively established a national myth hostile to the Irish Catholics" (178). While it is not within the scope of this essay to analyze fully the impact and effect of Temple's text, it is important to note that anti-Irish stereotyping reached its nadir here, in part, Barnard says, because "it accorded with Protestant preconceptions and expectations," and "Temple's magisterial tone was calculated to silence doubters" (174). Temple based his accounts on the depositions, which gave his own summative description an unprecedented force and credibility. "The mercies of the wicked are cruell," Temple reminded his English audience, and as evidence offered exaggerations and fabrications of alleged Catholic atrocities against Protestants, including how the Catholics herded thousands of Protestant women and children like cattle and threw them into rivers, sometimes pricking the hesitant ones with their swords and pikes (92). See also Norah Carlin, "Extreme or Mainstream? The English Independents and the Cromwellian Reconquest of Ireland 1649–51," in Bradshaw, Hadfield, and Maley, *Representing Ireland*, 209–26. For statistics on Protestants in Ireland, see Barnard, "1641: A Bibliographical Essay," 175–76.

33. *Modern Intelligencer*, no. 215 (May 2, 1649).

34. Milton uses "reduction" in this way in several instances. For additional examples, see YP 1:648, 853.

35. Abbott, *Writings and Speeches of Oliver Cromwell*, 118, 224, 227.

36. Stevens, "Milton's Janus-Faced Nationalism," 268.

37. "For the Honorable William Lenthall, Esquire, Speaker of the Parliament of England: These . . ." (Dublin, September 17, 1649). Reprinted in Abbott, *Writings and Speeches of Oliver Cromwell*, 125–28.

38. See also, for example, the lengthy *Declaration to the Irish Prelates*, in which he declares, "I can give you a better reason for the army's coming over than this. England hath had experience of the blessing of God in prosecuting just and righteous causes, whatever the cost and hazard be," and "But as for those who, notwithstanding all this, persist and continue in arms, they must expect what the Providence of God (in that which is falsely called the chance of war) will cast upon them," in Abbott, *Writings and Speeches of Oliver Cromwell*, 204–5.

39. Paul Stevens also argues cogently that Milton's sense of the superiority of English law and civility drives his justification of just retribution, which Milton "so often articulates in terms of the Hebrew Law." See Stevens, "Milton's Janus-Faced Nationalism," 262.

40. For an extensive discussion on the history of the approximate number, see also YP 3:168.

41. Further, in several instances Milton notes Parliament's advice to Charles not to arm the Irish in a war against the Scots (YP 3:471) and how, despite Parliament's counsel, Charles did not later disarm or disband those Irish forces. Milton notes Parliament's "having put *Strafford* to death," an act the Puritans saw as a corrective and just measure for his abuses of power in Ireland and his "inclination to Popery" (YP 3:474).

42. To underscore Charles's liability, Milton indicts Charles as the "Author" of the rebellions no fewer than six times. For example: "Seeing then the maine incitement and Autority for this Rebellion must be needs deriv'd from *England*, it will be next inquir'd who was the prime Author" (YP 3:472); "And that he himself was the Author of that Rebelion, he denies . . . with many imprecations, but no solid evidence" (YP 3:472); and "I suppose no understanding Man could longer doubt who was *Author or Instigator* of that Rebellion" (YP 3:477).

43. It is not within the scope of this discussion to undertake an analysis of Milton's attitudes toward war, per se, and much excellent scholarship has already addressed this topic. See, for example, Michael Lieb, *Milton and the Culture of Violence* (Ithaca, NY, 1996); Robert Thomas Fallon, *Captain or Colonel: The Soldier in Milton's Life and Art* (Columbia, MO, 1984), and Shawcross, *John Milton*. Shawcross reminds us that Milton "reputedly carried a sword, [and] was not the pacifist some readers of the War in Heaven in *Paradise Lost* would make him" (164).

44. On "right reading," see Sharon Achinstein, *Milton and the Revolutionary Reader* (Princeton, 1994), p. 162. On the new republican rhetoric, see Thomas Corns, "Milton's *Observations upon the Articles of Peace*: Ireland under English Eyes," in Loewenstein and Turner, *Politics, Poetics, and Hermeneutics*, 123–34. See also Loewenstein, *Representing Revolution*.

45. All references to Milton's poetry are from *The Riverside Milton*, ed. Roy Flannagan (Boston, 1998).

46. Abbott, *Writings and Speeches of Oliver Cromwell*, 257.

47. An Act of Settlement (1652) and an Act of Satisfaction (1653) were passed to authorize confiscation of all Catholic lands east of the Shannon River. In 1653, the English Parliament confiscated Counties Dublin, Kildare, Carlow, and Cork in addition to ten other counties established for division among the Adventurers and soldiers: 1.1 million acres, or 5 percent of total profitable land, were divided by January 1654. See *The Oxford Companion to Irish History*, ed. S. J. Connolly (Oxford, 1999), 128–29. In the end, "the English confiscated something like 11 million out of 20 million acres in Ireland, and transplanted 3,000 Catholic landowners and over 40,000 of their servants and families to Connacht," according to James Scott Wheeler, *Cromwell in Ireland* (Dublin, 1999), 230.

48. Note the interesting difference between Milton's translation and the King James version, which uses the word "inheritance" where Milton instead uses "conquest," that is, "Ask of me, and I shall give *thee* the heathen for thine inheritance, and the uttermost parts of earth for thy possession. / Thou shalt break them with a rod of iron; thou shalt dash them in pieces like a potter's vessel."

49. Terry Eagleton, *Heathcliff and the Great Hunger* (London, 1995).

50. For a description of the importance of Jones's preemptive victories, see Abbott, *Writings and Speeches of Oliver Cromwell*, 101–2, 105–6, 257; on the siege of Clonmel, see 250–53.

51. See, for example, "A Perfect Table of one hundred forty and Five Victories obtained by the Lord Lieutenant of Ireland, and the Parliaments Forces under his Command, since his Excellency was made Governour Generall by the Parliament of England; From Wednesday August 1. 1649. to March the last, 1650" (Thomason Tract 669f.15 [27] Reel 246).

52. There have been several excellent commentaries on Milton's ambivalence about Cromwell, but the most circumspect and discerning is Stevens's "Milton's 'Renunciation' of Cromwell," in which he argues that Milton's increasing disenchantment with Cromwell has been oversimplified by Miltonists, and that Milton's Protestant nationalism ultimately overrides his republicanism, but that very nationalism is what "best explains both his loyalty to Cromwell and his decision to publish a book of aphorisms by Sir Walter Raleigh in the midst of a war against England's enemies" (388).

53. In his *Sonnet XVIII*, "On the Late Massacher in Piemont," Milton calls the French and Irish who persecuted the Waldensians, the "Babylonian wo," with its associations of the "Babylonian Whore," an age-old synonym for Catholicism. While Milton was certainly exposed to the accounts of the actual Piedmont massacres, his sonnet also echoes some of the discourse of the earlier Irish massacres, as he reiterates some of the common imagery of atrocity associated with the Irish rebellions that circulated throughout the 1640s and 1650s: "Slayn by the bloody Piemontese that roll'd / Mother with Infant down the Rocks" (7–8). See John T. Shawcross, "A Note on the Piedmont Massacre," in *Milton Quarterly* 6 (1972): 36. Shawcross observes that Milton knew of contemporary, often vivid, descriptions of the massacres. See also Elizabeth Sauer, "Culture of Intolerance: Re-reading Milton's 'On the Late Massacre in Piemont,'" in *Comparing Imperialisms: Early Modern to Late Romantic*, ed. Elizabeth Sauer and Balachandra Rajan (forthcoming). Sauer makes important connections between the massacres of the Waldensians and Cromwell's actions against the Irish, and she argues that Milton uses the sonnet to promote his English nationalism as well as his desired reformations. Further, even in *The Second Defense* (1654), Milton says little directly about the Irish. While several critics argue that Milton was by then discontented with Cromwell, Robert T. Fallon, "*A Second Defense*: Milton's Critique of Cromwell," in *Milton Studies* 39, ed. Albert C. Labriola (Pittsburgh, 2000), argues that "No artful reading of the silences in or reading between the lines of *A Second Defense* can disguise Milton's admiration for Cromwell at the time and his clear preference for the Protectorate over the bungling government that preceded it" (180).

54. In *The Readie and Easie Way to Establish a Commonwealth,* 2nd ed., April 1–10, 1660, Milton discusses the nature of covenant, and uses the Irish massacres as retroactive examples of monarchical abuses of power and breach of covenant. Milton here repeats accusations that the monarch abetted the Irish rebels:

> They covnanted *to preserve the Kings person and autoritie in the preservation of the true religion and our liberties;* not in his endeavoring to bring in upon our consciences a Popish religion, upon our liberties thraldom, upon our lives destruction, by his occasioning, in not complotting, as was after discoverd, the *Irish* massacre, his fomenting and arming the rebellion, his covert leaguing with the rebels against us, his refusing more then seaven times, propositions most just and necessarie to the true religion and our liberties, tenderd him by the Parlament both of *England* and *Scotland.* (YP 7:409–11)

55. The Oxford Companion to Irish History, 482–83. For property settlement history, see The Rebellion began and how disposed in 1653. When the War and Rebellion was declared. The State of the Papist and Protestant Proprieties in the Kingdom of Ireland in the Year 1641. When at an End, and how disposed in 1662, upon the Acts of Settlement (London, 1698). See also Kevin McKenny, "The Seventeenth-Century Land Settlement in Ireland: Towards a Statistical Interpretation," in Ohlmeyer, Ireland from Independence to Occupation, 181–200; Raymond Gillespie, "The Irish Economy at War, 1641–1652," in ibid., 160–80. Despite Charles II's assurances that the Cromwellian land settlement would be reversed, it was left mainly intact. See Wheeler, Cromwell in Ireland, 229.